BARRON'S

MSAT

HOW TO PREPARE FOR THE MULTIPLE SUBJECTS ASSESSMENT FOR TEACHERS

by
Robert D. Postman, Ed.D.
Professor
Mercy College

To my wife
Liz
and my children
Chad, Blaire and Ryan
This book is dedicated to you

Some material in this book was adapted from Barron's *How to Prepare for the Praxis* by Robert D. Postman.

All inquiries should be addressed to:
Barron's Educational Series, Inc.
250 Wireless Boulevard
Hauppauge, New York 11788
http://www.barronseduc.com

Library of Congress Catalog Card No. 97-30119

International Standard Book No. 0-7641-0268-0

Library of Congress Cataloging-in-Publication Data

Postman, Robert D.
How to prepare for the MSAT : multiple subjects assessment for teachers / by Robert D. Postman.
p. cm.
ISBN 0-7641-0268-0
1. Multiple Subjects Assessment for Teachers. 2. Elementary school teachers— United States—Examinations. I. Title.
LB1766.M64P67 1998
379. 1′57—dc21 97-30119
CIP

PRINTED IN THE UNITED STATES OF AMERICA

9 8 7 6 5 4 3 2 1

CONTENTS

PREFACE

This book shows you how to get a passing score on the MSAT Teacher Certification Examination and helps you get started in a teaching career. The book has been field-tested by college students and prospective teachers and reviewed by experienced teachers and subject matter specialists.

The practice tests in this book have the same question types and the same question-and-answer formats as the real tests. Review sections provide a clear overview of subject matter, strategies for passing the MSAT, and extra MSAT practice items.

My wife, Liz, a teacher, was a constant source of support, and she made significant contributions to this book. I hope she accepts my regrets for the lost months and believes my promises that it won't happen again. My children, Chad, Blaire, and Ryan have also been a source of support as I worked on this and other books over the years.

I can attest that Barron's is simply the best publisher of test preparation books. The editorial department, under the leadership of Grace Freedson, spared no effort to assure that this book is most helpful to you, the test taker.

Max Reed, Senior Editor at Barron's, did another masterful job with this manuscript. This is the third book that Max and I have worked on together, and many special touches in the book are due to her caring attention. Credit is also due to Wendy Wood and Ted Kula.

I also am grateful to several colleagues. Dominic Angiello, professor of English and a published poet, reviewed the language and literature items. James Melville, professor of science and science department chair, reviewed the science items. Sean Dugan, professor of English and English department chair, reviewed the language and literature section.

Special thanks to the undergraduate and graduate students and those changing careers who field-tested sections of this book, and to those at the Educational Testing Service and the Metropolitan Museum of Art for their assistance. I am also grateful to those at the California and Oregon Education Departments and to those at colleges and other organizations in California and Oregon who talked to me about the MSAT.

During the past three decades, teaching opportunities have shifted from promising to sparse to promising again. You are entering teaching during a time of tremendous opportunity, and I wish you well in your pursuit of a rewarding and fulfilling career. The next generation awaits. You will help them prepare for a vastly different, technological world.

Robert D. Postman
October 1997

MSAT 1998–1999 TEST DATES

Test Date	Regular Registration	Late Registration
February 7, 1998	January 6, 1998	January 13, 1998
May 2, 1998	March 31, 1998	April 7, 1998
July 11, 1998	June 9, 1998	June 16, 1998
October 17, 1998*	September 16, 1998	September 23, 1998
February 6, 1999*	January 5, 1999	January 12, 1999
May 1, 1999*	March 30, 1999	April 6, 1999
July 10, 1999*	June 8, 1999	June 15, 1999

*Tentative dates.

Additional administrations of the MSAT may be scheduled. Check with ETS at 800-772-9476 for details and for test center information.

PART I

Introduction

HOW TO USE THIS BOOK

TEST INFO BOX

Every chapter begins with a Test Info Box. Read it for information about the MSAT and for test item examples.

The MSAT consists of two tests. The Content Knowledge Test has 120 multiple choice items. The Content Area Exercises Test has 18 short answer items. Each test has questions about seven liberal arts areas at an introductory level. You may use a calculator on any test. California and Oregon currently require passing MSAT scores for certain teacher certification candidates.

PASSING SCORES

California

California requires a minimum score on each test and an overall passing score. About 62 correct on the Content Knowledge test and about 50 points on the Content Area Exercises test should earn a minimum score. There are many passing score combinations.

Oregon

Oregon requires a passing score on the Content Knowledge test. About 60 correct on the Content Knowledge test should earn a passing score. You must submit a Content Area Exercise score, but there is no required score.

More information about MSAT passing scores is found in this chapter.

PREPARING FOR THE MSAT

This book has all the subject matter, review, strategies, and test practice you need to pass the MSAT. The subject review is keyed directly to the test. The strategies and practice will help you improve your score.

READ ME FIRST

This section describes the MSAT, discusses scoring, and explains the steps you should take in the beginning of your preparation. Read it before going on.

WHAT'S GOING ON WITH THE MSAT?

The Multiple Subjects Assessment Test (MSAT) is a test about the introductory level liberal arts courses you took in college. You have five hours to complete the MSAT. So with breaks and lunch it will take a day. The MSAT consists of a two-hour Content Knowledge multiple choice test and a Content Area Exercises constructed-response (short answer) test.

Both the multiple choice and constructed-response tests cover seven liberal arts areas as shown in the table below.

MSAT ITEM DISTRIBUTION

Area	Content Knowledge (Two hours)	Content Exercises 1 (Two hours)	Content Exercises 2 (One hour)
Literature and Language Studies	24 items	3 items	
Mathematics	24 items	3 items	
History/Social Studies	22 items		3 items
Science	22 items		3 items
Visual and Performing Arts	12 items	2 items	
Human Development	8 items	2 items	
Physical Education	8 items	2 items	
TOTAL	120 items	12 items	6 items

The MSAT yields two scores, one for Content Knowledge and one for Content Area Exercises. The MSAT is given through the Educational Testing Service as one of its Praxis Tests. So you sign up for the MSAT using the regular ETS Praxis Registration Form.

THE GOOD NEWS

The good news is that the MSAT focuses on a central core of information. The information covered by the test is at an introductory level. You can use a calculator for the mathematics section. This book will show you how to successfully prepare for this test.

At the end of the book you will learn how to begin your career in teaching, how to get certified, how to write your first resume, and how to look for your first job.

GETTING A PASSING SCORE IN CALIFORNIA AND OREGON

Raw Scores and Scale Scores

Your raw score is the number of items you answer correctly, or the number of points you actually earn. Your scale score shows your raw score on a single scale compared to everyone else who has taken the MSAT.

It works this way. MSAT test items and different forms of the test have different difficulty levels. For example, a mathematics item on one form of the MSAT might be harder than a mathematics item on another form. To make up for this difference in difficulty, the harder mathematics item might earn 0.9 scale points, while the easier item might earn 0.8 scale points.

This is the fair way to do it. To maintain this fairness, MSAT passing scores are given as scale scores. The scale scores for the Content Knowledge test and the Content Area Exercises test each range from 100 to 200.

Test Scoring

The highest Content Knowledge raw score is 120 (1 point for each item correct.) The highest Content Area Exercises raw score is 54 (a maximum of 3 points for each of the 18 items.) Your response to each Content Area Exercises item is rated 0–3 by two readers. The score for that item is the average of their ratings.

No one can be absolutely sure what raw scores will convert to what scale scores. However, we can make some reasonable estimates. These estimates are based on reports from those who have previously taken the test, and from those at ETS who like to be helpful.

California Passing and Minimum Scores

Scale Scores

You pass if your overall scale score is 311 or better, and if your individual scale scores are at or above the minimums shown below. The overall scale score is the sum of the individual scale scores. You can use Content Knowledge scores and Content Area Exercise scores from different administrations to achieve a passing score.

CALIFORNIA PASSING AND MINIMUM SCALE SCORES

Overall Passing Score	311
Content Knowledge Minimum Score	148
Content Area Exercises Minimum Score	147

As long as you get the minimum scale score on each test, there are a large number of passing score combinations. You can make up for a lower score on one test with a higher score on the other test.

Raw Scores

The table below shows the raw scores likely to earn minimum scale scores. These are estimates and somewhat higher or somewhat lower raw scores may be passing for the test you take.

ESTIMATED RAW SCORES NEEDED FOR CALIFORNIA MINIMUM SCORES

Content Knowledge	72–74 correct out of 120 items
Content Area Exercises	26–27 points out of a possible 54 points

Get the minimum raw score on each test and there are a large number of passing score combinations. You can make up for a lower score on one test with a higher score on the other test.

Some passing raw score combinations are shown below. There are many other passing combinations. These are estimates, and somewhat higher or lower raw score combinations may be passing for the test you take.

ESTIMATED PASSING RAW SCORE COMBINATIONS

Combination	Content Knowledge	Content Area Exercises
Passing Combination with the Content Knowledge Minimum Score	72–74 correct (60%–62%)	33–34 points (60%–63%)
Passing Combination with the Content Area Exercises Minimum Score	88–90 correct (73%–75%)	26–27 points (48%–50%)
Passing Combination with Half the Scale Points from each Test	80–82 correct (67%–68%)	30–31 points (56%–58%)

Oregon Passing Score

You pass if your Content Knowledge score is 147 or better. You can pass with from 71 to 73 correct on the Content Knowledge Test. You have to submit a Content Area Exercises score, but no minimum score is required. I still urge you to do your best on the Content Area Exercises, in case you want to submit scores to California.

OREGON PASSING SCALE SCORE AND ESTIMATED RAW SCORE NEEDED TO PASS

	Passing Scale Score	Estimated Passing Raw Scores
Content Knowledge	147	71–73 correct
Content Area Exercises	Submit any score	

Finding Out If You Passed

You don't have to wait for the score report. ETS will tell you if your score is passing. Call the Educational Testing Service at (800) 772-9476 (24 hours) or TTY for the deaf (800) 275-1391 (during business hours). Tell the operator the test, the test date, your name, and your social security number. The operator will tell you whether your score is passing or not passing. The operator will not tell you your actual score.

FOLLOW THESE STEPS

Follow the chapters in this book—one after another. They are arranged to take you right through the review process and right up to test day. First you'll find out how to register for the tests, how to set up a study plan, and how to use test taking strategies that work.

Then you'll go through chapters that review the MSAT subject matter. Review chapters provide a clear overview of subject matter and specific strategies for passing the MSAT. These chapters also give you extra MSAT questions to practice.

Finally there are two complete practice MSATs to get you ready for the real thing. These practice tests give you a chance to find out how well you will do on the actual MSAT. An extra section at the end of the book helps you get started in a teaching career.

So just relax. Let this book guide you to successful scores on the MSAT.

REGISTERING FOR THE MSAT

The Praxis Bulletin contains registration forms for the MSAT and other Praxis tests. The Praxis Bulletin is available in late July for the following school year. If you are attending college, you can usually find copies of the bulletin in the school or department of education. If not, you can call to obtain the bulletin and other information. If you live in California, get a copy of the Praxis California Registration Bulletin.

in the United States:	(800) 772-9476 (24 hours)
TTY for the deaf:	(800) 275-1391
outside the United States:	(609) 771-7395

You can also get a bulletin by writing to:

Praxis Bulletin
Educational Testing Service
CN 6501
Princeton, NJ 08541-6051

When you get the Praxis Bulletin, check the location and schedule for the tests you want to take. Complete the registration form and send it in with the correct fee.

ON THE WEB

The Educational Testing Service has a web site with comprehensive information about teacher tests (www.ets.org). Go to the web site and click on Teacher Testing for up-to-date information about test dates and state-by-state testing requirements. You can also download booklets that describe the tests and the Praxis Registration Bulletin. Test scores are not available through this site.

TEST LOCATION

Where you take the MSAT is very important. Check the bulletin for locations near you and list as your first choice the location in which you feel most comfortable. Remember to list acceptable alternative locations but never list any alternates you really don't want to go to. If you do, you can be sure that's where you'll end up.

Send in the registration form as soon as possible. Early registrants are more likely to get their first choice location. Each test date has a cutoff usually one month before the test is given. You may still be able to register at Ticketron, Teletron, or other computerized ticketing agencies after the deadline has passed.

You will receive a registration ticket from ETS several weeks before the test. If you don't like your test site, you can call (800) 772-9476 (TTY for the deaf, (800) 275-1391) to try to have it changed.

If you are too late for regular registration or computerized ticketing, don't give up. Most MSAT sites accept walk-ins for registrants who don't show up. Call sites until you find one that can accept you. If you still have no luck, go directly to a site early on the test day and hope for the best. With persistence, you should be able to take the test somewhere.

TEST SCHEDULE

The MSAT takes about seven hours with breaks and instructions. It is usually scheduled for a Saturday in October, February, May, and July. Additional administrations by states, colleges, and universities may be scheduled.

WHERE TO SEND YOUR SCORES

The MSAT Bulletin lists a code for each organization that can receive scores. You should list the code for each certification agency or college you want to receive your scores. The scores must usually be sent directly to the agencies from ETS.

You may feel that you should wait until you know you have gotten a passing score before sending it in, but that's not necessary. You will just slow down the process and incur extra expense. Certification agencies do not use these scores for evaluative purposes. They just need to see a passing score, and ETS reports only your highest score.

You will receive your own report and you are entitled to have four score reports sent to the certification agency or colleges you choose. Any extra reports will be sent to you in sealed envelopes.

SPECIAL TEST ARRANGEMENTS

ETS offers special arrangements or considerations for the following categories. If you qualify for special test arrangements, take advantage of the opportunity.

Do You Have a Disability (a Learning Disability or a Physical, Visual, or Hearing Handicap)?

You may qualify for additional time to complete the test, for someone to read the test to you, or for other special circumstances to accommodate your handicap. You must use the Certification of Documentation form from the Registration Bulletin or write directly to ETS to receive these special considerations. Your letter should describe your disability and the special arrangements you desire. Also enclose a note from a school counselor or employer to verify that these arrangements have previously been made for you, or a note from a health professional documenting your disability. Call ETS if you have any questions.

Do You Celebrate Your Sabbath on Saturday?
Do Your U.S. Military Duties Prevent You from Taking the Test on a Saturday?

You may qualify to take the MSAT on the Monday following the Saturday administration. Complete the MSAT registration form indicating this special situation. If you are unable to take a test for religious reasons, include a note from the head of the religious group where you worship, on that group's letterhead, stating that your Sabbath is on Saturday. If you cannot take a test for military reasons, include a copy of your orders.

Do You Live More Than 100 Miles from an MSAT Test Site?

You may qualify for an alternative test site. Send in the registration form with a note explaining your circumstances. There is an additional fee for taking the MSAT at an alternative test site.

MSAT PREPARATION AND TEST TAKING STRATEGIES

TEST INFO BOX

The chapter shows you how to set up a test preparation schedule and shows you test taking strategies that will help you improve your score.

The two most important test taking strategies are discussed below.

Content Knowledge (Multiple Choice)

- **Eliminate and then guess.**
- **There is no penalty for wrong answers on the MSAT. Never leave any answer blank.**
- **Say you eliminate just one incorrect answer choice on each item and you guess every answer. On average you would get 33 percent correct. Say you eliminate two incorrect answer choices on each item and you guess every answer. On average, you would get 50 percent correct.**

Content Area Exercises (Short Answer)

- **Get at least one point for each item.**
- **Don't leave any items blank. If you get 1 point on half the items and 2 points on the other half, you are very close to the California mini-**

PREPARING FOR THE MSAT

By now you've sent in the registration form and the test is at least four to nine weeks away. This section describes how to prepare for the MSAT. The next chapter describes test taking strategies. Before we go on, let's think about what you are preparing for.

Wait! Why Test Me? I'm a Good Person!

Why indeed? Life would be so much easier without tests. If anyone tells you that they like to take tests, don't believe them. Nobody does. Tests are imperfect. Some people pass when they should have failed, while others fail when they should have passed. It may not be fair, but it is very real. So sit back and relax. You're just going to have to do it, and this book will show you how.

Who Makes Up These Tests and How Do They Get Written?

Consider the following scenario. It is late in the afternoon in Princeton, New Jersey. Around a table sit teachers, deans of education, parents, and representatives of state education departments. In front of each person is a preliminary list of skills and knowledge that teachers should possess. The list comes from comments by an even larger group of teachers and other educational professionals.

Those around the table are regular people just like the ones you might run into in a store or on the street. They all care about education. They also bring to the table their own strengths and weaknesses—their own perspectives and biases. What's that? An argument just broke out. People are choosing up sides and, depending on the outcome, one item on the list will stay or go.

The final list goes to professional test writers to prepare test items. These items are tried out, refined, and put through a review process. Eventually the test question bank is established, and a test is born. These test writers are not geniuses. They just know how to write questions. You might get a better score on this test than some of them would.

The test writers want to write a test that measures important things. They try not to ask dumb or obscure questions that have strange answers. For the most part, they are successful. You can count on the test questions to ask about things you should know.

You can also be sure that the test writers will ask questions that will make you think. Their questions will ask you to use what you know. They will not ask for rote responses.

Keep those people around the table and the test writers in mind as you use this book. You are preparing for their test. Soon, you will be like one of those people around the table. You may even contribute to a test like this one.

Get Yourself Ready for the Test

Most people feel at least a little bit uncomfortable about tests. You are probably one of them. No book is going to make you feel comfortable. But here are some suggestions.

Most people are less tense when they exercise. Set up a reasonable exercise program for yourself. The program should involve exercising in a way that is appropriate for you 30 to 45 minutes each day. This exercise may be just as important as other preparation.

Prepare with another person. You will feel less isolated if you have a friend or colleague to study with.

Accept these important truths. You are not going to get all the answers correct. You don't have to. You can take this test over again if you have to. Remember the score you have to get. There is no penalty for taking the test again. This is not a do or die, life or death situation.

Follow This Study Plan

Begin working four to ten weeks before the test. Use the study plan that follows.

Most review chapters start with a review quiz. Take each review quiz. Use the answer key to mark the review quiz. Each incorrect answer will point you to a specific portion of the review. Use the subject matter review indicated by the review quiz. Don't spend your time reviewing things you already know.

Each review chapter ends with MSAT practice items. Complete these items to help you get ready for the Practice MSATs.

MSAT STUDY PLAN

This plan starts ten weeks before the test. Adjust the time line if you have less time to study or if you have particular subject matter strengths or needs. Write your target completion date for each step of the review in the space provided.

Ten weeks to go **Target Completion Date**________

Review the test preparation strategies on pages 11–13 in this chapter.
Review the test taking strategies on pages 14–21 in this chapter.

Nine weeks to go **Target Completion Date**________

Review Chapter 3–Language and Literature Studies

Eight weeks to go **Target Completion Date**________

Review Chapter 4–Mathematics

Seven weeks to go **Target Completion Date**________

Review Chapter 5–History and Social Studies

Six weeks to go **Target Completion Date**________

Review Chapter 6–Science

Five weeks to go **Target Completion Date**________

Review Chapter 7–Visual and Performing Arts
Chapter 8–Human Development
Chapter 9–Physical Education
Review the test taking strategies on pages 14–21.
Review the special test taking strategies on pages 52–54, 98–101, 137–140, 197.

Four weeks before the actual test **Target Completion Date**________

Take Practice MSAT I (page 273)
Try to take the test on Saturday under exact test conditions.
Score the test and review the answer explanations.

Four weeks to go and
Three weeks to go **Target Completion Date**________

Review the errors you made on Practice MSAT I.
Review the test taking strategies on pages 14–21.

Two weeks before the actual test ***Target Completion Date***__________
Take Practice MSAT II (page 314)
Try to take the test on Saturday under exact test conditions.
Score the test and review the answer explanations.

Two weeks to go ***Target Completion Date***__________
During this week look over those areas you got wrong on the second Practice MSAT. Go over the answer explanations and go back to the review sections. Read the newspaper every day until the day before the test.

One week to go ***Target Completion Date***__________
The hard work is over. You're coasting in for a landing. You know the material on the test. You don't even have to get an A. You just have to pass.

Get up each day at the time you will have to get up the following Saturday. Sit down at the time the test will start and spend about one hour answering questions on practice tests. It's okay that you have answered these questions before.

MONDAY

Make sure you have your admission ticket.
Make sure you know where the test is given.
Make sure you know how you're getting there.

TUESDAY

Visit the test site, if you haven't done it already. You don't want any surprises this Saturday.

WEDNESDAY

Get some sharpened No. 2 pencils, a digital watch or pocket clock, your calculator, and a good big eraser and put them aside.

THURSDAY

Take a break from preparing for the test, and relax.

FRIDAY

Complete any forms you have to bring to the test.
Prepare any snacks or food you want to bring with you.
Talk to someone who makes you feel good or do something enjoyable and relaxing.
Have a good night's sleep.

SATURDAY—TEST DAY

Dress comfortably. There are no points for appearance.
Eat the same kind of breakfast you've been eating each morning.
Don't stuff yourself. You want your blood racing through your brain, not your stomach.
Get together things to bring to the test including: registration ticket, identification forms, pencils, calculator, eraser, and snacks or food.

Get to the test room, not the parking lot, about 10 to 15 minutes before the start time.
Remember to leave time for parking and walking to the test site.
Hand in your forms–you're in the door. You're ready. This is the easy part.
Follow the test taking strategies in the next section.

PROVEN TEST TAKING STRATEGIES

Testing companies like to pretend that test taking strategies don't help that much. They act like that because they want everyone to think that their tests only measure your knowledge of the subject. Of course, they are just pretending; knowing test taking strategies can make a big difference.

However, there is nothing better than being prepared for the subject matter on this test. These strategies will do you little good if you lack this fundamental knowledge. If you are prepared, then these strategies can make a difference. Use them. Other people will be. Not using them may very well lower your score.

Be Comfortable

Get a good seat. Don't sit near anyone or anything that will distract you. Stay away from your friends. If you don't like where you are sitting, move or ask for another seat. You paid money for this test, and you have a right to favorable test conditions.

You Will Make Mistakes

You are going to make mistakes on this test. The people who wrote the test expect you to make them.

You Are Not Competing with Anyone

Don't worry about how anyone else is doing. Your score does not depend on theirs. When the score report comes out it doesn't say, "Nancy got a 661, but Blaire got a 670." You just want to get the score required for your certificate. If you can do better, that's great. Stay focused. Remember your goal.

MULTIPLE CHOICE STRATEGIES

It's Not What You Know That Matters, It's Just Which Circle You Fill In

No one you know or care about will see your test. An impersonal machine scores all multiple choice questions. The machine just senses whether the correct circle on the answer sheet is filled in. That is the way the test makers want it. If that's good enough for them, it should be good enough for you. Concentrate on filling in the correct circle.

You Can Be Right but Be Marked Wrong

If you get the right answer but fill in the wrong circle, the machine will mark it wrong. We told you that filling in the right circle was what mattered. We strongly recommend that you follow this strategy.

Write the letter for your answer big in the test booklet next to the number for the problem. If you change your mind about an answer, cross off the "old" letter and write the "new" one. At the end of each section, transfer all the answers together from the test booklet to the answer sheet.

Do Your Work in the Test Booklet

You can write anything you want in your test booklet. The test booklet is not used for scoring and no one will look at it. You can't bring scratch paper to the test so use your booklet instead.

Some of the strategies we recommend involve writing in and marking up the booklet. These strategies work and we strongly recommend that you use them.

Do your work for a question near that question in the test booklet. You can also do work on the cover or wherever else suits you. You may want to do calculations, underline important words, mark up a picture, or draw a diagram.

Watch That Answer Sheet

Remember that a machine is doing the marking. Fill in the correct answer circle completely. Don't put extra pencil marks on the answer section of the answer sheet. Stray marks could be mistaken for answers.

Some Questions Are Traps

Some questions include the words *not*, *least*, or *except*. You are being asked for the answer that doesn't fit with the rest. Be alert for these types of questions.

Save the Hard Questions for Last

You're not supposed to get all the questions correct, and some of them will be too difficult for you. Work through the questions and answer the easy ones. Pass the other ones by. Do these more difficult questions the second time through. If a question seems really hard, draw a circle around the question number in the test booklet. Save these questions until the very end.

They Show You the Answer

Every multiple choice test shows you the correct answer for each question. The answer is staring right at you. You just have to figure out which one it is. There is a 20 or 25 percent chance you'll get it right by just closing your eyes and pointing.

Some Answers Are Traps

When someone writes a test question, they often include distracters. Distracters are traps—incorrect answers that look like correct answers. It might be an answer to an addition problem when you should be multiplying. It might be a correct answer to a different question. It might just be an answer that catches your eye. Watch out for this type of incorrect answer.

Eliminate the Incorrect Answers

If you can't figure out which answer is correct, then decide which answers can't be correct. Choose the answers you're sure are incorrect. Cross them off in the test booklet. Only one left? That's the correct answer.

Guess, Guess, Guess

If there are still two or more answers left, then guess. Guess the answer from those remaining. Never leave any item blank. There is no penalty for guessing.

SHORT ANSWER STRATEGIES

Here's How They Score You

Two readers rate short answer items 0–3. Your score is the average of their ratings. The raters use these guidelines.

3–Shows a thorough understanding of the topic. Responds to all parts of the item. Clear explanations that are well supported.
2–Shows an adequate understanding of the topic. Responds to most parts of the item. Clear explanations that are somewhat well supported.
1–Shows little if any understanding of the topic. Does not respond to most parts of the item. Unclear explanations that are not supported.
0–Blank response sheet, completely off the topic, or just repeats or rephrases the question.

Your Responses Are Graded Holistically

Holistic rating means the raters assign a score based on their informed sense about your writing. Raters have a lot of answers to look at and they do not do a detailed analysis.

Write for a 2. Avoid a 0

Try to write enough to get a 2 on each item. You can get a 2 with a solid paragraph or two with about 80 to 100 words. Write enough to be considered for a 1. You can usually think of something to write about the topic. Two sentences on the topic is usually good enough for a 1.

If you get nine 2's and nine 1's you're right at the California minimum score.

Your Answer Will Usually Be One or Two Short Paragraphs

You will usually write a few short paragraphs for each item. You may have to draw a diagram, and some mathematics items may call for computations.

First Step—Review All the Items

Take about five minutes to read over all the items. Form an initial impression of each item. Write any initial thoughts on the test next to the item. You may decide to respond to the items out of order. Just write your own numbering next to each item.

WRITING YOUR RESPONSES

Use Your Nine Minutes Wisely

You have about nine minutes to write the response for each item. Do not spend more time than this on any one item. You can come back to a item if you have time at the end of the test.

Allocate your time in the following way.

1. **Read and Understand the Item (1 minute).**
   Identify the topic. Read the item carefully. The item may have several parts. Read carefully to ensure that you understand each of the parts. You have to stay on topic. If you write a great answer but it is not about the item, the rater will give you a score of 0. Don't waste your time supplying information not called for in the item. Extraneous information will not improve your score.
2. **Write Your Response (6 minutes).**
   Write clearly and directly. Plan to write one or two paragraphs. The raters are used to reading responses like yours. Don't waste any words. Don't restate the item. The next section gives detailed steps for writing your response.

   Use This Approach When You Write Your Response:

   Write a topic sentence. Raters expect one clear statement about the topic. Choose and write yours and stick to it. Make sure the topic sentence directly addresses the topic.
   Write one or two sentences with details to support the topic sentence. Details support the topic sentence. Details tell how, what, or why the topic sentence is true. Details can be explanations or examples.
   Write a second topic sentence to begin another paragraph. Write one sentence with details to support that topic sentence.
3. **Edit and Revise. (2 minutes)**
   Delete, add, or change words if you want to. Leave time to read your essay over. Raters understand that your essay is a first draft and they expect to see corrections. However, don't spend time correcting minor grammatical or punctuation errors. Do not attempt to copy your answer; you will not have time.

APPLYING THE STEPS

Let's see how to apply these steps to a particular item.

Item: Discuss the difference between a metaphor and a simile.

1. **Read and Understand the Item (1 minute).**
   The topic is: difference between a metaphor and a simile. We will discuss simile and metaphor, but the emphasis will be on the difference.
2. **Write Your Response (6 minutes).**
   Write a topic sentence.
   A metaphor discusses one thing as though it were something else, while a simile compares two different things.
   This sentence summarizes the difference between a metaphor and a simile. The word *while* emphasizes the difference.
   Write one or two sentences with details to support the topic sentence.
   For example, "dawn crept out of night" is a metaphor, while "dawn opened like a flower" is a simile. The metaphor discusses day and night as though they were people or animals, but the simile compares dawn to a flower.
   We gave an example of the difference between a simile and a metaphor, and then we explained the difference between the examples.
   Write a second topic sentence to begin another paragraph.
   Write one sentence with details to support that topic sentence.
   You can usually tell the difference between a metaphor and a simile because a simile uses the words like *and* as. *A metaphor does not use these words.*

3. Edit and Revise (2 minutes).

We'll take this response as it is.

This response has 85 words. It should be good for a solid 2 or a 3.

A *metaphor* discusses one thing as though it were something else, while a *simile* compares two different things. For example, "dawn crept out of night" is a *metaphor*, while "dawn opened like a flower" is a *simile*. The *metaphor* discusses day and night as though they were people or animals. The *simile* compares dawn to a flower.

You can usually tell the difference between a *metaphor* and a *simile* because a *simile* uses the words *like* or *as*. A *metaphor* does not use these words.

A response rated a 1 might look like this.

A *metaphor* and a *simile* are different because a *simile* uses the words like or as. A *metaphor* does not use these words.

Responses rated a 0 might look like this.

A *metaphor* and a *simile* are both figures of speech. Figures of speech are not supposed to be taken literally.

This response is off the topic. It will be rated 0 even though it contains correct information.

A discussion of the differences between a *simile* and a *metaphor* means understanding that they are not the same. And they must be different because they refer to different things.

This response just restates the question. It will be rated 0.

USING A CALCULATOR

You may use any nonprogrammable calculator on all parts of the MSAT. You should definitely bring an appropriate calculator with you. Here are some basic tips.

What Type of Calculator Can't I Bring to the MSAT?

You can't bring a programmable calculator. This type of calculator lets you enter and store special programs. It could also be used to enter test questions and answers into the calculator's memory. Educational Testing Service doesn't want you to have access to these questions.

It is pretty easy to tell if a calculator can be programmed. This type of calculator usually has a program (PRGM) key. This type of calculator will also have all the letters of the alphabet somewhere on the keypad and an alpha key to enter letters.

What Type of Calculator Should I Bring?

At a minimum, you should bring a four-function calculator with a memory key. The test is not written to require an advanced calculator, and you don't need one.

All calculators sold today have LCD displays (black symbols with a silver background) and so should yours. It is better to have a solar rather than a battery-operated calculator. If you have a battery-operated calculator, be sure the batteries are fresh.

If you have a calculator with these minimum features, and you're accustomed to using it, that's great. Do not go out and buy a new calculator. Bring the one you have. If you are going to learn about a new calculator for the test, then consider these choices.

The *Texas Instruments Math Explorer Plus* is an inexpensive solar calculator with the basic functions and some interesting features. You can enter, add, subtract, multiply, and divide fractions and mixed numbers. The calculator converts between fractions/mixed numbers and decimals and does integer operations. The calculator also has a square root key and a power key. The calculator keys are laid out in a clear manner with distinguishing colors. For a mix of simplicity, usefulness, and cost, this is the type of calculator that I would use.

Key Entry Errors

Many calculator mistakes come from key entry errors. I would want to avoid that at all costs. Let me explain.

When you work with paper and pencil, you see all your work. On most calculators, you see only the last entry or the last answer. So it is possible to make a key entry error and, in a flurry of entries, never catch your mistake. We all put an enormous amount of trust in the calculator answer, and we don't usually question the answer it produces. This makes us particularly vulnerable to the results of these key entry errors.

Nonprogrammable Graphing Calculator

A nonprogrammable graphing calculator such as the *FX6300* will help eliminate this type of error. Just as the name implies, graphing calculators show graphs of equations. But more important for you, these calculators show from five to eight lines of symbols. This means that you can review all your key entries as well as your answer. But the calculator has a very busy keypad, and it is also difficult to work with fractions.

Choose the calculator you are most comfortable using.

How Should I Use a Calculator?

Use your calculator to calculate. Remember that the calculator is best at helping you find answers quickly. Use it to calculate the answers to numerical problems. Use it to try out answers quickly to find which is correct. Whenever you come across a problem involving calculation, you can use the calculator to do or check your work.

Estimate before you calculate. Earlier in this section we mentioned that many calculator errors are caused by key entry mistakes. You think you put in one number, but you really put in another. One way to avoid this type of error is to estimate before you calculate. Then compare the estimate to your answer. If they aren't close, then either your estimate or your calculation is off.

Recognize when your calculator will be helpful. Let's think of problems in three categories. The calculator can be a big help, some help, or no help. The idea is to use your calculator on the first two types of problems and not to use it when it won't help.

Big Help

P Q R S T

The segment $\overline{PT}$ has a length of 31.5. What is the length of segment $\overline{QS}$?

A calculator is a big help here. There are 9 units from *P* to *T*. So divide 31.5 by 9 = 3.5 to find the length of each unit. Multiply 3.5 by 5 = 17.5 to find the length of *QS*.

Some Help

A rectangle has a length 3 and width 5. What is the area?

You can do this computation in your head. A calculator could help you check the answer, but you don't absolutely need it.

No Help

Calculators are no help with problems involving equations or nonnumerical solutions. Using a calculator when it won't help will cause trouble and waste time.

How Are Calculator Keys Used?

Press the numeral keys and the decimal point to represent numbers.

Press the [+], [–], [×], and [÷] keys to add, subtract, multiply, and divide.

Press the equal [=] key when you are through to get the final answer.

4 [×] 7 [+] 9 [=] ***13.7*** **12 [–] 18 [=]** ***-6***

6 [×] 4 [×] 3 [=] ***25.8*** **10 [÷] 3 [=]** ***3.3333333***

The [CE] key clears the current display.

The [C] key clears the entry and all the work you have done.

Pressing [C] means you are starting all over.

You will find these special keys on the TI Math Explorer Plus.

Square Root. The calculator may have a [√] key. To find the square root of 38.44 enter 38.44 [√] =. Note also that the square root key will not simplify a square root. So the square root shows up as 2.8284, not $2\sqrt{2}$.

Integers. The subtraction key on the calculator cannot be used to represent negative integers. Use the [+/–] key on the calculator after a number to change the sign. For example, to subtract $^{-}62 - {}^{+}25$, enter 62 [+/–] [–] 25 [=]. To multiply $^{-}8 \times {}^{-}6$, enter 8 [+/–] [×] 6 [+/–] [=].

Some calculators have these special keys.

Memory. The calculator may have [M+] and [MR] keys. Use the [M+] key to store a number in the calculator memory. Use the [MR] key to recall the number from memory and show it on the display.

Power. The power key looks like this [y^x]. Use this key to raise a number to a power.

To find the cube of 4 enter **4** [y^x] **3** [=]. The answer is 64.

Percent. The percent key helps you find taxes, mark-ups, and discounts directly.

For example, to find the 6.5% tax on a \$48 bill enter 48 $\boxed{+}$ 6.5 $\boxed{\%}$ $\boxed{=}$.

To find the cost of a \$92 item after a 15% discount enter 92 $\boxed{-}$ 15 $\boxed{\%}$ $\boxed{=}$.

Fractions. The TI Math Explorer Plus and other calculators show the answer to fraction and mixed number problems as fractions and mixed numbers. If you don't have this type of calculator, use the division sign in place of the fraction bar. Your answers will be displayed as decimals. When you do operations with fractions on the TI Math Explorer Plus, the fraction answer is shown in simplest form. For example, to add $^1/_4$ and $^1/_6$ enter **1** $\boxed{/}$ **4** + **1** $\boxed{/}$ **6** $\boxed{=}$.

Other keys. The calculator may have parentheses keys $\boxed{(}$ $\boxed{)}$. Use these keys to enter an expression such as: $\boxed{(}$ **2** $\boxed{+}$ **3** $\boxed{)}$ $\boxed{\times}$ 4. If you don't use the parentheses keys, you will not get the correct answer.

The calculator may have a $\boxed{10^n}$ key, to raise 10 to a power. For example, to find 10 to the 6th power enter $\boxed{10^n}$ **6** $\boxed{=}$. To find $^1/_{10^6}$ enter $\boxed{10^n}$ **6** $\boxed{+/-}$ $\boxed{=}$.

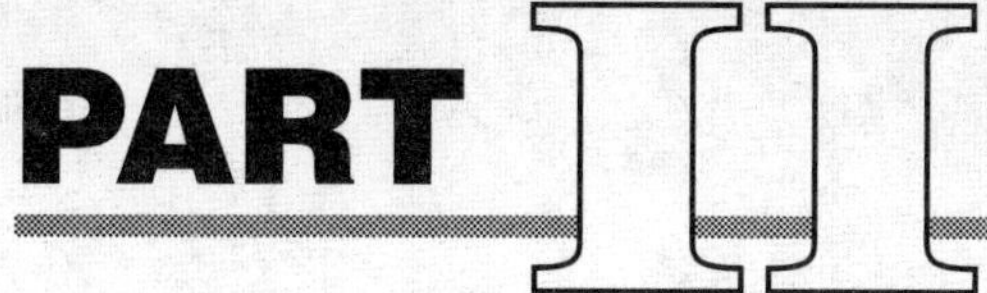

PART II

Subject Matter Preparation, Strategies, and Practice for the MSAT

3 LITERATURE AND LANGUAGE STUDIES

TEST INFO BOX

24 of 120 Multiple Choice items — 20% of Content Knowledge items
3 of 18 Short Answer items — 17% of Content Area Exercise items

LITERATURE AND LANGUAGE ITEMS

Literature and Language multiple choice items look like this.

In which sentence is the underlined word used correctly?

(A) The rider grabbed the horse's reign.
(B) The teacher had just begun her lessen.
(C) The dog's collar showed its address.
(D) The road offered a steep assent to the plateau.

Literature and Language short answer items look like this.

Write two brief paragraphs, one using argumentation and one using narration, to support Pacific Coast ecological movements.

USING THIS CHAPTER

This chapter prepares you to take the Literature and Language Studies part of the MSAT. Choose one of these approaches.

I want a thorough Literature and Language Studies review.

- ❑ Read the entire Literature and Language Review.
- ❑ Go over the Special Strategies for Answering the Literature and Language items on pages 52–54.
- ❑ Complete the Literature and Language MSAT Practice Questions on page 55.

I want to practice Literature and Language Studies items.

- ❑ Go over the Special Strategies for Answering the Literature and Language items on pages 52–54.
- ❑ Complete the Literature and Language MSAT Practice Questions on page 55.

I don't need any Literature and Language Studies review.

- ❑ OK. If you're sure, skip this chapter.

LITERATURE AND LANGUAGE STUDIES REVIEW

VOCABULARY

This vocabulary review will help you prepare for the Literature and Language items. It will also help you prepare to read all the other MSAT items. This section begins with roots and prefixes followed by a vocabulary list. It shows you how to find the meaning of a word from context clues, roots, and prefixes.

CONTEXT CLUES

Many times you can figure out a word from its context. Look at these examples. Synonyms, antonyms, examples, or descriptions may help you figure out the word.

1. The woman's mind wandered as her two friends *prated* on. It really did not bother her though. In all the years she had known them, they had always *babbled* about their lives. It was almost comforting.
2. The wind *abated* in the late afternoon. Things were different yesterday when the wind had *picked up* toward the end of the day.
3. The argument with her boss had been her *Waterloo*. She wondered if the *defeat* suffered by Napoleon *at this famous place* had felt the same.
4. The events swept the politician into a *vortex* of controversy. The politician knew what it meant to be spun around like a toy boat in the *swirl of water* that swept down the bathtub drain.

Passage 1 gives a synonym for the unknown word. We can tell that *prated* means babbled. *Babbled* is used as a synonym of *prated* in the passage.

Passage 2 gives an antonym for the unknown word. We can tell that *abated* means slowed down or diminished because *picked up* is used as an antonym of *abated.*

Passage 3 gives a description of the unknown word. The description of *Waterloo* tells us that the word means *defeat.*

Passage 4 gives an example of the unknown word. This example of a *swirl of water* going down the bathtub drain gives us a good idea of what a *vortex* is.

ROOTS

A root is the basic element of a word. The root is usually related to the word's origin. Roots can often help you figure out the word's meaning. Here are some roots that may help you.

Root	Meaning	Examples
bio	life	biography, biology
circu	around	circumference, circulate
frac	break	fraction, refract
geo	earth	geology, geography
mal	bad	malicious, malcontent
matr, mater	mother	maternal, matron
neo	new	neonate, neoclassic
patr, pater	father	paternal, patron
spec	look	spectacles, specimen
tele	distant	telephone, television

PREFIXES

Prefixes are syllables that come at the beginning of a word. Prefixes usually have a standard meaning. They can often help you figure out the word's meaning. Here is a list of prefixes that may help you figure out a word.

Prefix	Meaning	Examples
a-	not	amoral, apolitical
il-, im-, ir-	not	illegitimate, immoral, incorrect
un-	not	unbearable, unknown
non-	not	nonbeliever, nonsense
ant-, anti-	against	antiwar, antidote
de-	opposite	defoliate, declaw
mis-	wrong	misstep, misdeed
ante-	before	antedate, antecedent
fore-	before	foretell, forecast
post-	after	postfight, postoperative
re-	again	refurbish, redo
super-	above	superior, superstar
sub-	below	subsonic, subpar

THE VOCABULARY LIST

Here is a list of a few hundred vocabulary words. This list includes everyday words and a few specialized education terms. Read through the list and visualize the words and their definitions. After a while you will become very familiar with them.

Of course, this is not anywhere near all the words you need to know for the MSAT. But they will give you a start. These words also will give you some idea of the kinds of nonspecialized words you may encounter on the MSAT.

Another great way to develop a vocabulary is to read a paper every day and a news magazine every week, in addition to the other reading you are doing. There are also several inexpensive books, including *1100 Words You Need to Know*, *Pocket Guide to Vocabulary*, and *Vocabulary Success* from Barron's, which may help you develop your vocabulary further.

abhor To regard with horror
I abhor violence.
abstain To refrain by choice
Ray decided to abstain from fattening foods.
abstract Not related to any object, theoretical
Mathematics can be very abstract.
acquisition An addition to an established group or collection
The museum's most recent acquisition was an early Roman vase.
admonish To correct firmly but kindly
The teacher admonished the student not to chew gum in class.
adroit Skillful or nimble in difficult circumstances
The nine year old was already an adroit gymnast.
adversary A foe or enemy
The wildebeast was ever-alert for its ancient adversary, the lion.
advocate To speak for an idea; a person who speaks for an idea
Lou was an advocate of gun control.
aesthetic Pertaining to beauty
Ron found the painting a moving aesthetic experience.
affective To do with the emotional or feeling aspect of learning
Len read the Taxonomy of Educational Objectives: Affective Domain.
alias An assumed name
The check forger had used an alias.
alleviate To reduce or make more bearable
The hot shower helped alleviate the pain in her back.
allude To make an indirect reference to, hint at
Elaine only alluded to her previous trips through the state.
ambiguous Open to many interpretations
That is an ambiguous statement.
apathy Absence of passion or emotion
The teacher tried to overcome their apathy toward the subject.
apprehensive Fear or unease about possible outcomes
Bob was apprehensive about visiting the dentist.
aptitude The ability to gain from a particular type of instruction
The professor pointed out that aptitude alone was not enough for success in school.
articulate To speak clearly and distinctly, present a point of view
Chris was chosen to articulate the group's point of view.
assess To measure or determine an outcome or value
There are many informal ways to assess learning.
attest To affirm or certify
I can attest to Cathy's ability as a softball pitcher.
augment To increase or add to
The new coins augmented the already large collection.

belated Past time or tardy
George sent a belated birthday card.
benevolent Expresses good will or kindly feelings
The club was devoted to performing benevolent acts.
biased A prejudiced view or action
The judge ruled that the decision was biased.
bolster To shore up, support
The explorer sang to bolster her courage.

candid Direct and outspoken
Lee was well known for her candid comments.
caricature Exaggerated, ludicrous picture, in words or a cartoon
The satirist presented world leaders as caricatures.
carnivorous Flesh eating or predatory
The lion is a carnivorous animal.
censor A person who judges the morality of others; act on that judgment
Please don't censor my views!
censure Expression of disapproval, reprimand
The senate acted to censure the congressman.
cessation The act of ceasing or halting
The eleventh hour marked the cessation of hostilities.
chronic Continuing and constant
Asthma can be a chronic condition.
clandestine Concealed or secret
The spy engaged in clandestine activities.
cogent Intellectually convincing
He presented a cogent argument.
cognitive Relates to the intellectual area of learning
Lou read the Taxonomy of Educational Objectives: Cognitive Domain.
competency Demonstrated ability
Bert demonstrated the specified mathematics competency.
complacent Unaware self-satisfaction
The tennis player realized she had become complacent.

concept A generalization
The professor lectured on concept development.

congenital Existing at birth but nonhereditary
The baby had a small congenital defect.

contemporaries Belonging in the same time period, about the same age
Piaget and Bruner were contemporaries.

contempt Feeling or showing disdain or scorn
She felt nothing but contempt for their actions.

contentious Argumentative
Tim was in a contentious mood.

corroborate To make certain with other information, to confirm
The reporter would always corroborate a story before publication.

credence Claim to acceptance or trustworthiness
They did not want to lend credence to his views.

cursory Surface, not in depth
Ron gave his car a cursory inspection.

daunt To intimidate with fear
Harry did not let the difficulty of the task daunt him.

debacle Disastrous collapse or rout
The whole trip had been a debacle.

debilitate To make feeble
He was concerned that the flu would debilitate him.

decadent Condition of decline/decay
Joan said in frustration, "We live in a decadent society."

deductive Learning that proceeds from general to specific
He proved his premise using deductive logic.

demographic Population data
The census gathers demographic information.

denounce To condemn a person or idea
The diplomat rose in the United Nations to denounce the plan.

deter To prevent or stop an action, usually by some threat
The president felt that the peace conference would help deter aggression.

diligent A persistent effort; a person who makes such an effort
The investigator was diligent in her pursuit of the truth.

discern To perceive or recognize, often by insight
The principal attempted to discern which student was telling the truth.

discord Disagreement or disharmony
Gail's early promotion led to discord in the office.

discriminate To distinguish among people or groups based on their characteristics
It is not appropriate to discriminate based on race or ethnicity.

disdain To show or act with contempt
The professional showed disdain for her amateurish efforts.

disseminate To send around, scatter
The health organization will disseminate any new information on the flu.

divergent Thinking that extends in many directions, is not focused
Les was an intelligent but divergent thinker.

diverse Not uniform, varied
Alan came from a diverse neighborhood.

duress coercion
He claimed that he confessed under duress.

eccentric Behaves unusually, different from the norm
His long hair and midnight walks made Albert appear eccentric.

eclectic Drawing from several ideas or practices
Joe preferred an eclectic approach to the practice of psychology.

eloquent Vivid, articulate expression
The congregation was spellbound by the eloquent sermon.

emanate To flow out, come forth
How could such wisdom emanate from one so young?

embellish To make things seem more than they are
Art loved to embellish the truth.

empirical From observation or experiment
The scientist's conclusions were based on empirical evidence.

employment A job or professional position (paid)
You seek employment so you can make the big bucks.

enduring Lasting over the long term
Their friendship grew into an enduring relationship.

enhance To improve or build up
The mechanic used a fuel additive to enhance the car's performance.

enigma A mystery or puzzle
The communist bloc is an "enigma wrapped inside a mystery." (Churchill)

equity Equal attention or treatment
The workers were seeking pay equity with others in their industry.

equivocal Uncertain, capable of multiple interpretations
In an attempt to avoid conflict, the negotiator took an equivocal stand.

expedite To speed up, facilitate
Hal's job at the shipping company was to expedite deliveries.

exploit Take maximum advantage of, perhaps unethically
Her adversary tried to exploit her grief to gain an advantage.

extrinsic Coming from outside
The teacher turned to extrinsic motivation.

farce A mockery
The attorney objected, saying that the testimony made the trial a farce.

feign To pretend, make a false appearance of
Some people feign illness to get out of work.

fervent Marked by intense feeling
The spokesman presented a fervent defense of the company's actions.

fiasco Total failure
They had not prepared for the presentation, and it turned into a fiasco.

formidable Difficult to surmount
State certification requirements can present a formidable obstacle.

fracas A noisy quarrel or a scrap
The debate turned into a full-fledged fracas.

gamut Complete range or extent
Waiting to take the test, her mind ran the gamut of emotions.

glib Quickness suggesting insincerity
The glib response made Rita wonder about the speaker's sincerity.

grave Very serious or weighty
The supervisor had grave concerns about the worker's ability.

guile Cunning, crafty, duplicitous
When the truth failed, he tried to win his point with guile.

handicapped Having one or more disabilities
The child study team classified Loren as handicapped.

harass Bother persistently
Some fans came to harass the players on the opposing team.

heterogeneous A group with normal variation in ability or performance
Students from many backgrounds formed a heterogeneous population.

homogeneous A group with little variation in ability or performance
The school used test scores to place students in homogeneous groups.

hypocrite One who feigns a virtuous character or belief
Speaking against drinking and then driving drunk make him a hypocrite!

immune Protected or exempt from disease or harm
The vaccination made Ray immune to measles.

impartial Fair and objective
The contestants agreed on an objective, impartial referee.

impasse Situation with no workable solution
The talks had not stopped, but they had reached an impasse.

impede To retard or obstruct
Mason did not let adversity impede his progress.

implicit Understood but not directly stated
They never spoke about the matter, but they had an implicit understanding.

indifferent Uncaring or apathetic
The teacher was indifferent to the student's pleas for an extension.

indigenous Native to an area
The botanist recognized it as an indigenous plant.

inductive Learning that proceeds from specific to general
Science uses an inductive process, from examples to a generalization.

inevitable Certain and unavoidable
After the rains, the collapse of the dam was inevitable.

infer To reach a conclusion not explicitly stated
The advertisement sought to infer that the product was superior.

inhibit To hold back or restrain
The hormone was used to inhibit growth.

innovate To introduce something new or change established procedure
Mere change was not enough, they had to innovate the procedure.

inquiry Question-based Socratic learning
Much of science teaching uses inquiry-based learning.

intrinsic inherent, the essential nature
The teacher drew on the meaning of the topic for an intrinsic motivation.

inundate To overwhelm, flood
It was December, and mail began to inundate the post office.

jocular Characterized by joking or good nature
The smiling man seemed to be a jocular fellow.

judicial Relating to the administration of justice
His goal was to have no dealings with the judicial system.

knack A talent for doing something
Ron had a real knack for mechanical work.

languid Weak, lacking energy
The sunbather enjoyed a languid afternoon at the shore.

liaison An illicit relationship or a means of communication
The governor appointed his chief aid liaison to the senate.

lucid Clear and easily understood
The teacher answered the question in a direct and lucid way.

magnanimous Generous in forgiving
Loretta is a magnanimous to a fault.

malignant Very injurious, evil
Crime is a malignant sore on our society.

malleable Open to being shaped or influenced
He had a malleable position on gun control.

meticulous Very careful and precise
Gina took meticulous care of the fine china.

miser A money hoarder
The old miser had more money than he could ever use.

monotonous Repetitive and boring
Circling the airport, waiting to land, became monotonous.

mores Understood rules of society
Linda made following social mores her goal in life.

motivation Something that creates interest or action
Most good lessons begin with good motivation.

myriad Large indefinite number
Look skyward and be amazed by the myriad of stars.

naive Lacking sophistication
Laura is unaware, and a little naive, about the impact she has on others.

nemesis A formidable rival
Lex Luthor is Superman's nemesis.

novice A beginner
Her unsteady legs revealed that Sue was a novice skater.

nullified Removed the importance of
The penalty nullified the 20-yard gain made by the running back.

objective A goal
The teacher wrote an objective for each lesson.

oblivious Unaware and unmindful
Les was half asleep and oblivious to the racket around him.

obscure Vague, unclear, uncertain
The lawyer quoted an obscure reference.

ominous Threatening or menacing
There were ominous black storm clouds on the horizon.

palatable Agreeable, acceptable
Sandy's friends tried to make her punishment more palatable.

panorama A comprehensive view or picture
The visitors' center offered a panorama of the canyon below.

pedagogy The science of teaching
Part of certification tests focus on pedagogy.

perpetuate To continue or cause to be remembered
A plaque was put up to perpetuate the memory of the retiring teacher.

pompous Exaggerated self-importance
Rona acted pompous, but Lynne suspected she was very empty inside.

precarious Uncertain, beyond one's control
A diver sat on a precarious perch on a cliff above the water.

precedent An act or instance that sets the standard
The judge's ruling set a precedent for later cases.

preclude To act to make impossible or impracticable
Beau did not want to preclude any options.

precocious Very early development
Chad was very precocious and ran at six months.

prolific Abundant producer
Isaac Asimov was a prolific science fiction writer.

prognosis A forecast or prediction
The stock broker gave a guarded prognosis for continued growth.

provoke To stir up or anger
Children banging on the cage would provoke the circus lion to growl.

psychomotor Relates to the motor skill area of learning
I read the Taxonomy of Behavioral Objectives: Psychomotor Domain.

quagmire Predicament or difficult situation
The regulations were a quagmire of conflicting rules and vague terms.

qualm Feeling of doubt or misgiving
The teacher had not a single qualm about giving the student a low grade.

quandary A dilemma
The absence of the teacher aide left the teacher in a quandary.

quench To put out, satisfy
The glass of water was not enough to quench his thirst.

rancor Bitter continuing resentment
A deep rancor had existed between the two friends since the accident.

rationale The basis or reason for something
The speeder tried to present a rationale to the officer who stopped her.

reciprocal Mutual interchange
Each person got something out of their reciprocal arrangement.

refute To prove false
The lawyer used new evidence to refute claims made by the prosecution.

remedial Designed to compensate for learning deficits
Jim spent one period a day in remedial instruction.

reprove Criticize gently
The teacher would reprove students for chewing gum in class.

repudiate To reject or disown
The senator repudiated membership in an all male club.

resolve To reach a definite conclusion
A mediator was called in to resolve the situation.

retrospect Contemplation of the past
Ryan noted, in retrospect, that leaving home was his best decision.

revere To hold in the highest regard
Citizens of the town revere their long time mayor.

sanction To issue authoritative approval or a penalty
The boxing commissioner had to sanction the match.

scrutinize To inspect with great care
You should scrutinize any document before signing it.

siblings Brothers or sisters
The holidays give me the chance to spend time with my siblings.

skeptical Doubting, questioning the validity
The principal was skeptical about the students' reason for being late.

solace Comfort in misfortune
Her friends provided solace in her time of grief.

solitude Being alone
Pat enjoyed her Sunday afternoon moments of solitude.

stagnant Inert, contaminated
In dry weather the lake shrank to a stagnant pool.

stereotype An oversimplified generalized view or belief
We are all guilty of fitting people into a stereotype.

subsidy Financial assistance
Chris received a subsidy from her company so she could attend school.

subtle Faint, not easy to find or understand
Subtle changes in the teller's actions alerted the police to the robbery.

subterfuge A deceptive strategy
The spy used subterfuge to gain access to the secret materials.

superficial Surface, not profound
The inspector gave the car a superficial inspection.

tacit Not spoken, inferred
They had a tacit agreement.

taxonomy Classification of levels of thinking or organisms
I read each Taxonomy of Educational Objectives.

tenacious Persistent and determined
The police officer was tenacious in pursuit of a criminal.

tentative Unsure, uncertain
The athletic director set up a tentative basketball schedule.

terminate To end, conclude
He wanted to terminate the relationship.

transition Passage from one activity to another
The transition from college student to teacher was not easy.

trepidation Apprehension, state of dread
Erin felt some trepidation about beginning her new job

trivial Unimportant, ordinary
The seemingly trivial occurrence had taken on added importance.

ubiquitous Everywhere, omnipresent
A walk through the forest invited attacks from the ubiquitous mosquitoes.

ultimatum A final demand
After a trying day, the teacher issued an ultimatum to the class.

usurp To wrongfully and forcefully seize and hold, particularly power
The association vice president tried to usurp the president's power.

vacillate To swing indecisively
He had a tendency to vacillate in his stance on discipline.

valid Logically correct
The math teacher was explaining a valid mathematical proof.

vehement Forceful, passionate
The child had a vehement reaction to the teacher's criticism.

vestige A sign of something no longer there or existing
Old John was the last vestige of the first teachers to work at the school.

vicarious Experience through the activities or feelings of others
He had to experience sports in a vicarious way through his students.

virulent Very poisonous or noxious
The coral snake has a particularly virulent venom.

vital Important and essential
The school secretary was a vital part of the school.

waffle To write or speak in a misleading way
The spokesperson waffled as she tried to explain away the mistake.

wary Watchful, on guard
The soldiers were very wary of any movements in the field.

Xanadu An idyllic, perfect place
All wished for some time in Xanadu.

yearned Longed or hoped for
Liz yearned for a small class.

zeal Diligent devotion to a cause
Ron approached his job with considerable zeal.

LITERATURE

Children's Literature

Children's literature, as we know it, did not exist until the late 1700s. Jean Rousseau, in his influential *Emile*, was among the first writers to popularize the view that children were not just small adults. A collection of age-old fairy tales, *The Tales of Mother Goose*, was published in France about 1700. The first illustrated book was probably *The Visible World in Pictures*, which was written in Latin about 1760 by John Comenius.

Before this time, most children's literature conveyed a religious or moral message or was designed for instruction. A few adult books appealed to children including *Robinson Crusoe* and the satirical *Gulliver's Travels*.

In the United States during the 1800s, James Fenimore Cooper wrote *The Last of the Mohicans*, Washington Irving wrote *The Legend of Sleepy Hollow*, and Nathaniel Hawthorne wrote *A Wonder Book for Boys and Girls*. Louisa May Alcott wrote *Little Women* and Samuel Clemens, writing as Mark Twain, wrote *The Adventures of Huckleberry Finn*. Horatio Alger wrote a series of "rags to riches" books at the end of the century.

On the European continent, the Brothers Grimm published *Grimm's Fairy Tales*, which included "Snow White and the Seven Dwarfs." Hans Christian Anderson published a number of stories including "The Ugly Duckling." *Heidi* and the *Adventures of Pinocchio* were also published about this time.

In England, Charles Dodgson, writing as Lewis Carroll, penned *Alice's Adventures in Wonderland*. John Tenniel provided the illustrations for this famous work. Robert Louis Stevenson wrote *Treasure Island*, Rudyard Kipling wrote *The Jungle Book*, and Edward Lear wrote the *Nonsense Book*.

At the beginning of this century, Frank Baum wrote the first *Wizard of Oz* book and Lucy Maud Montgomery wrote *Anne of Green Gables*. Also in this century, Hugh Loftig penned the famous Dr. Doolittle books, A. A. Milne published a series of Winnie-the-Pooh books and P. L.

Travers wrote the Mary Poppins books. Albert Payson Terhune wrote a series of dog stories, most notably *Lad a Dog*.

The Little Prince and *Charlotte's Web* were published in the mid 1900s. About this time, Theodore Geisel, writing as Dr. Seuss, began to write a popular series of books, including *Green Eggs and Ham*. Notable books of the past twenty years include *The Snowy Day*, and *Where the Wild Things Are*.

The Newbery Award and Caldecott Medal are given annually to the most notable American children's books. The Newbery Award is named after publisher John Newbery and is awarded to the best American children's book. The Caldecott Medal is named after illustrator Randolph Caldecott and is given to the best picture book.

Poetry

Poetry usually communicates through linguistic imagery, sounds of words, and a rhythmic quality. Poetry and poems are among the oldest forms of literature and date to ancient Greece. Ancient poems were originally sung, and poetry has been slowly emancipated from this reliance on music, replacing it with a linguistic cadence.

Poetry is often associated with rhyming. However, many poems do not rhyme. Some poems rely on their rhythmic patterns alone, others are composed of open verses, while still others, such as Japanese haiku, rely on special features such as the number of syllables in a line.

The epic, the lyric, and some romances are examples of early poetry.

Epic

The epic is a very long narrative poem, usually about a single heroic person. Epics have a monumental sweep, embrace the essence of an entire nation, and frequently include mythical forces that influence the inevitable battles and conflicts. Epics include the *Odyssey* and the *Illiad*, which were written by Homer and embrace Greek national themes, as well as the Scandinavian *Beowulf*.

Lyric

The lyric is related to the epic, but it is shorter and presents profound feelings or ideas. The terms elegy and ode both refer to lyric poems. Lyric poems were called rondeaus when sung by French troubadours and madrigals when sung by English balladeers. During the 1800s both Robert Browning and Tennyson wrote lyrics. Modern lyrics are still written but no longer occupy a central place in culture.

Romance

The romance and the epic are similar. However, the romance is concerned with love and chivalry and, originally, was written in one of the romance languages. This genre of literature dates from the 1100s and was most popular during the 1200s. Stories of *King Arthur and the Knights of the Round Table* are romances.

Satire

Satire exposes the frailty of the human condition through wit, irony, mockery, sarcasm, or ridicule. For example, the sentence, "The doctor looked down at the man sneaking away from the impending flu shot and said, 'At least he knows to avoid sharp objects,'" is an example of satire. Occasionally, entire works such as Jonathan Swift's *Gulliver's Travels* are satirical.

Short Story

The short story is a short fictional piece, usually with a single theme. The first short stories date from ancient Egypt. O. Henry and Mark Twain were famous writers who penned short stories in the early 1900s. Hemingway and Faulkner wrote short stories before mid-century with John Cheever and Eudora Welty noted as prominent short story writers in the latter half of the century.

Novel

The novel is a fictional story that depicts characters in a plot. The novel builds on the epic and the romance. The first novels were written during the Renaissance (1300–1600) and were developed more fully during the 1700s and 1800s in England.

The modern novel developed in the 1800s. Novels with strong historical and social themes, including dialogue, were written by the English authors Dickens, Thackeray, and Eliot. American novels written during this time tended to be allegorical.

American novels in the early 1900s focused on social ills. These novels include *The Jungle* by Sinclair Lewis, *Studs Lonigan* by James Farrell, and *The Grapes of Wrath* by John Steinbeck. In the late 1900s American novels of great strength appeared including *The Naked and the Dead* by Norman Mailer and *Catch-22* by Joseph Heller.

APPROACHES TO READING AND INTERPRETING LITERATURE

This section shows how to interpret passages on the Literature and Language Studies sections of the MSAT.

Recognize the Author's Purpose

The author's primary purpose explains why the author wrote the passage. The purpose is closely related to the main idea. You might think. "Fine, I know the main idea. But why did the author take the time to write about that main idea?" "What is the author trying to make me know or feel?"

The author's purpose will be in one of the following five categories.

Describe	Present an image of physical reality or a mental image.
Entertain	Amuse, Perform
Inform	Clarify, Explain, State
Narrate	Relate, Tell a story
Persuade	Argue, Convince, Prove

There is no hard and fast rule for identifying the author's purpose. Rely on your informed impression of the passage. Once in a while a passage may overtly state the author's purpose. But you must usually figure it out on your own. Remember, one of the answer choices will be correct. Your job is to decide which one it is.

Distinguish Between Fact and Opinion

Facts can be proven true *or* false by some objective means or method. *A fact refers to persons, things, or events that exist now or existed at some time in the past.* Note that a fact does not have to be true. For example, the statement "The tallest human being alive today is 86 inches tall" is false. This statement is a fact because it can be proven false.

Opinions, however, cannot be proved or disproved by some objective means or method.

Opinions are subjective and include attitudes and probabilities. Some statements, which seem true, may still be opinions. For example, the statement "A car is easier to park than a bus" seems true. However, this statement is an opinion. There is no way to objectively prove this statement true or false.

Examples:

Fact: Abraham Lincoln was President of the United States during the Civil War. We can check historical records and find out if the statement is true. This statement of fact is true.

Fact: Robert E. Lee went into exile in Canada after the Civil War. We can check historical records. This factual statement is true. Lee later became president of Washington College, now called Washington and Lee University.

Fact: It is more than 90°F. outside. We can use a thermometer to prove or disprove this statement.

Fact: More people were born in November than in any other month. We can check statistical records to prove or disprove this statement.

Opinion: If Lincoln had lived, Reconstruction would have been better. This sounds true, but there is no way to prove or disprove this statement.

Opinion: Lee was the Civil War's most brilliant general. Sounds true, but there is no way to prove it.

Opinion: It will always be colder in November than in July. Sounds true! But we can't prove or disprove future events.

Detect Bias

Bias

A statement or passage reveals bias if the author has prejudged or has a predisposition to a doctrine, idea, or practice. Bias means the author is trying to convince or influence the reader through some emotional appeal or slanted writing.

Bias can be positive or negative.

Positive Bias: She is so lovely, she deserves the very best.
Negative Bias: She is so horrible, I hope she gets what's coming to her.

Forms of Bias

Biased writing can often be identified by the presence of one or more of the following forms of bias.

Emotional Language Language that appeals to the reader's emotions, and not to common sense or logic.

Positive: If I am elected, I will help your family get jobs.
Negative: If my opponent is elected, your family will lose their jobs.

Inaccurate Information	Language that presents false, inaccurate, or unproved information as though it were factual. Positive: My polls indicate that I am very popular. Negative: My polls indicate that a lot of people disagree with my opponent.
Name Calling	Language that uses negative, disapproving terms without any factual basis. Negative: I'll tell you, my opponent is a real jerk.
Slanted Language	Language that slants the facts or evidence toward the writer's point of view. Positive: I am a positive person, looking for the good side of people. Negative: My opponent finds fault with everyone and everything.
Stereotyping	Language that indicates that a person is like all the members of a particular group. Positive: I belong to the Krepenkle party, the party known for its honesty. Negative: My opponent belongs to the Perplenkle party, the party of increased taxes.

Recognize the Author's Tone

Tone

The author's tone is the author's attitude as reflected in the passage. Answering this question means choosing the correct tone word. How do you think the author would sound while speaking? What impression would you form about the speaker's attitude or feeling? The answer to the latter question will usually lead you to the author's tone. A partial list of tone words is given below.

absurd	excited	outraged
amused	formal	outspoken
angry	gentle	pathetic
apathetic	hard	pessimistic
arrogant	impassioned	playful
bitter	indignant	prayerful
cheerful	intense	reverent
comic	intimate	righteous
compassionate	joyous	satirical
complex	loving	sentimental
concerned	malicious	serious
cruel	mocking	solemn
depressed	nostalgic	tragic
distressed	objective	uneasy
evasive	optimistic	vindictive

Recognize Valid Arguments

The terms valid and invalid have very special meaning on the MSAT. Valid arguments are reasonable. Valid arguments are objective and supported by evidence. Invalid arguments are *not* reasonable. They are not objective. Invalid arguments usually reflect one of the following fallacies.

Ad hominem	Arguing against a person to discredit their position, rather than an argument against the position itself
Ad populum	An argument that appeals to the emotions of the person
Bandwagon	Arguing for position because of its popularity
Begging the question	Assuming that an argument, or part of an argument, is true without providing proof
Circular logic	Using a statement of a position to argue in favor of that position
Either/or	Stating that the conclusion falls into one of two extremes, when there are more intermediate choices
Faulty analogy	Using an analogy as an argument when the analogy does not match the situation under discussion
Hasty generalization	Reaching a conclusion too quickly, before all the information is known
Non sequitur	A conclusion that does not logically follow from the facts
Post hoc, ergo propter hoc	Falsely stating that one event following another is caused by the first event (faulty cause and effect)
Red herring	An irrelevant point, diverting attention from the position under discussion

GLOSSARY OF LITERARY TERMS

allegory Expression in which the characters, story, and setting actually represent other people, settings, or abstract ideas. This symbolic meaning is more important than the literal meaning. For example, Jonathan Swift's *Gulliver's Travels* is allegorical when it uses horses and other creatures to represent people. *Aesop's Fables* use allegory to represent moral or ethical ideas. Parables such as the Prodigal Son use allegory to teach a lesson.

alliteration The repetition of an initial consonant in nearby words. For example, the selections "Neither rain, nor sleet nor dark of night," and "Peas?—Please. Peanuts?—Possibly. Potatoes?—Potentially. Pigs knuckles?—Please!" use alliteration.

anthropomorphism Attributing the human body or human qualities to nonhuman things or entities. Initially, anthropomorphism meant depicting a god or gods as humans with human qualities.

biography A full account of a person's life. An autobiography is a biography written by the person.

connotation The secondary meanings that the word represents.

couplet Two successive poetic lines that form a single unit because they rhyme.

denotation Actual meaning of the word

doggerel A work that features awkward or rough verbiage. Most often, this clumsy verse is the result of an inept writer, although it may occasionally be intended as humor.

essay A fairly brief work that tries to get across a particular point of view or to persuade the reader about the correctness of a point of view.

fable A short literary piece designed to present a moral or truth. Fables frequently involve animals. The most famous fables are attributed to a reputed Greek slave, Aesop, who lived in the sixth century.

figures of speech Figurative language that is not meant to be taken literally. Figures of speech are used to create some special meaning or imagery.

euphemism Figure of speech in which an inoffensive term is substituted for one that may be offensive or cause distress. For example, *pass away* may be substituted for *die*, and *indisposed* may be substituted for *ill*.

hyperbole Figure of speech in which a drastic overstatement or understatement is used. Hyperbole may be used to emphasize a point or for comic effect. For example, after an argument between friends one might exclaim, "You are the worst person who has ever lived." In another example, the winner of the Olympic decathlon may be referred to as "Not that bad an athlete."

metaphor Figure of speech in which one thing is discussed as though it were something else. The words *like* or *as* are not used. For example, "My life's a tennis match, but I never get to serve" and "The night crept through til dawn" are metaphors.

mixed metaphor Figure of speech in which two or more unrelated metaphors are combined. For example, "Running on empty, the soccer player plowed through the rest of the match" is a mixed metaphor.

onomatopoeia Figure of speech that refers to words that imitate natural sounds. Onomatopoeia appears in the words of a once popular song, "*Buzz, buzz, buzz* goes the bumble bee, *twiddely, diddely, dee* goes the bird."

simile Figure of speech that compares two different things, usually using the words *like* or *as*. For example, "Her eyes are like deep, quiet pools" or "Her nails are like tiger claws" are similes.

haiku Poetry of Japanese origin with three nonrhyming lines with a pattern of five-seven-five syllables.

legend A heroic story or collection of stories about a specific person or persons. Legends are presented as fact but are actually a combination of fact and fiction. Legends with differing degrees of factual content have been built around Davy Crockett, who "kilt him a bar when he was only three," and the gigantic logger Paul Bunyan and his blue ox Babe. Paul Bunyan reputedly cleared out entire Maine forests with one swing of the ax.

LANGUAGE AND LINGUISTICS

We use language, including gestures and sounds, to communicate. Humans first used gestures, but it was spoken language that opened the vistas for human communication. Language consists of two things: the thoughts that language conveys and the physical sounds, writing, and structure of the language itself.

Human speech organs (mouth, tongue, lips, etc.) were not developed to make sounds but they uniquely determined the sounds and words humans could produce. Human speech gradually came to be loosely bound together by unique rules of grammar.

Many believe that humans developed their unique ability to speak with the development of a specialized area of the brain called Broca's area. If this is so, human speech and language probably developed in the past 100,000 years.

The appearance of written language about 3500 B.C. separates prehistoric from historic times. Written language often does not adequately represent the spoken language. For example, English uses the 26-letter Latin alphabet, which does not represent all the English sounds.

The English Language

The English language emerged 1500 years ago from Germanic languages on the European continent and developed primarily in England. American English is based on the English language and includes words from every major language including Latin, Greek, and French.

English is spoken throughout Australia, Canada, the United Kingdom, and the United States. It is the most universally accepted language in the world, and only Chinese is spoken by more people. In all likelihood, English will become even more prominent as the world's primary language.

Some experts estimate that there are over 1,000,000 English words, more than any other language in the world. Sounds and letters do not match in the English language. For example the word spelled t-o-u-g-h is pronounced *tuf*. The rock group Phish also reminds us of this variation, which often makes English words difficult to pronounce and spell.

Linguistics

Linguistics is the scientific study of language. Linguistics studies the development of languages and language groups, vocabulary and meaning, the structure of contemporary languages, and how speech and language is learned and taught. A list of the areas of language studied by linguistics follows.

Morphology studies morphemes, the building blocks of language. These building blocks include words and roots, word endings, prefixes and suffixes, case, number, and tense.

Phonetics studies all speech sounds in a language and the way speech sounds are produced. Phonetics is reflected in many school curricula.

Phonology studies the important sounds in a language.

Transformational grammar is an approach to understanding language developed by Noam Chomsky, an American linguist. He posited that a universal linguistic structure was present in all humans. He further said that this structure naturally leads people to "transform" their thoughts into sentences that follow natural grammatical rules. There are also grammatical rules for individual languages. Chomsky pointed out that many errors found in children's grammar follow these natural grammatical rules.

LANGUAGE DEVELOPMENT

Language has a structure and a function. The structure of a language refers to the way words and sentences are combined to create effective communication. The function of a language is the ability to use language to think and communicate. Understanding language development means understanding how each of these aspects develops.

Much of the recent work on structural language development is related to Chomsky's work. Chomsky says that the "old" explanations of language development, modeling and reinforcement, were incorrect. This is not to say that language cannot be learned through these methods because this task is accomplished every day as people learn a foreign language. Rather, Chomsky says that this model-repeat-reinforce approach is not the way that children actually learn language.

Chomsky holds that children possess an innate ability to learn language, both words and structure, merely through exposure. To bolster his argument, Chomsky points out that most grammatical mistakes made by children actually follow the general grammatical rules of the language and that the children's errors represent exceptions to these rules.

For example, a child may say "Lisa goed to the store" instead of "Lisa went to the store." Chomsky would say, *goed* is structurally sound and represents a good grasp of the English language. The child would certainly say *hopped* if Lisa had gotten to the store that way. The problem is created because the past tense for *go* is an exception to the past tense formation rule.

Vygotsky is a prominent psychologist who studied the relationship between thought and language. A contemporary of Piaget, he pointed out that thought and language are not coordinated during the sensorimotor and most of the preoperational stages. That is, from birth through about age 6 or 7, thought and language develop independently, with language being primarily functional.

As students move toward the concrete operational stage, their language also becomes operational. That is, thought and the structural and functional aspects of language become integrated, and students can use language to think and solve problems.

Teachers can foster language development most effectively by constantly encouraging and enabling students to express themselves by speaking and writing. Students should be encouraged to integrate writing and speaking with all subject matter, and writing and speaking should be the overarching classroom objectives to be developed in every lesson. In all cases, teachers should help children communicate in standard English while in school.

ORAL AND WRITTEN COMMUNICATION

This review section begins with a review of English conventions that may be tested on the MSAT.

NOUNS AND VERBS

Every sentence has a subject and a predicate. Most sentences are statements. The sentence usually names something (subject). Then the sentence describes the subject or tells what that subject is doing (predicate). Sentences that ask questions also have a subject and a predicate. Here are some examples.

Subject	Predicate
The car	moved.
The tree	grew.
The street	was dark.
The forest	teemed with plants of every type and size.

Many subjects are nouns. Every predicate has a verb. A list of the nouns and verbs from the preceding sentences follows.

Noun	Verb
car	moved
tree	grew
street	was
forest, plants	teemed

Nouns

Nouns name a person, place, thing, characteristic, or concept. Nouns give a name to everything that is, has been, or will be. Here are some simple examples.

Person	Place	Thing	Characteristic	Concept (Idea)
Abe Lincoln	Lincoln Memorial	beard	mystery	freedom
judge	courthouse	gavel	fairness	justice
professor	college	chalkboard	intelligence	number

Singular and Plural Nouns

Singular nouns refer to only one thing. Plural forms refer to more than one thing. Plurals are usually formed by adding an *s* or dropping a *y* and adding *ies*. Here are some examples.

Singular	Plural
college	colleges
professor	professors
Lincoln Memorial	Lincoln Memorials
mystery	mysteries

Possessive Nouns

Possessive nouns show that the noun possesses a thing or a characteristic. Make a singular noun possessive by adding *'s*. Here are some examples.

The *child's* sled was in the garage ready for use.
The *school's* mascot was loose again.
The rain interfered with *Jane's* vacation.
Ron's and *Doug's* fathers were born in the same year.
Ron and *Doug's* teacher kept them after school.

Make a singular noun ending in *s* possessive by adding *'s* unless the pronunciation is too difficult.

The teacher read *James's* paper several times.
The angler grabbed the *bass'* fin.

Make a plural noun possessive by adding an apostrophe (') only.

The *principals'* meeting was delayed.
The report indicated that *students'* scores had declined.

Verbs

Some verbs are action verbs. Other verbs are linking verbs that link the subject to words that describe it. Here are some examples.

Action Verbs	Linking Verbs
Blaire *runs* down the street.	Blaire *is* tired.
Blaire *told* her story.	The class *was* bored.
The crowd *roared.*	The players *were* inspired.
The old ship *rusted.*	It *had been* a proud ship.

Tense

A verb has three principal tenses: present tense, past tense, and future tense. The present tense shows that the action is happening now. The past tense shows that the action happened in the past. The future tense shows that something will happen. Here are some examples.

Present: I *enjoy* my time off.
Past: I *enjoyed* my time off.
Future: I *will enjoy* my time off.

Present: I *hate* working late.
Past: I *hated* working late.
Future: I *will hate* working late.

Regular and Irregular Verbs

Regular verbs follow the consistent pattern noted previously. However, a number of verbs are irregular. Irregular verbs have their own unique forms for each tense. A partial list of irregular verbs follows. The past participle is usually preceded by *had, has* or *have.*

SOME IRREGULAR VERBS

Present Tense	Past Tense	Past Participle
am, is, are	was, were	been
begin	began	begun
break	broke	broken
bring	brought	brought
catch	caught	caught
choose	chose	chosen
come	came	come
do	did	done
eat	ate	eaten
give	gave	given
go	went	gone
grow	grew	grown
know	knew	known
lie	lay	lain
lay	laid	laid
raise	raised	raised
ride	rode	ridden
see	saw	seen
set	set	set
sit	sat	sat
speak	spoke	spoken
take	took	taken
tear	tore	torn
throw	threw	thrown
write	wrote	written

PRONOUNS

Pronouns take the place of nouns or noun phrases and help avoid constant repetition of the noun or phrase. Here is an example.

Blaire is in law school. *She* studies in *her* room every day.
[The pronouns *she* and *her* refer to the noun *Blaire.*]

SUBJECT-VERB AGREEMENT

Singular and Plural

Singular nouns take singular verbs. Plural nouns take plural verbs. Singular verbs usually end in *s*, and plural verbs usually do not. Here are some examples.

Singular: My father want*s* me home early.
Plural: My parents want me home early.

Singular: Ryan run*s* a mile each day.
Plural: Ryan and Chad run a mile each day.

Singular: She trie*s* her best to do a good job.
Plural: Liz and Ann try their best to do a good job.

Correctly Identify Subject and Verb

The subject may not be in front of the verb. In fact, the subject may not be anywhere near the verb. Say the subject and the verb to yourself. If it makes sense, you probably have it right.

- Words may come between the subject and the verb.

    Chad's final exam score, which he showed to his mother, improved his final grade.

  The verb is *improved*. The word *mother* appears just before improved.

  Is this the subject? Say it to yourself. [Mother improved the grade.]

  That can't be right. Score must be the subject. Say it to yourself. [Score improved the grade.] That's right. *Score* is the subject, and *improved* is the verb.

    The racer running with a sore arm finished first.

  Say it to yourself. [Racer finished first.] *Racer* is the noun, and *finished* is the verb.

  It wouldn't make any sense to say the arm finished first.

- The verb may come before the subject.

    Over the river and through the woods romps the merry leprechaun.

  Leprechaun is the subject, and *romps* is the verb. [Think: Leprechaun romps.]

    Where are the car keys?

  Keys is the subject, and *are* is the verb. [Think: The car keys are where?]

Examples of Subject-Verb Agreement

Words such as *each, neither, everyone, nobody, someone,* and *anyone* are singular pronouns. They always take a singular verb.

> Everyone *needs* a good laugh now and then.
> Nobody *knows* more about computers than Bob.

Words that refer to number such as *one-half, any, most,* and *some* can be singular or plural.

> One-fifth of the students *were* absent. [*Students* is plural.]
> One-fifth of the cake *was* eaten. [There is only one cake.]

ADJECTIVES AND ADVERBS

Adjectives

Adjectives modify nouns and pronouns. Adjectives add detail and clarify nouns and pronouns. Frequently, adjectives come immediately before the nouns or pronouns they are modifying. At other times, the nouns or pronouns come first and are connected directly to the adjectives by linking verbs. Here are some examples.

Direct	With a Linking Verb
That is a *large* dog.	That dog is *large*.
He's an *angry* man.	The man seems *angry*.

Adverbs

Adverbs are often formed by adding *ly* to an adjective. However, many adverbs don't end in *ly* (for example, *always*). Adverbs modify verbs, adjectives, and adverbs. Adverbs can also modify phrases, clauses, and sentences. Here are some examples.

Modify verb:	Ryan *quickly* sought a solution.
Modify adjective:	That is an *exceedingly* large dog.
Modify adverb:	Lisa told her story *quite* truthfully.
Modify sentence:	*Unfortunately*, all good things must end.
Modify phrase:	The instructor arrived *just* in time to start the class.

always is always an adverb.

CONJUNCTIONS

Conjunctions are words that connect and logically relate parts of a sentence.

- These conjunctions connect words: *and, but, for, or, nor.*

  Dan *and* Dorie live in Pittsburgh.
  Tim *or* Sarah will get up to feed the baby.

- These conjunctive pairs establish a relationship among words: *either-or, neither-nor, not only-but also*. Words in these pairs should not be mixed.

  Neither David *nor* Noel wants to get up to feed the baby.

  The baby cries *not only* when she is hungry, *but also* when she is thirsty.

- These conjunctions connect and modify clauses in a sentence: nevertheless, however, because, furthermore.

  Matt's mother was coming to visit; *however*, a snow storm prevented the trip.
  Because the baby was sleeping, Julie and Bill decided to get some sleep too.

PREPOSITIONS

Prepositions connect a word to a pronoun, noun, or noun phrase called the object of the preposition. A partial list of prepositions follows.

PREPOSITIONS

above	across	after	among
as	at	before	below
beside	by	except	for
from	in	into	near
of	on	over	to
toward	up	upon	without

A prepositional phrase consists of a preposition, its object and any modifiers. Here are some examples.

Preposition	**Object**
in	the book
with	apparent glee
without	a care

Some sentences with prepositional phrases follow.

Chad found his book *in the room.*
Liz rode *on her horse.*
Trix is the dog *with the brown paws.*
Over the river and *through the woods to grandmother's house* we go.

NEGATION

Words such as *no, never, nobody, nothing,* and *not* (with contractions such as *would not—wouldn't*) are used to express a negative. However, only one of these words is needed to express a negative thought. Two negative words create a double negative, which is not standard English.

Incorrect:	The politician *didn't say nothing* that made sense.
Revised:	The politician *didn't say anything* that made sense.
Revised:	The politician *said nothing* that made any sense.
Incorrect:	The politician *wouldn't do nothing* that did no good. [A triple negative.]
Revised:	The politician *would do nothing* good.
Revised:	The politician *wouldn't do* good things.

CHOOSING THE CORRECT WORD

Homonyms

Homonyms are words that sound alike but do not have the same meaning. These words can be confusing and you may use the incorrect spelling of a word. If words are homonyms, be sure you choose the correct spelling for the meaning you intend.

HOMONYMS

accept (receive) except (other than)	ascent (rise) assent (agreement)
board (wood) bored (uninterested)	fair (average) fare (a charge)
led (guided) lead (metal)	lessen (make less) lesson (learning experience)
past (gone before) passed (moved by)	peace (no war) piece (portion)
rain (precipitation) reign (rule) rein (animal strap)	to (toward) too (also) two (a number)

their (possessive pronoun)	its (shows possession)
there (location)	it's (it is)
they're (they are)	

OTHER RESOURCES

Retrieval of Information from Print and Nonprint Sources

Information can be retrieved from books, magazines, and other print sources by simply picking up the reading materials and turning and flipping through the pages. The book, newspaper, or periodical remains one of the most efficient ways to access print information.

Print materials are also found in libraries or other repositories on microfilm and microfiche. Microfilms are 35mm films of books, while microfiche are flat and can contain hundreds of pages of text material. Microfilm and microfiche are read with specialized readers.

Other information can be retrieved on or through the computer. Written materials can be entered on a computer, usually with a word processor. This information can be accessed directly through the computer's hard disk. Special features of most word processors and other utilities permit the user to search electronically for words and phrases. Sound, graphics, and animation may also be stored on a computer's hard disk. These sounds and images may be accessed using specialized computer programs.

Print materials, images, sounds and animation may also be stored on CD-ROMs designed for computer use. Information on these CD-ROMs may be accessed through a CD-ROM player that is connected to the computer. Images and sounds on videotapes, audiotapes, music CD-ROMs, and videodisk may also be accessed through the computer.

Computers can be connected to telephone lines and television cables using a modem. Modems allow computers to upload and download data from other computers, usually via the Internet. "Going on line" has become a popular way to gather information.

The Internet is a vast collection of computers around the world. These computers are connected by cables and phone lines, forming a huge net. Once on the Internet, a person can have access to enormous amounts of information.

Browsers such as Microsoft Explorer and Netscape Navigator turn the Internet's electronic signals into viewable text and images. You can retrieve text, pictures, video, and sound with these browsers. Almost all periodical and newspaper information is available on line, and you can hold Internet conversations and Internet videoconferences.

The World Wide Web is the collection of sites on the Internet. Web addresses identify the different sites and the information contained at these sites. For example the Web address http://www.barronseduc.com connects you directly to the Barron's Web site.

Search engines such as Excite and Yahoo help you to find sites containing the information you want. If you entered "teacher testing," these search engines would return a list of WWW sites in their catalog containing these key words.

Rhetorical Conventions of Argumentation, Exposition, Narration, and Reflection

In **argumentation** the writer or speaker tries to convince the readers or listeners to accept a particular view or idea. There are several rules to follow to construct a well-ordered argument. Your presentation should appear moderate and reasoned, and you should acknowledge the reasonableness of those who differ with you.

The statements must be believable in form and in fact. That is, the statements must distinguish among fact, opinion, and the conclusions you have drawn. The presentation should clarify the meanings of key ideas and words. The presentation must also squarely address the question and not beg the question as described in the preceding example.

The presentation must support any views or conclusions with solid evidence and arguments. The arguments can be inductive or deductive. However, these arguments must avoid the invalid and fallacious arguments noted previously.

Expository presentations simply explain. This book is essentially expository presentation. It explains about the MSAT and how to pass it.

Narration presents a factual or fictional story. A written fictional account or a spoken presentation about your life as a child is a narration.

Reflection describes a scene, person, or emotion. A spoken description of your neighborhood or a written note describing how you felt when you graduated from high school are reflections.

Assessment Instruments

Tests have long been used to determine what students have learned and to compare students. Every test is imperfect. Many tests are so imperfect that they are useless. It is important to realize how this imperfection affects test results.

Some students are poor test takers. Every test assumes that the test taker has the opportunity to demonstrate what he or she knows. A student may know something but be unable to demonstrate it on a particular test. We must also consider alternative assessment strategies for these students.

Familiarize yourself with these basic assessment concepts.

- Errors of Measurement—Every test contains errors of measurement. In other words, no one test accurately measures a student's achievement or ability. Carefully designed standardized tests may have measurement errors of 5 percent or 10 percent. Teacher-designed tests typically have large errors of measurement.

  A test result shows that a student falls into a range of scores and not just the single reported score. Focusing on a single score and ignoring the score range is among the most serious of score-reporting errors.
- Reliability—A reliable test is consistent. That is, a reliable test will give similar results when given to the same person in a short time span. You can't count on unreliable tests to give you useful scores. Use only very reliable standardized tests and be very aware of how important reliability is when you make up your own tests.
- Validity—Valid tests measure what they are supposed to measure. There are two important types of validity: content validity and criterion validity.

  A test with high content validity measures the material covered in the curriculum or unit being tested. Tests that lack high content validity are unfair. When you make up a test it should have complete content validity. This does not mean that the test has to be unchallenging. It does mean that the questions should refer to the subject matter covered.

  A test with high criterion validity successfully predicts the ability to do other work. For example, a test to be an automobile mechanic with high criterion validity will successfully predict who will be a good mechanic.

Norm-Referenced and Criterion-Referenced Tests

Norm-referenced tests are designed to compare students. Intelligence tests are probably the best-known norm-referenced tests. These tests yield a number that purports to show how one person's intelligence compares to everyone else's. The average IQ score is 100.

Standardized achievement tests yield grade-level equivalent scores. These tests purport to show how student achievement compares to the achievement of all other students of the same grade level.

A fifth grader who earns a grade level equivalent of 5.5 might be thought of as average. A second-grade student with the same grade equivalent score would be thought of as above average. About half of all the students taking these tests will be below average.

Standardized tests also yield percentile scores. Percentile scores are reported as a number from 0 through 100. A percentile of 50 indicates that the student did as well as or better than 50 percent of the students at that grade level who took the test. The higher the percentile, the better the relative performance.

Criterion-referenced tests are designed to determine the degree to which an objective has been reached. Teacher made tests and tests found in teachers' editions of texts are usually criterion referenced tests. Criterion referenced tests have very high content validity.

Authentic Assessment

Standardized and teacher-made tests have significant drawbacks. These types of tests do not evaluate a student's ability to perform a task or demonstrate a skill in a real-life situation. These tests do not evaluate a student's ability to work cooperatively or consistently.

In authentic assessment, students are asked to demonstrate the skill or knowledge in a real-life setting. The teacher and students collaborate in the learning assessment process and discuss how learning is progressing and how to facilitate that learning. The idea is to get an authentic picture of the student's work and progress.

The student has an opportunity to demonstrate what he or she knows or can do in a variety of settings. Students can also demonstrate their ability to work independently or as part of a group.

Portfolio assessment is another name for authentic assessment. Students evaluated through a system of authentic assessment frequently keep a portfolio of their work. Authentic assessment might include the following approaches.

- The student might be observed by the teacher, or occasionally by other students. The observer takes notes and discusses the observation later with the students.
- Students establish portfolios that contain samples of their work. Students are told which work samples they must include in their portfolios. The students place their best work for each requirement in the portfolio. Portfolios are evaluated periodically during a conference between the teacher and the student.
- Students maintain journals and logs containing written descriptions, sketches, and other notes that chronicle their work and the process they went through while learning. The journals and logs are reviewed periodically during a conference between the teacher and the student.

Grading and Interpreting Test Scores

The grade level at which you are teaching determines the approach you will take to grading. In the primary grades, you are often asked to check off a list of criteria to show how a student is progressing. Starting in intermediate grades, you will usually issue letter grades.

You should develop a consistent, fair, and varied approach to grading. Students should understand the basis for their grades. You should give students an opportunity to demonstrate what they have learned in a variety of ways.

It is not necessary to adopt a rigid grading system in the elementary grades. Remember, the purpose of a grading system should be to help students learn better, not just to compare them to other students.

Beginning about sixth or seventh grade, the grade should reflect how students are doing relative to other students in the class. By this age, students need to be exposed to the grading system they will experience through high school and college. The grading system should always be fair, consistent, and offer students a variety of ways to demonstrate their mastery.

You will need to interpret normed scores. These scores may be reported as grade equivalents or as percentiles. You may receive these results normed for different groups. For example, one normed score may show performance relative to all students who took the test. Another normed score may show performance relative to students from school districts that have the same Socioeconomic Status (SES) as your school district.

When interpreting normed scores for parents, point out that the student's performance falls into a range of scores. A student's score that varies significantly from the average score from schools with a similar SES requires attention followed by remediation or enriched instruction.

When interpreting district-wide normed scores, remember that these scores correlate highly with SES.

SPECIAL STRATEGY FOR ANSWERING LITERATURE AND LANGUAGE STUDIES ITEMS

How to Critique Literature

When you critique a literary passage, you should consider both the literal meaning of the passage and the imagery it evokes. Consider this sentence: "The beggar pushed his way through the crowds in the squalid slum." We can tell from the sentence that the person is poor and is in a run-down area. However, what imagery does the passage evoke? That is, what sights, sounds, tactile experiences, smells, taste, and experiences of temperature and movement do you have?

The beggar pushed his way through the crowds in the squalid slum.

Sight. Try to visualize the beggar. Do you see a person on a street or sidewalk in an urban slum? Do you see a beggar with tattered clothes in the streets of India? Write what you visualize about the beggar.

I see a white man, wearing a dirty red shirt, greasy black pants, showing a smile that exposed teeth colored "yellow, black, and brown". I see the beggar asking people for spare change.

Try to visualize the surroundings. Do you see apartment houses with boarded-up windows and crowds of people sitting on corners and outside doors? Do you see the crowded streets of India teeming with people? Write what you visualize.

The beggar's in run-down ghetto section of downtown Sacramento. The bus station is across the street, where the old black man and his young son sit on the bus bench.

Sound. Try to hear the sounds. Do you hear the honking of horns or do you hear the cries of hawkers? Write about the sounds you hear.

I hear people talking, car horns beeping, whistles blowing, And vender's hawking their wares.

Tactile. Try to feel the tactile experience. Can you feel the pavement beneath the beggar's feet or the press of the crowds? Write about the tactile experience.

Smell. Explore your sense of smell. Do you smell exhaust fumes or can you smell the odor of decaying food left in the sun? Write about the odors you smell.

Taste. Explore your sense of taste. Can you taste food cooking or a bit of food just eaten? Write about your taste experience.

Temperature. Explore your sensation of temperature. Can you feel the cold of night or do you experience a hot day? Write about your experience of temperature.

Movement. What movement do you experience? Can you sense the beggar's movement through the crowd? Write about your experience of movement.

Write below the imagery you experience from the following passage.

The pilot swung the plane around in an attempt to make an emergency landing on the small field.

Sight. Write what you visualize.

The pilot face expresses grave concern

Sound. Write about the sounds you hear.

Tactile. Write about the tactile experience.

Smell. Write about the odors you smell.

Taste. Write about your taste experience.

Temperature. Write about your temperature experience.

Movement. Write about your movement experience.

LITERATURE AND LANGUAGE STUDIES MSAT PRACTICE ITEMS

These items will help you practice for the real MSAT. These items have the same form and test the same material as MSAT items. The items you encounter on the MSAT may have a different emphasis and may be more complete.

Instructions

Mark your answers on the sheet provided below. Complete the items in 20 minutes or less. Correct your answer sheet using the answers on page 59.

1 Ⓐ Ⓑ Ⓒ Ⓓ	5 Ⓐ Ⓑ Ⓒ Ⓓ	9 Ⓐ Ⓑ Ⓒ Ⓓ	13 Ⓐ Ⓑ Ⓒ Ⓓ	17 Ⓐ Ⓑ Ⓒ Ⓓ
2 Ⓐ Ⓑ Ⓒ Ⓓ	6 Ⓐ Ⓑ Ⓒ Ⓓ	10 Ⓐ Ⓑ Ⓒ Ⓓ	14 Ⓐ Ⓑ Ⓒ Ⓓ	18 Ⓐ Ⓑ Ⓒ Ⓓ
3 Ⓐ Ⓑ Ⓒ Ⓓ	7 Ⓐ Ⓑ Ⓒ Ⓓ	11 Ⓐ Ⓑ Ⓒ Ⓓ	15 Ⓐ Ⓑ Ⓒ Ⓓ	19 Ⓐ Ⓑ Ⓒ Ⓓ
4 Ⓐ Ⓑ Ⓒ Ⓓ	8 Ⓐ Ⓑ Ⓒ Ⓓ	12 Ⓐ Ⓑ Ⓒ Ⓓ	16 Ⓐ Ⓑ Ⓒ Ⓓ	20 Ⓐ Ⓑ Ⓒ Ⓓ

Questions 1–3

The United States National Park system is extensive, although most land dedicated to the park system is in the western states. This is no doubt the case because these lands are occupied by states most recently admitted to the union. I have some very happy personal memories about Yellowstone National Park, having visited there on several occasions. All of my visits came before the series of fires, which burned much of the park's forested areas. My most unusual recollection dates back a number of years when I was part of a group waiting for the Old Faithful geyser to erupt. A young child was standing about twenty yards away looking at something on the ground. The group gathered around where the child was standing. And while Old Faithful _____, we all watched a small, rusty water pipe leak onto the ground. I never understood what about the pipe drew everyone's interest. It must have to do with a child's wonder.

1. Which of the following best characterizes the preceding passage?
   (A) A person describes the American National Park System.
   (B) A person describes his childhood in Yellowstone National Park.
   (C) A person describes group behavior with an example from his or her own experience.
   (D) A person describes an unusual memory from Yellowstone Park.

2. Why does the writer discuss the Yellowstone fires in lines 9-11?
   (A) to discuss the destruction of the park
   (B) to give a time frame to the writer's visits
   (C) to warn against careless use of fire
   (D) to describe the burned areas

3. Which of the following words would be most appropriate to fill the blank space in line 18?
   (A) burned
   (B) gurgled
   (C) foamed
   (D) gushed

4. This passage is best characterized as
   (A) argumentation.
   (B) exposition.
   (C) narration.
   (D) reflection.

5. What is the subject of the sentence "My most unusual recollection dates back . . .," which begins at the end of line 10 and ends on line 13?
   (A) My
   (B) recollection
   (C) I
   (D) group

6. These are the first two lines from a haiku poem:

   The waves on the beach
   Are a-rhythmically crashing.

   Which of the following choices could be the third line in the poem?
   (A) Like the precarious fate
   (B) Like the sands of time
   (C) Like the love clinging
   (D) Like the deafening quiet

7. Which of the following examples would Chomsky (transformational grammar) identify as an error demonstrating children possess an innate grammatical sense?
   (A) "Jim told me I ain't going to no picnic."
   (B) "Lynne goed to the picnic already."
   (C) "Not right to make me stay home."
   (D) "I hollers and screams if I can't go to that picnic."

Questions 8–11 are based on the following passages.

(A) The tires screeched, and the car spun uncontrollably. I gripped the wheel in fear as the car swung around again and again. My body was thrown against the side of the car—my heart pounded. A horn blared in my ear, and images of cars, buildings, and light poles went whizzing by. It seemed that I would careen into the car just ahead of me. Then everything stopped. I'm not going on that ride again.

(B) A soft and silent breeze swept across the field carrying with it the sweet smell of blooming flowers, the delightful chirping of circling birds, and small bits of pollen and newly cut grass. The breeze softly passed unfelt by all but the few standing at the field's edge. Life is like that breeze in that field for all who will but stop to experience it.

(C) The seat was hard, the room was crowded, and the perspiration flowed. All eyes were on the proctor who was handing out tests and on the air conditioner, which wasn't working. They all wanted to be teachers, and they were all ready to take the test, but they were not ready for the hottest day of the year and the stuffiest room imaginable. Someone sighed. What were they to do?

(D) "I object your honor," called out the lawyer. "I object to the way that my rights and my client's rights have been systematically, outrageously, and impermissibly denied by this court, by the incredibly irresponsible reporting of the tawdry tabloid shows, and by the second-rate journalists who control the newspapers in this town."
"I guess the evidence is against that lawyer," thought the judge.

8. Which passage includes a metaphor for life?

9. Which passage describes a person's reaction to an amusement park ride?

10. Which passage includes a rhetorical question?

11. Which of the following choices describes a common element of these five passages?
(A) Each passage draws a conclusion.
(B) Each passage describes a feeling.
(C) Each passage includes dialogue.
(D) Each passage is descriptive.

<u>Questions 12–14</u> are based on the following reading.

I remember my childhood vacations at a bungalow colony near a lake. Always barefoot, my friend and I spent endless hours playing and enjoying our fantasies. We were pirates, rocket pilots, and detectives. Everyday objects were transformed into swords, ray guns, and two-way wrist radios. With a lake at hand, we swam, floated on our crude rafts made of old lumber, fished, and fell in. The adult world seemed so meaningless while our world seemed so full. Returning years later I saw the colony for what it was—tattered and torn. The lake was shallow and muddy. But the tree that had been our lookout was still there. And there was the house where the feared master spy hid from the FBI. There was the site of the launching pad for our imaginary rocket trips. The posts of the dock we had sailed from many times were still visible. But my fantasy play did not depend on this place. My child-mind would have been a buccaneer wherever it was.

12. Which of the following choices best characterizes this passage?
(A) An adult describes disappointment at growing up.
(B) A child describes the adult world through the child's eyes.
(C) An adult discusses childhood viewed as a child and as an adult.
(D) An adult discusses the meaning of fantasy play.
(E) An adult describes a wish to return to childhood.

13. The sentence "The adult world seemed so meaningless while our world seemed so full" on lines 10 and 11 is used primarily to
(A) emphasize the emptiness of most adult lives.
(B) provide a transition from describing childhood to describing adulthood.
(C) show how narcissistic children are.
(D) describe the difficulty this child had relating to adults.
(E) emphasize the limited world of the child compared to the more comprehensive world of the adult.

14. Which of the following best characterizes the last sentence in the passage?
(A) The child would have been rebellious, no matter what.
(B) Childhood is not a place but a state of mind.
(C) We conform more as we grow older.
(D) The writer will always feel rebellious.
(E) A part of us all stays in childhood.

<u>Questions 15–18</u> are based on the following passages.

(A) Swept along the gnarly road of life,
Abounding with its traffic laden strife.
Rest you now upon the yonder hill,
Tis there that you'll finally be still.

I am about the richest man there is,
(B) 'Cause I was ever so great at biz.
The biz that I was great at though,
Was little more than blowing snow.

(C) Birds in the meadow—
chirp, chirp, chirp,
Too full a tummy—
burp, burp, burp,
Cats at the milk saucer—
slurp, slurp, slurp,
Don't have another rhyme—
gulp, gulp, gulp.

(D) They say that fame and fortune
comes,
From starring in some fil-e-ums.
But it seems to me that you end up,
Just taking lots of pill-e-ums.

15. Which passage provides a contrast between two possible outcomes?

16. Which passage appears to be a metaphor for the end of life?

17. Which passage relates a person's success to obscuring or hiding?

18. Which of the following best explains why the author of selection (C) chose the words that appear at the end of each line?
(A) For poetic effect
(B) To have a particular number of beats in each line
(C) To emphasize the *urp* sound
(D) To conform to the rules for haiku

Questions 19–20 are based on the passages preceding them.

Japanese students have always been considered to be well-prepared for life in the world's business and engineering communities. The mathematics and science curricula of Japanese schools are considered to be superior to those in American schools. With the daily advancement of Japanese technological prowess, how can American children ever hope to compete with their Japanese counterparts?

19. Which of the following is the best descriptor of the author's tone in this passage?
(A) disbelief
(B) anger
(C) pride
(D) concern

The retired basketball player said that, while modern players were better athletes because there was so much emphasis on youth basketball and increased focus on training, he still believed that the players of his day were better because they were more committed to the game, better understood its nuances, and were more dedicated to team play.

20. The retired basketball player attributes the increased athletic prowess of today's basketball players to
(A) better nutrition.
(B) youth basketball programs.
(C) salary caps.
(D) more athletic scholarships.

Answers

1. **D**	5. **B**	9. **C**	13. **B**	17. **B**
2. **B**	6. **B**	10. **D**	14. **B**	18. **C**
3. **D**	7. **B**	11. **C**	15. **D**	19. **A**
4. **D**	8. **B**	12. **C**	16. **A**	20. **B**

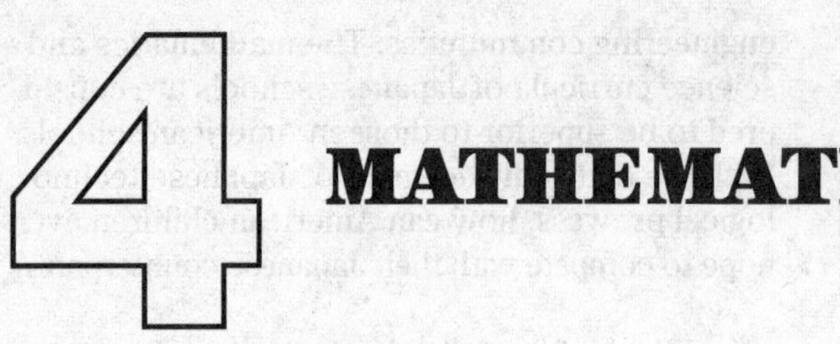

4 MATHEMATICS

TEST INFO BOX

24 of 120 Multiple Choice items	**20% of Content Knowledge items**
3 of 18 Short Answer items	**17% of Content Area Exercise items**

MATHEMATICS ITEMS

Mathematics multiple choice items look like this.

If $x = 5/6$, which of the following inequalities is correct?

(A) $5/9 \le x < 7/9$
(B) $5/8 < x < 3/4$
(C) $3/4 < x < 7/8$
(D) $7/8 < x < 15/16$

Mathematics short answer items look like this.

You have a one-inch hollow paper cube and a pair of scissors. Display the different flat designs you can make by cutting the cube along the

USING THIS CHAPTER

This chapter prepares you to take the Mathematics part of the MSAT. Choose one of the approaches.

I want all the Mathematics review I can get.

- ❑ Skip the Review Quiz and read the entire review section.
- ❑ Take the Mathematics Review Quiz on page 62.
- ❑ Correct the Review Quiz and reread the indicated parts of the review.
- ❑ Go over the Special Strategies for Answering the Mathematics items on pages 98–101.
- ❑ Complete the Mathematics MSAT Practice items on page 103.

I want a thorough Mathematics review.

- ❑ Take the Mathematics Review Quiz on page 62.
- ❑ Correct the Review Quiz and reread the indicated parts of the review.
- ❑ Go over the Special Strategies for Answering the Mathematics items on pages 98–101.
- ❑ Complete the Mathematics MSAT Practice items on page 103.

I want a quick Mathematics review.

- ❑ Take and correct the Mathematics Review Quiz on page 62.
- ❑ Go over the Special Strategies for Answering the Mathematics items on pages 98–101.
- ❑ Complete the Mathematics MSAT Practice items on page 103.

I want to practice Mathematics questions.

- ❑ Go over the Special Strategies for Answering the Mathematics items on pages 98–101.
- ❑ Complete the Mathematics MSAT Practice items on page 103.

I don't need any Mathematics review.

- ❑ OK. If you're sure, skip this chapter.

MATHEMATICS REVIEW QUIZ

This quiz uses a short answer format to help you find out what you know about the Mathematics topics reviewed in this chapter. The quiz results direct you to the portions of the chapter you should reread.

This quiz will also help focus your thinking about Mathematics, and these questions and answers are a good review in themselves. It's not important to answer all these questions correctly, and don't be concerned if you miss many of them.

The answers are found immediately after the quiz. It's to your advantage not to look at them until you have completed the quiz. Once you have completed and corrected this review quiz, use the answer checklist to decide which sections of the review to study.

> Write the answers in the space provided or on a separate sheet of paper.

1. Which number is missing from this sequence?

   3 6 ______ 12

<u>Questions 2–4:</u> *Use symbols for less than, greater than, and equal to, and compare these numbers:*

2. 23 ______ 32
3. 18 ______ 4 + 14
4. 9 ______ 10 ______ 11
5. Write the place value of the digit 7 in the numeral 476,891,202,593.

   ____
6. Write this number in words: 6,000,000,000,000.

   ____
7. $4^3 =$ ______
8. $2^2 \times 2^3 =$ ______
9. $6^9 \div 6^7 =$ ______
10. $3^2 \times 2^3 =$ ______
11. Write the place value of the digit 4 in the numeral 529.354.

    ____

<u>Questions 12–13:</u> *Use symbols for less than, greater than, and equal to, and compare these numbers:*

12. 9,879 ______ 12,021
13. 98.1589 ______ 98.162

<u>Questions 14–17:</u>

Round 234,489.0754 to the:

14. thousands place ______________
15. hundredths place ______________
16. tenths place ______________
17. hundreds place ______________
18. Write these fractions from least to greatest.

    $^7/_8$, $^{11}/_{12}$, $^{17}/_{20}$

    ______, ______, ______
19. $5 + 7 \times 3^2$ ______________
20. $5 \times 8 - (15 - 7 \times 2)$ ______________
21. Write a seven-digit number divisible by 4.

    ____
22. Write the GCF and LCM of 6 and 14.

    ____

23. Ron had 20 more baseball cards than he started out with. Then he gave half the cards away and was left with 19. How many baseball cards did Ron start out with?
______

24. 203.61 + 9.402 + 0.78 ______

25. 30.916 – 8.72 ______

26. 3.4 × 0.0021 ______

27. 0.576 ÷ 0.32 ______

28. $1^{2}/_{3} \times 3^{3}/_{4}$ ______

29. $1^{2}/_{3} \div {}^{3}/_{8}$ ______

30. $1^{4}/_{9} + {}^{5}/_{6}$ ______

31. $4^{5}/_{6} - 2^{3}/_{5}$ ______

32. Simplify this square root $\sqrt{98}$ = ______

33. Complete the following ratio so that it is equivalent to 4 : 5:

28 : ______

34. Use a proportion and solve this problem. Bob uses jelly and peanut butter in a ratio of 5 : 2. He uses 10 teaspoons of jelly. How much peanut butter will he use?
______

Questions 35-40: *Change among decimals, percents, and fractions to complete the table.*

Decimal	Percent	Fraction
0.56	35. ______	36. ______
37. ______	15.2%	38. ______
39. ______	40. ______	$^{3}/_{8}$

41. What is 35 percent of 50? ______

42. What percent of 120 is 40? ______

43. 15 percent of what number is 6? ______

44. What is the probability of rolling one die and getting a 7? ______

45. You flip a fair coin five times in a row and it comes up heads each time. What is the probability that it will come up tails on the next flip?
______

46. You pick one card from a deck. Then you pick another one without replacing the first. Are these dependent or independent events? Explain.
______

Questions 47-49: *Find the mean, median, and mode of this set of data.*

10, 5, 2, 1, 8, 5, 3, 0

47. Mean ______

48. Median ______

49. Mode ______

50. Draw a stem and leaf plot that shows these data: 12, 12, 23, 25, 36, 38.

51. $^{-}8 + {}^{+}4 =$ ______

52. $^{+}85 + {}^{-}103 =$ ______

53. $^{-}12 - {}^{+}7 =$ ______

54. $^{-}72 - {}^{-}28 =$ ______

55. $^{-}9 \times {}^{+}8 =$ ______

56. $^{-}12 \times {}^{-}6 =$ ______

57. $^{-}28 \div {}^{+}7 =$ ______

58. $^{-}72 \div {}^{-}9 =$ ______

59. Find the area of a triangle with a base of 3 and a height of 2.
______

60. Find the area of a square with a side of 5.
______

61. Find the area of a circle with a radius of 6.
______

62. Find the volume of a cube with a side of 5.
______

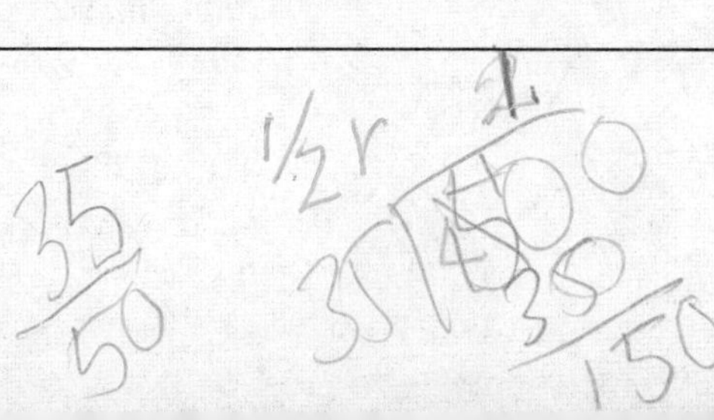

Write the value of the variable.

63. $x - 35 = 26$ ______

64. $x + 81 = 7$ ______

65. $y \div 8 = 3$ ______

66. $3z = 54$ ______

67. $4y - 9 = 19$ ______

68. $k \div 6 + 5 = 17$ ______

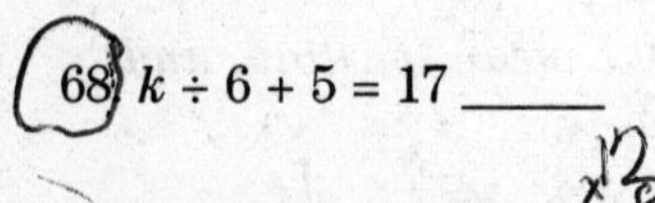

Questions 68-74: *Draw a model of:*

69. a point

70. a line

71. a ray

72. an acute angle

73. complementary angles

74. an isosceles triangle

75. a rectangle

76. Use this coordinate grid and plot these points: A (3,2) B (–4, –2).

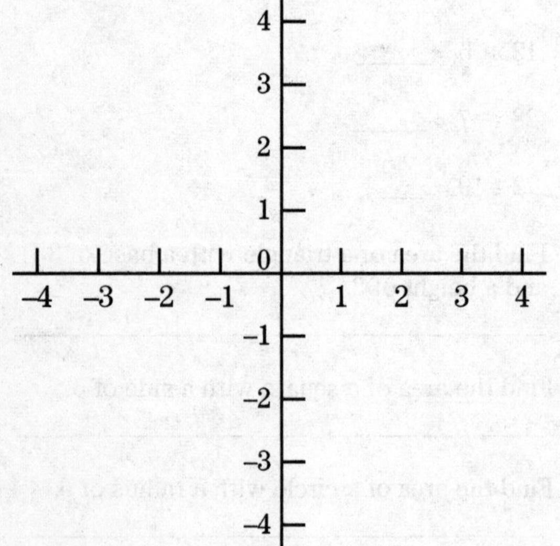

77. Draw a diagram to show that all vowels (*a, e, i, o, u*) are letters and that all consonants are letters, but that no vowels are consonants.

78. What is the difference between the mass of an object on earth and the mass of the same object on the moon?

______

79. How many inches would it take to make 5 yards? ______

80. How many cups would it take to make 3 quarts? ______

81. A kilogram is how many grams? ______

82. A centimeter is how many meters? ______

83. It's 1:00 P.M. in Los Angeles. What time is it in New York? ______

84. It's 32° Celsius. How would you describe a day with that temperature?

______

ANSWER CHECKLIST

The answers are organized by review sections. Check your answers. If you miss any questions in a section, check the box and review that section. Always review the calculator section on pages 18–21.

Number Sense and Numeration

❑ *Understanding and Ordering Whole Numbers, page 68*

1. 9
2. <
3. =
4. <, <

❑ *Place Value, page 68*

5. 10 billion
6. six trillion

❑ *Positive Exponents, page 69*

7. 64
8. 32
9. 36
10. 72

❑ *Understanding and Ordering Decimals, page 69*

11. thousandths

❑ *Comparing Whole Numbers and Decimals, page 69*

12. <
13. <

❑ *Rounding Whole Numbers and Decimals, page 70*

14. 234,000
15. 234,489.08
16. 234,489.1
17. 234,500

❑ *Understanding and Ordering Fractions, page 70*

18. $\frac{17}{20}$, $\frac{7}{8}$, $\frac{11}{12}$

❑ *How and When to Add, Subtract, Multiply, and Divide, page 72*

19. 68
20. 39

❑ *Number Theory, page 73*

21. The last 2 digits have to be divisible by 4.
22. GCF is 2. LCM is 42.

Real Number Systems and Subsystems

❑ *Add, Subtract, Multiply, and Divide Decimals, page 76*

23. 18
24. 213.792
25. 22.196
26. 0.00714
27. 1.8

❑ *Multiplying, Dividing, Adding, and Subtracting Fractions and Mixed Numbers, page 77*

28. $6\frac{1}{4}$
29. $4\frac{4}{9}$
30. $2\frac{5}{18}$
31. $2\frac{7}{30}$

❑ *Square Roots, page 78*

32. $7\sqrt{2}$

❑ *Ratio and Proportion, page 78*

33. 35
34. 4

❑ *Percent, page 79*

Decimal	Percent	Fraction
0.56	**35.** 56%	**36.** 14/25
37. 0.152	15.2%	**38.** 19/125
39. 0.375	**40.** 37.5%	3/8

❑ *Three Types of Percent Problems, page 80*

41. 17.5
42. $33\frac{1}{3}$%
43. 40

Probability and Simple Statistics

❑ *Probability, page 81*

44. Zero
45. $^1/_2$

❑ *Dependent and Independent Events, page 82*

46. Dependent. The outcome of one event affects the probability of the other event.

❑ *Statistics, page 82*

47. 4.25
48. 4
49. 5

❑ *Stem-and-Leaf and Box-and-Whisker Plots, page 83*

50.

Stem	Leaf
1	2,2
2	3,5
3	6,8

Algebra

❑ *Adding and Subtracting Integers, page 84*

51. –4
52. –18
53. –19
54. –44

❑ *Multiplying and Dividing Integers, page 84*

55. –72
56. +72
57. –4
58. +8

❑ *Formulas, page 85*

59. 3
60. 25
61. about 113 (113.097...)
62. 125

❑ *Equations, page 86*

63. 61
64. –74
65. 24
66. 18
67. 7
68. 72

Geometry

❑ *Two-Dimensional Geometry, page 88*

69. •
70. ⟷
71. •⟶

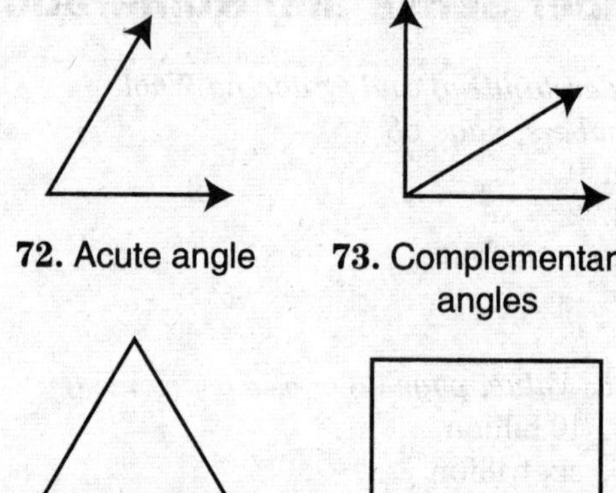

72. Acute angle **73.** Complementary angles

74. Isosceles triangle **75.** Rectangle

❑ *Coordinate Grid, page 91*

76.

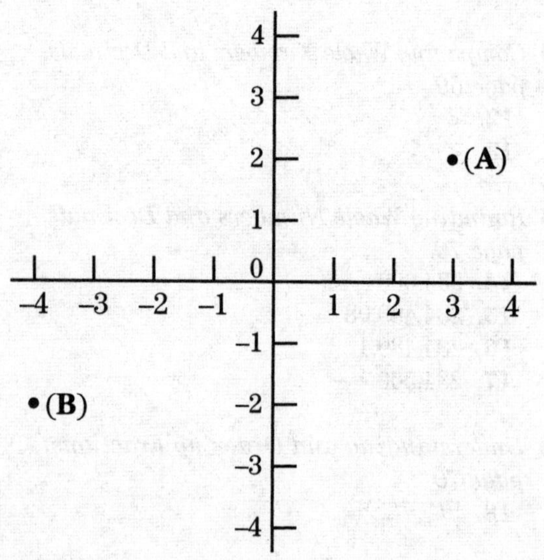

❑ *Using Diagrams, page 91*

77.

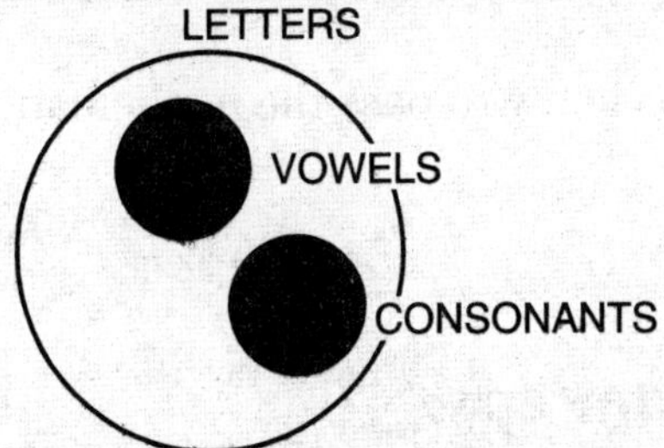

Measurement

❑ *Measuring with a Ruler and a Protractor, page 92*

❑ *Weight and Mass, page 93*

78. None. Mass remains constant.

❑ *Customary (English) Units, page 93*

79. 180 inches

80. 12

❑ *Metric System, page 94*

81. 1,000

82. 0.01

❑ *Time and Temperature, page 94*

83. 4:00 P.M.

84. Hot — about 90°F.

☑ *Problem Solving, page 96*

MATHEMATICS REVIEW

This review section targets the skills and concepts you need to know to pass the mathematics part of the MSAT.

NUMBER SENSE AND NUMERATION

UNDERSTANDING AND ORDERING WHOLE NUMBERS

Whole numbers are the numbers you use to tell how many. They include 0, 1, 2, 3, 4, 5, 6 . . . . The dots tell us that these numbers keep going on forever. There are an infinite number of whole numbers, which means you will never reach the last one.

Cardinal numbers such as 1, 9, and 18 tell how many. There are 9 players on the field in a baseball game. Ordinal numbers such as 1st, 2nd, 9th, and 18th tell about order. For example, Lynne batted 1st this inning.

You can visualize whole numbers evenly spaced on a number line.

You can use the number line to compare numbers. Numbers get smaller as we go to the left and larger as we go to the right. We use the terms *equal to* (=), *less than* (<), *greater than* (>), and between to compare numbers.

12 equals 10 +2	2 is less than 5	9 is greater than 4	6 is between 5 and 7
$12 = 10 + 2$	$2 < 5$	$9 > 4$	$5 < 6 < 7$

PLACE VALUE

We use ten digits, 0–9 to write out numerals. We also use a place value system of numeration. The value of a digit depends on the place it occupies. Look at the following place value chart.

millions	hundred thousands	ten thousands	thousands	hundreds	tens	ones
3	5	7	9	4	1	0

The value of the 9 is 9,000. The 9 is in the thousands place. The value of the 5 is 500,000. The 5 is in the hundred thousands place. Read the number three million, five hundred seventy-nine thousand, four hundred ten.

Some whole numbers are very large. The distance from earth to the planet Pluto is about six trillion (6,000,000,000,000) yards. The distance from earth to the nearest star is about 40 quadrillion (40,000,000,000,000,000) yards.

POSITIVE EXPONENTS

You can show repeated multiplication as an exponent. The exponent shows how many times the factor appears.

[Exponent]

$$\text{Base—}3^5 = 3 \times 3 \times 3 \times 3 \times 3 = 243$$

[Factors]

Rules for Exponents

Use these rules to multiply and divide exponents with the *same base.*

$$7^8 \times 7^5 = 7^{13} \qquad a^n \times a^m = a^{m+n}$$
$$7^8 \div 7^5 = 7^3 \qquad a^n \div a^m = a^{n-m}$$

Scientific Notation

Sometimes we use scientific notation to represent very large numbers. For example, 6,000,000,000,000 has 12 zeros. We can write 6,000,000,000,000 as 6×10^{12}.

UNDERSTANDING AND ORDERING DECIMALS

Decimals are used to represent numbers between 0 and 1. Decimals can also be written on a number line.

0 0.1 0.2 0.3 0.4 0.5 0.6 0.7 0.8 0.9 1

We also use ten digits 0–9 and a place value system of numeration to write decimals. The value of a digit depends on the place it occupies. Look at the following place value chart.

ones	tenths	hundredths	thousandths	ten-thousandths	hundred-thousandths	millionths	ten-millionths	hundred-millionths	billionths
0.	3	6	8	7					

The value of 3 is three tenths. The 3 is in the tenths place. The value of 8 is eight thousandths. The 8 is in the thousandths place.

COMPARING WHOLE NUMBERS AND DECIMALS

To compare two numbers line up the place values. Start at the left and keep going until the digits in the same place are different.

Compare	9,879 and 16,459	23,801 and 23,798	58.1289 and 58.132
Line up the place values	9,879 **1**6,459	23,**8**01 23,798	58.1289 58.1**3**2
	9,879 < 16,459 Less than	23,801 > 23,798 Greater than	58.1289 < 58.132 Less than

ROUNDING WHOLE NUMBERS AND DECIMALS

Follow these steps to round a number to a place.

- Look at the digit to the right of that place.
- If the digit to the right is 5 or more, round up. If the digit is less than 5, leave the numeral to be rounded as written.

Round 859,465 to the thousands place.

Underline the thousands place.

Look to the right. The digit 4 is less than 5 so leave as written.

859,465 rounded to the thousands place is 859,000.

859,465 rounded to the ten-thousands place 860,000.

Round 8.647 to the hundredths place.

Underline the hundredths place.

Look to the right. The digit 7 is 5 or more so you round up.

8.647 rounded to the *hundredths* place is 8.65.

8.647 rounded to the *tenths* place is 8.6.

UNDERSTANDING AND ORDERING FRACTIONS

A fractions names a part of a whole or of a group. A fraction has two parts, a numerator and a denominator. The denominator tells how many parts in all. The numerator tell how many parts you identified.

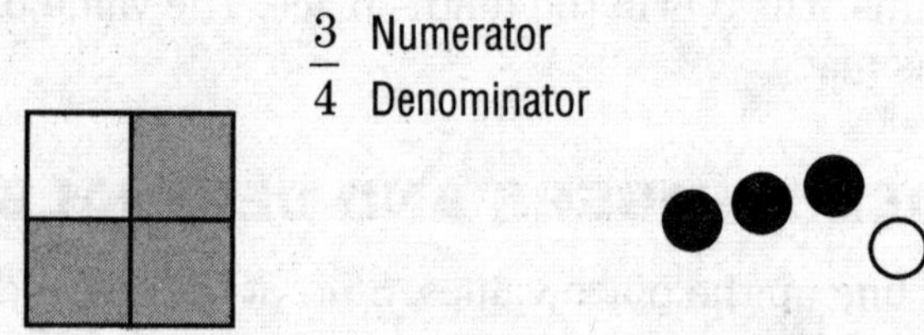

Equivalent Fractions

Two fractions that stand for the same number are called equivalent fractions. Multiply or divide the numerator and denominator by the same number to find an equivalent fraction.

$$\frac{2\times3}{5\times3}=\frac{6}{15} \qquad \frac{6\div3}{9\div3}=\frac{2}{3} \qquad \frac{6\times4}{8\times4}=\frac{24}{32} \qquad \frac{8\div2}{10\div2}=\frac{4}{5}$$

Fractions can also be written and ordered on a number line. You can use the number line to compare fractions. Fractions get smaller as we go to the left and larger as we go to the right. We use the terms equivalent to (=), less than (<), greater than (>), and between to compare fractions.

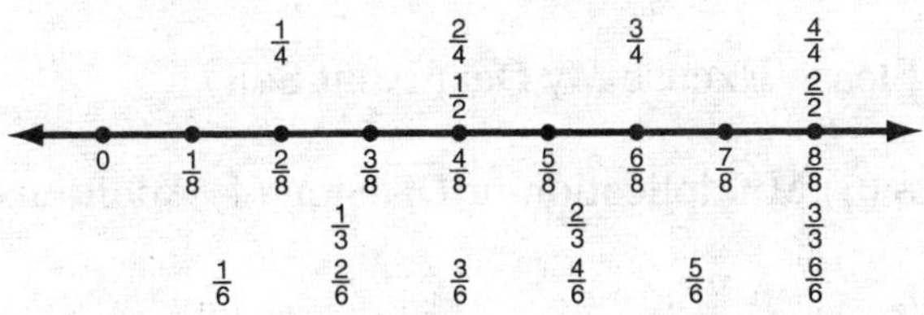

$^1/_2$ is equivalent to $^2/_4$ $\qquad$ $^2/_3$ is less than $^3/_4$ $\qquad$ $^5/_8$ is greater than $^1/_2$ $\qquad$ $^1/_3$ is between $^1/_4$ and $^3/_8$

$$\frac{1}{2}=\frac{2}{4} \qquad \frac{2}{3}<\frac{3}{4} \qquad \frac{5}{8}>\frac{1}{2} \qquad \frac{1}{4}<\frac{1}{3}<\frac{3}{8}$$

Compare Two Fractions

Use this method to compare two fractions. For example, compare $^{13}/_{18}$ and $^5/_7$. First write the two fractions and cross multiply as shown. The larger cross product appears next to the larger fraction. If cross products are equal then the fractions are equivalent.

$$91 = \quad \frac{13}{18} \times \frac{5}{7} \quad = 90$$

$$91 > 90 \text{ so } \frac{13}{18} > \frac{5}{7}$$

Mixed Numbers and Improper Fractions

Change an improper fraction to a mixed number:

$$\frac{23}{8} = 8\overline{)23} \quad \text{quotient: } 2\frac{7}{8}$$

Change a mixed number to an improper fraction:

$$3\frac{2}{5}=\frac{17}{5}$$

Multiply denominator and whole number. Then add the numerator.

$$\frac{(3 \times 5) + 2}{5} = \frac{15 + 2}{5} = \frac{17}{5}$$

HOW AND WHEN TO ADD, SUBTRACT, MULTIPLY, AND DIVIDE

Order of Operations

Use this phrase to remember the order in which we do operations:

Please **E**xcuse **M**y **D**ear **A**unt **S**ally

(1) **P**arentheses (2) **E**xponents (3) **M**ultiplication or **D**ivision (4) **A**ddition or **S**ubtraction

For example,

$$4 + 3 \times 7^2 = 4 + 3 \times 49 = 4 + 147 = 151$$

$$(4 + 3) \times 7^2 = 7 \times 7^2 = 7 \times 49 = 343$$

$$(6 - 10 \div 5) + 6 \times 3 = (6 - 2) + 6 \times 3 = 4 + 6 \times 3 = 4 + 18 = 22$$

Decide Whether to Add, Subtract, Multiply, or Divide

Before you can solve a problem, you should know which operation to use. You can use key words to decide which operation to use, or you can use a problem-solving strategy called choosing the operation. We'll discuss both of them here.

Key Words

Addition	sum, and, more, increased by
Subtraction	less, difference, decreased by
Multiplication	of, product, times
Division	per, quotient, shared, ratio
Equals	is, equals

You can't just use these key words without thinking. You must check to be sure that the operation makes sense when it replaces the key word. For example,

19 and 23 is 42	16 is 4 more than 12	What percent of 19 is 5.7
$19 + 23 = 42$	$16 = 4 + 12$	____% $\times$ 19 = 5.7

Choosing the Operation

To use the choosing-the-operation strategy, you think of each situation in this way. What do I know? What am I trying to find? The answers to these questions lead you directly to the correct operation.

You Know	You Want to Find
Add	
1. How many in two or more groups	How many in all
2. How many in one group How many join it	The total amount
3. How many in one group How many more in the second group	How many in the second group
Subtract	
4. How many in one group Number taken away	How many are left
5. How many in each of two groups	How much larger one group is than the other
6. How many in one group How many in part of that group	How many in the rest of the group
Multiply	
7. How many in each group There is the same number in each group How many groups	How many in all
Divide	
8. Same number in each group How many in all How many in each group	How many groups
9. Same number in each group How many in all How many groups	How many in each group

NUMBER THEORY

Number theory explores the natural numbers {1, 2, 3, 4, . . .}. We'll review just a few important number theory concepts.

Factors

The factors of a number evenly divide the number with no remainder. For example, 2 is a factor of 6, but 2 is not a factor of 5.

The number 1 is a factor of every number. Each number is a factor of itself.

1 The only factor is 1
2 Factors 1, 2
3 1, 3

4 1, 2, 4
5 1, 5
6 1, 2, 3, 6
7 1, 7
8 1, 2, 4, 8
9 1, 3, 9
10 1, 2, 5, 10

Prime Numbers and Composite Numbers

A prime number has exactly two factors, itself and 1.

2 is prime. The only factors are 1 and 2.
3 Prime. Factors 1, 3.
5 Prime. Factors 1, 5.
7 Prime. Factors 1, 7.

A composite number has more than two factors.

4 is composite. The factors are 1, 2, 4.
6 is composite. Factors: 1, 2, 3, 6.
8 is composite. Factors: 1, 2, 4, 8.
9 is composite. Factors: 1, 3, 9.
10 is composite. Factors: 1, 2, 5, 10.

The number 1 has only one factor, itself. The number 1 is neither prime nor composite.

Least Common Multiple (LCM), Greatest Common Factor (GCF)

Multiples. The multiples of a number are all the numbers you get when you count by that number. Here are some examples.

Multiples of 1: 1, 2, 3, 4, 5, . . .
Multiples of 2: 2, 4, 6, 8, 10, . . .
Multiples of 3: 3, 6, 9, 12, 15, . . .
Multiples of 4: 4, 8, 12, 16, 20, . . .
Multiples of 5: 5, 10, 15, 20, 25, . . .

Least Common Multiple is the smallest multiple shared by two numbers.

The least common multiple of 6 and 8 is 24.

List the multiples of 6 and 8. Notice that 24 is the smallest multiple common to both numbers.

Multiples of 6: 6, 12, 18, **24**, 30, 36
Multiples of 8: 8, 16, **24**, 32, 40

Greatest Common Factor is the largest factor shared by two numbers.

The greatest common factor of 28 and 36 is 4.
List the factors of 28 and 36.

Factors of 28: 1, 2, **4**, 7, 28
Factors of 36: 1, 2, 3, **4**, 9, 12, 18, 36

Divisibility Rules

Use these rules to find out if a number is divisible by the given number. *Divisible* means the given number divides evenly with no remainder.

2 Every even number is divisible by 2.

3 If the sum of the digits is divisible by 3, the number is divisible by 3.

347 $3 + 4 + 7 = 14$ 14 is not divisible by 3 so 347 is not divisible by 3

738 $7 + 3 + 8 = 18$ 18 is divisible by 3 so 738 is divisible by 3

4 If the last two digits are divisible by 4, the number is divisible by 4.

484,842 42 is not divisible by 4 so 484,842 is not divisible by 4.

371,956 56 is divisible by 4 so 372,956 is divisible by 4.

5 If the last digit is 0 or 5, then the number is divisible by 5.

6 If the number meets the divisibility rules for both 2 *and* 3 then it is divisible by 6.

8 If the last three digits are divisible by 8, then the number is divisible by 8.

208,513,114 114 is not divisible by 8 so 208,513,114 is not divisible by 8.

703,628,920 920 is divisible by 8 so 703,628,920 is divisible by 8.

9 If the sum of the digits is divisible by 9 then the number is divisible by 9.

93,163 $9 + 3 + 1 + 6 + 3 = 22$ 22 is not divisible by 9 so 93,163 is not divisible by 9.

86,715 $8 + 6 + 7 + 1 + 5 = 27$ 27 is divisible by 9 so 86,715 is divisible by 9.

10 If a number ends in 0, the number is divisible by 10.

REAL NUMBER SYSTEMS AND SUBSYSTEMS

ADD, SUBTRACT, MULTIPLY, AND DIVIDE DECIMALS

Add and Subtract Decimals

Line up the decimal points and add or subtract.

Add: 14.9 + 3.108 + 0.16

```
  14.9
   3.108
+ 0.16
-------
 18.168
```

Subtract 14.234 - 7.14

```
 14.234
 -7.14
-------
  7.094
```

Multiply Decimals

Multiply as with whole numbers. Count the total number of decimal places in the factors. Put that many decimal places in the product. You may have to write leading zeros.

Multiply: 17.4 × 1.3

```
  17.4
 × 1.3
 -----
   522
  174
 -----
  22.62
```

Multiply: 0.016 × 1.7

```
  0.016
 ×  1.7
 ------
    112
    16
 ------
  .0272
```

Divide Decimals

Make the divisor a whole number. Match the movement in the dividend and then divide.

$0.16\overline{)1.328}$ $\qquad$ $0.16\overline{)1.328}$ $\qquad$ $16\overline{)132.8}$

```
       8.3
16 ) 132.8
     128
     ----
       48
       48
       --
        0
```

MULTIPLYING, DIVIDING, ADDING, AND SUBTRACTING FRACTIONS AND MIXED NUMBERS

Multiplying Fractions and Mixed Numbers

Write any mixed number as an improper fraction. Multiply numerator and denominator. Write the product in simplest form. For example, Multiply $^3/_4$ and $^1/_6$.

$$\frac{3}{4} \times \frac{1}{6} = \frac{3}{24} = \frac{1}{8}$$

Now, multiply $3^1/_3$ times $^3/_5$.

$$3\frac{1}{3} \times \frac{3}{5} = \frac{10}{3} \times \frac{3}{5} = \frac{30}{15} = 2$$

Dividing Fractions and Mixed Numbers

To divide $1^4/_5$ by $^3/_8$:

$$1\frac{4}{5} \div \frac{3}{8} = \frac{9}{5} \div \frac{3}{8} = \frac{9}{5} \times \frac{8}{3} = \frac{72}{15} = 4\frac{12}{15} = 4\frac{4}{5}$$

Write any mixed numbers as improper fractions; Invert the divisor and multiply; Write the product; Write in simplest form

Adding Fractions and Mixed Numbers

Write fractions with common denominators. Add and then write in simplest form.

Add: $\frac{3}{8}+\frac{1}{4}$

$$\frac{3}{8}=\frac{3}{8}$$
$$+\frac{1}{4}=\frac{2}{8}$$
$$\frac{5}{8}$$

Add: $\frac{7}{8}+\frac{5}{12}$

$$\frac{7}{8}=\frac{21}{24}$$
$$+\frac{5}{12}=\frac{10}{24}$$
$$\frac{31}{24}=1\frac{7}{24}$$

Add: $2\frac{1}{3}+\frac{5}{7}$

$$2\frac{1}{3}=2\frac{7}{21}$$
$$+\frac{5}{7}=\frac{15}{21}$$
$$2\frac{22}{21}=3\frac{1}{21}$$

Subtracting Fractions and Mixed Numbers

Write fractions with common denominators. Subtract and then write in simplest form.

Subtract: $\frac{5}{16}-\frac{1}{3}$

$$\frac{5}{6}=\frac{5}{6}$$
$$-\frac{1}{3}=\frac{2}{6}$$
$$\frac{3}{6}=\frac{1}{2}$$

Subtract: $\frac{3}{8}-\frac{1}{5}$

$$\frac{3}{8}=\frac{15}{40}$$
$$-\frac{1}{5}=\frac{8}{40}$$
$$\frac{7}{40}$$

Subtract: $3\frac{1}{6}-1\frac{1}{3}$

$$3\frac{1}{6}=3\frac{1}{6}=2\frac{7}{6}$$
$$-1\frac{1}{3}=1\frac{2}{6}=1\frac{2}{6}$$
$$1\frac{5}{6}$$

SQUARE ROOTS

The square root of a given number, when multiplied by itself, equals the given number. This symbol means the square root of 25 $\sqrt{25}$. The square root of 25 is 5. $5 \times 5 = 25$.

Some Square Roots Are Whole Numbers

The numbers with whole-number square roots are called perfect squares.

$$\sqrt{1}=1 \quad \sqrt{4}=2 \quad \sqrt{9}=3 \quad \sqrt{16}=4 \quad \sqrt{25}=5 \quad \sqrt{36}=6$$

$$\sqrt{49}=7 \quad \sqrt{64}=8 \quad \sqrt{81}=9 \quad \sqrt{100}=10 \quad \sqrt{121}=11 \quad \sqrt{144}=12$$

Use This Rule to Write a Square Root in Its Simplest Form

$$\sqrt{a \times b} = \sqrt{a} \times \sqrt{b} \qquad \sqrt{5 \times 3} = \sqrt{5} \times \sqrt{3}$$

$$\sqrt{72} = \sqrt{36 \times 2} = \sqrt{36} \times \sqrt{2} = 6 \times \sqrt{2}$$

RATIO, PROPORTION, AND PERCENT

Ratio

A ratio is a way of comparing two numbers with division. It conveys the same meaning as a fraction. There are three ways to write a ratio.

Using words 3 to 4 As a fraction 3/4 Using a colon 3 : 4

Proportion

A proportion shows two ratios that have the same value; that is, the fractions representing the ratios are equivalent. Use cross multiplication. If the cross products are equal, then the two ratios form a proportion.

$^{3}/_{8}$ and $^{27}/_{72}$ form a proportion. The cross products are equal. ($3 \times 72 = 8 \times 27$)

$^{3}/_{8}$ and $^{24}/_{56}$ do not form a proportion. The cross products are not equal.

Solving a Proportion

You may have to write a proportion to solve a problem. For example, the mason mixes cement and sand using a ratio of 2 : 5. Twelve bags of cement will be used. How much sand is needed?

To solve, use the numerator to stand for cement. The denominator will stand for sand.

$$\frac{2}{5}=\frac{12}{S}$$

Write the proportion

$$\frac{2}{5}=\frac{12}{S}$$

$$2\times S=5\times 12$$
$$2S=60$$
$$S=30$$

Cross multiply to solve

Thirty bags of sand are needed.

PERCENT

Percent comes from per centum, which means per hundred. Whenever you see a number followed by a percent sign it means that number out of 100.

Decimals and Percents

To write a decimal as a percent, move the decimal point two places to the right and write the percent sign.

0.34 = 34% 0.297 = 29.7% 0.6 = 60% 0.001 = 0.1%

To write a percent as a decimal, move the decimal point two places to the left and delete the percent sign.

51% = 0.51 34.18% = 0.3418 0.9% = 0.009

Fractions and Percents

Writing Fractions as Percents

- Divide the numerator by the denominator. Write the answer as a percent.

Write $^{3}/_{5}$ as a percent.

$$5\overline{)3.0}\quad 0.6$$

0.6 = 60%

Write $^{5}/_{8}$ as a percent.

$$8\overline{)5.000}\quad 0.625$$

0.625 = 62.5%

- Write an equivalent fraction with 100 in the denominator. Write the numerator followed by a percent sign.

Write $^{13}/_{25}$ as a percent.

$$\frac{13}{25} = \frac{52}{100} = 52\%$$

- Use these equivalencies.

$\frac{1}{4} = 25\%$	$\frac{1}{2} = 50\%$	$\frac{3}{4} = 75\%$	$\frac{4}{4} = 100\%$
$\frac{1}{5} = 20\%$	$\frac{2}{5} = 40\%$	$\frac{3}{5} = 60\%$	$\frac{4}{5} = 80\%$
$\frac{1}{6} = 16\frac{2}{3}\%$	$\frac{1}{3} = 33\frac{1}{3}\%$	$\frac{2}{3} = 66\frac{2}{3}\%$	$\frac{5}{6} = 83\frac{1}{3}\%$
$\frac{1}{8} = 12\frac{1}{2}\%$	$\frac{3}{8} = 37\frac{1}{2}\%$	$\frac{5}{8} = 62\frac{1}{2}\%$	$\frac{7}{8} = 87\frac{1}{2}\%$

Writing Percents as Fractions

Write a fraction with 100 in the denominator and the percent in the numerator. Simplify.

$$18\% = \frac{18}{100} = \frac{9}{50} \qquad 7.5\% = \frac{7.5}{100} = \frac{75}{1000} = \frac{3}{40}$$

THREE TYPES OF PERCENT PROBLEMS

Finding a Percent of a Number

To find a percent of a number, write a number sentence with a decimal for the percent and solve.

Find 40% of 90.

$$0.4 \times 90 = 36$$

It may be easier to write a fraction for the percent.

Find $62^1/_2$% of 64.

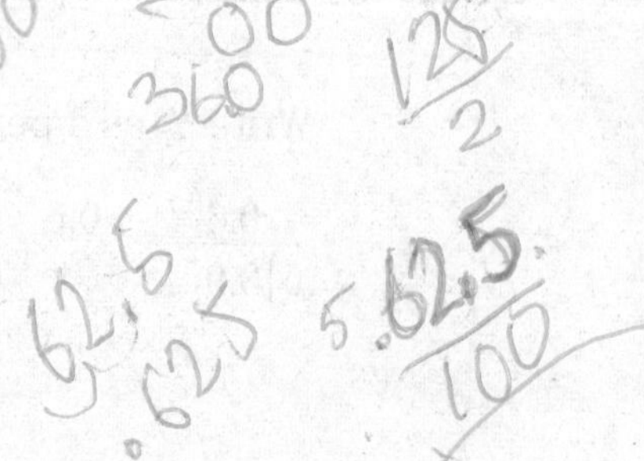

$$\frac{5}{8} \times 64 = 5 \times 8 = 40$$

Finding What Percent One Number Is of Another

To find what percent one number is of another, write a number sentence and solve to find the percent.

What percent of 5 is 3?

$$n \times 5 = 3$$

$$n = {}^{3}/_{5} = 0.6 = 60\%$$

Finding a Number When a Percent of It Is Known

To find a number when a percent of it is known, write a number sentence with a decimal or a fraction for the percent and solve to find the number.

5% of what number is 2?

$$0.05 \times n = 2$$

$$n = 2 \div 0.05$$

$$n = 40$$

PROBABILITY AND SIMPLE STATISTICS

PROBABILITY

The probability of an occurrence is the likelihood that it will happen. Most often, we write probability as a fraction.

Flip a fair coin and the probability that it will come up heads is 1/2. The same is true for tails. Write the probability this way.

P (H) = 1/2 *P* (T) = 1/2

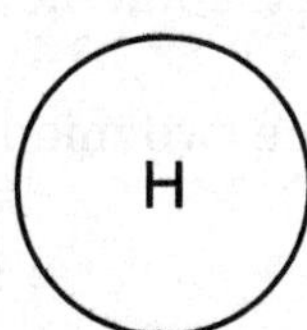

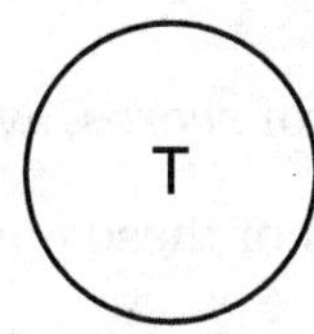

If something will never occur the probability is 0. If something will always occur, the probability is 1. Therefore, if you flip a fair coin,

P (7) = 0 *P* (H or T) = 1

DEPENDENT AND INDEPENDENT EVENTS

Events are *independent* when the outcome of one event does not affect the probability of the other event. Each coin flip is an independent event. No matter the outcome of one flip, the probability of the next flip remains the same.

Flip heads 10 times in a row with a fair coin. On the next flip, the *P* (H) is still 1/2. Coin flips are independent events.

Events are *dependent* where the outcome of one event does affect the probability of the other event. For example, you have a full deck of cards. The probability of picking the Queen of Hearts is 1/52.

You pick one card and it's not the Queen of Hearts. You don't put the card back. The probability of picking the Queen of Hearts is now 1/51. Cards picked without replacement are dependent events.

STATISTICS

Descriptive statistics are used to explain or describe a set of numbers. Most often we use the mean, median, or mode to describe these numbers.

Mean (Average)

The mean is a position midway between two extremes. To find the mean:

1. Add the items or scores.

2. Divide by the number of items.

For example, find the mean of 24, 17, 42, 51, 36.

$$24 + 17 + 42 + 51 + 36 = 170 \qquad 170 \div 5 = 34$$

The mean or average is 34.

Median

The median is the middle number. To find the median:

1. Arrange the numbers from least to greatest.

2. If there are an odd number of scores, then find the middle score.

3. If there is an even number of scores, average the two middle scores.

For example, find the median of these numbers.

6, 9, 11, <u>17</u>, <u>21</u>, 33, 45, 71

There are an even number of scores.

$$17 + 21 = 38 \qquad 38 \div 2 = 19$$

The median is 19.

Don't forget to arrange the scores in order before finding the middle score!

Mode

The mode is the number that occurs most often.

For example, find the mode of these numbers.

6, 3, 7, 6, 9, 3, 6, 1, 2, 6, 7, 3

The number 6 occurs most often so 6 is the mode.

Not all sets of numbers have a mode. Some sets of numbers may have more than one mode.

STEM-AND-LEAF AND BOX-AND-WHISKER PLOTS

Stem-and-Leaf Plots

Stem-and-leaf plots represent data in place value-oriented plots. Each piece of data is shown in the plot. The following stem-and-leaf plot shows test scores. The stem represents 10, and the leaves represent 1. You can read each score. In the 50s the scores are 55, 55, and 58. There are no scores in the 60s. You can find the lowest score, 40, and highest score, 128.

Stem	Leaves
4	0 7
5	5 5 8
6	
7	1 4 4 6
8	2 3 4 5
9	9 9
10	
11	
12	3 4 8

Example: 7 | 4 means 74 people

Box-and-Whisker Plots

Box-and-whisker plots show the range and quartiles of scores. The plot is a box divided into two parts with a whisker at each end. The ends of the left and right whiskers show the lowest and highest scores. Quartiles partition scores into quarters. The left and right parts of the box show the upper and lower quartiles; the dividing line shows the median.

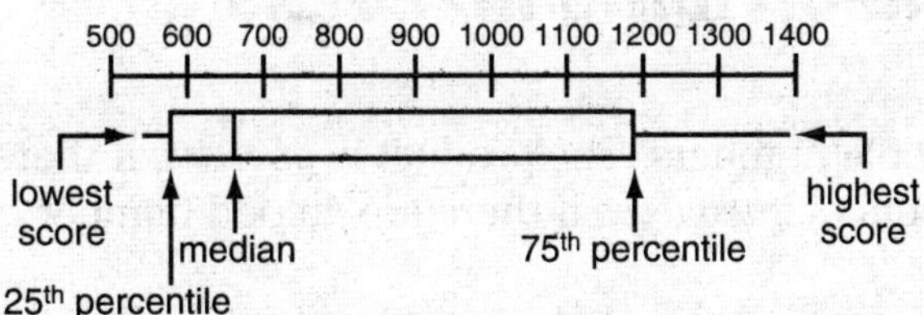

ALGEBRA

The number line can also show negative numbers. There is a negative whole number for every positive whole number. Zero is neither positive nor negative. The negative whole numbers and the positive whole numbers together are called integers.

ADDING AND SUBTRACTING INTEGERS

Addition

When the signs are the same keep the sign and add.

$$\begin{array}{r} {}^{+}7 \\ +\ {}^{+}8 \\ \hline {}^{+}15 \end{array} \qquad \begin{array}{r} {}^{-}3 \\ +\ {}^{-}11 \\ \hline {}^{-}14 \end{array}$$

When the signs are different, disregard the signs, subtract the numbers, and keep the sign of the larger number.

$$\begin{array}{r} {}^{+}28 \\ +\ {}^{-}49 \\ \hline {}^{-}21 \end{array} \qquad \begin{array}{r} {}^{-}86 \\ +\ {}^{+}135 \\ \hline {}^{+}49 \end{array}$$

Subtraction

Change the sign of the number being subtracted. Then add using the preceding rules.

$$\begin{array}{r} {}^{+}13 \\ -\ {}^{-}18 \\ \hline \downarrow \\ {}^{+}13 \\ +\ {}^{+}18 \\ \hline {}^{+}31 \end{array} \qquad \begin{array}{r} {}^{-}43 \\ -\ {}^{-}17 \\ \hline \downarrow \\ {}^{-}43 \\ +\ {}^{+}17 \\ \hline {}^{-}26 \end{array} \qquad \begin{array}{r} {}^{+}29 \\ -\ {}^{-}49 \\ \hline \downarrow \\ {}^{+}29 \\ +\ {}^{+}49 \\ \hline {}^{+}78 \end{array} \qquad \begin{array}{r} {}^{-}92 \\ -\ {}^{+}135 \\ \hline \downarrow \\ {}^{-}92 \\ +\ {}^{-}135 \\ \hline {}^{-}227 \end{array}$$

MULTIPLYING AND DIVIDING INTEGERS

Multiply

Multiply as you would whole numbers. The product is *positive* if there are an even number of negative factors. The product is *negative* if there are an odd number of negative factors.

$${}^{-}2 \times {}^{+}4 \times {}^{-}6 \times {}^{+}3 = {}^{+}144 \qquad {}^{-}2 \times {}^{-}4 \times {}^{+}6 \times {}^{-}3 = {}^{-}144$$

Divide

Forget the signs and divide. The quotient is *positive* if both integers have the same sign. The quotient is *negative* if the integers have different signs.

$^{+}24 \div {}^{+}4 = {}^{+}6$ $^{-}24 \div {}^{-}4 = {}^{+}6$ $^{+}24 \div {}^{-}4 = {}^{-}6$ $^{-}24 \div {}^{+}4 = {}^{-}6$

FORMULAS

Evaluating an Expression

Evaluate an expression by replacing the variables with values. Remember to use the correct order of operations. For example, evaluate

$$3x - \frac{y}{z} \text{ for } x = 3,\ y = 8, \text{ and } z = 4$$

$$3\left(3\right) - \frac{8}{4} = 9 - 2 = 7$$

Using Formulas

Using a formula is like evaluating an expression. Just replace the variables with values. Here are some important formulas to know. The area of a figure is the amount of space it occupies in two dimensions. The perimeter of a figure is the distance around the figure. Use 3.14 for π.

Figure	Formula	Description
Triangle	Area = $\frac{1}{2}bh$ Perimeter = $s_1 + s_2 + s_3$	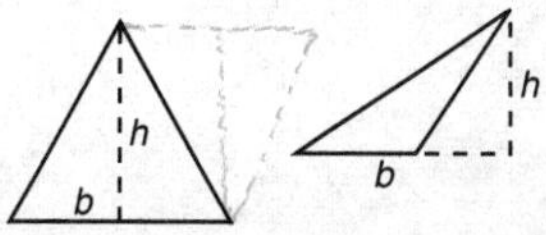 h, b
Square	Area = s^2 Perimeter = $4s$	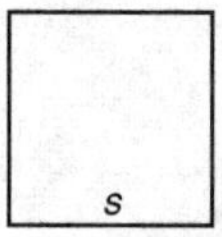 s
Rectangle	Area = lw Perimeter = $2l + 2w$	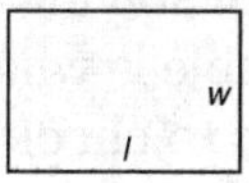 w, l
Parallelogram	Area = bh Perimeter = $2s + 2h$	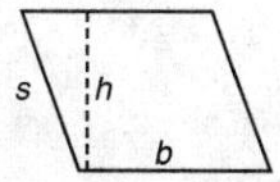 s, h, b
Trapezoid	Area = $\frac{1}{2}h(b_1 + b_2)$ Perimeter = $b_1 + b_2 + s_1 + s_2$	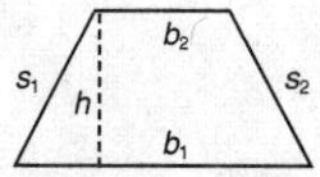 b_2, s_1, s_2, h, b_1

Figure	Formula	Description
Circle	Area = πr^2 Circumference = $2\pi r$ or = πd	
Cube	Volume = s^3	
Rectangular Prism	Volume = lwh	
Sphere	Volume = $\frac{4}{3}\pi r^3$	

Pythagorean Formula

The Pythagorean formula for right triangles states that the sum of the square of the legs equals the square of the hypotenuse:

$$a^2 + b^2 = c^2$$

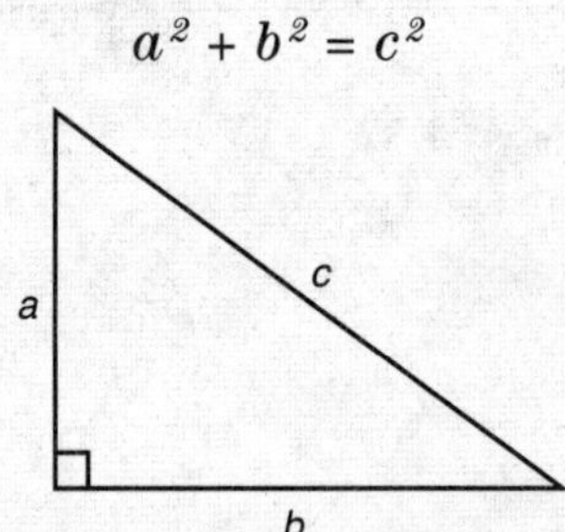

EQUATIONS

The whole idea of solving equations is to isolate the variable on one side of the equal sign. The value of the variable is what's on the other side of the equal sign. Substitute your answer into the original equation to check your solution.

Solving Equations by Adding or Subtracting

Solve: $y + 19 = 23$

Subtract 19 $\quad y + 19 - 19 = 23 - 19$

$y = 4$

Check: Does **4** + 19 = 23? Yes. It checks.

$$\text{Solve: } x - 23 = 51$$
$$\text{Add 23} \quad x - 23 + 23 = 51 + 23$$
$$x = 74$$

Check: Does **74** – 23 = 51. Yes. It checks.

Solving Equations by Multiplying or Dividing

$$\text{Solve: } \frac{z}{7} = 6$$

$$\text{Multiply by 7} \quad \frac{z}{7} \times 7 = 6 \times 7$$

$$z = 42$$

Check: Does $\frac{42}{7} = 6$? Yes. It checks.

$$\text{Solve: } 21 = -3x$$

remember to divide

$$\text{Divide by } {}^-3 \quad \frac{21}{-3} = \frac{-3x}{-3}$$

$$-7 = x$$

Check: Does 21 = (–3)(–7)? Yes. It checks.

Solving Two-Step Equations

Add or subtract before you multiply or divide.

$$\text{Solve: } 3x - 6 = 24$$

$$\text{Add 6} \quad 3x - 6 + 6 = 24 + 6$$
$$3x = 30$$

$$\text{Divide by 3} \quad \frac{3x}{3} = \frac{30}{3}$$

$$x = 10$$

Check: Does $3 \times \mathbf{10} - 6 = 24$? Yes. It checks.

$$\text{Solve: } \frac{y}{7} + 4 = 32$$

$$\text{Subtract 4} \quad \frac{y}{7} + 4 - 4 = 32 - 4$$

$$\frac{y}{7} = 28$$

$$\text{Multiply by 7} \quad \frac{y}{7} \times 7 = (28)(7)$$

$$y = 196$$

Check: Does $\frac{\mathbf{196}}{7} + 4 = 32$? Yes. It checks.

GEOMETRY

TWO-DIMENSIONAL GEOMETRY

We can think of geometry in two or three dimensions. A two-dimensional model is this page. A three-dimensional model is the room you'll take the test in.

Definition	Model	Symbol
Point—a location	. *A*	*A*
Plane—a flat surface that extends infinitely in all directions	A• •B •C	plane *ABC*
Space—occupies three dimensions and extends infinitely in all directions	z y x	space *xyz*
Line—a set of points in a straight path that extends infinitely in two directions	A B	$\overleftrightarrow{AB}$
Line segment—part of a line with two endpoints	B A	$\overline{AB}$
Ray—part of a line with one endpoint	A B	$\overrightarrow{AB}$
Parallel lines—lines that stay the same distance apart and never touch	A B / D F	

Definition	Model	Symbol
Perpendicular lines—lines that meet at right angles		
Angle—two rays with a common endpoint, which is called the vertex	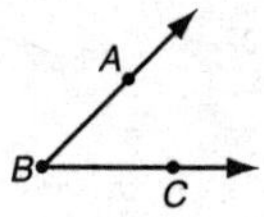	$\angle ABC$
Acute angle—angle that measures between 0° and 90°		
Right angle—angle that measures 90°		
Obtuse angle—angle that measures between 90° and 180°		
Complementary angles—angles that have a total measure of 90°		
Supplementary angles—angles that have a total measure of 180°		

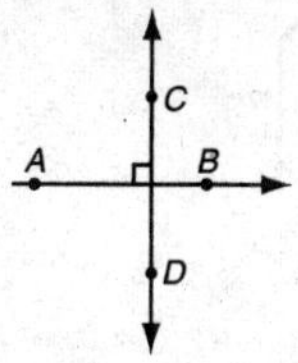

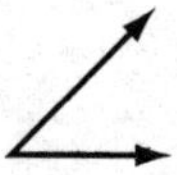

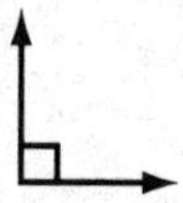

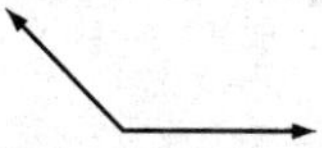

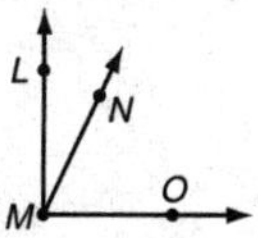

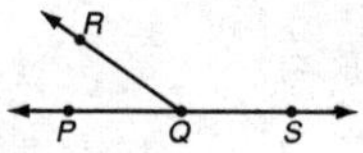

Polygon—a closed figure made up of line segments; if all sides are the same length, the figure is a regular polygon

Pentagon

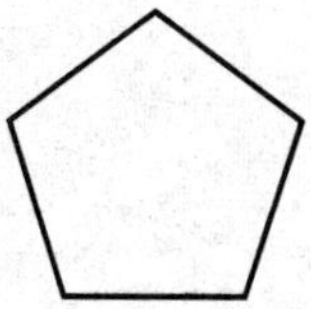

Five Sides

Hexagon

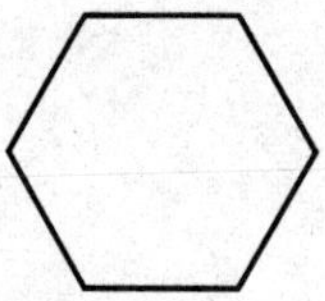

Six Sides

Octagon

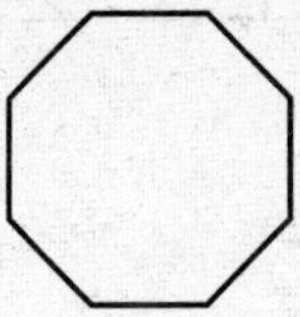

Eight Sides

Triangle—polygon with three sides and three angles; the sum of the angles is always 180°.

Equilateral triangle—all the sides are the same length; all the angles are the same size, 60°.

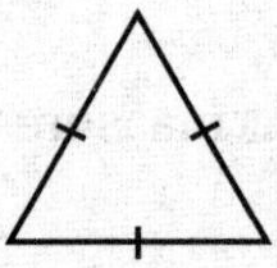

Isosceles triangle—two sides the same length; two angles the same size.

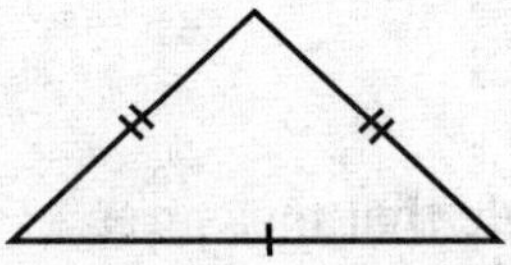

Scalene triangle—all sides different lengths; all angles different sizes.

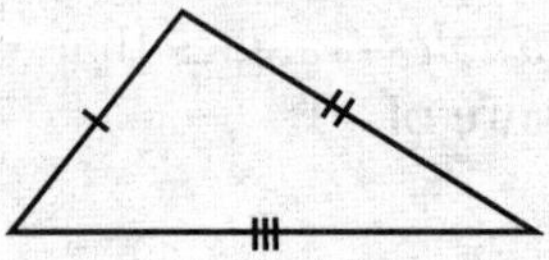

Quadrilateral—polygon with four sides

Square

Rhombus

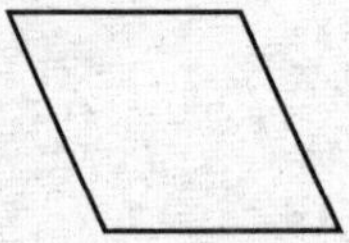

Rectangle

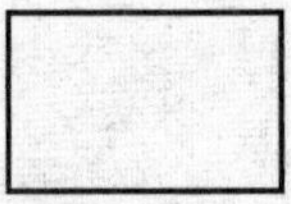

Parallelogram

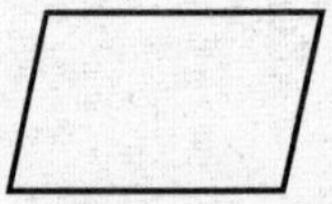

Trapezoid

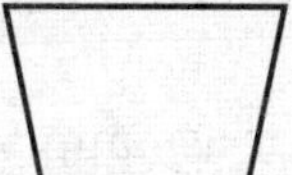

COORDINATE GRID

You can plot ordered pairs of numbers on a coordinate grid.

The x axis goes horizontally from left to right. The first number in the pair tells how far to move left or right from the origin. A minus sign means move left. A plus sign means move right.

The y axis goes vertically up and down. The second number in the pair tells how far to move up or down from the origin. A minus sign means move down. A plus sign means move up.

Pairs of numbers show the x coordinate first and the y coordinate second (x, y). The origin is point (0, 0) where the x axis and the y axis meet.

Plot these pairs of numbers on the grid.

A ($^{+}3$, $^{-}7$) **B** ($^{+}5$, $^{+}3$) **C** ($^{-}6$, $^{+}2$) **D** ($^{-}3$, $^{-}6$)

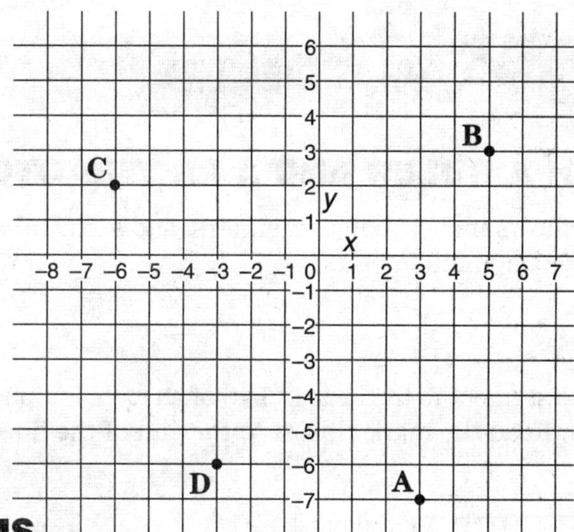

USING DIAGRAMS

All, Some, and None

Diagrams can show the logical connectives all, some, and none. View the following diagrams for an explanation.

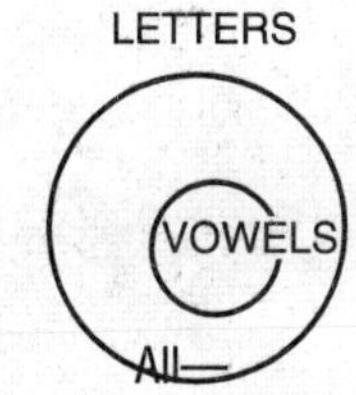

All vowels are letters.

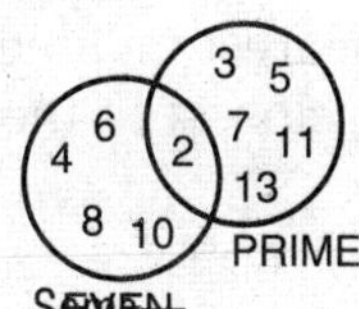

Some prime numbers are even.

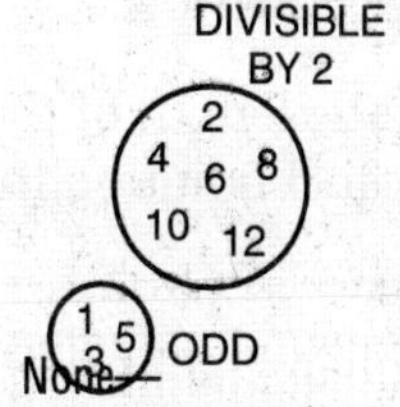

No odd numbers are divisible by two.

Deductive Reasoning

Deductive reasoning draws conclusions from statements or assumptions. Diagrams may help you draw a conclusion. Consider this simple example.

Assume that all even numbers are divisible by two and that all multiples of ten are even. Draw a diagram:

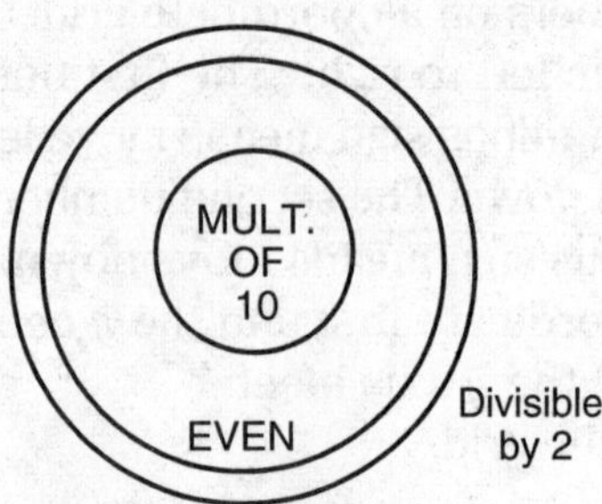

The multiple of ten circle is entirely within the divisible by two circle. Conclusion: All multiples of ten are divisible by two.

MEASUREMENT

MEASURING WITH A RULER AND A PROTRACTOR

You may use a ruler that shows inches, halves, quarters, and sixteenths, or you may use a ruler that shows centimeters and millimeters.

Customary Rulers

Measure the length of a line segment to the nearest 1/16 of an inch. Put one end of the line segment at the 0 point on the ruler. Read the mark closest to the end of the line

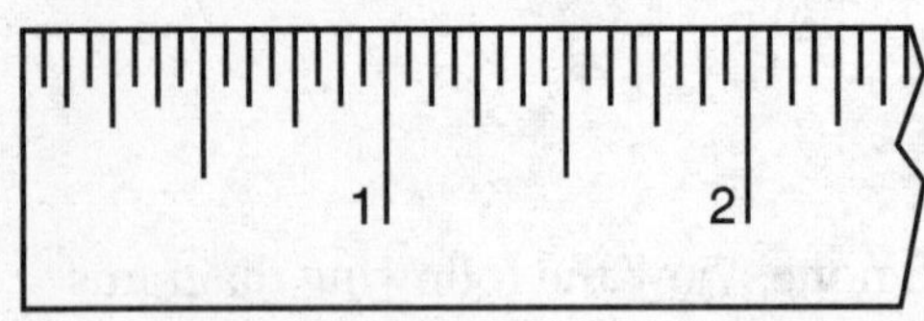

The line segment is $1^{11}/_{16}$ inches long.

Metric Rulers

Measure the length of the line segment to the nearest millimeter. Put one end of the line segment at the 0 point on the ruler. Read the mark closest to the end of the line.

The line segment is 45 mm long.

Protractors

Most protractors are half circles and show degrees from 0° to 180°.

Put the center of the protractor on the vertex of the angle. Align one ray of the angle on the inner or outer 0° point on the scale. Read the measure of the angle on that scale.

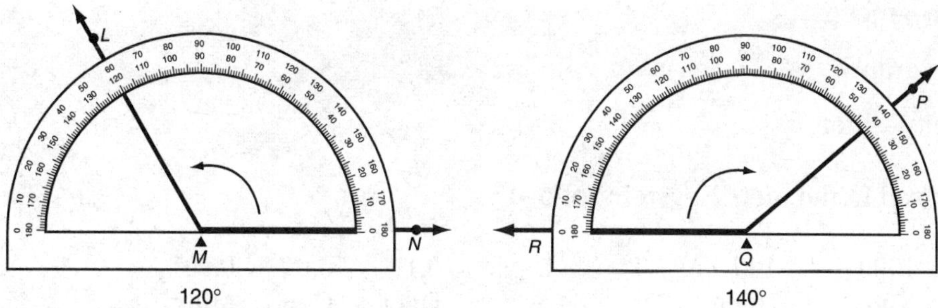

WEIGHT AND MASS

Mass is the amount of matter in a body. Weight is a measure of the force of gravity on a body. Mass is the same everywhere, but weight depends on its location in a gravitational field. That is, an object has the same mass whether on the moon or on earth. However, the object weighs less on the moon than on earth.

CUSTOMARY (ENGLISH) UNITS

Length

12 inches (in.) = 1 foot (ft)
3 feet = 1 yard (yd)
36 inches = 1 yard
1,760 yards = 1 mile (mi)
5,280 feet = 1 mile

Weight

16 ounces (oz) = 1 pound (lb)
2,000 pounds = 1 ton (T)

Capacity

2 cups = 1 pint (pt)
2 pints = 1 quart (qt)
4 quarts = 1 gallon (gal)

METRIC SYSTEM

The metric system uses common units of measure. The system uses prefixes that are powers of 10 or 0.1.

The common units used in the metric system follow:

Length—meter

Mass—gram

Capacity—liter

The prefixes used in the metric system follow:

1000	100	10	Unit	0.1	0.01	0.001
Kilo	Hecto	Deka		Deci	Centi	Milli

Notice that prefixes less than 1 end in *i*.

References for commonly used metric measurements

Unit	Description
Length	
Meter	A little more than a yard
Centimeter (0.01 meter)	The width of a paper clip (About 2.5 per inch)
Millimeter (0.001 meter)	The thickness of the wire on a paper clip
Kilometer (1000 meters)	About 0.6 of a mile
Mass	
Gram	The weight of a paper clip
Kilogram (1000 grams)	About 2.2 pounds
Capacity	
Liter	A little more than a quart
Milliliter	The amount of water in a cubic centimeter

TIME AND TEMPERATURE

Time

Each of the 24 hours in a day is partitioned into 60 minutes. Each minute is partitioned into 60 seconds. In the United States we use a 12-hour clock. The time between midnight and noon is called A.M., while the time between noon and midnight is called P.M. In other countries and in the scientific and military communities, a 24-hour clock is used. Both analog and digital clocks are used to keep track of time.

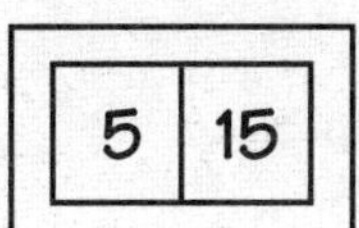

Digital 12-hour clock
5:15 P.M.

Analog 24-hour clock
1715 hours (5:15 P.M.)

There are 24 time zones in the world and four time zones in the continental United States. The United States time zones are shown in the following map. As you travel west, the sun rises later and the time gets earlier—10 A.M. in New York is 7 A.M. in Los Angeles.

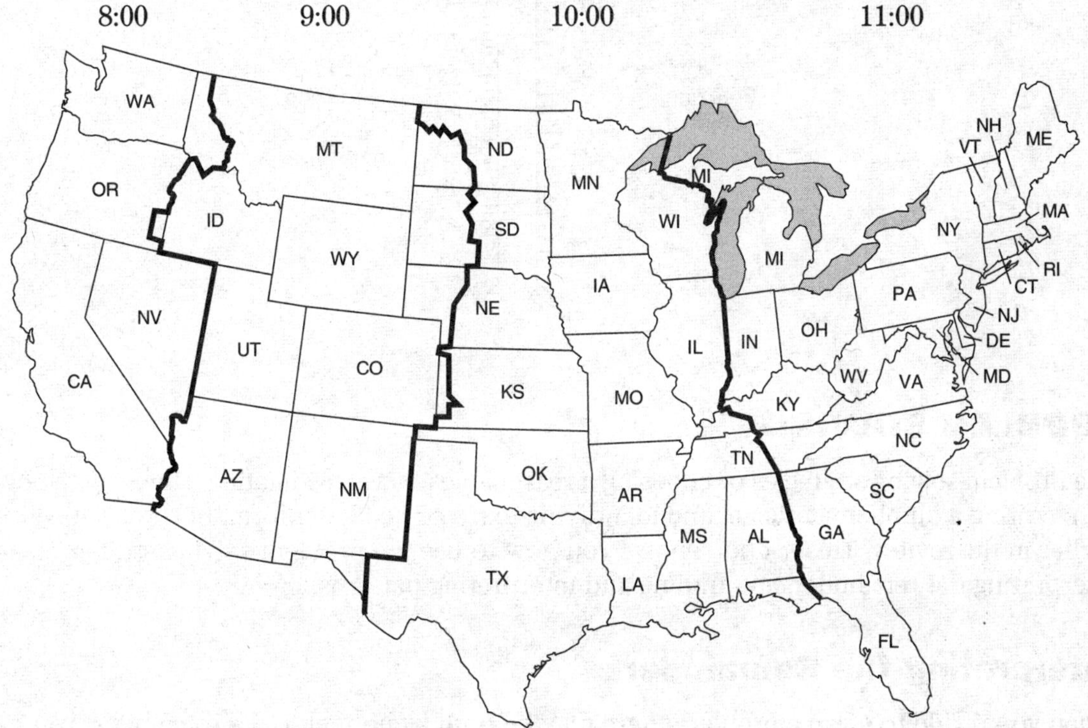

Temperature

Temperature is the degree of warmth or cold. We use Fahrenheit and Celsius thermometers to measure warmth. On a Fahrenheit thermometer water freezes at 32° and boils at 212°. A temperature of 98.6° Fahrenheit is normal body temperature and 90° Fahrenheit is a hot day. On the Celsius thermometer water freezes at 0° and boils at 100°. A temperature of 37° is normal body temperature and about 32° is a hot day.

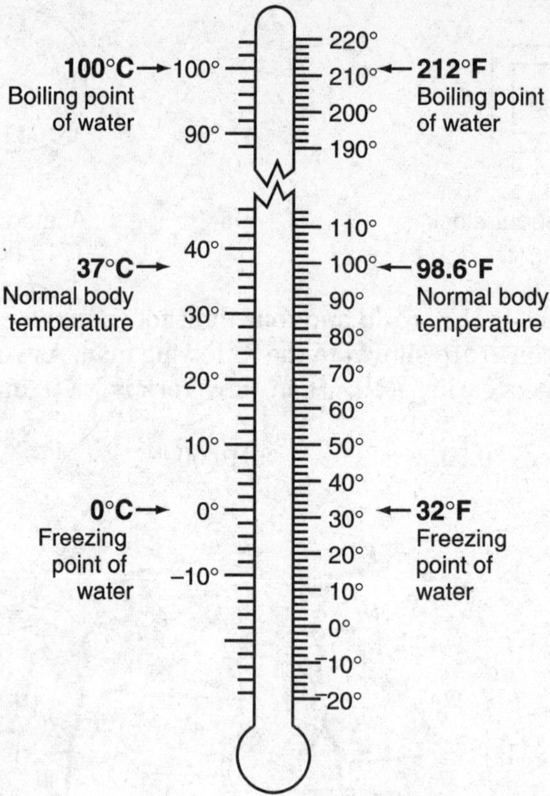

PROBLEM SOLVING

The problem-solving strategies of choosing a reasonable answer, estimating, choosing the operation, writing a number sentence, and identifying extra or needed information were discussed earlier in the review. This section shows you how to use the problem-solving strategies for interpreting the remainder, and finding and interpreting patterns.

Interpreting the Remainder

When you divide to solve a problem there may be both a quotient and a remainder. You may need to (1) use only the quotient, (2) round the quotient to the next greater whole number, or (3) use only the remainder.

Example:

Stereo speakers are packed 4 to a box. There are 315 stereo speakers to be packed.

Questions:

1. How many boxes can be filled?

2. How many boxes would be needed to hold all the stereo speakers?

3. How many stereo speakers will be in the box that is not completely full?

Divide 315 by 4.

$$\begin{array}{r} 78 \text{ R3} \\ 4\overline{)315} \\ \underline{28} \\ 35 \\ \underline{32} \\ 3 \end{array}$$

Answers:

1. Use only the quotient—78 of the boxes can be filled.
2. Round the quotient to the next higher number. It would take 79 boxes to hold all the stereo speakers.
3. Use only the remainder. Three stereo speakers would be in the partially filled box.

Finding and Interpreting Patterns

Sometimes you may be able to use a pattern to find a rule or make a generalization and solve a problem. This approach is also called inductive reasoning. You proceed from information, data, to the rule.

For example, a meteorologist placed remote thermometers at sea level and up the side of the mountain at 1,000, 2,000, 5,000, and 6,000 feet. Readings were taken simultaneously and entered in the following table. What temperatures would you predict for the missing readings?

TEMPERATURE

0	1,000	2,000	3,000	4,000	5,000	6,000	7,000	8,000	9,000	10,000
52°	49°	46°			37°	34°				

The temperatures drops 3° from 52° to 49°. If it drops at the same rate, the temperature drop at 3,000 would be 43° and 4,000 feet would be 40° (followed by 37° and 34°). Continue to fill in the table accordingly, as follows.

TEMPERATURE

0	1,000	2,000	3,000	4,000	5,000	6,000	7,000	8,000	9,000	10,000
52°	49°	46°	*43°*	*40°*	37°	34°	*31°*	*28°*	*25°*	*22°*

Consider another example. A space capsule is moving in a straight line and is being tracked on a grid. The first four positions on the grid are recorded in the following table. Where will the capsule be on the grid when the x position is 13?

x Value	*1*	*2*	*3*	*4*
y Value	1	4	7	10

To solve, multiply three times the x value, subtract 2, and that gives the y value. The rule is y equals three times $x - 2$ so that the equation is $y = 3x - 2$. Substitute 13 for x:

$$y = 3(13) - 2 = 39 - 2 = 37$$

The capsule will be at position (13, 37).

SPECIAL STRATEGIES FOR ANSWERING MATHEMATICS ITEMS

The mathematics tested is the kind you probably had in high school and in college. It is the kind of mathematics you will use as you teach and go about your everyday life. Computational ability alone is expected but is held to a minimum. Remember to use the general test strategies discussed in the Introduction.

WRITE IN THE TEST BOOKLET

It is particularly important to write in the test booklet while taking the mathematics portion of the test. Use these hints for writing in the test booklet.

Do Your Calculations in the Test Booklet

Do all your calculations in the test booklet to the right of the question. This makes it easy to refer to the calcuations as you choose the correct answer.

This example should make you feel comfortable about writing in the test booklet.

What number times 0.00708 is equal to 70.8?

~~(A) 100,000 × 0.00708 = 708~~

B (B) 10,000 × 0.00708 = 70.8

(C) 1,000

(D) 0.01

(E) 0.0001

The correct answer is (B) 10,000

Draw Diagrams and Figures in the Test Booklet

When you come across a geometry problem or related problem, draw a diagram in the test booklet to help.

All sides of a rectangle are shrunk in half. What happens to the area?

(A) Divided by two

(B) Divided by four

(C) Multiplied by two

(D) Multiplied by six

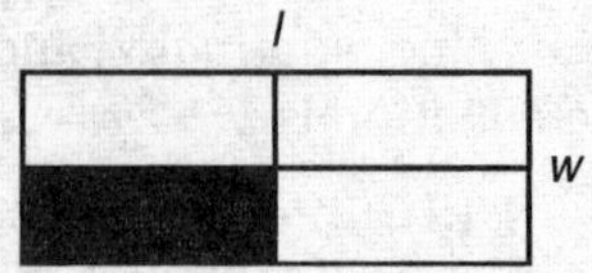

Answer (B), divided by 4, is the correct answer. The original area is evenly divided into four parts.

Circle Important Information and Key Words and Cross Out Information You Don't Need

This approach will draw your attention to the information needed to answer the question. A common mistake is to use from the question information that has nothing to do with the solution.

Example:

In the morning, a train travels at a constant speed over an 800 kilometer distance. In the afternoon the train travels back over this same route. There is less traffic and the train travels four times as fast as it did that morning. However, there are more people on the train during the afternoon. Which of the following do you know about the train's afternoon trip?

(A) The time is divided by four

(B) The time is multiplied by four

(C) The rate and time are divided by four

(D) The distance is the same so the rate is the same

To solve the problem you just need to know that the speed is constant, four times as fast, and the same route was covered. Circle the information you need to solve the problem.

The distance traveled or that there were more people in the afternoon is extra information. Cross off this extra information, which may interfere with your ability to solve the problem.

In the morning, a train travels at a constant speed ~~over an 800 kilometer distance.~~ In the afternoon the train travels back over this same route. ~~There is less traffic~~ and the train travels four times as fast as it did that morning. ~~However, there are more people on the train during the afternoon.~~ Which of the following do you know aobut the train's afternoon trip?

The correct answer is (A), the time is divided by four. The route is the same, but the train travels four times as fast. Therefore, the time to make the trip is divided by four. Rate means the same thing as speed, and we know that the speed has been multiplied by four.

OTHER STRATEGIES

Estimate to Be Sure Your Answer Is Reasonable

You can use estimation and common sense to be sure that the answer is reasonable. You may make a multiplication error or misalign decimal points. You may be so engrossed in a problem that you miss the big picture because of the details. These difficulties can be headed off by making sure your answer is reasonable.

A few examples follow.

A question involves dividing or multiplying. Multiply: 28×72.

Estimate first: $30 \times 70 = 2{,}100$. Your answer should be close to 2,100. If not, then your answer is not reasonable. A mistake was probably made in multiplication.

A question involves subtracting or adding. Add: $12.9 + 0.63 + 10.29 + 4.3$

Estimate first: $13 + 1 + 10 + 4 = 28$. Your answer should be close to 28. If not, then your answer is not reasonable. The decimal points may not have been aligned.

A question asks you to compare fractions to $^{11}/_{10}$.

Think: $^{11}/_{10}$ is more than 1. Any number 1 or less will be less than $^{11}/_{10}$. Any number $1^1/_8$ or larger will be more than $^{11}/_{10}$. You have to look closely only at numbers between 1 and $1^1/_8$.

A question asks you to multiply two fractions or decimals.

The fractions or decimals are less than 1. The product of two fractions or decimals less than 1 is less than either of the two fractions or decimals. If not, you know that your answer is not reasonable.

Stand back for a second after you answer each question and ask, "Is this reasonable? Is this at least approximately correct? Does this make sense?"

Check answers to computation, particularly division and subtraction. When you have completed a division or subtraction example, do a quick, approximate check. Your check should confirm your answer. If not, your answer is probably not reasonable.

Work from the Answers

If you don't know how to solve a formula or relation try out each answer choice until you get the correct answer. Look at this example.

What percent times $^1/_4$ is $^1/_5$?

(A) 25%

(B) 40%

(C) 80%

(D) 120%

Just take each answer in turn and try it out.

$$0.25 \times \frac{1}{4} = \frac{1}{4} \times \frac{1}{4} = \frac{1}{16}$$ That's not it.

$$0.40 \times \frac{1}{4} = \frac{4}{10} \times \frac{1}{4} = \frac{4}{40} = \frac{1}{10}$$ That's not it either.

$$0.8 \times \frac{1}{4} = \frac{4}{5} \times \frac{1}{4} = \frac{4}{20} = \frac{1}{5}$$

You know that 0.8 is the correct answer, so choice (C) is correct.

Try Out Numbers

Look at the preceding question.

Work with fractions at first. Ask: What number times $^1/_4$ equals $^1/_5$?

Through trial and error you find out that $^4/_5 \times {}^1/_4 = {}^1/_5$.

The answer in fractions is $^4/_5$.

$$\frac{4}{5} = 0.8 = 80\%$$

The correct choice is (C).

In this example, we found the answer without ever solving an equation. We just tried out numbers until we found the one that works.

Eliminate and Guess

Use this approach when all else has failed. Begin by eliminating the answers you know are wrong. Sometimes you know with certainty that an answer is incorrect. Other times, an answer looks so unreasonable that you can be fairly sure that it is not correct.

Once you have eliminated incorrect answers, a few will probably be left. Just guess among these choices. There is no method that will increase your chances of guessing correctly.

MATHEMATICS MSAT PRACTICE ITEMS

These items will help you practice for the real MSAT. These items have the same form and test the same material as the MSAT items and test material. The items you encounter on the real MSAT may have a different emphasis and may be more complete.

Instructions

Mark your answers on the sheet provided below. Complete the items in 20 minutes or less. Correct your answer sheet using the answers on page 107.

1 Ⓐ Ⓑ Ⓒ Ⓓ	5 Ⓐ Ⓑ Ⓒ Ⓓ	9 Ⓐ Ⓑ Ⓒ Ⓓ	13 Ⓐ Ⓑ Ⓒ Ⓓ	17 Ⓐ Ⓑ Ⓒ Ⓓ
2 Ⓐ Ⓑ Ⓒ Ⓓ	6 Ⓐ Ⓑ Ⓒ Ⓓ	10 Ⓐ Ⓑ Ⓒ Ⓓ	14 Ⓐ Ⓑ Ⓒ Ⓓ	18 Ⓐ Ⓑ Ⓒ Ⓓ
3 Ⓐ Ⓑ Ⓒ Ⓓ	7 Ⓐ Ⓑ Ⓒ Ⓓ	11 Ⓐ Ⓑ Ⓒ Ⓓ	15 Ⓐ Ⓑ Ⓒ Ⓓ	19 Ⓐ Ⓑ Ⓒ Ⓓ
4 Ⓐ Ⓑ Ⓒ Ⓓ	8 Ⓐ Ⓑ Ⓒ Ⓓ	12 Ⓐ Ⓑ Ⓒ Ⓓ	16 Ⓐ Ⓑ Ⓒ Ⓓ	20 Ⓐ Ⓑ Ⓒ Ⓓ

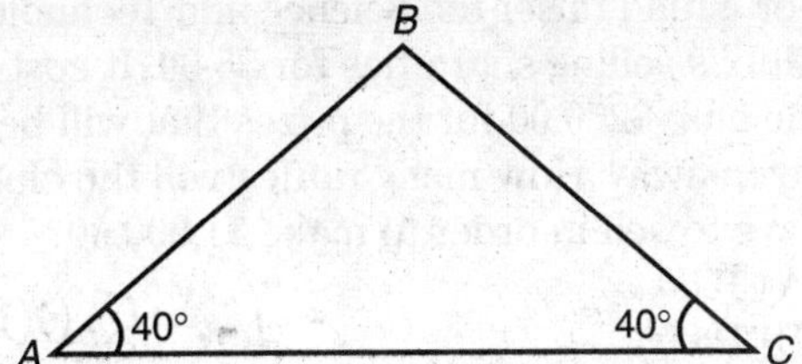

1. What is the measure of angle B?
   (A) 10
   (B) 40
   (C) 80
   (D) 100

2. After a discount of 25%, the savings on a pair of roller blades was $12.00. What was the sale price?
   (A) $48.00
   (B) $36.00
   (C) $24.00
   (D) $25.00

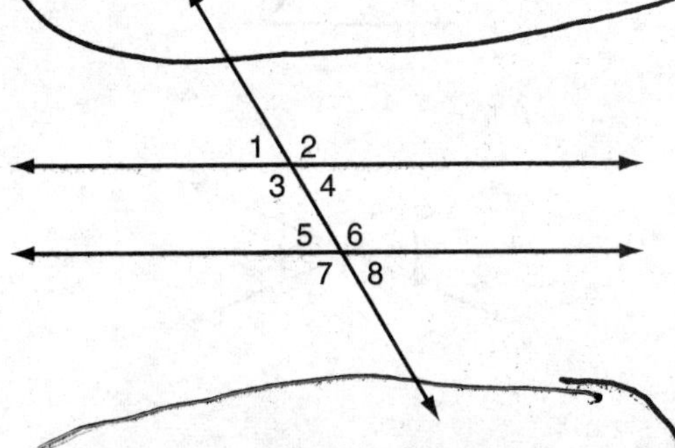

3. Which two angles are supplementary?
   (A) 6 & 7
   (B) 1 & 4
   (C) 3 & 6
   (D) 2 & 4

4. Chad rolls a fair die. The sides of the die are numbered from 1 to 6. Ten times in a row, he rolls a 5. What is the probability that he will roll a 5 on his next roll?
   (A) $1/5$
   (B) $1/6$
   (C) $1/50$
   (D) $1/11$

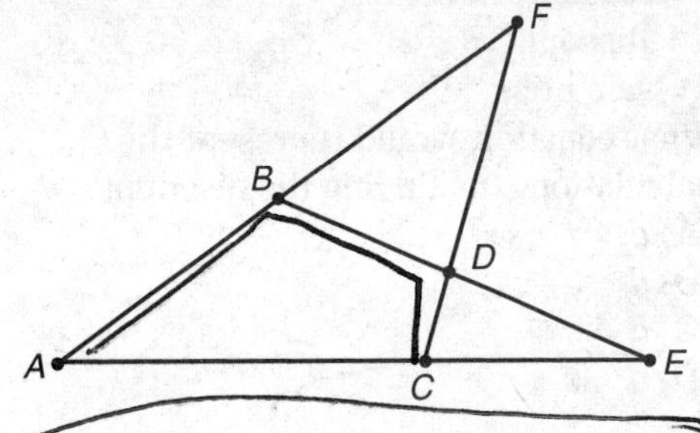

5. Which of the following set of points do not form an angle in the diagram?
   (A) ABF
   (B) ABE
   (C) AFC
   (D) ABC

6. An apple costs (C). You have (D) dollars. What equation would represent the amount of apples you could buy for the money you have?
   (A) C/D
   (B) CD
   (C) $C + D$
   (D) D/C

7. If a worker gets $144.00 for 18 hours' work, how much would that worker get for 32 hours' work?
   (A) $200.00
   (B) $288.00
   (C) $256.00
   (D) $432.00

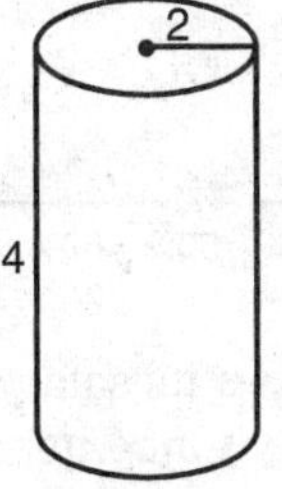

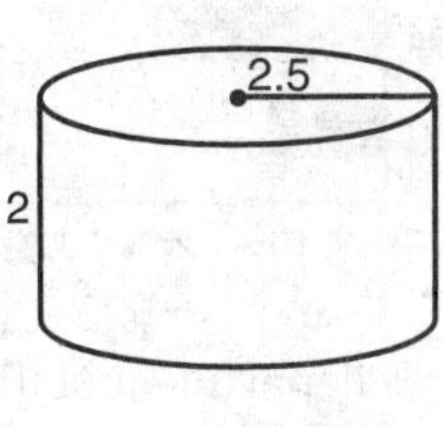

$V = \pi r^2 h$

8. What is the combined volume of these two cylinders?
   (A) 12.5π
   (B) 16π
   (C) 26.5π
   (D) 28.5π

9. r = regular price
   d = discount
   s = sale price
   What equation would represent the calculations for finding the discount?
   (A) $d = r - s$
   (B) $d = s - r$
   (C) $d = sr$
   (D) $d = s + r$

10. A printing company makes pamphlets that cost $.75 per copy plus $5.00 as a setter's fee. If $80 were spent printing a pamphlet, how many pamphlets were ordered?
    (A) 50
    (B) 75
    (C) 100
    (D) 150

11. Which is furthest from $\frac{1}{2}$ on a number line?
    (A) $\frac{1}{12}$
    (B) $\frac{7}{8}$
    (C) $\frac{3}{4}$
    (D) $\frac{2}{3}$

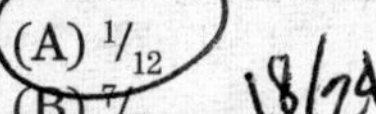

12. Which of the following could be about 25 centimeters long?
    (A) a human thumb
    (B) a doorway
    (C) a car
    (D) a notebook

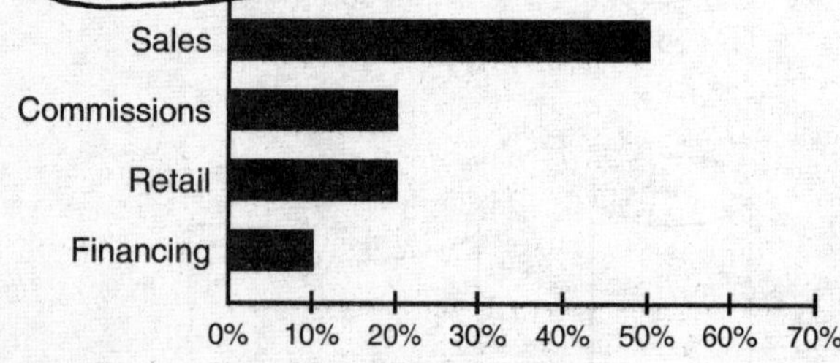

13. The sales department staff draws its salary from four areas of the company's income, as shown in the above graph. What percentage is drawn from the retail fund?
    (A) 10%
    (B) 20%
    (C) 25%
    (D) 30%

14. What percentage of 250 is 25?
    (A) 5%
    (B) 10%
    (C) 20%
    (D) 25%

15. For a fund raiser the Science and Technology Club is selling six raffles for $5.00. It costs the club $250.00 for the prizes that will be given away. How many raffles will the club have to sell in order to make $1,000.00?
    (A) 1500
    (B) 1200
    (C) 600
    (D) 300

16. $5.3 \times 10^4 =$
    (A) 0.0053
    (B) 0.00053
    (C) 5,300
    (D) 53,000

17. Which of the following represents supplementary angles?

(A)

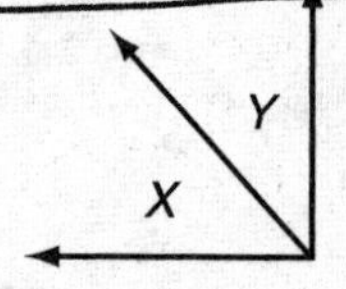

(B)

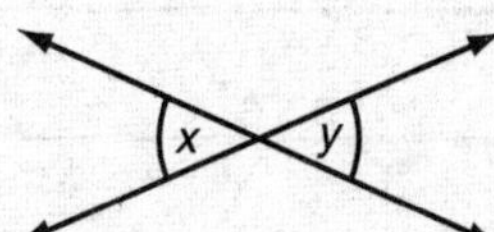

(C)

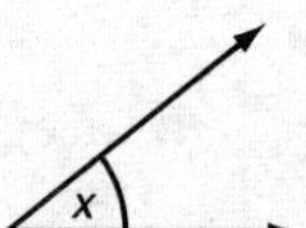

(D)

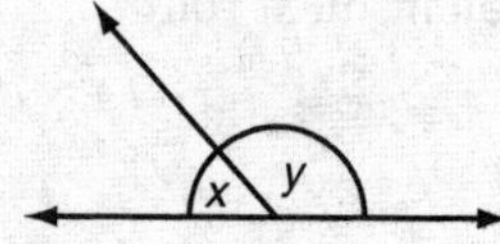

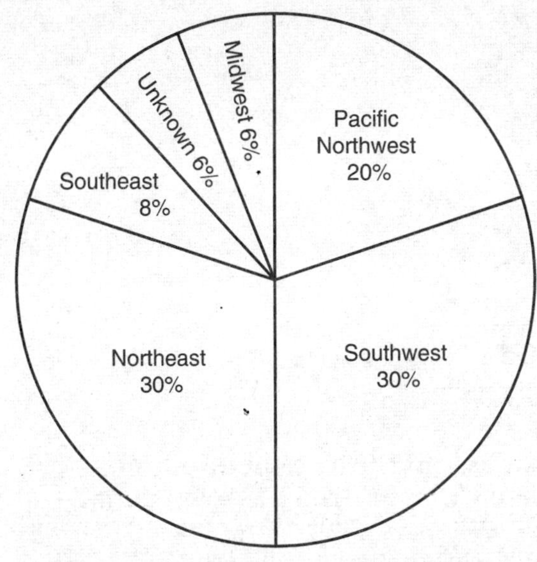

18. The above graph shows the percentage of students that attend a college according to the area of the United States that they come from. How many more college students come from the Northeast than come from the Midwest?
    (A) twice as many
    (B) three times as many
    (C) half as many
    (D) five times as many

19. Each of these rectangles has a total area of 1 square unit. What number represents the area of the shaded regions?
    (A) $^5/_6$ square units
    (B) $^7/_8$ square units
    (C) $1^3/_4$ square units
    (D) $1^5/_{24}$ square units

20. Which diagram shows that the set of whole numbers between 1 and 20 contains multiples of 5?
    (A)
    (B)
    (C)

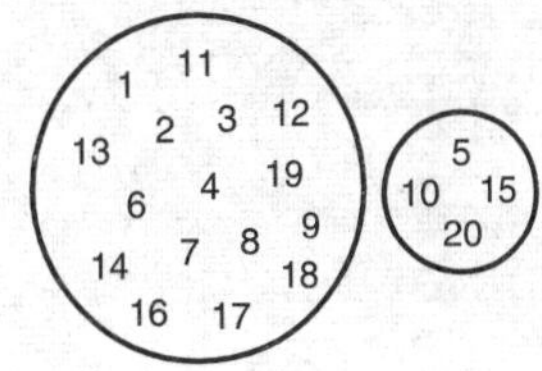

    (D)

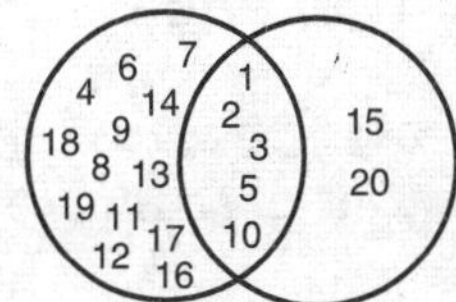

Answers

1. **D**	5. **D**	9. **A**	13. **B**	17. **D**
2. **B**	6. **D**	10. **C**	14. **B**	18. **D**
3. **D**	7. **C**	11. **A**	15. **A**	19. **D**
4. **B**	8. **D**	12. **D**	16. **D**	20. **B**

5 SCIENCE

TEST INFO BOX

22 of 120 Multiple Choice items
3 of 18 Short Answer items

18% of Content Knowledge items
17% of Content Area Exercise items

SCIENCE ITEMS

Science multiple choice items look like this.

During which period did the dinosaurs appear on earth?

(A) Cambrian
(B) Carboniferous
(C) Triassic
(D) Tertiary

Science short answer items look like this.

Sophisticated technological processes permit a very precise DNA typing for organic material. Describe two uses of this process.

USING THIS CHAPTER

This chapter prepares you to take the Science part of the MSAT. Choose one of these approaches.

I want all the Science review I can get.

- ❑ Skip the Science Review Quiz and read the entire review section.
- ❑ Take the Science Review Quiz on page 110.
- ❑ Correct the Review Quiz and reread the indicated parts of the review.
- ❑ Go over the Special Strategies for Answering Science Test items on pages 137–140.
- ❑ Complete the Science MSAT Practice Questions on page 141.

I want a thorough Science review.

- ❑ Take the Science Review Quiz on page 110.
- ❑ Correct the Review Quiz and reread the indicated parts of the review.
- ❑ Go over the Special Strategies for Answering Science Test items on pages 137–140.
- ❑ Complete the Science MSAT Practice Questions on page 141.

I want a quick Science review.

- ❑ Take and correct the Science Review Quiz on page 110.
- ❑ Go over the Special Strategies for Answering Science Test items on pages 137–140.
- ❑ Complete the Science MSAT Practice Questions on page 141.

I want to practice Science questions.

- ❑ Go over the Special Strategies for Answering Science Test items on pages 137–140.
- ❑ Complete the Science MSAT Practice Questions on page 141.

I don't need any Science review.

- ❑ OK. If you're sure, skip this chapter.

SCIENCE REVIEW QUIZ

This quiz uses a short answer format to help you find out what you know about the Science topics reviewed in this chapter. The quiz results direct you to the portions of the chapter you should read.

This quiz will also help focus your thinking about Science, and these questions and answers are a good review in themselves. It's not important to answer all these questions correctly, and don't be concerned if you miss many of them.

The answers are found immediately after the quiz. It's to your advantage not to look at them until you have completed the quiz. Once you have completed and corrected this review quiz, use the answer checklist to decide which sections of the review to study.

Write the answers in the space provided or on a separate sheet of paper.

1. What name is given to the cells that make up most living things?

2. Name the two methods of cell reproduction.

3. What does photosynthesis create?

4. What do cells create when they respire?

5. Where are genes located?

6. What type of organism could have developed spontaneously in earth's early atmosphere?

7. What is the name of the very first cells to develop?

8. What is the dominant invertebrate animal species?

9. Which animal has the most striking genetic similarity to humans?

10. What types of organisms make up the Protistae kingdom?

11. What three main functions do bacteria perform?

12. How many pairs of chromosomes do humans usually have?

13. How is AIDS transmitted?

14. What part of the circulatory system carries blood back to the heart?

15. What part of a cell transmits signals?

16. What does the endocrine system consist of?

17. What function do granulocytes perform in the immune system?

18. What do ecologists study?

19. What survival options do subdominant individuals have?

20. How do plants and animals balance the carbon cycle?

21. What do cosmologists study?

22. About how long does it take for light to travel from the North Star to the earth?

23. What causes seasons on earth?

____

____

24. What percent of earth's atmosphere is nitrogen? ________ oxygen? __________

25. About what percent of the earth's surface is covered by water?

____

____

26. What is the temperature in the earth's inner core?

____

____

27. In which direction does Coriolis force pull air in the Southern Hemisphere?

____

____

28. About what percent of sea water is salt?

____

____

29. How were the earth's continents arranged during the Permian period about 280,000,000 years ago?

____

____

30. How are metamorphic rocks formed?

____

____

31. What subatomic particles do atoms consist of?

____

____

32. How can matter be destroyed?

____

____

33. When do chemical reactions occur?

____

____

34. Does a body's mass vary?

____

____

35. What two factors determine a body's velocity?

____

____

36. How does Newton's Second Law describe the relationship between mass and acceleration?

____

____

37. What type of energy does fuel in a car's gas tank represent?

____

____

38. What must happen for work to occur?

____

____

39. What method of transfer moves heat from a heating pad to a person's back?

____

____

40. What determines a wave's frequency?

____

____

41. What three things may happen when light strikes a surface?

____

____

42. Through which medium does sound travel most quickly?

____

____

43. What charges may an object possess?

____

____

44. What does an ampere measure?

____

____

45. Where is the magnetic North Pole?

____

____

46. Name the three types of energy radioactive material can release.

____

____

47. What is the advantage of nuclear fusion over nuclear fission?

____

____

ANSWER CHECKLIST

The answers are organized by review sections. Check your answers. If you miss any question in a section, check the box and review that section.

Biology

Cellular Biology

❑ *Cells, page 114*
1. eukaryotes

❑ *Reproduction, page 114*
2. mitosis and meiosis

❑ *Photosynthesis, page 115*
3. carbohydrates, water, and oxygen

❑ *Cell Activities, page 115*
4. energy

❑ *Genes, page 115*
5. Genes are located on chromosomes.

Biology of Organisms and Evolution

❑ *Evolution, page 116*
6. molecule
7. prokaryotes
8. insects
9. African apes

❑ *Cell Classification, page 117*
10. single-celled eukaryotes including algae and protozoa
11. Bacteria live on dead material, are helpful in human bodies, and function as parasites.

❑ *Human Biology, page 118*
12. 23
13. blood and bodily fluids
14. veins
15. dendrites
16. glands that secrete hormones
17. They ingest antigens already killed by cell enzymes.

❑ *Ecology, page 121*
18. the relationship between organisms and their ecosystems
19. They accept a poorer habitat, give up resources, immigrate, or perish.

❑ *Life Cycles, page 122*
20. Plants use carbon dioxide and give off oxygen. Animals use oxygen and give off carbon dioxide.

Geosciences

❑ *Astronomy, page 123*
21. the universe
22. 300 years
23. the tilt of the Earth's axis

❑ *Meteorology, page 127*
27. Southeast

❑ *Oceanography, page 128*
28. 3.5 percent (0.035)

❑ *Geology, page 129*
29. Earth's land mass consisted of a single continent.
30. Existing rocks are subjected to enormous pressure.

❑ *The Earth's Parts, page 129*
24. 78 percent nitrogen, 21 percent oxygen
25. about 75 percent
26. 10,000° F

Physical Sciences

Chemistry

❑ *Atoms, page 131*
31. protons, neutrons, and electrons

❑ *Matter, page 132*
32. Matter cannot be destroyed; it can only be converted.

❑ *Chemical Reactions, page 132*
33. when bonds between atoms form or break

Physics

❑ *Matter and Mass, page 132*
34. A body's mass is constant.

❑ *Motion, page 133*
35. magnitude and direction
36. The more the mass, the less the acceleration.

- ❑ *Energy, page 133*
  37. potential
- ❑ *Work, page 134*
  38. There must be some movement.
- ❑ *Heat, page 134*
  39. conduction
- ❑ *Wave Phenomena, page 135*
  40. vibrations per second
- ❑ *Light, page 135*
  41. Light can be reflected, absorbed, or scattered.
- ❑ *Sound, page 135*
  42. solid

Electricity and Magnetism

- ❑ *Electricity, page 135*
  43. positive, negative, neutral
  44. rate of current flow
- ❑ *Magnetism, page 136*
  45. northeastern Canada
- ❑ *Modern Physics and Radioactivity, page 137*
  46. alpha, beta, and gamma
  47. Fusion is much safer because it releases less radioactivity.

SCIENCE REVIEW

BIOLOGY

CELLULAR BIOLOGY

Cells

The cell is the basic unit of all living things. A cell may be an organism by itself or the basic building block of a multicell living organism. Animal and plant cells are different.

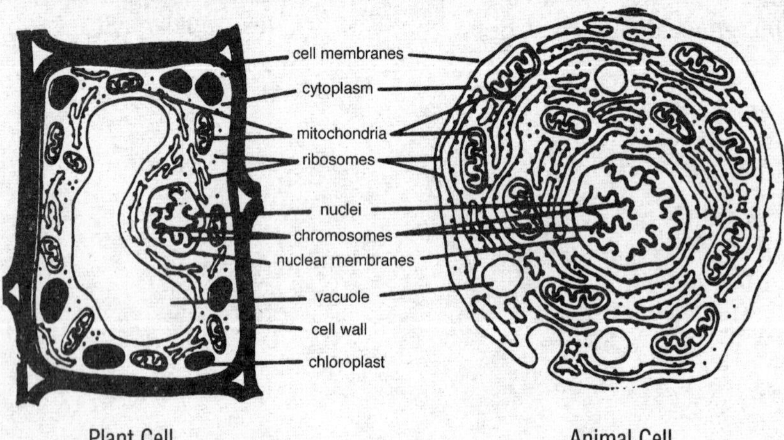

Most cells that make up living things are eukaryotes. The second type of cells are called prokaryotes. Most prokaryotes are bacteria or blue-green algae.

All cells have a cell membrane at the outer edge of the cell. A gel-like cytoplasm throughout the interior of the cell protects the different organelles (cell organs) inside the cell. A nucleus, the cell's brain, inside the cytoplasm is protected by a nuclear membrane. The nucleus contains chromosomes. The golgi apparatus make, store, and distribute hormone and enzyme materials. The mitochondria process food into energy.

Plant cells have a thicker cell wall outside the membrane. Plant cells also contain chloroplasts where photosynthesis takes place.

Reproduction

Cells must reproduce to survive. There are two methods of cell reproduction—mitosis and meiosis.

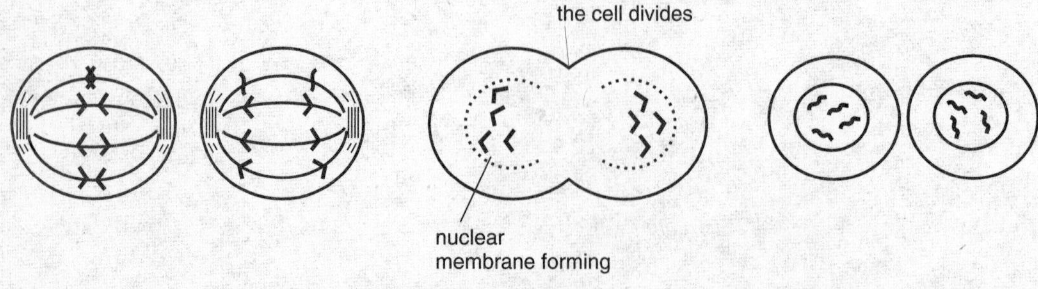

Mitosis

In mitosis, cells make a carbon copy of themselves and create duplicate chromosomes. The chromosomes migrate to opposite sides of the cell; then the cell splits, making an exact copy of itself.

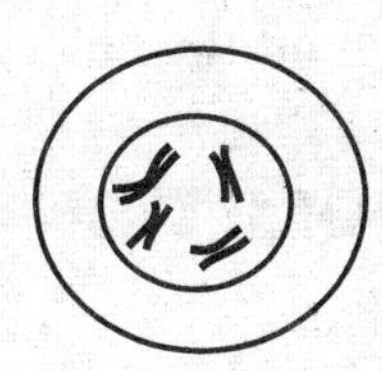
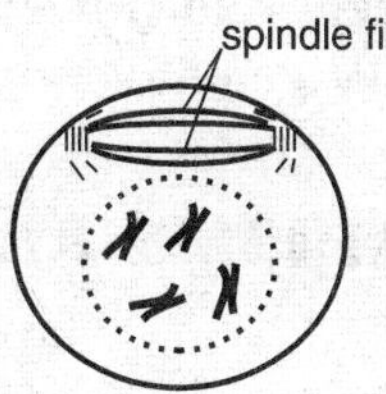

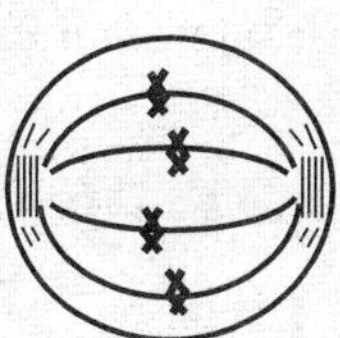

Meiosis

Higher multicell organisms reproduce sexually. In these organisms, the sperm and egg cells combine in a process called meiosis. Meiosis begins with egg and sperm cells, each with half the number of chromosomes. When the sperm and egg cells combine, a single cell, zygote, is created with a complete set of chromosomes. This single cell develops into the advanced organism.

Photosynthesis

Photosynthesis occurs within plant cells to create carbohydrates, water, and oxygen needed by the plant. Photosynthesis occurs in two stages.

1. In the presence of light and chlorophyll, carbon dioxide and water are broken down.

2. Carbon combines with oxygen and hydrogen to form carbohydrates. Light is not needed for this stage.

Cell Activities

Respiration

Cells create energy through respiration. This process, which occurs in the mitochondria, can be either aerobic or anaerobic. Aerobic respiration is the oxidation of food, which takes place in the presence of oxygen. Anaerobic respiration is fermentation, which takes place without oxygen.

Other Cell Activities

Ingestion	Take in food
Digestion	Break down food to usable forms
Secretion	Create and release useful substances
Excretion	Eliminate waste material
Homeostasis	Maintain the cell's equilibrium

Genes

A chromosome is a rodlike structure located in the cell nucleus. Each gene occupies a specific location on one of the chromosomes. Genes carry specific bits of genetic information.

Deoxyribonucleic acid (DNA) is the genetic material found tightly coiled in a gene. DNA provides the genetic codes that determine many traits of an organism. The gene also contains very large quantities of noncoding DNA, which does not affect the makeup of an organism.

The DNA creates ribonucleic acid (RNA). The DNA cannot leave the nucleus; RNA serves as the messenger that carries the genetic code throughout the cell.

BIOLOGY OF ORGANISMS AND EVOLUTION

Early Life

There was very little oxygen in the earth's atmosphere about 3.5 billion years ago. Research has shown that atoms can combine spontaneously in this type of environment to form molecules. This is how life may have begun on earth about 3.4 billion years ago.

Eventually these molecules linked together in complex groupings to form organisms. These earliest organisms must have been able to ingest and live on nonorganic material. Over a period of time, these organisms adapted and began using the sun's energy. When photosynthesis released oxygen into the oceans and the atmosphere, the stage was set for more advanced life forms.

First Cells

The first cells were prokaryotes (bacteria), which created energy (respired) without oxygen (anaerobic). The next cells to develop were blue-green algae prokaryotes, which were aerobic (created energy with oxygen) and used photosynthesis. Advanced eukaryotes developed from these primitive cells.

It took about 2.7 billion years for algae to develop. When this simple cell appeared 950 million years ago, it contained an enormous amount of DNA. This very slow process moved somewhat faster in the millennia that followed as animal and plant forms slowly emerged.

Animals

Animals developed into vertebrate (backbone) and invertebrate (no backbone) species. Mammals became the dominant vertebrate species, and insects became the dominant invertebrate species. As animals developed, they adapted to their environment. Those species that adapted best survived. This process is called natural selection. Entire species have vanished from the earth.

Mammals and dinosaurs coexisted for over 100 million years. During that time, dinosaurs were the dominant species. When dinosaurs became extinct 65 million years ago, mammals survived. Freed of dinosaurian dominance, mammals evolved into the dominant creatures they are today. Despite many years of study, it is not known what caused the dinosaurs to become extinct or why mammals survived.

Humans

Humans are in the primate (upright) family of mammals. Very primitive primates, along with other mammals, were found on earth before the dinosaurs became extinct. Modern humans demonstrate striking genetic similarities to other members of the primate group, particularly to African apes.

Tools are a mark of the advanced adaptation of a species. Stone tools found in association with early humanoids date back about 2 million years. Sites dated 1 million years old show marks caused by humanlike use of tools.

Scientists believe that early sapiens developed about 250,000 years ago and that modern Homo sapiens developed about 75,000 years ago.

The ability to communicate is a sign of advanced development. Many forms of nonverbal communication have probably existed since the appearance of Homo sapiens. Scientists speculate that speech distinct from animal sounds probably occurred about 30,000 years ago. Writing first appeared about 5,500 years ago.

Era	Period	Epoch	Approximate Beginning Date	Life Forms Originating
Cenozoic	Quaternary	Recent	10,000	Humans
		Pleistocene	2,500,000	
	Tertiary	Pilocene	12,000,000	Grazing and Meat-eating Mammals
		Miocene	26,000,000	
		Oligocene	38,000,000	
		Eocene	54,000,000	
		Paleocene	65,000,000	
Mesozoic	Cretaceous		136,000,000	Primates-Flowering Plants
	Jurassic		195,000,000	Birds
	Triassic		225,000,000	Dinosaurs-Mammals
Paleozoic	Permian		280,000,000	
	Carbonifurous	Pennsylvanian	320,000,000	Reptiles
		Mississippian	345,000,000	Ferns
	Devonian		395,000,000	Amphibians-insects
	Silurian		430,000,000	Vascular Land Plants
	Ordovician		500,000,000	Fish-Chordates
	Cambrian		570,000,000	Shellfish-Trilobites
Precambrian			(700,000,000)	Algae
			(1,500,000,000)	Eukaryotic Cells
			(3,500,000,000)	Prokaryotic Cells

The History of Life

CELL CLASSIFICATION

Living things are generally classified into five kingdoms. Two kingdoms are dedicated to one-celled living things (prokaryote or eukaryote). There are three kingdoms of multicelled eukaryotes based on whether nutrition is obtained through absorption, photosynthesis, or ingestion.

Single Cells

The Moneran kingdom includes all prokaryotes. The organisms include bacteria and blue-green algae. These microscopic organisms are limited to respiration and reproduction.

The Protistae kingdom includes all single-celled eukaryotes. These organisms include algae and protozoa. These cells have a fully functional organ system and get their nutrition through photosynthesis.

Multi Cells

The Fungi kingdom includes multicelled eukaryotes that gain their nutrition through absorption. These organisms include mushrooms and are rootlike with caps and filaments.

The Plantae kingdom includes multicelled eukaryotes that gain their nutrition through photosynthesis. These organisms have thicker cellulose cell walls.

The Animalae kingdom includes multicelled eukaryotes that gain their nutrition through ingestion. Most of these organisms are mobile at some time in their existence.

Bacteria

Bacteria are small, single-celled organisms (prokaryotes) found everywhere in the environment. As noted already, bacteria were among the earliest organisms to develop. Bacteria are classified as bacilli (rod-shaped), cocci (circular or spherical), and spirilla (coiled). Bacteria that can move "swim" with flagella.

One type of bacteria live on dead animal and vegetable material. Without the decomposition these bacteria bring, the earth would quickly be covered with dead organic material. A second type of bacteria is a normal part of living tissues and is often needed for regular physiological processes. The third type, parasites, destroy the organisms in which they live. About 200 types of bacteria cause diseases in humans.

Viruses

A virus is a bit of genetic material surrounded by a protective coat of protein. The virus itself is lifeless, lacks the ability to reproduce, and is not classified in one of the five kingdoms. Viruses cannot be seen in even the most powerful regular microscope. The smallest virus is about one millionth of a centimeter long.

Viruses are parasitic and remain a major challenge in battling infectious diseases. Once in a living cell, a virus can send its own genetic material into the cell, reproduce, and do significant damage to the host cell and the host organism.

HUMAN BIOLOGY

Humans have 23 pairs of chromosomes. Females typically have 23 similar pairs including a pair of X chromosomes. Males typically have 22 similar pairs and one X and one Y chromosome.

Genes carry specific bits of genetic information. Each gene occupies a specific location on one of the chromosomes. Researchers today have identified and mapped the exact location of more than 200 genes. Scientists can even identify whether or not a person has certain hereditary traits. For example, scientists have identified a gene linked to hereditary breast cancer.

Disease

Diseases compromise the body's defense system. Most diseases can be recognized by symptoms that may include fever, aches and pains, fatigue, growths, changes in blood cell composition, and high blood pressure.

Many infectious diseases, including pneumonia and infections in cuts, are caused by bacteria. Other infectious diseases, including measles and influenza (flu), are caused by viruses. Environmental causes of disease include smoking, a high-fat diet, and pollution. Other diseases may result from genetic or occupational causes and abnormal cell growth. Many diseases are related to mental disorders or stress.

Acquired Immune Deficiency Syndrome (AIDS) is a disease caused by the HIV virus that attacks the body's immune system. Current research indicates that all those with AIDS will die as a result of this virus. The HIV virus is transmitted through blood and bodily fluids, including those fluids associated with intimate sexual contact. Intravenous drug users who share needles may become infected with the virus by injecting small amounts of contaminated blood.

The Human Body

Parts of the human body are made up of highly specialized cells. These cells combine to make tissue. Some tissues combine to form organs. Various organs combine in systems that enable the body to function.

Cells → Tissue → Organ → Organ System → Body

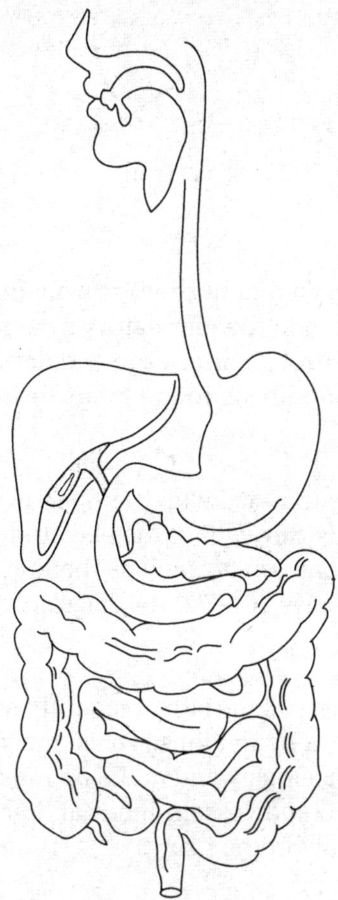

The Human Digestive System

Digestive System

Food is usually taken in through the mouth. The teeth and tongue break the food down mechanically, and the saliva begins the digestive process. When food reaches the stomach, the stomach churns to mix the food while digestive enzymes break down the proteins. The semiliquid, digested food moves into the small intestine.

Nutrients are absorbed through the small intestine into the bloodstream. Waste and undigested food move into the large intestine. The large intestine carries the waste and undigested food to the rectum.

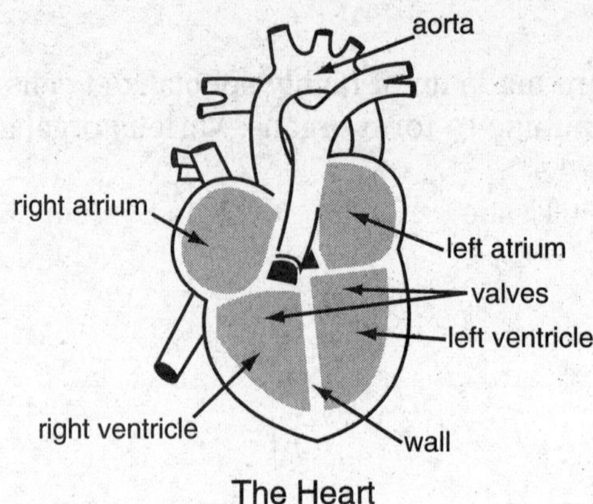

The Heart

Circulatory System

The circulatory system carries oxygen and nutrients throughout the body. A four-chambered heart (see above) pumps blood through the circulatory system. Oxygenated blood is pumped through the right side of the heart, through arteries to capillaries and then to cells. The left side of the heart pumps oxygen-poor blood back to the lungs through veins.

Skeletal System

The bones (about 200) and cartilage that make up the skeletal system provide form and rigidity to the human body. A series of joints throughout the skeleton provide flexibility. Bone is living, rigid tissue. Cartilage is found at bone joints, such as the knee, and makes up the nose and other rigid parts of the body. (See pages 261–262 for diagrams of the skeletal system and spine.)

Muscular System

The muscular system consists of skeletal (striated), smooth, and cardiac muscles. Most skeletal muscles are attached to the skeleton by tendons. These muscles are called voluntary muscles because they can be controlled consciously and make up most of human flesh. Smooth muscle is involuntary and is found in large blood vessels, internal organs, and the skin. Cardiac muscles are an involuntary muscle found only in the heart.

Nervous System

The nervous system receives stimuli, transmits electrochemical signals, and activates muscles. Receptors in the skin and elsewhere in the body receive stimuli. Nerve cells, called neurons, send signals to the central nervous system. Dendrites in the cell transmit signals, while axons receive stimuli.

The central and peripheral nervous systems form a single operating system. The central nervous system includes the brain and spinal cord. The peripheral nervous system connects the central nervous system to the rest of the body. The autonomic nervous system is connected to the central nervous system and controls circulation, respiration, digestion, and elimination.

Excretory System

The excretory system consists of the kidney, bladder, and connecting tubes. Nephrons in the kidney collect liquid wastes. The liquid wastes are transferred to the bladder and leave the body as urine through the urethra.

Respiratory System

Respiration delivers oxygen to the bloodstream. Nasal passages clean and warm the air on its way to the lungs through the trachea and bronchi. Air is collected in the alveoli, which transfers oxygen and other gases to the bloodstream. (See page 263 for a diagram of the respiratory system.)

Endocrine System

The endocrine system is a complex system that produces and distributes hormones through the bloodstream. The system consists of glands that secrete hormones and other substances.

The **pituitary gland** is located near the brain and is the primary gland in the body. Hormones from this gland control the operation of other endocrine glands, sex glands, milk production, and pigmentation.

The **adrenal glands** are found near the kidney. Hormones from these glands effect heart rate, blood pressure, blood vessels, and blood sugar.

The **thyroid** is found in the neck. It regulates mental and physical alertness. The parathyroid glands are found near or inside the thyroid and regulate calcium in the blood.

Ovaries are located near the uterus. These glands produce eggs, control the development of secondary sex characteristics, and maintain pregnancy.

Testes produce sperm and control the development of secondary sex characteristics.

The **pancreas** secretes insulin and facilitates digestion.

Immune System

The immune system resists the spread of disease by destroying disease-causing agents (antigens). This system is exceptionally complex and not fully understood. Normally, a combination of the following immune responses is needed to defeat an antigen.

The lymphatic system produces lymphocytes in bean-sized lymph glands located throughout the body. The lymphocytes are transported throughout bodily tissue by lymphatic capillaries. Lymphocytes control the immune system and kill antigens directly.

Granulocytes are very numerous. They ingest antigens already killed by cell enzymes. Monocytes exist in small numbers. They ingest and kill antigens and more importantly alter antigens in a way that makes it easier for lymphocytes to destroy them.

Immunoglobins (antibodies) combine with antigens to remove them from the body. There are thousands of antibodies, each targeted for a specific antigen. Other proteins called cytokines complement proteins and aid the immune response.

ECOLOGY

Ecology refers to the relationship between organisms and their ecosystem (habitat). An ecosystem includes interdependent life forms and supports life through food, atmosphere, energy, and water. Organisms, including plants and animals, interact with and adapt to their ecosystem.

Earth is surrounded by a thin layer of atmosphere. Within that atmosphere lies earth's biosphere where life exists. The biosphere contains a number of biomes or living areas. Aquatic biomes include ocean, shallow water, and tidal marshes. Land biomes are classified by the predominant form of plant life and include forest, grassland, and desert.

Each organism in a biome occupies a place in the food web. Each organism, at some point in its life or death, is food for some other organism. In this way, energy is transferred among organisms in the biome.

A community refers to the interdependent populations of plants and animals. The dominance of one species in a community can affect the diversity (number of species and specie members). The community includes the habitat where a particular plant or animal lives and its niche (role).

Within a community, the primary interactions are predation (including parasitism) and cooperation. Predators and prey adapt and develop more effective ways of hunting or defense. Cooperation may develop due to the dependence of one organism on another.

Organisms may compete within their species or with other species for resources. Successful competitors survive and become dominant. Subdominant individuals either accept poorer habitats, give up the resources, migrate, or perish.

LIFE CYCLES

A number of essential life cycles take place on earth.

Water Cycle

Most of the earth's water is salty, but humans need fresh water to survive. Fresh water is renewed through the water cycle. The cycle consists of three phases: evaporation, condensation, and precipitation.

Evaporation occurs when heat from the sun changes ocean water, and some water from other sources, into water vapor. Condensation follows when water vapor turns into water droplets, which form clouds. Precipitation occurs when the droplets become too heavy and water falls as rain, snow, sleet, or hail.

Oxygen Cycle

Humans and other animal organisms need oxygen to survive. Plants give off oxygen. An appropriate balance between plant photosynthesis and animal respiration ensures that enough oxygen is available.

Carbon Cycle

Carbon is used by all living things. Plants need carbon dioxide for photosynthesis. Animals get the carbon from the plant tissues they eat and exhale carbon dioxide as a by product of respiration. Here again, the balance between animal respiration and plant photosynthesis ensures that enough carbon will be available. In recent times, however, industrialization has added extra carbon to the atmosphere, jeopardizing the balance of this cycle.

Pollution

Air, water, and soil pollution are serious environmental problems. Some lakes, rivers, and streams are so polluted they can not be used by humans. Fish from many of these waters cannot be eaten. Air in some areas has been very polluted by factories and power plants, which use sulfur based fuels such as oil and coal. Land has been polluted by dumping hazardous wastes, including radioactive wastes. All forms of pollution lead to disease and premature death.

GEOSCIENCES

ASTRONOMY

Astronomy is the study of space and the relationship of objects in space. Astronomers use optical telescopes and radio telescopes, including the orbiting Hubble Telescope, to study space and objects in space.

Solar System

Our solar system has one star (the sun), nine planets, some comets, and lots of satellites (moons), asteroids, and meteors. A diagram of the solar system is shown below. Only the planets are shown to rough scale in this diagram.

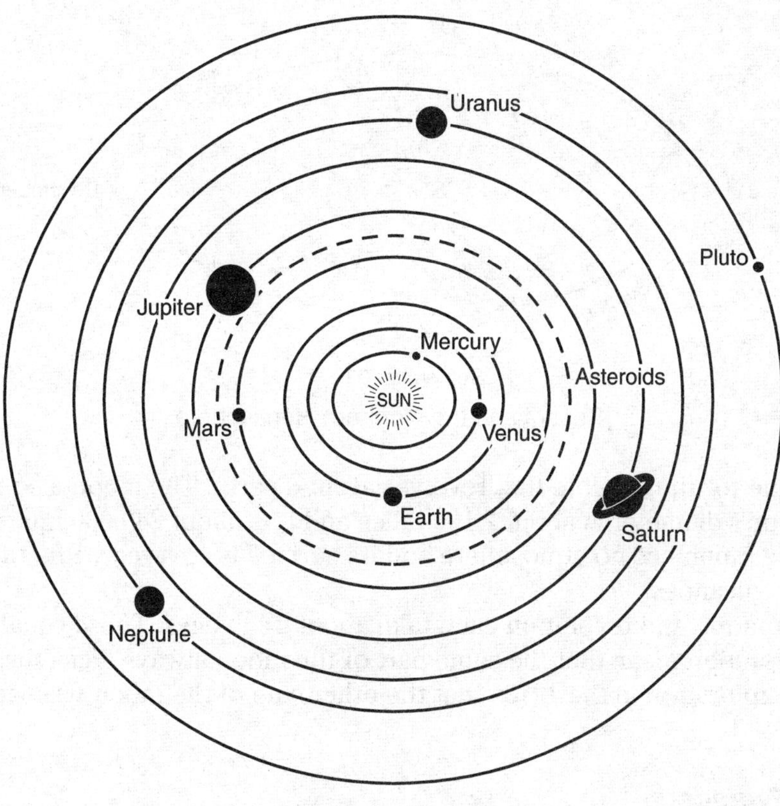

Our Solar System

The Sun

Our sun is a star, a turbulent mass of incredibly hot gases exploding with repeated nuclear fusion reactions. Without the heat and light from the sun, our universe would not exist as we know it. About 1,000,000 earths could fit inside the sun. The sun's diameter is about 864,000 miles, and the surface temperature is over 10,000° Fahrenheit. Still, the sun is just average size by galactic standards.

The sun is at the center of our solar system, although this was not realized until the time of Copernicus in the 1500s. The most noticeable features of the sun's surface are the sunspots, cooler areas that move across the sun's surface. Sunspots appear in somewhat predictable cycles and are associated with interruptions in radio and television transmissions.

The Earth and the Moon

Earth is the name of our planet. The earth is the third plant from the sun. The earth's distance from the sun ranges from about 91,000,000 to 95,000,000 miles. It takes light about eight minutes to travel from the sun to earth. The earth's diameter is about 7,900 miles. The earth's rotation and revolution have a tremendous impact on life here.

Rotation. The earth *rotates* around its axis, which roughly runs through the geographic north and south poles. This rotation creates day and night as parts of the earth are turned toward and then away from the sun.

Revolution. The earth *revolves* in an orbit (path) around the sun. The earth's axis is tilted about 23° from perpendicular with the orbit around the sun. The tilting and revolving creates seasons as regions of the earth are tilted toward the sun and away from the sun.

The diagram here shows the earth's tilt and earth's relation to the sun at the beginning of each season in the Northern Hemisphere. Seasons are opposite in the Southern Hemisphere.

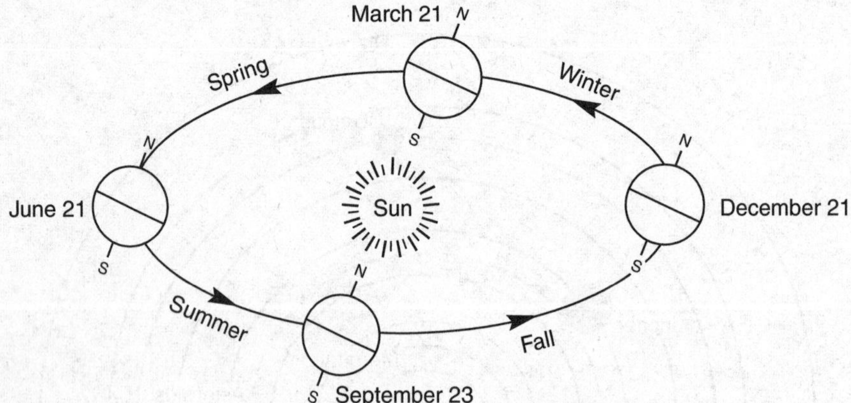

Seasons in the Northern Hemisphere

Moon is the name for the satellite that revolves around earth. The moon also rotates around its axis. The moon's diameter is about 2,100 miles and it is about 240,000 miles from the earth to the moon. The moon has no atmosphere and its surface is covered with craters from meteorites and from volcanoes.

The moon's rotation and revolution each take about 27 ½ days. These equal periods of rotation and revolution mean that the same part of the moon always faces the earth. It was not until lunar exploration in the 1970s that the other side of the moon was viewed and photographed.

The Moon's Phases

Different parts of the moon's surface reflect light to the earth, creating the different phases of the moons as shown on the next page.

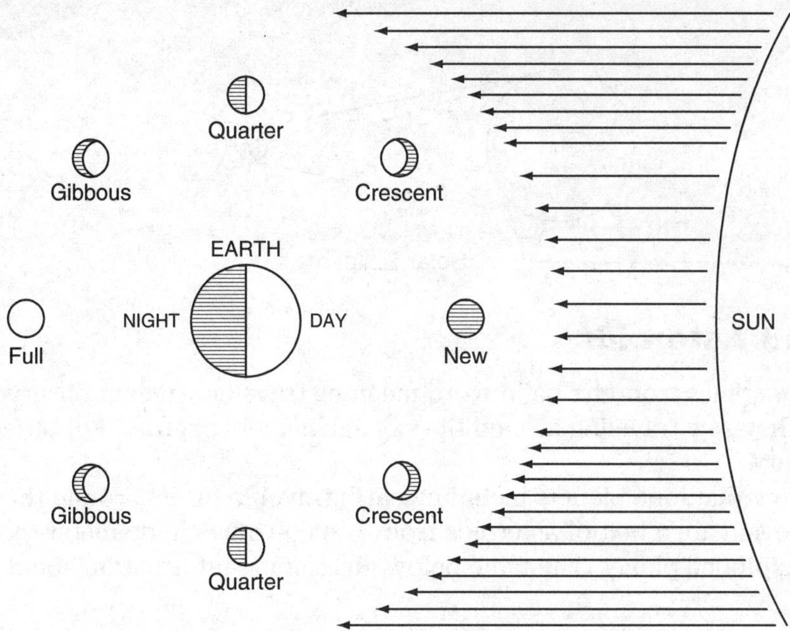

Appearance of the Moon During Different Phases

Tides

The phases of the moon are also integrally related to tides on earth. High tides occur on the parts of earth directly under the moon and on the other side of earth directly opposite this point. Low tides occur halfway between the two high tides. The tides move around the earth as the moon revolves around the earth, creating two high and two low tides each day at each place on earth.

The lowest and highest tides occur when the sun and the moon are in a straight line. These tides are called spring tides. The moon is either new or full during this direct alignment.

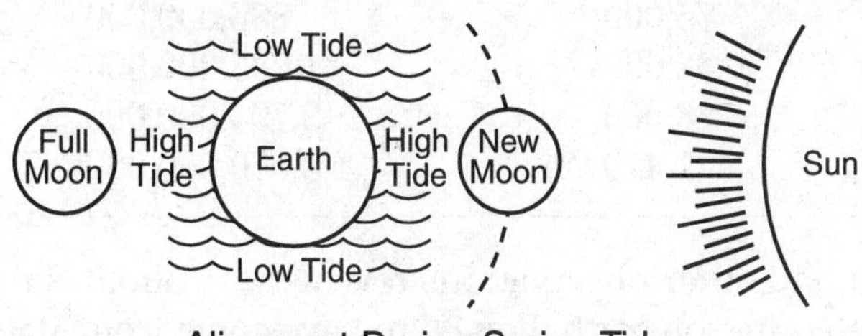

Alignment During Spring Tides

Eclipses

The position of the sun, earth, and moon can create eclipses. A lunar eclipse occurs when the moon is in the earth's shadow. A solar eclipse occurs when the sun is "hidden" behind the moon. Look at the diagrams below.

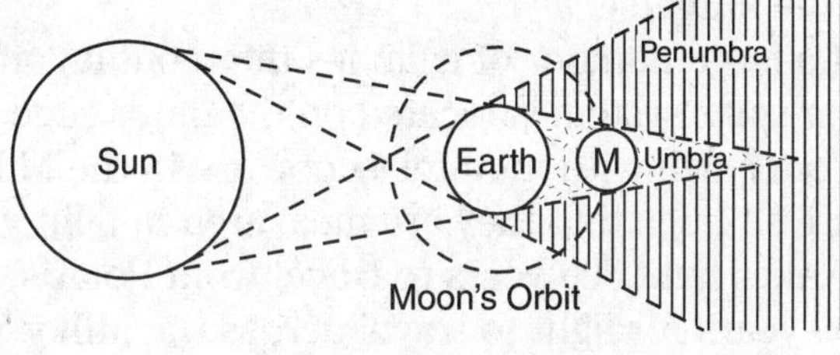

Lunar Eclipse

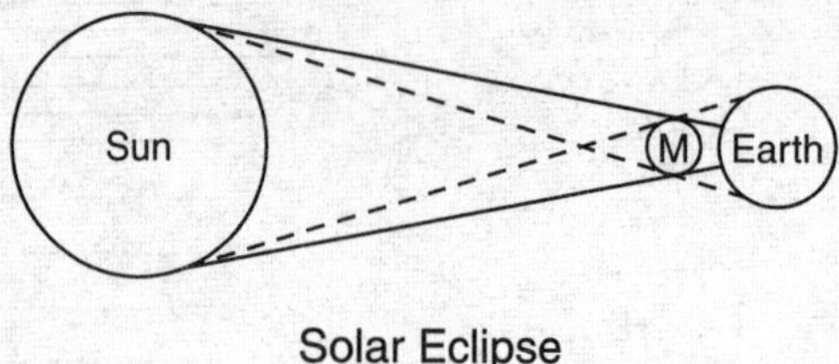

Solar Eclipse

Planets and Asteroids

The word planet comes from the Latin word meaning traveler. Ancient observers were taken by the "lights" they saw traveling around the sky against a background of other "lights" that seemed stationary.

Today we know that nine planets including earth travel in orbits around the sun. Also in orbit around the sun are a belt of asteroids from 1 to 500 miles in diameter that may be the remains of an exploded planet. The table below gives some information about the planets and asteroids.

BODIES IN SOLAR ORBIT

Name	Approximate diameter in miles	Approximate distance from sun in miles	Revolution Period
Mercury	3,100	36,000,000	88 days
Venus	7,700	67,000,000	225 days
Earth	7,900	93,000,000	365¼ days
Mars	4,200	142,000,000	687 days
Asteroids		161,000,000	
Jupiter	88,700	483,000,000	12 years
Saturn	75,000	886,000,000	29½ years
Uranus	32,000	1,783,000,000	84 years
Neptune	28,000	2,794,000,000	165 years
Pluto	1,420 (?)	3,670,000,000	248 years

Unmanned spacecraft and other observations reveal more about the planets each year. Recent discoveries of meteorites on earth thought to have come from Mars have fueled speculation that some life forms might exist, or might have existed, on Mars.

COSMOLOGY

Cosmology is the study of the universe. Cosmological theories are about the origin, development, and ultimate fate of the universe.

The universe consists of a large number of galaxies that contain an enormous number of stars and other material. Our solar system is located on the outer edge of the Milky Way galaxy. All the stars you can see from earth without a telescope are in the Milky Way galaxy.

Intergalactic distances are so huge that they are measured in light years. Light travels about 6 trillion miles in a year. It takes light 300 years to travel from Polaris, the North Star, to earth. It would take about 100,000 years for light to travel across the Milky Way galaxy.

Scientists have discovered a great many other galaxies. The Andromeda galaxy is over 2 million light years away from earth. The most distant detectable galaxies are about 10 to 15 billion light years from earth.

Scientists have discovered that galaxies are moving away from each other. This, among other factors, has led most scientists to embrace the Big Bang theory. This theory proposes that helium and hydrogen combined to create a gigantic explosion 15 billion to 20 billion years ago. This explosion led to the development of the stars, galaxies, and eventually planets.

METEOROLOGY

Meteorology is the study of the earth's atmosphere. We are most attentive to meteorologist's predictions about weather.

Weather observations are taken on the ground, in the upper atmosphere, and from satellites in space. All these observations inform us about likely weather events and add to our knowledge about the atmosphere.

The complex movement of air masses creates our weather. This movement begins because air around the equator is heated and air at the poles is cool. Air in the lower atmosphere moves toward the equator, while upper air moves toward the poles. Added to this is the effect of Coriolis force, caused by the rotation of the planet. Coriolis force pulls air to the right in the Northern Hemisphere and to the left in the Southern Hemisphere.

Weather fronts move from west to east in the United States. High pressure systems are usually associated with good weather. Wind circulates to the right (left in the Southern Hemisphere) around a high pressure system. Low pressure systems are usually associated with bad weather. Wind circulates to the left (right in the Southern Hemisphere) around a low pressure system.

Humidity

Humidity refers to the percent of water vapor in the air. Dew point is the temperature below which the air will become so humid that it is saturated with water. Humidity above 60 or 65 percent makes us more uncomfortable because perspiration evaporates slowly.

Fog and Clouds

When the temperature is below the dew point, the air is saturated with water droplets or ice crystals, and fog or clouds are formed. Fog is a cloud that touches the ground. Clouds are formed well above the ground.

Stratus clouds refer to low-hanging clouds. Rain or snow may fall from nimbostratus clouds. Other stratus clouds can appear after rain has fallen. Stratus clouds may be just a few thousand feet above the ground.

Cumulus can be puffy cotton-like clouds that appear in the afternoon. The base of these clouds is about a mile above the ground. Cumulonimbus clouds are huge dark cumulus clouds that produce thunderstorms and hail. All cumulus clouds have strong convective, upward wind currents.

Cirrus clouds are high wispy clouds made up of ice crystals. Cirrus clouds are frequently three to five miles above the ground.

Precipitation

When condensed water or ice crystals become too dense for the air to support the precipitate, they fall toward the ground. *Rain* is water droplets that fall to the ground. *Snow* crystallizes from water droplets in clouds and falls to the earth. *Sleet* begins as rain and freezes or partially freezes as it falls to the earth. *Freezing rain* is rain that freezes when it strikes the surface. *Hail* is rain that freezes in cumulonimbus clouds and is blown up and falls only to be blown up again. This cycle is repeated many times, forming noticeable layers of ice in a hailstone.

Lightning

Lightning is an instantaneous, high energy electrical discharge in the atmosphere. Lightning occurs when positive and negative charges are separated in the atmosphere. While this occurs most often in violent thunderstorms it can occur also in sandstorms or in clouds above volcanoes. Lightning can be from cloud to cloud, or from cloud to ground.

Weather Maps

Weather maps show the position of pressure systems and fronts. A *warm front* signals that the air behind the front is warmer than the air in front. A *cold front* signals that the air behind the front is colder. The map below shows the symbols for fronts and pressure systems.

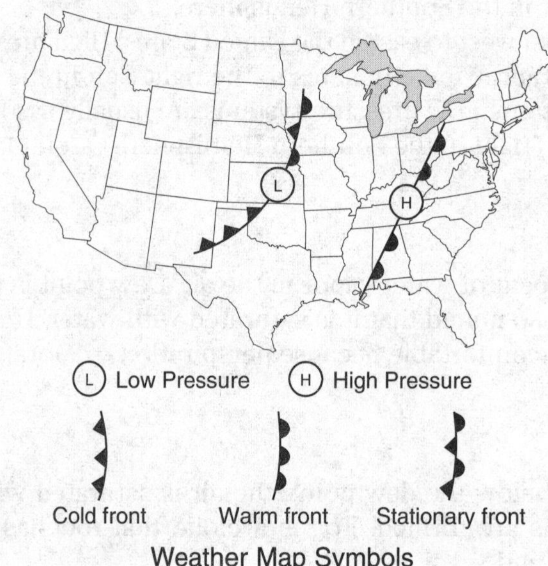

Weather Map Symbols

OCEANOGRAPHY

Oceanography is the study of the world's oceans and ocean beds. Oceanographers are concerned with 71 percent of the earth's surface. The ocean floor is covered by sediment, which reveals information about life on earth. Midocean ridges are the source of many volcanic eruptions.

Seawater itself is about 3.5 percent salt. Ocean currents, such as the Gulf Stream, are like rivers of water within the ocean. The sea provides over one-quarter of the protein needed in the world. Off-shore wells provide about 15 percent of the world's petroleum. Pollution by petroleum spills and other factors has had a noticeable impact on the oceans and on marine life.

GEOLOGY

Geology is the study of the earth, its development and origin. The History of Life table on page 117 shows the different periods in earth's development and when living organisms appeared on earth.

Using this time scale, geologists are fairly certain that, during the Permian period, earth's land mass consisted of a single continent called Pangea. During the Triassic period, Pangea split into two continents. During the Jurassic period, the Atlantic Ocean was formed. During the Cretaceous period, the Rocky Mountains rose. During the Tertiary period, the land bridge between North America and Europe disappeared. During the Quaternary period, glaciers covered most of North America.

THE EARTH'S PARTS

The earth has five parts—atmosphere, crust, mantle, outer core, and inner core.

The atmosphere is the gaseous region that surrounds the earth; it consists of 78 percent nitrogen and 21 percent oxygen. The remaining 1 percent consists of carbon dioxide, argon, water vapor, and other gases. The atmosphere extends out about 650 miles. But air becomes thinner as you travel away from earth and only the bottom 3 ½ miles or so of the atmosphere is habitable by humans without special equipment. The ozone layer, which protects earth from ultraviolet rays, is about 20 miles up.

The hydrosphere is the layer of water that covers about three-quarters of earth's surface. Ocean water, salt water, makes up about 95 percent of all earth's water. Oceans average about 12,400 feet deep. Below 100 feet, water temperature decreases rapidly. At 5,000 feet, the ocean temperature is near freezing.

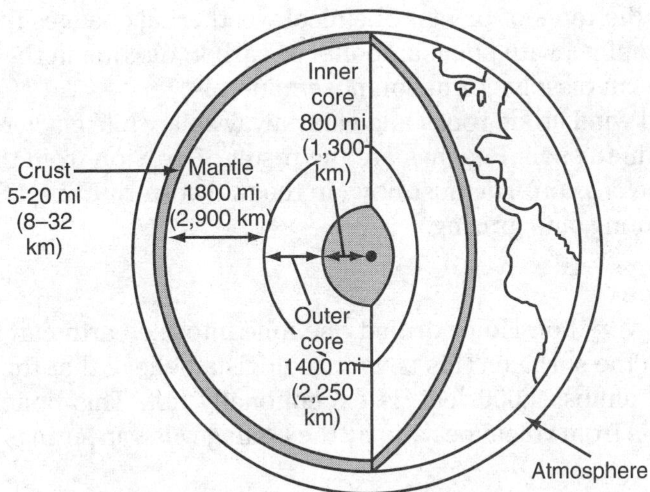

It is about 4,000 miles from the surface to the center of earth. Pressure and density increase with depth.

The lithosphere includes the rigid crust (20 miles thick) and upper mantle (40 miles thick) of the earth. The lithosphere is divided into a number of tectonic plates, which drift across earth's surface on the partially molten asthenosphere. The asthenosphere separates the lithosphere from the mantle.

The rigid mantle reaches to a depth of about 1,800 miles. The outer core is about 1,400 miles thick and consists of dense rigid materials. The inner core has a radius of about 800 miles and is very dense and hot with temperatures over 10,000° F. The heat generated in the inner core is transferred to the surface and provides the energy for continental drift and for molten rock, which erupts on land and in the ocean.

Rocks

Geologists study rocks. Three types of rocks are found in the earth's crust—sedimentary, igneous, and metamorphic. Sedimentary rocks form in water when sediments and remains of dead organisms harden. Igneous rocks form when molten rock, magma, crystallizes. Metamorphic rocks form when other rocks are subjected to extreme pressure. Sedimentary rocks are found near the surface of the earth while igneous and metamorphic rocks are usually found beneath the surface.

Fossils

Fossils are evidence of living organisms. Geologists and other scientists use fossils to learn about earth's history. Fossils usually form when organisms die and are buried in the sediment that forms sedimentary rocks. Other fossils include footprints or tracks of animals. Fossils of animals help us date rocks and other layers of the earth.

Geologic Processes

External Processes

As new rocks are being created, old ones are being destroyed, and earth's surface is being worn away. This process is called erosion.

Most erosion begins with weathering. Weathering disintegrates rocks physically and chemically. Physical weathering breaks up rocks and may be caused by intense heat or cold, by frost, or by the action of vines or the roots of plants. Chemical weathering changes the composition of the rocks. Rain water combines with small amounts of carbon dioxide in the atmosphere to form carbonic acid, which can dissolve or decompose minerals.

Streams, rivers, and wind erode rocks and carry away soil, while glaciers can gouge out huge grooves in rocks and in the soil. Beaches are the result of erosion from the pounding surf or oceans. Humans cause erosion. The dust bowl in the midwestern United States was caused by careless plowing, planting, and grazing.

Internal Processes

The earth's interior is very hot. Holes drilled one mile into the earth can be 85° to 90° warmer at the bottom than on the surface. This is why geologists believe that the interior of the earth, which extends down almost 4,000 feet, is exceptionally hot. This belief is bolstered by the molten rock that erupts from volcanoes and by the boiling water in springs at the earth's surface.

New Land Masses

New mountains and land are constantly being created. Hot magma comes to the surface, seeps out, and is cooled. Land masses also rise as the land is eroded and pushed up from below.

PHYSICAL SCIENCES

CHEMISTRY

Chemistry refers to the composition, properties, and interactions of matter. Organic chemistry is about living things. Inorganic chemistry deals with all other substances.

Atoms

Matter consists of atoms, which are so small they have never been seen—not even with the most powerful microscope. Atoms contain three subatomic particles—protons, neutrons, and electrons. The nucleus contains positively charged protons and neutrons with a neutral charge. Negatively charged electrons revolve around the nucleus.

Elements

Elements are the building blocks of chemistry. They cannot be broken by chemical means into other elements. Over 100 chemical elements are known today. Some have been produced artificially and have not been found in nature. Atoms are the smallest piece of an element.

Each element is classified by its atomic number, which is the total number of protons in the nucleus. Every element has its own symbol. Therefore, every substance can be represented by symbols that show how many atoms of each element it contains.

PERIODIC TABLE OF THE ELEMENTS

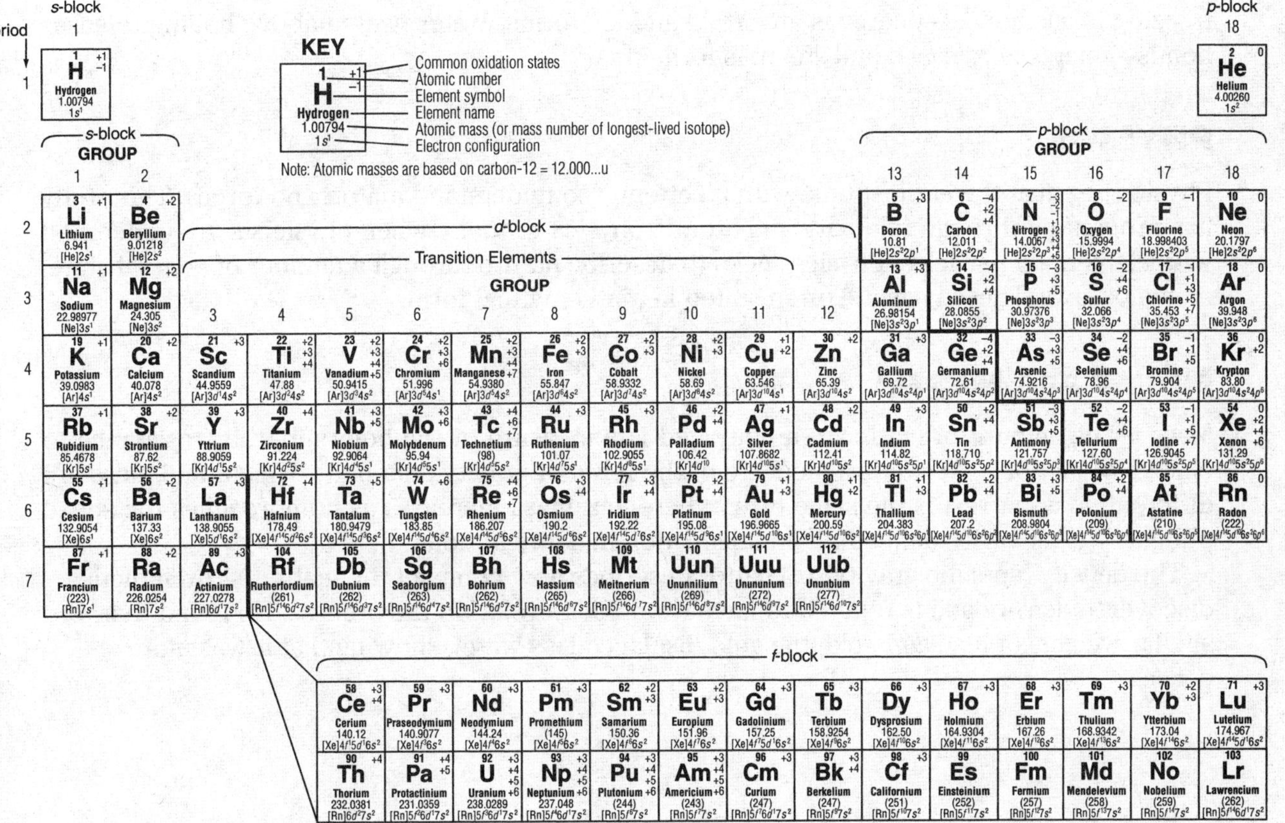

Matter

Matter is anything that has mass and takes up space. Matter can exist as a solid, liquid, or gas. The form of matter may change. For example, water becomes solid below freezing, and lead can be heated to a liquid.

All matter is made up of atoms. The weight of matter is a measure of the force that gravity places on its mass. Matter is conserved. That is, it cannot be created or destroyed, but it can be converted into energy.

Compound

A compound is formed when two or more elements unite chemically. A molecule is the smallest part of a compound with the properties of that compound.

There are three important types of chemical compounds—acids, bases, and salt. Acids dissolved in water produce hydrogen. Bases dissolved in water produce hydroxide. When acids and bases are combined chemically, they form salt.

Solution

A solution is formed when element(s) or compound(s) are dissolved in another substance. Club soda is a solution with carbon dioxide dissolved in water. Lemonade is a solution of lemon juice and sugar dissolved in water.

Chemical Reactions

Chemical reactions occur when bonds between atoms form or break. Energy, usually as heat, is absorbed when bonds are formed and released when bonds are broken. Water cooled below freezing forms bonds—energy is absorbed and ice forms. Water heated above boiling releases bonds—energy is released and steam is formed.

PHYSICS

Physics began at the earliest time with an attempt to understand matter and forces. This study has progressed through relativity and atomic physics to today when physicists are concerned with elementary particles. Physics seeks to describe nature through a number of general statements or laws. These laws are often stated in mathematical form.

Matter and Mass

Mass is the amount of matter in a body and is a measure of the body's inertia (resistance to change of motion). Weight is a measure of the force of gravity on a body. Weight and mass are different. Mass at rest is the same everywhere, but mass increases as it approaches the speed of light. Weight varies depending on its location in a gravitational field.

The density (specific gravity) of matter describes how compact the matter is. Archimedes discovered density and is reputed to have shouted "Eureka" in the process. He found that, in similar weights of lead and gold, the gold displaced less water, showing that it was more dense.

Motion

Physics is concerned with an object's response to force and the resulting movement. Force is energy that causes a change in an object's motion or shape. To explain force completely, you must describe both the magnitude and the direction. For example, two forces of the same magnitude pushing in the same direction are different from these same forces pushing at one another.

Velocity is described as magnitude (e.g., miles per hour) and direction (e.g., from 220 degrees). The magnitude portion of velocity is speed. The following formula describes the distance traveled for a constant velocity and a known time. For a time t and a constant velocity v the distance traveled d is:

$$d = vt$$

Newton's three laws of motion are still most important in everyday life. We must remember, though, that recent theories have shown that these laws do not apply to objects traveling near the speed of light or for very small subatomic particles.

Newton's First Law (Inertia). A body maintains its state of rest or uniform motion unless acted upon by an outside force.

Newton's Second Law (Constant Acceleration). As force is applied to an object, the object accelerates in the direction of the force. Both the mass and the force affect how the object accelerates. The more the mass the less the acceleration. The formula for this law follows:

$$F(\text{orce}) = M(\text{ass}) \times A(\text{cceleration}) \text{ or } A(\text{cceleration}) = \frac{F(\text{orce})}{M(\text{ass})}$$

Newton's Third Law (Conservation of Momentum). This law states that for every action there is an equal and opposite reaction. If two objects bump into each other, they are pushed away from each other with an equal force. The net effect of this event is 0, and the momentum is conserved.

Energy

Energy is the ability to do work. Energy can be mechanical, solar, thermal, chemical, electrical, or nuclear. Potential energy is stored energy or energy ready to be released. Kinetic energy is energy resulting from motion. Activation energy converts potential energy into kinetic energy.

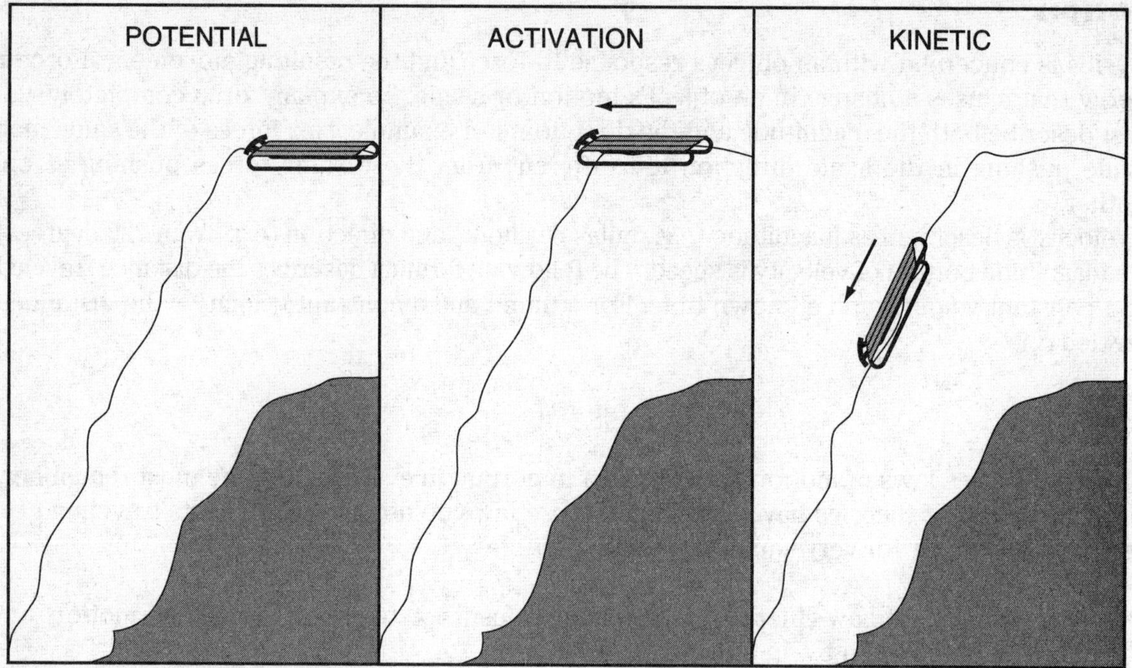

In one simple example, a sled at the top of a hill possesses potential energy. The push of the sledder is the activation energy needed to set the sled in motion. While in motion, the sled possesses kinetic energy.

In another example, the fuel in a rocket car has potential energy. This potential energy is activated by energy from a flame and transformed into the kinetic energy of the moving car.

Work

Work is the movement of a body by a force. If there is no movement, there is no work. Work occurs when you pick up an object. Trying without success to move a heavy object or holding an object steady involves no work. It does not matter that a lot of effort was involved. The rate of work is power. Power is measured in foot-pounds. A foot-pound is the amount of work it takes to raise one pound, one foot at sea level.

Heat

In physics, heat is energy in motion. Heat transfers energy within a body or from one body to the other when there is a temperature difference. Heat moves from higher temperature to lower temperature, lowering the former and raising the latter. Heat is measured in calories.

Temperature measures how fast the molecules in a substance are moving. The faster the molecules move, the hotter the substance. Temperature is commonly measured on two scales, Fahrenheit (freezing 32 degrees, boiling [water] 212 degrees) and Celsius (freezing 0 degrees and boiling [water] 100 degrees). The Kelvin scale is used in science. Zero on the Kelvin scale is absolute zero—molecules are not moving at all—and is equal to –273°C or –460°F.

Heat is transferred by conduction (physical contact), convection (from moving liquid or gas), and radiation (no physical contact). A heating pad *conducts* heat to your back. Moving hot water transfers heat to the radiator by *convection*. The sun *radiates* heat to the earth.

Wave Phenomena

Waves transfer energy without transferring matter. Microwaves, radio waves, sound waves, and x-rays are examples of waves in action. Most waves resemble the one below. The frequency of a wave is the vibrations per second. The wavelength is the distance between crests.

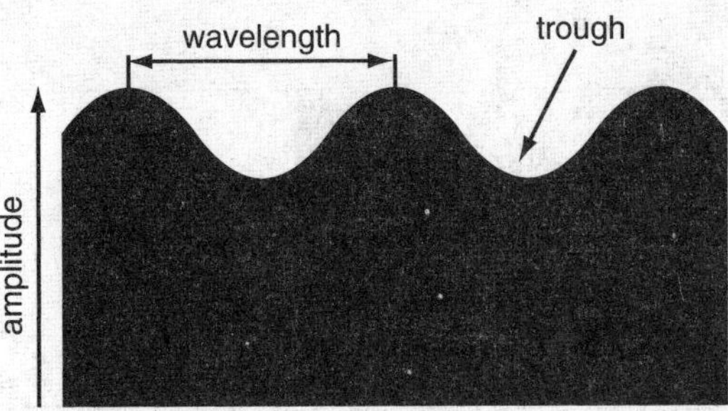

Light

Most light is produced by heated electrons vibrating at high frequencies. Light makes it possible for us to see things and to observe colors. Plants need light to carry out photosynthesis.

Light travels in straight lines and spreads out as it travels. When light strikes a rough surface it may be absorbed or scattered. When light strikes a highly polished surface it is reflected away at the angle of the original ray (angle of incidence equals the angle of reflection). Black surfaces absorb all light, while white surfaces scatter all light. This is why white clothes are recommended for sunny, warm days.

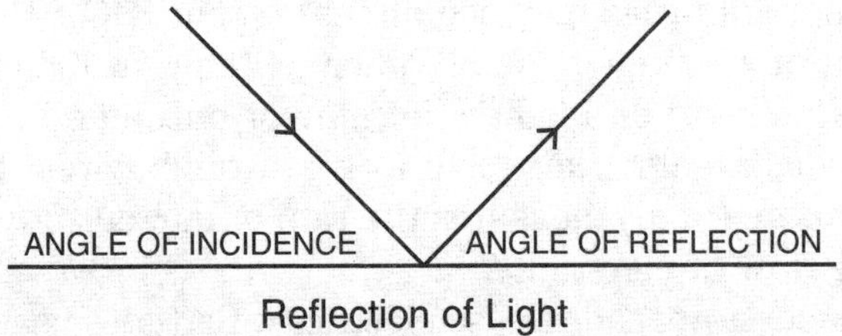

Reflection of Light

Sound

Sounds are waves. For the human ear to hear a sound it must travel through a medium—a gas, a solid, or a liquid. As the sound waves travel through the medium, molecules in the medium vibrate.

Sound travels more quickly through solid media because the molecules are more closely packed together. Sound travels through air at about 1,100 feet per second, through water at about 5,000 feet per second, and through stone at about 20,000 feet per second.

ELECTRICITY AND MAGNETISM

Atoms are composed of protons (positive charge), electrons (negative charge), and neutrons (neutral charge). All things have either a positive (more protons), negative (more electrons), or neutral (balance of protons and electrons) charge.

Electricity

Electricity is based on these charges and follows these rules. Like charges repel, unlike charge attract. Neutral charges are attracted by both positive and negative charges, but not as strongly as opposite charges.

In a static electricity experiment, the experimenter shows that the glass rod does not attract bits of paper. Then the glass rod is rubbed with a piece of silk. This process removes electrons from the rod, creating a negative charge. Then the rod attracts the neutral bits of paper.

Electricity speeds through conductors such as copper. Electricity moves slower through semiconductors such as ceramics. Electricity does not move through nonconductors or insulators such as rubber and glass.

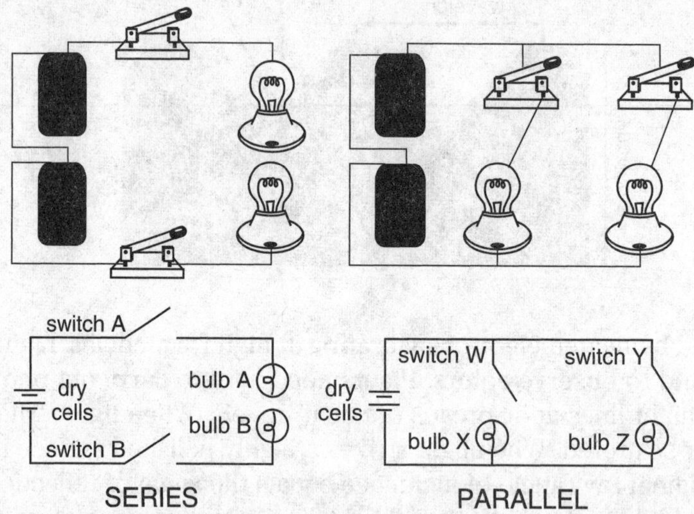

Electricity moves through wires to form circuits. Most circuits in this country use alternating current (AC). Circuits in other countries may use direct current (DC). Most circuits are wired parallel—if a light burns out, or a switch is off, all other switches or lights work. Some circuits are wired in series—if a switch is off or a light is missing or burned out, all lights go out.

Three units are used to measure electricity as it flows through wires. The volt measures the force of the current. The ampere (amp) measures the rate of current flow. The ohm tells the resistance in the wire to the flow of electricity.

Batteries are used to produce, store, and release electricity. Batteries used in a toy or flashlight are dry cell batteries. Car batteries are wet cell batteries.

Magnetism

Magnets occur naturally in magnetite, although most magnets are manufactured from iron. Magnetism is very similar to electricity, and electromagnets can be made from coils of wire. Magnets have a north and south pole—like poles repel, while opposite poles attract. The magnetic field is strongest around the poles.

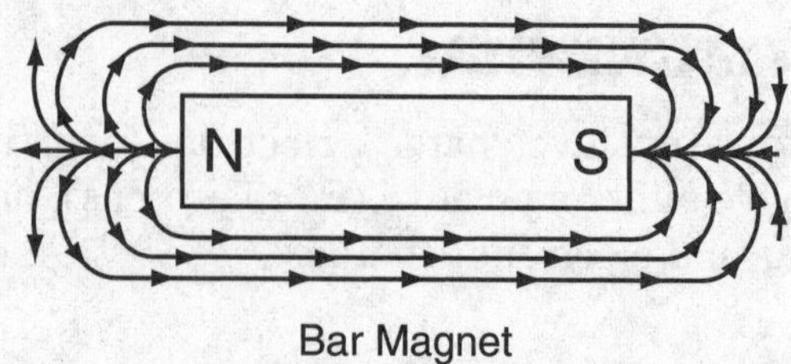

Bar Magnet

Earth has a magnetic field that aids navigation. Magnetic north is located in northeastern Canada. It is not located at the North Pole. Compass needles point to magnetic north, not to the geographic North Pole.

MODERN PHYSICS AND RADIOACTIVITY

MODERN PHYSICS

Modern physics studies very small particles of energy. Energy as very small discrete quantities gives scientists a different view than energy as a continuous flow. Particle physics is particularly useful as scientists study atomic energy. For example, scientists study light as the transmission of tiny particles called photons. In fact, it is believed that energy is transmitted as both particles and waves.

Modern physics also studies the conversion of matter into energy and energy into matter. Einstein's famous equation quantifies the conversion between mass to energy.

$$E = mc^2$$

(E is energy, m is mass, and c is the speed of light, 186,000 miles per second.)

Calculations with this equation reveal that very small amounts of mass can create huge amounts of energy. Similarly, calculations reveal it would take huge amounts of energy to create a very small amount of mass.

RADIOACTIVITY

Materials are radioactive when they have unstable nuclei. Uranium is an example of a naturally occurring radioactive substance. Radioactive materials decay, losing their radioactivity at a certain rate. The decay of radioactive materials is very useful for dating rocks and other materials.

Other radioactive material is created through nuclear fission in nuclear power plants. The energy from the reaction can be used as a power source.

Radioactive materials release energy including alpha, beta, and usually gamma radiation. Gamma rays penetrate living organisms very deeply and can destroy living cells and lead to the death of humans.

Fusion

The sun creates energy through fusion. Attempts are underway to create energy through nuclear fusion. Fusion creates much less radioactivity and could be fueled by deuterium, which is found in limitless quantities throughout the ocean.

SPECIAL STRATEGIES FOR ANSWERING SCIENCE ITEMS

Interpreting Graphs

You will encounter four main types of graphs on the test.

The Pictograph

The pictograph uses symbols to stand for numbers. In the following graph, each picture represents 1,000 phones.

Number of Phones in Five Towns
(in thousands)

Try these questions:

1. According to this graph, about how many more phones are there in Bergenfield than in Emerson?
   (A) 10,000
   (B) 15,000
   (C) 1,000
   (D) 1.5 thousand

2. This graph *best* demonstrates which of the following?
   (A) More people live in Bergenfield.
   (B) People in Alpine make the fewest calls.
   (C) There are about twice as many phones in Emerson as in Alpine.
   (D) There are about four times as many phones in Bergenfield as in Alpine.

Answers are on page 140.

The Bar Graph

The bar graph represents information by the length of a bar. The graph below shows the rainfall during two months in each of five towns.

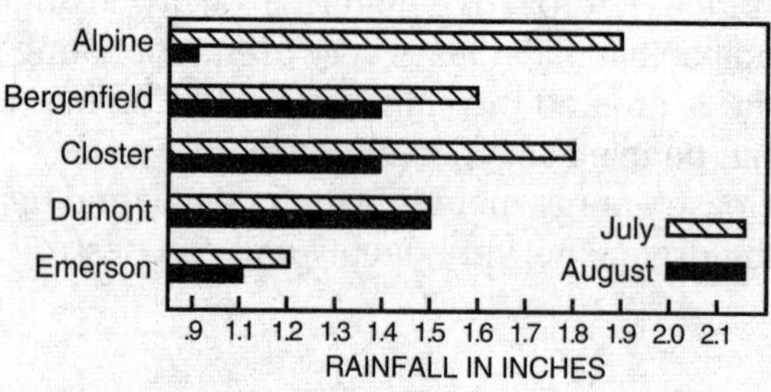

Rainfall in July and August for Five Towns

Try these questions:

3. You wanted to get the least rainfall. Based on this graph, which town would you go to in July and which town would you go to in August?
   (A) Closter, Bergenfield
   (B) Alpine, Dumont
   (C) Closter, Alpine
   (D) None of the above

4. This graph *best* demonstrates which of the following?
   (A) The rainiest town yearly is Closter.
   (B) Alpine has the largest rainfall difference between July and August.
   (C) The driest town yearly is Emerson.
   (D) In August, Alpine has more rain than Emerson.

The Line Graph

The line graph plots information against two axes. The graph below shows monthly sales for two corporations.

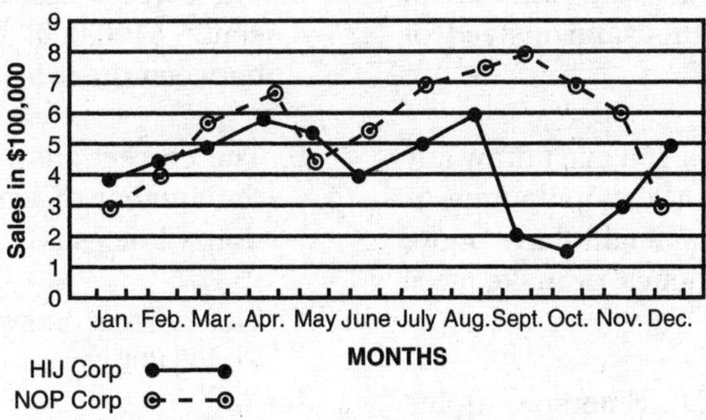

Sales for Two Companies During the Year

You might be asked two types of questions.

5. What was the approximate difference in sales between the HIJ and the NOP Corporations in June?
   (A) $15,000
   (B) $150,000
   (C) $400,000
   (D) $4.5 million

6. This graph *best* demonstrates which of the following?
   (A) NOP has more employees.
   (B) From August to September, the differences in sales grew by 400%.
   (C) In October, NOP had over $600,000 more in sales than HIJ.
   (D) In total, HIJ had more sales this year than NOP.

The Circle Graph

The circle represents an entire amount. In the graph below, each wedge-shaped piece of the graph represents the percent of tax money spent on different town services.

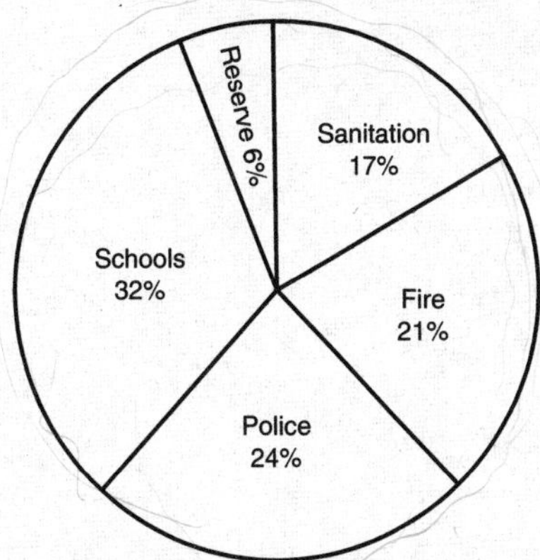

Percent of Tax Money Spent for Town Services

Use the circle graph to answer these questions.

7. The town collects $1,400,000 in taxes. How much will the town spend on schools?
   (A) $320,000
   (B) $60,000
   (C) $600,000
   (D) $448,000

8. The town collects $1,400,000 in taxes. The town needs to spend $392,000 for police. Any needed money will come from sanitation. The percents in the pie chart are recalculated. What percent is left for sanitation?
   (A) 21%
   (B) 17%
   (C) 13%
   (D) 10%

EXPLAINED ANSWERS

1. The correct answer is (D). Writing answers in a different format (1.5 thousand instead of 1,500) is common.

2. The correct answer is (D). You can't draw any valid conclusions about the populations or calls made. Some towns might have more businesses, own fewer phones, or make more calls per household.

3. The correct answer is (D). Emerson, Alpine are the towns you would choose. No need to compute. Find the smallest bar for each month.

4. The correct answer is (B). That fact is clear. We only have information about July and August, so we can't be sure about (A) or (C). Choice (D) is not true.

5. The correct answer is (B). Each space represents \$100,000 and there are 1.5 spaces between the sales figures in June.

6. The correct answer is (B). You can't predict the number of employees from this information. Choices (C) and (D) are false.

7. The correct answer is (D). Multiply 0.32 × \$1,400,000.

8. The correct answer is (C). It takes 28 percent of the taxes to get \$392,000. That's 4 percent more than the police get now. Sanitation loses 4 percent, leaving 13 percent.

SCIENCE MSAT PRACTICE ITEMS

These items will help you practice for the real MSAT. These items have the same form and test the same material as MSAT items and test material. The items you encounter on the real MSAT may have a different emphasis and may be more complete.

Instructions

Mark your answers on the sheet provided below. Complete the items in 20 minutes or less. Correct your answer sheet using the answers on page 144.

1 Ⓐ Ⓑ Ⓒ Ⓓ	5 Ⓐ Ⓑ Ⓒ Ⓓ	9 Ⓐ Ⓑ Ⓒ Ⓓ	13 Ⓐ Ⓑ Ⓒ Ⓓ	17 Ⓐ Ⓑ Ⓒ Ⓓ
2 Ⓐ Ⓑ Ⓒ Ⓓ	6 Ⓐ Ⓑ Ⓒ Ⓓ	10 Ⓐ Ⓑ Ⓒ Ⓓ	14 Ⓐ Ⓑ Ⓒ Ⓓ	18 Ⓐ Ⓑ Ⓒ Ⓓ
3 Ⓐ Ⓑ Ⓒ Ⓓ	7 Ⓐ Ⓑ Ⓒ Ⓓ	11 Ⓐ Ⓑ Ⓒ Ⓓ	15 Ⓐ Ⓑ Ⓒ Ⓓ	19 Ⓐ Ⓑ Ⓒ Ⓓ
4 Ⓐ Ⓑ Ⓒ Ⓓ	8 Ⓐ Ⓑ Ⓒ Ⓓ	12 Ⓐ Ⓑ Ⓒ Ⓓ	16 Ⓐ Ⓑ Ⓒ Ⓓ	20 Ⓐ Ⓑ Ⓒ Ⓓ

1. The following are parts of all cells EXCEPT:
   (A) chloroplasts
   (B) cytoplasm
   (C) nucleus
   (D) cell membrane

2. Cells may reproduce through
   (A) photosynthesis.
   (B) mitochondria.
   (C) mitosis.
   (D) eukaryotes.

3. All the following are cell activities EXCEPT:
   (A) homeostasis
   (B) respiration
   (C) ingestion
   (D) chromosome

4. The genetic material termed DNA has the following function:
   (A) It divides the nucleus acid in genes.
   (B) It provides the genetic codes that determine many traits of an organism.
   (C) It carries the genetic code throughout the cell.
   (D) It arranges rodlike structures located in the cell nucleus.

5. All the following belong to the class called mammals EXCEPT:
   (A) moles
   (B) humans
   (C) monkeys
   (D) carp

6. Which of the following is not one of the five kingdoms living things are generally classified into?
   (A) Moneran
   (B) Fungi
   (C) Plantae
   (D) Reptilae

7. Find the statement about bacteria that is not true.
   (A) Bacteria help decompose dead matter.
   (B) Bacteria cause disease.
   (C) Bacteria help regular physiological processes.
   (D) Bacteria are lifeless and lack the ability to reproduce.

8. Which is the correct hierarchy of the body makeup:
   (A) tissues-cells-organs-systems-body
   (B) cells-tissues-organs-systems-body
   (C) cells-tissues-systems-organs-body
   (D) tissues-cells-systems-organs-body

9. Which of the following is considered to be the primary gland in the male body?
   (A) testes
   (B) thyroid
   (C) pituitary
   (D) pancreas

10. Which of the following definitions best describes the meaning of ecology?
    (A) Recycling to keep the human habitat as pure as possible.
    (B) The relationship between organisms and their habitat.
    (C) Making use of natural materials from our habitat.
    (D) Keeping the biosphere free of toxic materials.

11. When the elements of hydrogen and oxygen combine they form
    (A) coal
    (B) diamond
    (C) carbon dioxide
    (D) water

12. Which is a false statement about matter?
    (A) Matter is anything that has mass and takes up space.
    (B) Matter is made up of atoms.
    (C) Matter cannot be changed, created, or destroyed.
    (D) The weight of matter depends on gravitational force.

13. Which of the following is not a planet of our solar system?
    (A) Pluto
    (B) Uranus
    (C) Neptune
    (D) Polaris

14. Which is not part of the gaseous make-up of our atmosphere?
    (A) nitrogen
    (B) water vapor
    (C) argon
    (D) ozone

15. Approximately what percent of the earth's surface is covered with water?
    (A) 90 percent
    (B) 75 percent
    (C) 60 percent
    (D) 45 percent

16. Which of the following is a stage in the water cycle?
    (A) photosynthesis
    (B) respiration
    (C) condensation
    (D) accumulation

17. Magnitude and direction together are needed to describe
    (A) work.
    (B) motion.
    (C) mass.
    (D) force.

18. A person is driving a car; what types of energy are represented respectively by the gas in the tank and the motion of the car?
    (A) kinetic, potential
    (B) activation, kinetic
    (C) potential, activation
    (D) potential, kinetic

19. Which of the following is the description of heat?
    (A) temperature
    (B) energy in motion
    (C) radiation
    (D) a temperature measurement

20. Which of the following would be the best conductor of electricity?
    (A) paper
    (B) copper
    (C) hair
    (D) rubber

Answers

1. **A**	5. **D**	9. **C**	13. **D**	17. **D**
2. **C**	6. **D**	10. **B**	14. **D**	18. **D**
3. **D**	7. **D**	11. **D**	15. **B**	19. **B**
4. **B**	8. **B**	12. **C**	16. **C**	20. **B**

6 HISTORY AND SOCIAL STUDIES

TEST INFO BOX

22 of 120 Multiple Choice items — 18% of Content Knowledge items
3 of 18 Short Answer items — 17% of Content Area Exercise items

HISTORY AND SOCIAL STUDIES ITEMS

History and Social Studies multiple choice items look like this.

The main effect of the Treaty of Utrecht in 1742 was that

(A) France lost North American possessions to England.
(B) the Spanish Empire was partitioned.
(C) Britain recognized the United States after the Revolutionary War.
(D) Holland and Switzerland were officially formed.

Social Studies short answer items look like this.

Describe the view supported by the *Federalist Papers* and the impact of the debate between the Jeffersonians and the Federalists on the American political system.

USING THIS CHAPTER

This chapter prepares you to take the History and Social Studies part of the MSAT. Choose one of these approaches.

I want all the History and Social Studies review I can get.

- ❑ Skip the Review Quiz and read the entire review section.
- ❑ Take the History and Social Studies Review Quiz on page 147.
- ❑ Correct the Review Quiz and reread the indicated parts of the review.
- ❑ Go over the Special Strategies for Answering the History and Social Studies items on page 196.
- ❑ Complete the History and Social Studies MSAT Practice Questions on page 197.

I want a thorough History and Social Studies review.

- ❑ Take the History and Social Studies Review Quiz on page 147.
- ❑ Correct the Review Quiz and reread the indicated parts of the review.
- ❑ Go over the Special Strategies for Answering the History and Social Studies items on page 196.
- ❑ Complete the History and Social Studies MSAT Practice Questions on page 197.

I want a quick History and Social Studies review.

- ❑ Take and correct the History and Social Studies Review Quiz on page 147.
- ❑ Go over the Special Strategies for Answering the History and Social Studies items on page 196.
- ❑ Complete the History and Social Studies MSAT Practice Questions on page 197.

I want to practice History and Social Studies questions.

- ❑ Go over the Special Strategies for Answering the History and Social Studies items on page 196.
- ❑ Complete the History and Social Studies MSAT Practice Questions on page 197.

I don't need any History and Social Studies review.

- ❑ OK. If you're sure, skip this chapter.

HISTORY AND SOCIAL STUDIES REVIEW QUIZZES

These quizzes use a short answer format to help you find out what you know about the History and Social Studies topics reviewed in this chapter. The quiz results direct you to the portions of the chapter you should read. There are three quizzes—United States, World History, and Other Social Studies Topics.

These quizzes will also help focus your thinking about History and Social Studies, and these questions and answers are a good review in themselves. It's not important to answer all these questions correctly, and don't be concerned if you miss many of them.

The answers are found immediately after the quiz. It's to your advantage not to look at them until you have completed the quiz. Once you have completed and corrected the review quizzes, use the answer checklist to decide which sections of the review to study.

UNITED STATES HISTORY REVIEW QUIZ

Write the answers in the space provided or on a separate sheet of paper.

1. Which Indian group established a culture off southern Alaska about 7,000 years ago?

2. In what structure did plains Indians live?

3. Name a nonindigenous group that established North American settlements before Columbus.

4. In what year did Columbus reach the mainland of North America?

5. Where were African slaves first brought to America?

6. What did Spanish explorers bring that caused great devastation to Native Americans?

7. Which nation established the first settlement in Manhattan?

8. How many English colonies were there in the 1740s?

9. Which things frequently used by colonists were taxed by the original Townsend Acts?

10. What was the Boston Tea Party and why was it held?

11. Which riders spread the word about the English march on Concord?

12. Name two of the self-evident truths found in the Declaration of Independence.

13. Where did the Colonial army winter in 1777?

14. Which two main forces trapped Cornwallis at Yorktown, Virginia?

15. What was the first governing document for the United States?

16. Describe the effect of three of the first ten amendments to the Constitution.

17. Briefly describe the theory of nullification.

18. What tract of land did Jefferson purchase from France?

19. What action started the War of 1812?

20. What famous national song was written during the War of 1812?

21. What impact did the Missouri Compromise have on the state of Missouri?

22. What governmental group did Jackson ignore when he moved Native Americans onto reservations?

23. What was the status of Texas after it gained independence from Mexico?

24. What did the Underground Railroad transport?

25. What states seceded from the Union before hostilities began?

26. What action began the Civil War?

27. What was the effect of the Emancipation Proclamation?

28. What type of government did Lincoln call for in his Gettysburg Address?

29. Describe one of the three civil rights amendments adopted from 1865 and 1870.

30. Until what year were Northern troops in the South following the Civil War?

31. Who was the only president to be elected and re-elected during this period?

32. What was the goal of the Dawes Severalty Act?

33. What inventions drew women to the workplace?

34. Name a territory the United States gained in the treaty ending the Spanish American War.

35. Teddy Roosevelt was awarded the Nobel Prize for helping to end what war?

36. Who did the United States army pursue in Mexico following the Mexican Revolution?

37. What act led to the beginning of World War I?

38. What occurred during World War I to remove an Ally from the conflict?

39. What German war policy brought the United States into the war?

40. Exactly when did World War I officially end?

41. What was the highest unemployment rate during the Depression?

42. Name and describe two of FDR's New Deal programs.

43. What main factor led to Hitler's rise to power in Germany?

44. What conflict provided a proving ground for World War II?

45. What were Russia's first actions when World War II began?

46. What power did Roosevelt gain from the Lend-Lease Act?

47. What was the outcome of Operation Barbarosa?

48. Why was Roosevelt criticized for his actions at Yalta?

49. What was the effect of the war on unemployment?

50. How did Truman use the Smith Act following World War II?

51. What led to China's involvement in the Korean War?

52. Describe the essence of the Supreme Court ruling in *Brown v. Board of Education.*

53. Describe the effectiveness of Presidents Kennedy and Johnson in passing War on Poverty legislation.

54. What happened after World War II to foster an alliance between Ho Chi Minh and Mao Tse-tung?

55. Through what process did Gerald Ford become president?

56. What major new programs did Carter introduce?

57. What is supply-side economics?

58. What "read my lips" promise led to Bush's defeat in 1992?

59. What type of question dogged the Clinton presidency?

WORLD HISTORY REVIEW QUIZ

Write the answers in the space provided or on a separate sheet of paper.

1. Give the approximate population of the world in 1 A.D.______ 1992 A.D.________

2. Approximately when was writing invented?

3. What is the name of the justice codes formulated in ancient Mesopotamia?

4. Approximately when were most Egyptian pyramids built?

5. Who fought in the Peloponesian Wars?

6. Name two of the three greatest thinkers of the Greek Classic age.

7. What event marked the beginning of the Greek Hellenistic age?

8. What was the outcome of the Punic wars?

9. Which leaders were defeated at the Battle of Acton?

10. Approximately when was Christianity declared the national religion of Rome?

11. Who was the original founder of Islam and approximately when was he born?

12. What was the original Japanese religion?

13. Why did the Samurai revolt in 1876?

14. Who was named emperor of the Holy Roman Empire in the late 700s A.D.?

15. What were the stated reasons for the Crusades?

16. Joan of Arc fought for which country in what war?

17. About what percent of the European population was killed by the bubonic plague?

18. Approximately when was Confucius born?

19. During what centuries did the Mongol Kahns rule China?

20. What was the cause of the Chinese-British Opium War?

21. What name was given to the earliest inhabitants of the Indus Valley in India?

22. What ideal did Buddha preach?

23. What was the beginning of Muslim and Hindu strife in India?

24. Where did the first towns in Africa appear?

25. During what century was Northern Africa predominately Islamic?

26. What role did African kingdoms play in the slave trade?

27. What was the dominant civilization of the Yucatan peninsula until about 900 A.D.?

28. What was the dominant civilization in South America in 1500 A.D.?

29. The ideas of which ancient civilization were dominant during the Renaissance?

30. Which practice of the Catholic church was particularly repugnant to Protestants?

31. What was the significant difference between the English queens Mary I and her successor Elizabeth I?

32. What was the main effect of European exploration on American Indians?

33. What major trade was begun during the Age of Exploration?

34. What major discovery did Copernicus make?

35. What was the average life expectancy in the early 1700s?

36. Who was the most famous Baroque painter?

37. Which Romanov leader began the modernization of Russia?

38. Which action began the French Revolution?

39. Which leader oversaw the reign of terror following the French Revolution?

40. Where was Napoleon exiled?

41. Which industries were the first to develop after the Industrial Revolution?

42. Which ideals were stressed by the Romantic Movement?

43. With which country were Great Britain and France allied during the Crimean War?

44. What do anarchists believe?

45. What continent drew the most attention from European countries during the period of New Imperialism?

OTHER SOCIAL STUDIES TOPICS REVIEW QUIZ

Write the answers in the space provided or on a separate sheet of paper.

1. What do physical anthropologists study?

____

____

2. What are the three primary determinants of culture?

____

____

____

3. What is the relationship of the legislative and executive branches in a parliamentary government?

____

____

____

____

____

4. What percentage of United States Representatives are elected every two years?

____

____

5. What percent of the popular vote is required to elect the president of the United States?

____

____

ANSWER CHECKLIST

The answers are organized by review sections. Check your answers. If you miss any question in a section, check the box and review that section. Everyone should review the section on Interpreting Graphs and Maps.

United States History

Native American Civilizations

❑ *Primitive Cultures, page 158*
1. Aleuts

❑ *Recent Cultures, page 158*
2. tepees

European Exploration and Colonization

❑ *Visitors Before Columbus, page 159*
3. Celtic/Norse (Vikings)

❑ *Columbus, page 159*
4. never

❑ *English Colonization, page 159*
5. Jamestown in 1619

❑ *Spanish Exploration, page 159*
6. disease

❑ *Other Explorers, page 159*
7. Holland (Dutch)

❑ *Colonies in the 1700s, page 160*
8. thirteen

The American Revolution and the Founding of America

❑ *Road to the Revolutionary War, page 160*
9. just about everything
10. Tea was dumped in Boston harbor to protest the British tax on tea.

❑ *War's Beginnings, page 161*
11. Revere and Dawes
12. (1) equality of all persons; (2) inalienable rights of life, liberty, and the pursuit of happiness; (3) rights of government come from the governed; (4) the right of the people to alter or abolish a destructive government

❑ *Revolutionary War, page 161*
13. Morristown, N.J.
14. American army and the French fleet

Growth of the New Republic

❑ *The New Nation, page 163*
15. Articles of Confederation

❑ *First Constitutional Government, page 163*
16. I. Freedom of religion, speech, press, assembly, and petition
II. Right to bear arms
III No troops can be quartered in homes without permission
IV. Warrants and probable cause needed for search and seizure
V. Rights of the accused are assured
VI. Right to a speedy public trial and the right to a lawyer
VII. Right to a jury trial
VIII. Excessive bail, excessive fines, and cruel and unusual punishment are forbidden
IX. Rights not spelled out are retained by the people
X. Powers not specifically federal are retained by the states.

❑ *Adams to Madison, page 164*
17. States can nullify federal laws in that state.
18. Louisiana Purchase

❑ *War of 1812, page 164*
19. American invasion of Canada
20. "The Star Spangled Banner"

❑ *1830–1850, page 164*
21. Missouri was admitted as a slave state.
22. Supreme Court
23. sovereign nation, then a state

❑ *Movements and Accomplishments 1800–1850, page 165*
24. It moved slaves from the South to the North.

Civil War and Reconstruction: Causes and Consequences

❑ *Road to Civil War, page 166*

25. South Carolina, Alabama, Georgia, Florida, Louisiana, Mississippi, and Texas seceded before hostilities began. Other states seceded once hostilities had begun.

❑ *Civil War, page 166*

26. Confederate attack on Fort Sumter, S.C.
27. It freed slaves in Confederate states.
28. "A government of the people, by the people, for the people"

❑ *Reconstruction, page 167*

29. XIII. Prohibits slavery
XIV. Former slaves given citizenship
XV. Voting rights for former slaves
30. 1877

Industrialization of America

❑ *1877–1897, page 168*

31. McKinley
32. to move Indians from reservations into society
33. sewing machine, typewriter

❑ *Spanish-American War, page 169*

34. Puerto Rico, Guam, and the Philippines

❑ *1900–1916, page 169*

35. Russo-Japanese War
36. Pancho Villa

World War I: Causes and Consequences

❑ *War Begins, page 170*

37. assassination of Archduke Ferdinand
38. Russian Revolution

❑ *American Involvement, page 170*

39. unrestricted submarine warfare
40. 11/11/1918, 11:00 A.M.

Post-World War I America

Prohibition, Depression, FDR, page 171

41. 25 percent
42. The Civilian Conservation Corps (CCC) put unemployed young men to work building roads, stopping erosion, and reforesting the country.
The Works Project Administration (WPA) gave other public service jobs.
The Agricultural Adjustment Act paid farmers for not growing crops.
The Federal Deposit Insurance Company (FDIC) insured bank deposits.
The Securities and Exchange Commission (SEC) oversaw the stock market.
The Tennessee Valley Authority (TVA) built hydroelectric plants and dams.

World War II: Causes and Consequences

❑ *Road to World War II, page 172*

43. The Depression
44. Spanish Civil War

❑ *World War II, page 172*

45. to occupy Estonia, Latvia, and Lithuania.
46. power to lend or transfer arms to friendly countries
47. Germany occupied suburbs of Moscow but was defeated by the Russians.
48. He gave too much to Stalin.

❑ *The Home Front, page 174*

49. Unemployment was eliminated.

Post-World War II America

❑ *The Cold War, page 174*

50. He jailed Communist leaders.

❑ *Korean War, page 175*

51. UN troops reached the Yalu River border between North Korea and China.

❑ *Civil Rights, page 176*

52. Separate but equal schools are unconstitutional.

❑ *Kennedy and Johnson, page 176*

53. Kennedy was ineffective; Johnson was very effective.

❑ *Vietnam War, page 177*

54. The United States supported France in its effort to regain control of Indochina.

❑ *Nixon, Ford, page 178*

55. Vice President Spiro Agnew resigned; Nixon appointed Ford vice president, and he was confirmed by Congress; Nixon resigned, and Ford became president.

❑ *Carter, Reagan, Bush, and Clinton, page 178*

56. none
57. Tax cuts lead to investments, which lead to jobs.
58. "No new taxes."
59. questions about his personal integrity.

World History

Prehistory and Early Civilizations

❑ *World Population, page 179*

1. 1 A.D., 200 million; 1992 A.D., 5.7 billion

❑ *Early Civilizations, page 179*

2. 3500 B.C.

❑ *Mesopotamia (4000–500 B.C.), page 179*

3. Codes of Hammurabi

Classical Civilizations

❑ *Egypt (5000–30 B.C.), page 180*

4. 2600–2100 B.C.

❑ *Greece, page 180*

5. Athens and Sparta
6. There were three: Plato, Aristotle and Socrates.
7. the death of Alexander the Great

❑ *Rome, page 180*

8. Rome gained control of both sides of the Mediterranean.
9. Antony and Cleopatra

Development of World Religions

❑ *Judaism and Christianity, page 181*

10. 300s A.D.

❑ *Islam, Buddhism, Hinduism, page 182*

11. Mohammed, 570 A.D.

Feudalism in Japan and Europe

❑ *Japan, page 182*

12. Shinto
13. They had lost power and were forbidden to wear their swords.

❑ *Europe, page 183*

14. Charlemagne
15. to force Muslims from the Holy Land

The Middle and Late Ages

❑ *The Middle and Late Ages (1300–1500), page 184*

16. She fought for France in the Hundred Years War.
17. About 50 percent.

Chinese and Indian Empires

❑ *China to 1900, page 184*

18. 550 B.C.
19. 1200–1400 A.D.
20. The Chinese resisted importation of opium.

❑ *India to 1900, page 185*

21. Dravidians
22. Nirvana
23. the invasion of India about 1200 A.D. by Turk and Afghan Muslims

Sub-Saharan Kingdoms and Cultures

❑ *Early Africa, page 187*

24. around the Nile River

❑ *Sub-Saharan Africa, page 187*

25. 1000–1100 A.D.
26. They captured and sold African slaves.

Civilizations of the Americas

❑ *Mayan Culture, page 188*

27. Mayans

❑ *Aztec, Incan Culture, page 188*

28. Incas

Rise and Expansion of Europe

❑ *Renaissance (1300–1600), page 189*

29. Greece

❑ *Reformation (1500–1600), page 189*

30. selling indulgences
31. Mary killed Protestants; Elizabeth was a Protestant.

❑ *Age of Exploration (1500–1650), page 189*

32. death from disease
33. slaves

❑ *Scientific Revolution (1550–1650), page 190*

34. The sun is at the center of the solar system.

❑ *Enlightenment (c. 1650–1790), page 190*

35. about 30
36. Michelangelo

❑ *Romanov Russia, page 191*

37. Peter the Great

❑ *French Revolution, page 191*

38. storming of the Bastille
39. Robspierre

❑ *Napoleon, page 191*
40. to Elba and then to St. Helena

❑ *Industrial Revolution (1750–1850), page 192*
41. textiles and metal

❑ *Romanticism (1790–1850), page 192*
42. personal freedom and humanitarianism

European Developments

❑ *Crimean War, page 192*
43. Turkey

❑ *Capitalism, Marxism, and Anarchism, page 192*
44. There should be no authority.

❑ *New Imperialism, page 193*
45. Africa

Other Social Studies Topics

❑ *Anthropology, page 193*
1. the evolution of primates including humans
2. material aspects of life—food, energy, and technology

❑ *Government and Political Science, page 194*
3. The executive branch is subordinate to the legislative branch

❑ *United States Government, page 194*
4. 100 percent
5. There is no set percent. Presidents are not elected by popular vote.

SOCIAL STUDIES REVIEW

There is a lot of information here. Don't try to memorize it. For most readers, a quick skimming of the information will be sufficient test preparation.

UNITED STATES HISTORY

NATIVE AMERICAN CIVILIZATIONS

Immigration

Current scholarship indicates that Native Americans, "Indians," came to this continent about 30,000 years ago. They passed over a land bridge near what is now the Bering Strait between Siberia and Alaska. These Native Americans eventually spread throughout all of North, Central, and South America.

Primitive Cultures

Even with a glacier covering Alaska, the Aleuts had established a culture on the Aleutian islands off southern Alaska by 5000 B.C. This hunting/fishing society has retained much of its ancient character.

Primitive northern woodland cultures developed in the northeastern United States about 3000 B.C. These cultures included the Algonquin-speaking tribes, such as the Shawnee, and the Iroquois Federation. There is evidence that northern woodland Indians may have been exposed to outside contact hundred of years before the arrival of Columbus.

Also at about 3000 B.C., civilizations developed in southeast North America, in and around what is now Florida and Georgia. These sophisticated cultures built cities with central plazas. The tribes of this area included the Cherokee, Choctaw, and Seminole. These tribes had highly organized governments and economic systems.

Once glaciers melted in the area, the Eskimo and Inuit Indians established a culture in northern Alaska about 1800 B.C. Their use of igloos, kayaks, and dogsleds in harsh conditions was a remarkable adaptation to their environment.

Recent Cultures

In the Southwest United States the Anasazi (Pueblo) culture developed by about 500 A.D. Pueblo and Hopi Indians built walled towns, some on the sides of inaccessible mountains or on mesas.

Around 600 A.D. a mound-building culture developed from the Mississippi River into Ohio. This culture probably built a town with a population of over 30,000 on the east side of the Mississippi River near St. Louis.

Starting about 750 A.D., a nomadic culture was established on the great plains of the United States. These Native American nomads lived in tepees as they followed and hunted herds of bison. These are probably the most popularized of Native Americans. Original tribes of this area include the Blackfoot.

Around 1400 A.D., Native Americans who became the Navajos and the Apaches migrated from Canada to the southwestern United States.

Other western tribes included the Ute and Shoshone. The Nez Pierce and Walla Walla tribes inhabited the northwestern United States. Each had advanced agricultural and cultural traditions.

By 1500 advanced Native American cultures existed across North America. However, these cultures did not rival the Aztec, Inca, and Mayan cultures of Central and South America. They were nonetheless sophisticated, organized cultures that lacked only the technological developments of Europe and Asia.

EUROPEAN EXPLORATION AND COLONIZATION

Visitors Before Columbus

A number of groups visited what is now the United States before Columbus sailed. Whether by accident or design, sailors from Iceland, Europe, and Africa came to this continent before 1000 A.D. It appears that Celtic and Norse settlements were established in North America between 1000 and 1300 A.D. These settlements were not maintained.

Columbus

Notoriety greeted Columbus as he returned to Spain from the first of his four voyages. Columbus never reached the mainland of North America, but he landed throughout the Caribbean and established a settlement in what is now the Dominican Republic.

English Colonization

John Cabot reached the mainland in 1497 and claimed the land for England. In 1584 Sir Walter Raleigh established the "lost colony" on Roanoke Island just off the North Carolina coast. The settlement failed when all the settlers disappeared, leaving a cryptic message carved in a tree.

In 1607 the English established Jamestown, Virginia, under John Smith. Tobacco exports sustained the colony, and slaves from Africa were brought to Jamestown in 1619. In that same year, the House of Burgesses was formed as the first elected governing body in America.

In 1620 Pilgrims left England on the Mayflower to escape religious persecution. The Pilgrims established a colony at Provincetown and then a second colony at Plymouth in December 1620. The Pilgrims drafted and received popular approval for the Mayflower Compact as a way of governing their colony.

Spanish Exploration

Cortez conquered Mexico around 1520, and Pizarro conquered Peru around 1530. The Spaniards imported slaves from Africa at this time. Records of the native civilizations were destroyed, and natives were forced to convert to Catholicism. The Spanish also imported diseases, which effectively wiped out whole populations of natives. In North America the Spanish established a fort in St. Augustine, Florida, around 1565 and in Santa Fe, New Mexico, around 1610.

Other Explorers

In the 1500s the French through Cartier explored the Great Lakes. The French city of Quebec was founded about 1609.

Henry Hudson, under Dutch contract, explored the East Coast and the Hudson River in the 1600s. The Dutch established settlements under Peter Minuit in Manhattan about 1624. The Dutch built the first road for wheeled vehicles in America around 1650.

Colonies in the 1700s

By 1740 there were 13 English colonies, all located along the eastern seaboard. These colonies grew in size and prosperity and developed diversified populations by the time of the Revolutionary War. The colonists were in an almost constant state of conflict with Native Americans, with Spanish colonists, and with the French in the French and Indian wars.

THE AMERICAN REVOLUTION AND THE FOUNDING OF AMERICA

ROAD TO THE REVOLUTIONARY WAR

This chronology details the causes up to the Revolutionary War. Note how cumulative the causes are and how a change in English policy might have averted the conflict.

1763 Proclamation of 1763

After the English won the French and Indian War they signed the Proclamation of 1763, which forbade colonial expansion west of the current colonies. The proclamation was designed to avoid unnecessary expenditures and to appease France. It angered many colonists.

1764 Sugar Act

The English government was in serious financial debt after the French and Indian War. The English government levied a sugar tax on the colonies to help pay for the war. Colonists protested this tax saying it was "taxation without representation."

1765

In 1765 England passed a law called the Quartering Act. The act required colonial governments to pay for quarters and supplies for English troops and to quarter these troops in barracks and inns and taverns.

The Stamp Act required every legal piece of paper (college degrees, policies, licenses, etc.) to carry a tax stamp. The act was protested vehemently and eventually repealed by England.

These acts led to many colonial reactions. Patrick Henry spoke against the acts in the Virginia House of Burgesses. Revolutionary groups called Sons of Liberty were formed.

1767 Townsend Acts

The Townsend Acts were import duties on most things used by colonists. Colonists objected, and some tax officials in Boston were attacked. British troops were sent to Boston. Three years later, the British repealed all the Townsend duties except for the duties on tea!

1770 Boston Massacre

British troops fired on colonial protesters, killing five including Crispus Attucks in the Boston Massacre. The English soldiers were defended by patriots including John Adams. Other tensions continued for the next three years.

1773 Boston Tea Party

To protest the remaining import tax on tea, men dressed as Indians boarded English ships in Boston Harbor. They dumped hundreds of chests of tea into Boston Harbor in what has come to be known as the Boston Tea Party. In retaliation Britain closed Boston Harbor and took more direct control of the colony.

1774 First Continental Congress

In September, representatives from each colony except Georgia met at the First Continental Congress in Philadelphia. The congress called on the colonies to boycott goods from England until the English repealed the tax on tea and opened Boston Harbor. Massachusetts minutemen armed themselves and were declared in rebellion by Parliament.

WAR'S BEGINNINGS

1775

On April 18, 1775, English General Gage left Boston to commandeer arms at Concord. Revere and Dawes rode out to alert the minutemen. The English troops first encountered minutemen in Lexington. The first shot was fired, but no one knows by whom. There were American and English dead. British troops destroyed supplies at Concord but were decimated by minuteman attacks on the march back to Boston. Hostilities had begun.

The Second Continental Congress named George Washington commander-in-chief. The Congress asked England for negotiations but was rebuked.

Gage attacked colonists on the top of Breeds Hill (Bunker Hill because of the bunker on top). The British won the battle but at a tremendous loss, establishing the fighting ability of colonial forces.

1776

In this year Thomas Paine wrote his pamphlet *Common Sense*, which favored American independence. On July 4, 1776, the Continental Congress approved the Declaration of Independence authored by Jefferson.

The Declaration included four self-evident truths:

1. Equality of all persons.
2. Inalienable rights of life, liberty, and the pursuit of happiness.
3. Rights of the government come from the governed.
4. The right of the people to alter or abolish a destructive government.

REVOLUTIONARY WAR

1775

The battles of Bunker Hill and Concord and Lexington took place in 1775. Fighting also broke out in Virginia.

1776

In March, Washington laid siege to Boston. The British sent forces to New York. Washington failed in his attempt to drive the British out of New York and withdrew across New Jersey to Pennsylvania. Washington led a successful surprise attack against the British in Trenton, New Jersey, in December.

1777

In January, Washington followed up his Trenton victory with a successful attack at Princeton. Washington spent the remainder of the winter in camp at Morristown, New Jersey. The British, under Howe, attacked and occupied the American capital at Philadelphia. The fighting delayed Howe's planned move to Saratoga, New York. This action enabled American militia under Gates to defeat British troops from Canada at Saratoga.

The American victory at Saratoga and the British occupation of Philadelphia moved the French to recognize America. The French joined the war as allies in 1778. This action by France was the decisive moment in the Revolutionary War. Washington's forces spent the winter in Valley Forge, Pennsylvania.

1778

American forces suffered through a harsh winter in Valley Forge, while British forces were much better accommodated in New York and Philadelphia. The forces from Philadelphia marched to New York under the new British general, Clinton. They narrowly avoided defeat at the Battle of Monmouth in June. Late that year, British forces conquered Georgia.

1779

Fighting took place primarily around the British main headquarters in New York. Late in the year Clinton took the British army south.

1780

When Clinton captured Charleston, South Carolina, Cornwallis took over the southern army, while Clinton returned to New York. Cornwallis defeated American forces under Gates. Things were looking bleak for American forces, and American General Benedict Arnold became a traitor.

Then American forces under George Rogers Clark won a battle in the northwest while frontiersmen defeated Cornwallis in North Carolina.

1781

Cornwallis was beset by American guerrillas including Francis Marion, the swamp fox. Cornwallis moved into Virginia and maneuvered himself into a trap at Yorktown. Surrounded by American forces on the land and the French fleet in Chesapeake Bay, Cornwallis surrendered on October 17, 1781.

1782–1783

England decided to withdraw from the colonies. In 1783 Britain and the United States signed the Treaty of Paris, which gave the United States lands east of the Mississippi.

GROWTH OF THE NEW REPUBLIC

The New Nation

In 1781 the Articles of Confederation, drawn up in 1777, were approved. The Land Ordinance of 1785 established surveys of the Northwest Territories. (These territories became states such as Ohio and Illinois.) The Northwest Ordinance detailed the way in which states would be carved out of these territories.

The Articles of Confederation proved too weak and a Constitutional Convention convened during 1787 in Philadelphia. A compromise Constitution was written with special efforts by James Madison. The Constitution was sent to Congress, which approved it and in turn submitted it to the states for ratification.

The state ratification process fostered a brisk debate. Alexander Hamilton, John Jay, and James Madison authored *The Federalist Papers* to support ratification. Anti-Federalists were concerned that the Constitution did not sufficiently protect individual rights.

Delaware was the first state to ratify the Constitution in 1787 and Rhode Island was the last to ratify in 1790. Many of the ratification votes were very close. Strict versus loose construction of the Constitution has been a contentious issue since its ratification.

First Constitutional Government

New York was chosen as the temporary capital. Once the required nine states had ratified the Constitution, George Washington was sworn in as the first president on April 30, 1789. John Adams was sworn in as vice president.

The concern of the Anti-Federalists was partially answered in 1791 when the first ten amendments to the Constitution were ratified. A summary of the Bill of Rights follows.

I. Freedom of religion, speech, press, assembly, and petition
II. Right to bear arms
III. No troops can be quartered in homes without permission
IV. Warrants and probable cause needed for search and seizure
V. Rights of the accused are assured
VI. Right to a speedy public trial and the right to a lawyer
VII. Right to a jury trial
VIII. Excessive bail, excessive fines, and cruel and unusual punishment are forbidden
IX. Rights not spelled out are retained by the people
X. Powers not specifically federal are retained by the states.

The issue of a stronger versus a weaker central government was an active debate then as it is now. Washington was elected without opposition for his second term, the differences between Jeffersonians (less government, Democrat-Republicans) and Hamiltonians (more government, Federalists) led to a two party system.

In 1796 Washington bade farewell as president with three gems of advice for the country:

1. Avoid political parties based on geographic boundaries.
2. Avoid permanent alliances with foreign powers.
3. Safeguard the ability of America to pay its national debts.

Adams to Madison

In the 1796 presidential election, John Adams eked out a victory over Jefferson. In the controversial XYZ affair, France sought bribes from America. Concern about France led to the Alien and Sedition Acts. These acts put pressure on noncitizens and forbade writing that criticized the government.

Some western states opposed these acts and wanted to nullify the acts for their state. This Theory of Nullification, and the states' rights mentioned in the tenth amendment to the Constitution, raised issues still important today.

In 1800 Aaron Burr and Jefferson were tied for the presidency. Alexander Hamilton supported Jefferson. Jefferson won the vote in Congress and served a second term. Four years later, Burr killed Hamilton in a duel.

Jefferson resisted the demands of Barbary pirates for tribute. In 1801 Tripoli declared war on the United States, and Jefferson successfully blockaded the Tripoli coast. Tribute continued to be paid to other Barbary states.

Jefferson also purchased the Louisiana Territory from France, doubling the size of the country. In 1804 Jefferson sent Lewis and Clark to explore the territory and open it for settlement.

Madison was elected president in 1808 and again in 1812. For a number of years, British ships had been impressing American sailors at sea. In response to this practice, the war hawks pressed for war with Britain in 1811.

War of 1812

The War of 1812 began with a failed American invasion of Canada. The U.S.S. *Constitution* (Old Ironsides) and "Don't Give Up the Ship" Admiral Perry were active in this conflict. The British sacked and burned Washington and unsuccessfully attacked Fort McHenry. Francis Scott Key wrote "The Star Spangled Banner" while a prisoner on a British ship off Fort McHenry. After the war had been declared officially over, Andrew Jackson fought and defeated the British at the Battle of New Orleans.

Federalists had opposed the war and ceased to exist as a viable political party. In the wake of the Federalist collapse, Monroe was elected president in 1816 and again in 1820. In treaties with Spain and England, under the leadership of John Quincy Adams, the United States established borders with Canada, acquired Florida from Spain, and gave up any claims to Texas.

1830–1850

Missouri Compromise

The Missouri Compromise of 1820 was a response to rapid westward expansion and the slavery issue. It admitted Maine as a free state and Missouri as a slave state and excluded slavery in the northern part of the Louisiana Purchase. The compromise maintained the balance of free and slave states.

Monroe

James Monroe and John Quincy Adams established the Monroe Doctrine in 1823. The doctrine said: (1) the Americas were off limits for further colonization, (2) the political system in the United States was different from Europe, (3) the United States would see danger if European states meddled in the United States, and (4) the United States would not interfere in the internal affairs of other states or their established colonies.

Jackson

In 1824 Andrew Jackson entered the electoral college with a plurality of votes. He still lost in the House of Representatives to J.Q. Adams.

In 1828 Jackson was elected president. In this year, people voted directly for electors in all but 2 of 24 states. Jackson used a "kitchen cabinet" of friends to advise him on important issues. Jackson favored the removal of Native Americans to reservations and ignored Supreme Court decisions in favor of the Native Americans. This "trail of tears" is an uncomfortable American story. The age of Jackson marks a time of increased democracy in the United States.

Van Buren

Martin Van Buren was elected president in 1836. On the heels of the financial panic of 1837, Van Buren lost the presidency to William Harrison in 1840. Harrison died less than a month after his inauguration. John Tyler, the vice president, succeeded to the presidency.

Polk

James K. Polk was elected president in 1844. There had been conflict in Texas since 1836. Despite a loss at the Alamo, Texas became a sovereign country. After years of debate and in-fighting, Polk was able to get congressional approval, and Texas was admitted as a slave state in 1844.

Mexican-American War

Mexico objected, and the Mexican-American War started in 1846. U.S. generals, including Robert E. Lee, advanced into Mexico and captured Mexico City. The Treaty of Guadeloupe Hidalgo ended the war, and the United States acquired Texas south to the Rio Grande as well as the California and New Mexico Territories. Much of the manifest destiny of the United States to stretch from sea to sea had been achieved under Polk.

Taylor

Zachary Taylor, a general in the Mexican-American War, was elected president in 1848. Slavery remained a significant and contentious issue. In 1849 gold was discovered near Sutters Mill in California. The gold rush brought thousands of prospectors and settlers to California.

The Compromise of 1850 specified whether territories would be granted statehood as a free or slave state and contained a strict fugitive slave law. *Uncle Tom's Cabin* by Harriet Beecher Stowe was published in 1852.

Movements and Accomplishments 1800–1850

Horace Mann and others established public schools and training schools for teachers. The women's movement, featuring an 1848 meeting in Seneca Falls, New York, did not achieve much success. Abolitionists were active. The Underground Railroad helped slaves escape to the North. The temperance movement reduced the consumption of alcohol. Transcendentalist writers, who believed in the sanctity and importance of individual experience, were active during this period. These writers included James Fenimore Cooper, Ralph Waldo Emerson, Henry David Thoreau, and Herman Melville.

Large groups of non-English, Catholic immigrants arrived in New York. In the 1840s there was regular steamship travel between Liverpool, England, and New York City.

THE CIVIL WAR AND RECONSTRUCTION: CAUSES AND CONSEQUENCES

Road to Civil War

Pierce

Franklin Pierce was elected president in 1852. There was bloody warfare in Kansas over whether Kansas should enter the union as a free or slave state. Another significant event was Commodore Perry's visit to Japan, opening Japan to the West.

Buchanan

James Buchanan was elected president in 1856. In 1857 the Supreme Court decided the *Dred Scott* case. They found that Dred Scott, a slave, was property, not a citizen, and had no standing in the court.

John Brown

In 1859 an erratic John Brown launched an ill-prepared raid on the arsenal in Harpers Ferry, Virginia. Brown was tried, executed, and became a martyr in the abolitionist movement.

Lincoln

In 1860, and again in 1864, Abraham Lincoln was elected president. Southern states sought assurances about their right to hold slaves. Slaves were too important to the southern economy, and attempts at compromise failed. South Carolina seceded in December 1860. Alabama, Georgia, Florida, Louisiana, Mississippi, and Texas soon followed. In February 1861 the Confederate States of America (CSA) was formed with Jefferson Davis as its president.

Civil War

On April 12, 1861, Confederate forces attacked Fort Sumter in South Carolina. Arkansas, North Carolina, Tennessee, and Virginia seceded once hostilities began.

The war pitted brother against brother, and one in every 30 Americans was killed or wounded. The North had a larger population and an industrialized economy. The South had an agrarian economy.

Neither the English nor the French (who tried to conquer Mexico) supported the South. The English did build some Confederate ships.

While Northern troops performed poorly in initial battles, the North was too strong and too populous for the South. Lee's generalship during the early war years sustained the South.

Monitor *and* Merrimack

Northern ships blockaded Southern ports. This blockade effectively denied foreign goods to the South. The Confederate ironclad *Monitor* sailed out to challenge blockading ships in 1862, sinking several Union ships. The *Monitor* was challenged and repulsed by the Union ironclad *Merrimack* in March 1862.

Emancipation Proclamation

In 1862 Lincoln issued the Emancipation Proclamation. The proclamation freed all the slaves in Confederate states.

Sherman's March

The Union launched a successful attack on the South through Tennessee. New Orleans was captured in 1862. A final wedge was driven through the South with the capture of Vicksburg,

Mississippi, in 1863. Atlanta fell in 1864. Sherman then launched his infamous march to the sea, which cut a 20-mile wide swath of destruction through the South. Sherman reached the Gulf of Mexico in December 1864.

Gettysburg

Confederate forces did much better in and around Virginia, and there were draft riots in New York City during 1863. Lee brilliantly led his army and invaded Pennsylvania in 1863. The advance ended with Lee's questionable decision to launch Pickett's charge against the massed Union forces at Gettysburg.

Four months after the battle, Lincoln delivered the Gettysburg Address at the dedication of the Union Cemetery near Gettysburg. The brief transcendent address ends "...government of the people, by the people, for the people shall not perish from the earth."

War's End

In 1864 Grant took command of the Union Army of the Potomac. He waged a war of attrition against Lee. Richmond fell on April 2, 1865. On April 9, 1865, Lee surrendered at Appomattox Court House, Virginia.

Lincoln was assassinated five days later on April 15, 1865.

Homestead Act

In 1862 the Homestead Act made public lands available to Western settlers. Public lands were granted to the Union Pacific and Central Pacific companies to build rail lines from Omaha to California. After the war, farmers and settlers moved west.

Reconstruction

Three civil rights amendments were adopted between 1865 and 1870.

XIII. Prohibited slavery (1865)
XIV. Slaves given citizenship and rights (1868)
XV. Voting rights for former slaves (1870)

Johnson

Andrew Johnson became president after Lincoln was assassinated. During his administration, William Seward acquired Alaska (Seward's Folly) and occupied Midway Island. Johnson's dismissal of Secretary of War Stanton led to Johnson's impeachment (legislative indictment). Johnson survived the impeachment ballot by one vote.

Southern states slowly returned to the Union, but troops stayed in the South until 1877. During Reconstruction, former slaves gained some power in the South. This power did not last beyond 1877. Carpetbaggers from the North collaborated with white scalawags and former slaves to keep Confederates out of power. In turn, the Black Codes and the KKK emerged as ways to subjugate and terrorize former slaves. Grandfather clauses, which stated that you couldn't vote if your grandfather didn't, were used to deny former slaves the vote.

Grant

In 1868 and again in 1872, Ulysses S. Grant was elected president. Corruption was widespread in Grant's government. The "Whiskey Ring" involved members of Grant's administration in fraud. Boss Tweed and the Tweed Ring were looting the New York City treasury.

The Indian Wars continued. In 1876 Sioux chiefs Sitting Bull and Crazy Horse defeated Custer and his cavalry at the Little Big Horn River in Montana.

INDUSTRIALIZATION OF AMERICA

1877–1897

Individual presidents in the late 1800s were not notable, and this was the era of caretaker presidents. The highlights of this era were the growth of business, economic conditions, and other national events and issues. The presidents in this period were:

Rutherford B. Hayes	1876	Wins a close disputed election
James A. Garfield	1880	Shot and killed in 1881
Chester Arthur	1881	Succeeds Garfield
Grover Cleveland	1884, 1892	
William Henry Harrison	1888	
William McKinley	1896, 1900	Shot and killed in 1901

In 1877 Hayes directed the removal of troops from the South and southern whites reestablished their control over the South. Reconstruction was over.

Indian Wars

During this period most of the Indian Wars were concluded. Until now the government moved Indians onto reserved areas (reservations). But in 1887, under the Dawes Severalty Act, the federal government tried to move Indians from reservations into society. The act failed, and Indians continued to be treated poorly.

Railroads

The unfenced frontier, which had produced most of American western folklore, was shrinking. By 1890 railroads, settlers, and farmers had brought it to a final end.

The railroads brought other changes to American life. Chinese immigrants who came to work on the railroads were banned from immigration by 1890. Huge herds of buffalo were killed so that they could not interfere with train travel. Railroads stimulated the economy and created a unified United States.

Business and Commerce

Inventions during this period included the telephone (Alexander Graham Bell) and the light bulb (Thomas Alva Edison).

But it was business and profits that ruled the time. John D. Rockefeller formed the Standard Oil Trust. A trust could control many companies and monopolize business. Business owners cut wages and hired new workers if there was a strike. Social Darwinism, popular during this time, stressed the survival of the fittest. Trusts grew so rapidly that the Sherman Anti-Trust Act was passed in 1890. Any trust "in restraint of trade" was illegal.

Sewing machines and typewriters drew many women to the workforce. Clara Barton founded the Red Cross in 1881.

Unions

Unions tried to respond. In 1878 the Knights of Labor started to organize workers successfully. The union collapsed after the Chicago Haymarket Riot in 1888. The American Federation of Labor, under Samuel Gompers, successfully organized workers in 1886.

The government intervened in several strike situations. In 1894 Grover Cleveland used troops to break the Pullman Strike. In 1902 Teddy Roosevelt sided with coal miners in the Anthracite Coal Strike.

Another issue was hard versus cheap money. Hard money meant that currency was linked to something valuable (gold), limiting inflation. Cheap money removes the linkage, hastening inflation.

Immigration

Immigration increased dramatically after 1880. The new immigrants to the United States now came from eastern and southern Europe. Many immigrants settled in urban areas in the eastern United States. Living conditions were difficult in tenements. Urban gangs and crime were common during this period.

Literature

Horatio Alger's rags to riches stories were very popular. Mark Twain (Samuel Clemens) wrote *The Adventures of Tom Sawyer* (1876) and *The Adventures of Huckleberry Finn* (1884). Joseph Pulitzer (Pulitzer Prize) introduced a yellow comic page in his newspaper. "Yellow journalism" came to mean sensationalized journalism.

Temperance

The temperance movement was making steady progress to prohibition (enacted in 1919). Carrie Nation was famous for smashing liquor bottles with a hatchet. Elizabeth Cady Stanton and Susan B. Anthony led the women's suffrage movement. (Suffrage for women came with the Nineteenth Amendment in 1920, nearly 125 years after the U.S. Constitution was adopted.)

Spanish-American War

During Spanish suppression of a Cuban revolt in 1898, the battleship *Maine* was sunk in Havana Harbor. Popular reaction led to the Spanish-American War in Cuba and the Philippines. The war lasted eight months with most casualties coming from disease. The treaty ending the war gave the United States Puerto Rico, Guam, and the Philippines. In unrelated actions, the United States also annexed Wake Island and Hawaii.

1900–1916

Teddy Roosevelt

In 1901 Teddy Roosevelt succeeded McKinley. Roosevelt was re-elected in 1904. Roosevelt was a progressive opposed to monopolies. Roosevelt was particularly moved by the novel *The Jungle* (Upton Sinclair), which exposed abuses in the meat-packing industry. Roosevelt championed conservation. Roosevelt used "big stick diplomacy," and the United States started to become policeman of the world. Roosevelt earned the Nobel Peace Prize for arranging a cessation to the Russo-Japanese War.

Taft

William Howard Taft was elected president in 1908. Taft continued Roosevelt's campaign against monopolies and established the Bureau of Mines. Some of Taft's policies on conservation offended Teddy Roosevelt. Roosevelt established the Bull Moose Party for the 1912 election.

Wilson

In 1912 Woodrow Wilson was elected president with about 40 percent of the vote in a three way race with Roosevelt and Taft. Wilson was a scholarly man who hated war. Wilson established the Federal Reserve Banking System in 1913. His Federal Trade Commission Act helped unions and forbade monopolies. The Mexican Revolution in 1910 led to the U.S. army's pursuit of Pancho Villa in Mexico in 1916.

WORLD WAR I: CAUSES AND CONSEQUENCES

War Begins

Europe was ripe for war. The balance of power had been destroyed, and Germany had a military advantage. There was tremendous tension in and around the Slavic, Balkan area of southeastern Europe that was controlled by the German Austro-Hungarian Empire.

Then a single act occurred. Archduke Ferdinand of Austria was assassinated on June 28, 1914. The unrest that followed led to Germany declaring war on Russia on August 1, 1914. Woodrow Wilson declared U.S. neutrality. By 1915 the Central powers of Germany, Austria-Hungary, Bulgaria, and Turkey were at war with the Allies of England, France, Japan, and Russia. (The United States joined the Allies in 1917.)

So began the war that was to claim over 12,000,000 lives and decimate Europe. The war consisted of two fronts—Western (France, etc.) and Eastern (Russia, etc.). The war soon deteriorated into trench warfare, which led to a virtual stalemate for four destructive years. Airplanes, tanks, poison gas, and machine guns were all introduced during this conflict.

The Russian Revolution occurred in 1917 as World War I was underway. The Bolsheviks gained power. As they had promised, the Bolsheviks withdrew from the war, even though Russia gave up over 1,000,000 square miles of land with over 50,000,000 people in the peace settlement.

American Involvement

The sinking of the cruise liner *Lusitania* in 1915 with 139 Americans on board marked the beginning of American involvement in the war. Wilson was outraged when Germany started to use submarines and protested when the *Lusitania* was sunk. The Germans agreed to stop unrestricted submarine warfare. In 1917 the Germans resumed unrestricted submarine warfare, and the United States declared war on Germany. The American Expeditionary Force (AEF) arrived in France on June 25, 1917. The Allies fought back German attacks and launched their own offensive in 1918. Germany signed a very demanding armistice, and the war ended on the eleventh hour of the eleventh day of the eleventh month in 1918.

The Germans were forced to sign the Treaty of Versailles on June 28, 1919, which officially ended World War I. Japan and Italy (Allies) were not pleased with some of the terms of the Treaty of Versailles.

League of Nations

As the war was drawing to a close, Wilson presented his Fourteen Points. These points form a basis for the Treaty of Versailles, which ended the war, and for the League of Nations. The league was formed in 1919 and lasted until the 1940s. The forerunner of the United Nations was built on President Wilson's Fourteen Points. The United States' seat was never filled because the Senate did not ratify the Treaty of Versailles. The League of Nations sought to provide mechanisms for worldwide monetary control, conflict resolution, and humanitarian assistance.

POST-WORLD WAR I AMERICA

Prohibition

Warren G. Harding was elected president in 1920. Calvin Coolidge became president in 1923 when Harding died. Coolidge was elected in 1924. Herbert Hoover was elected president in 1928.

Prohibition dominated this period, and America entered the roaring twenties. Speakeasys had liquor for those who wanted in, and distilling became a huge underground industry. Gangsters such as Al Capone were prominent on the American scene.

Sigmund Freud's views of sexuality had become well known, and the country entered the sexual revolution. In the "Monkey Trial," John Scopes was tried and convicted of teaching evolution in a Tennessee school.

Depression

In October 1929 the stock market crashed. People lost their investments and often their homes. Banks failed, and people lost their deposits. Excessive borrowing, greed, and ineffective regulations were all factors in the collapse. The Depression began and spread throughout the world.

During the Depression, unemployment reached 25 percent. Some workers had no employment for years. Hoover took an ineffective hands-off approach. He did support the Reconstruction Finance Corporation, which lent money to employers in the hope that it would "trickle down" to the unemployed.

Franklin Delano Roosevelt

In 1932 Franklin Delano Roosevelt (FDR) was elected president in a landslide victory. He was reelected in 1936, 1940, and 1944. Roosevelt's Democratic Party enjoyed an enormous margin in the Congress during this time.

FDR offered the country a New Deal. He said, "the only thing we have to fear is fear itself," and held radio fireside chats that reassured the country. A summary of the New Deal actions follow in a sort of governmental alphabet soup.

- The Civilian Conservation Corps (CCC) put unemployed young men to work building roads, stopping erosion, and reforesting the country.
- The Works Project Administration (WPA) gave other public service jobs.
- The Agricultural Adjustment Act provided subsidies to farmers for not growing crops.
- The Federal Deposit Insurance Company (FDIC) insured bank deposits.
- The Securities and Exchange Commission (SEC) oversaw the stock market.
- The Tennessee Valley Authority (TVA) built hydroelectric plants and controlled floods.

The Second New Deal started in 1934 and included the following acts.

- The Social Security Act gave unemployment insurance and other humanitarian relief.
- The National Labor Relations Board (Wagner Act) gave the right of collective bargaining.
- The Fair Labor Standards Act set a minimum wage.

WORLD WAR II: CAUSES AND CONSEQUENCES

Road to World War II

Germany and Hitler

The Depression of the late 1920s ruined the German economy. Imports and exports fell while unemployment soared. Germany was also frustrated by what they saw as the harsh Treaty of Versailles.

Out of all this emerged Adolf Hitler, a would-be artist who had emerged from World War I as a decorated corporal. In 1920 he had founded the Nazi Party and put together a group of "brown shirts" to exert his will forcefully. With 50,000 or so followers he tried to take power in 1923 in the Beer Hall Putsch. He was arrested and jailed, where he dictated *Mein Kampf* to Rudolf Hess.

Between 1930 and 1932 Hitler's Nazi Party got increasing vote counts. Hitler was made Chancellor, and then his party gained control of the legislature. In 1933 all political parties were outlawed except the Nazi Party. In that same year the Gestapo was established, and Hitler became Fuhrer on August 2, 1934.

Anti-Semitism

Anti-Semitism was rampant in Germany, and Jews were declined civil service employment. The regime became a harsh dictatorship in which no dissent was tolerated. However, economic conditions improved dramatically under Hitler, and military manufacturing just about erased unemployment. Hitler was supported by the German people, and the world was moving toward war.

Spanish Civil War

The United States proclaimed neutrality in 1935, 1936, and 1937. No belligerents were permitted to purchase arms from America. The United States also stayed neutral in the Spanish Civil War.

The Spanish Civil War (1936–1939) provided a testing ground for Hitler and his military leaders. The German Air Force fought on the side of the Fascist leader Franco, and the war united Hitler and the Italian dictator Mussolini. In 1938 Hitler bullied and then captured Austria, and later annexed Czechoslovakia.

Japan

The Depression also caused great economic hardship in Japan, and military leaders gained more power. In 1931 Japan occupied Manchuria, and in 1937 war broke out between Japan and China. In 1938 Japan announced its intentions to establish a new order in Asia. In 1940 Japan signed a formal alliance with Germany and Italy.

World War II

On September 1, 1939, Hitler invaded Poland without provocation. England and France declared war on Germany a few days later, and World War II began.

World War II began with the Soviet Union on the sidelines. In fact, the Soviets used this time to occupy Estonia, Latvia, and Lithuania and to force concessions from Finland. The Allies included England, France, and eventually the United States. The Axis powers included Germany, Japan, and Italy.

German forces launched a major offensive against Belgium, France, and the Netherlands and attacked Denmark and Norway. The Germans by-passed the fortified Maginot line armament by attacking through Luxembourg. About 400,000 British and French troops were trapped but managed to escape without their equipment from around Dunkirk.

Germany tried to conquer Britain from the air in the Battle of Britain. While devastating, this tactic was unsuccessful. The Germans considered and then abandoned a plan to invade England.

Churchill

Just before this time, British Prime Minister Chamberlain was replaced by Winston Churchill. Churchill had long warned of German intentions. Once the war began, the United States began to cooperate with England. The Lend-Lease Act of 1941 allowed the president to sell, lend, or transfer arms to countries vital to American defense. Roosevelt used this act to aid England.

France

Paris fell in June 1940, and France surrendered. The Vichy government of France followed a policy of collaboration. Only a few Frenchmen joined the Free French movement led by Charles DeGaulle from London.

United States

In 1940 Charles Lindbergh, the first person to fly solo across the Atlantic (1927), supported Hitler's call for an expanded Germany. Roosevelt said the United States would not enter the war, and he was re-elected.

In 1941 Roosevelt met with Churchill off Newfoundland and signed the Atlantic Charter. The charter's postwar goals roughly incorporated Roosevelt's Four Freedoms: Freedom of Speech and Expression; Freedom of Religion; Freedom from Want; Freedom from Fear.

Second Front

Hitler turned his attention to Russia in June, 1941. He began Operation Barbarosa, an invasion of Russia with 3,000,000 Axis troops. The invasion was initially successful, and Axis troops actually entered the suburbs of Moscow in November 1941. A combination of the Russian winter, very long supply lines, and a Russian counterattack drove the Axis forces away from Moscow during the winter of 1941–1942.

The German army attacked Russia again and was stopped literally in the streets of Stalingrad. Hitler forbade a retreat, and German forces were surrounded and decimated. The German forces at Stalingrad surrendered in January 1943, and the Russians moved to the offensive.

Pearl Harbor

On December 7, 1941, Japan attacked the United States at Pearl Harbor. The attack brought the United States into war against Japan, Germany, and Italy. American involvement in the war ultimately led to the defeat of Axis forces.

North Africa

The Italians and the Afrika Corps under German General Rommel controlled North Africa. Combined British and American forces launched a combined offensive that trapped Axis forces and led to their surrender in 1943.

Battle of the Atlantic

During the early years of the war, German U-boats were winning the Battle of the Atlantic. Adequate supplies could not reach England and Europe. Improved ships, planes, and sonar reversed this trend, and by 1943 the Atlantic was an unsafe place for German submarines.

Invasion

In January 1943 Churchill and Roosevelt met at Casablanca and planned the future conduct of the war. On June 6, 1944, after the successful invasion of Italy, the Allied forces under Dwight

Eisenhower launched Operation Overlord, an invasion of France from England. It was the largest amphibious operation ever undertaken. The invasion was successful and by the end of 1944 all France had been recaptured and Allied forces were poised at German borders. Soviet forces had also been successful in their operations in Poland.

Resistance to Hitler's leadership developed in Germany. On July 20, 1944, Hitler survived a bomb blast designed to kill him. His survival meant that there would be no truce.

American, British, Russian, and other Allied forces attacked Germany simultaneously. Hitler committed suicide in his bunker, and the German army surrendered. Already, American and British leaders were questioning the results of their alliance with Stalin and the Soviet Union.

Yalta

In February 1945, Churchill, Roosevelt, and Stalin met at Yalta and agreements were reached about postwar political subdivisions. Many have criticized Roosevelt's participation in this meeting. In their view, Roosevelt made agreements too favorable to Stalin.

Potsdam

In July 1945 Stalin and Churchill met at Potsdam with newly inaugurated President Truman (Roosevelt had died after the Yalta meeting). While at the conference, Churchill was defeated for prime minister.

The Bomb and VJ Day

Truman learned of the successful test of the atomic bomb (Manhattan Project) while at Potsdam. After deciding that there was no practical way to demonstrate the bomb's force, it was dropped twice on Japan. The cities of Hiroshima and Nagasaki were obliterated. A new era of warfare had begun and the Japanese surrendered immediately. The surrender was taken on the battleship *Missouri* in Tokyo Bay under the leadership of General Douglas MacArthur.

The Home Front

With about 12,000,000 Americans in the armed forces during World War II, unemployment was eliminated. New businesses were created, and many new workers, particularly women, entered the work force. "Rosie the Riveter" became the symbol of these new workers. The Office of Price Administration (OPA) issued ration books and set prices. Other government boards regulated business and labor.

The only documented attack on the United States occurred when a Japanese submarine shelled a refinery in California. However, fear of Japanese Americans reached hysterical proportions. All Japanese Americans, most of them American citizens, were sent to internment camps. None were accused of wrongdoing. They were not released until the end of the war.

POST-WORLD WAR II AMERICA

The Cold War

The Cold War broke out immediately after WW II. Immediate divisions appeared between Russia and the other Allies. Speaking in Fulton, Missouri in 1946, Churchill said that an Iron Curtain had descended across the Continent, describing Soviet isolation from the rest of the world.

Occupation

Germany and Berlin were divided into four Occupation Zones—American, British, French, and Russian. Berlin was inside the Russian zone. The Russians blockaded land access to Berlin, but the blockade was overcome by the Berlin Airlift.

Truman

After succeeding Roosevelt, Harry Truman won an upset victory over New York Governor Thomas Dewey in 1948 and served as president until 1952.

Truman reacted to the Cold War and fear of communism by issuing the Truman Doctrine. The doctrine stipulated that the United States would help any free countries resisting armed minorities. The United States entered a period of Soviet containment designed to counter worldwide Soviet pressure.

At home, Truman used the Smith Act, designed for use against World War II subversives, to jail domestic Communist leaders. A Loyalty Board and the House UnAmerican Activities Committee also investigated Communist infiltration into government.

Marshall Plan

The Marshall Plan helped rebuild Europe with West Germany reaping the greatest benefits. The United Nations was established with a Security Council consisting mainly of Allied countries. Stalin pushed for recovery at home while taking further control of Eastern Europe. Germany remained under Allied occupation.

Israel

The mass killings of Jews in concentration camps during Hitler's regime gained support for a Jewish State in Palestine. In 1948 Israel was established and a series of conflicts with Egypt and other Arab states began.

NATO

Following the Berlin Airlift, the North Atlantic Treaty Organization was formed, which united the European allies in a military alliance. NATO was strengthened in the aftermath of the Korean War. The Cold War between the Western powers and Russia became a nuclear arms race.

Soviet Union

Brooding and paranoid, Stalin died in 1953. Khrushchev and his successors Brezhnev, Andropov, and Gorbachev attacked his ruthlessness and relaxed the political climate. Gradually, countries occupied or controlled by the Soviet Union sought freedom or autonomy. These freedom movements, such as in Hungary, were usually thwarted by a Soviet military reaction.

Later Developments

Britain and Western Europe formed a Common Market designed to create a free trade zone and to stimulate commerce. Soviet Communist influence decreased markedly in the 1980s. Countries occupied by Russia sought and gained freedom. East and West Germany were reunited at a great cost to West Germany. Satellites of Russia, such as Cuba, stopped receiving aid. Provinces of Russia were in revolt and there was open warfare between the Russian President Yeltsin and the Russian parliament. Some have concluded that the Cold War is over and that communism has fallen.

There are still tensions throughout the world, and open warfare raged during the 1990s in what was Yugoslavia, Albania, and African states.

Korean War

The undeclared war in Korea broke out with an invasion by North Korea in 1950. American troops were sent to fight on South Korea's side. Later the defense of South Korea was under United Nation auspices. As UN troops approached the Yalu River border with China, China entered the war and forced UN forces back to the 38th parallel, the original boundary between North and

South Korea. In a notable act of the war, Truman dismissed Douglas MacArthur as Commander-in-Chief of American forces because MacArthur advocated the nuclear bombing of North Korea and mainland China.

Eisenhower

In 1952 Dwight Eisenhower, former Allied supreme commander in Europe, was elected president. He was re-elected in 1956. After his election, Eisenhower went to Korea. Shortly thereafter, an armistice was established at the 38th parallel. Under Secretary of State John Foster Dulles, the United States embarked on a campaign of "brinkmanship." The policy was designed to show American resolve and toughness. In 1957 Congress approved the Eisenhower Doctrine, which gave the president the right to use force against aggressive acts by any country under the control of communism.

Concurrent with the beginning of the Korean War, Senator Joseph McCarthy used the red scare to propel himself to national prominence (McCarthyism). He accused many Americans of anti-American activities, and needlessly ruined many lives. Accusations against the army led to Army-McCarthy hearings and McCarthy's censure by the Congress.

Civil Rights

In 1954 the Supreme Court decided the landmark case of *Brown v. Board of Education.* The Court found that "separate but equal" schools were unconstitutional. In 1955 the Supreme Court ordered an end to school segregation.

In Little Rock, Arkansas, the governor ordered the National Guard to prevent minority students from entering the high school. President Eisenhower sent troops, nationalized the Guard, and the Little Rock nine entered school. In subsequent years, many public schools were closed in the South and replaced by private academies to escape desegregation laws.

In 1955 Dr. Martin Luther King, Jr., led the Montgomery bus boycott. In 1956 the Supreme Court found that segregation on local buses was unconstitutional. Civil disobedience and nonviolent protest were used throughout the South to gain civil rights victories.

Kennedy and Johnson

John F. Kennedy was elected president in 1960. After his assassination in 1963, Lyndon Johnson succeeded him, and Johnson was elected in 1964.

John Kennedy proclaimed the "New Frontier" but was unsuccessful in moving legislation through Congress. He also began the vigorous exploration of space and established the Peace Corps.

Kennedy eventually ordered troops to ensure that James Meredith was enrolled as a student in the University of Alabama. During his term, there were civil rights sit-ins in Birmingham, Alabama, and a civil rights march of 250,000 on Washington, D.C. It was at this march that Dr. King made his "I have a dream" speech.

In 1961 Kennedy supported the Bay of Pigs invasion of Cuba. The invasion was disastrous. Some months later, Soviet missiles were located in Cuba. Kennedy established a blockade of Cuba and entered into a confrontation with Soviet leader Khrushev. Eventually, the missiles were withdrawn, and Cuba maintained its sovereignty.

John Kennedy is the president best known for his assassination. On November 22, 1963, John Kennedy was killed while visiting Dallas, Texas. The Warren Commission was formed to investigate the assassination and found that Lee Harvey Oswald was the lone assassin. Many disagree with this finding.

Lyndon Johnson succeeded Kennedy. Johnson was very effective in getting Kennedy's, and his own, legislative proposals through Congress. He supported a number of laws designed to create the Great Society and to launch a War on Poverty.

The War on Poverty included the Job Corps and Project Head Start, Upward Bound for bright but poor high school students, and VISTA, the domestic version of the Peace Corps.

Other Great Society programs included:

- The Water Quality and Air Quality Acts
- The Elementary and Secondary Education Act
- The National Foundation for Arts and Humanities
- The Omnibus Housing Bill
- Highway Safety Act
- Medicare
- Cabinet-level departments Housing and Urban Development (HUD)
- Transportation

Vietnam War

The Vietnam War stretched across the 12 years of the Kennedy and Johnson presidencies and into the presidency of Richard Nixon. While the war officially began with Kennedy as president, its actual beginnings stretched back many years.

Causes

Before the war, Vietnam was called French Indochina. During World War II the United States supported Ho Chi Minh in Vietnam as he fought Japan. After the war, the United States supported the French over Ho Chi Minh as France sought to regain control of its former colony.

Fighting broke out between the French and Ho Chi Minh with support from Mao Tse-tung, the leader of mainland China. Even with substantial material aid from the United States, France could not defeat Vietnam. In 1950 the French were defeated at Dien Bien Phu.

Subsequent negotiations in Geneva divided Vietnam into North and South with Ho Chi Minh in control of the North. Ngo Dinh Diem was installed by the United States as a leader in the South. Diem never gained popular support in the South. Following a harsh crackdown by Diem, the Viet Cong organized to fight against him. During the Eisenhower administration, 2,000 American "advisors" were sent to South Vietnam.

War Begins

When Kennedy came to office, he approved a CIA coup to overthrow Diem. When Johnson took office, he was not interested in compromise. In 1964 Johnson started a massive buildup of forces in Vietnam until the number reached more than 500,000. The Gulf of Tonkin Resolution, passed by Congress, gave Johnson descretion to pursue the war.

Living and fighting conditions were terrible. Although American forces had many successes, neither that nor the massive bombing of North Vietnam led to victory. In 1968 the Vietcong launched the Tet Offensive. While ground gained in the offensive was ultimately recaptured, the offensive shook the confidence of military leaders.

The war cost 350,000 American casualties. The $175 billion spent on the war could have been used for Great Society programs.

Home Front

At home, there were deep divisions. War protests sprung up all over the United States. Half a million people protested in New York during 1967 and the tension between hawks and doves increased throughout the country.

Nixon

Richard Nixon was elected in 1970 in the midst of this turmoil. While vigorously pursuing the war, he and Secretary of State Henry Kissinger were holding secret negotiations with North Vietnam. In 1973 an agreement was finally drawn up to end the war. American prisoners were repatriated although there were still a number Mission in Action (MIA), and U.S. troops withdrew from Vietnam.

Nixon was elected again in 1972, only to resign on August 8, 1974, during the Watergate investigation. Richard Nixon was the only U.S. president in history to resign. Spiro Agnew, Nixon's vice president, had resigned before him in 1973, and Gerald Ford took Agnew's place as vice president. When Nixon resigned, Ford became president.

The economy deteriorated during Nixon's administration. The expensive Great Society programs and the Vietnam War had increased the federal deficit. The OPEC oil embargo forced inflation up and worsened the economic situation.

Nixon's greatest diplomatic contributions were in China and the Middle East. He opened a dialogue with China and, through Henry Kissinger, arranged a peace settlement to the 1973 Yom Kippur War between Egypt/Syria and Israel.

Watergate

Nixon is best known for the Watergate scandal and his resignation. The resignation was caused initially by an unnecessary break-in by Republican operatives into the Democratic campaign headquarters in the Watergate office complex. Nixon was later taped in his office as he ordered the FBI to call off their Watergate investigation. When the Supreme Court ordered that these tapes be made public, Nixon resigned.

Ford

Gerald Ford was the first American president not elected through the electoral college. Unemployment and interest rates grew dramatically under Ford. Responses to these problems were inadequate, and the country started to enter a recession.

Carter

In 1976 Jimmy Carter was elected president. Carter introduced no major programs. The economy worsened under Carter with interest rates over 21 percent and double-digit inflation. The federal deficit continued to grow, and domestic programs became more expensive.

Reagan

Ronald Reagan was elected president in 1980 and again in 1984. Reagan was a conservative ideologue who believed in supply-side economics. Supply-side theory held that tax cuts would result in more investment, and, in turn, these investments would create more jobs.

Under Reagan, tax rates were cut drastically. The economy emerged from recession, and the interest rates were reduced. However, government revenues did not increase, and the federal deficit sky-rocketed. Homelessness grew to significant proportions and became a major urban problem.

Deregulation of the savings and loans organizations during Reagan's presidency led to abuses with a multibillion dollar bankruptcy of these groups. The cost of the bankruptcies was borne by taxpayers.

Bush

In 1988 George Bush was elected president. Bush continued Reagan's economic programs but was forced to raise taxes in 1990. This reversal of his promise "read my lips, no new taxes" probably led to his defeat in the 1992 election. S & Ls continued to fail, and the national debt continued to grow dramatically. The Communist bloc was disintegrating, and the Cold War was coming to a close.

Clinton

Bill Clinton was elected president in 1992 and again in 1996. His administration was beset with questions related to his integrity. Health reform, deficit reduction, and crime were three major issues of his administration. Inflation was low and the stock market soared during Clinton's presidency.

WORLD HISTORY

PREHISTORY AND THE DEVELOPMENT OF EARLY CIVILIZATIONS

WORLD POPULATION

World population grew steadily from 1 A.D. through 1650 A.D. After 1650 A.D., world population exploded. Rapid population growth has made it more difficult to provide for everyone. A table showing population growth follows.

1 A.D.	500	1000	1650	1850	1930	1975	1992
200 million	220 million	300 million	500 million	1 billion	2 billion	4 billion	5.7 billion

EARLY CIVILIZATIONS

Current knowledge of human history stretches back about 8,000 years to 6000 B.C. The earliest established date is around 4200 B.C. Most historians agree that civilization began when writing was invented about 3500 B.C. This date separates prehistoric from historic times.

In prehistoric time, humans used calendars, invented and used the wheel, played flutes and harps, and alloyed copper. These humans also created pottery and colored ceramics. There was an active trade in the Mediterranean Sea with Cretan shipping most prominent. What follows is a brief summary of historic times.

MESOPOTAMIA (4000–500 B.C.)

The earliest recorded civilizations were in Mesopotamia. This region was centered near the Tigris and Euphrates Rivers in what is now Iraq and extended from the western Mediterranean to Palestine to the Persian Gulf. The Sumerians inhabited Mesopotamia from 4000 B.C. to 2000 B.C. and probably invented the first writing—wedge-shaped symbols called cuneiform.

The Old Babylonians (2000–1550 B.C.) inhabited this area and established a capital at Babylonia (hanging gardens). King Hammurabi, known for the justice code named after him, ruled during the middle of this period. The militaristic Assyrians ruled from 1000 to about 600 B.C. The Assyrians were followed by the New Babylonians under King Nebuchadnezzar from about 600 to 500 B.C. A defeat by the Persians in the fifth century B.C. led to a dissolution of Mesopotamia.

CLASSICAL CIVILIZATIONS

EGYPT (5000–30 B.C.)

Egyptian history is usually divided into seven periods. Pharaohs became deities during the Old Kingdom (2685–2180 B.C.). Most pyramids were built during the Fourth Dynasty of the Old Kingdom (about 2600–2500 B.C.) Our common vision of Egyptians in horse-drawn chariots marked the Second Intermediate Period (1785–1560 B.C.). The Egyptians invaded Palestine and enslaved the Jews during the New Kingdom (1560–1085 B.C.). King Tutankhamen reigned during this period. In the first millennium B.C. Egypt was controlled by many groups and leaders, including Alexander the Great. In about 30 B.C., Egypt came under control of the Roman Empire.

GREECE

Greece has always been linked to its nearby islands. One of these islands, Crete, was inhabited by the Minoans (about 2600–1250 B.C.). During this time the ancient city of Troy was built. The mainland, inhabited by the Myceneans since about 2000 B.C., eventually incorporated Crete and the Minoan Civilization about 1200 B.C.

Dorian invasions from the north around 1200 B.C. led to the defeat of the Myceneans and the Greek Dark Ages from 1200 to 750 B.C. The Trojan War, which occurred during this period, was described by Homer in the *Iliad*.

Athens (founded 1000 B.C.) and Sparta (founded 750 B.C.) were famous Greek city-states. Draco was a harsh Athenian leader and democracy was established only in 527 B.C. During this period, the Parthenon was built in Athens. In Sparta, each male citizen became a lifetime soldier at the age of 7.

Classic Age

The Classic Age of Greece began about 500 B.C. when Athens defeated Persia Marathon and declined with the Peloponnesian War (430–404 B.C.) between Athens and Sparta.

The Classic Age was a time for the development of great literature and great thought. During this period, Socrates, Plato, and Aristotle taught and wrote in Greece. (Aristotle tutored Alexander the Great after Alexander conquered Greece. Alexander spread Greek culture during his subsequent conquests.) In this relatively brief period, Aeschylus wrote his *Orestia Tiology* and Sophocles wrote *Oedipus Rex*. Also writing during this period were Aristophanes, Euripides, Herodotus, and Thucydides.

Hellenistic Age

This age begins with the death of Alexander the Great. Alexander lived for only 33 years (356–323 B.C.) but during his brief life he carved out a huge empire. His conquests led to the spread of Greek culture and thought to most of that region of the world. This age ended about 30 B.C. when Greece, like Egypt, was incorporated in the Roman Empire.

Epicurus and Zeno wrote during this time. The Hellenistic Age was a time of great scientific and mathematical development. Euclid wrote his *Elements* in the third century B.C. while Archimedes, and Erasthotenes made important discoveries later in the period.

ROME

Some say that Rome was founded between 700 and 800 B.C. The real founding of Rome may be closer to 500 B.C. The Roman Senate consisting of landowners was eventually replaced by the plebeian Assembly about 300 B.C. as the governing body of Rome.

Rome acquired all of Italy by about 300 B.C., defeated Carthage (in North Africa) during a series of Punic Wars, and controlled both sides of the Mediterranean by about 150 B.C. The Roman victories were marked by one defeat at the hands of the Carthaginian general Hannibal. Julius Caesar and Pompeii were leaders in the first century B.C. and Spartacus led a rebellion by slaves. Caesar was assassinated on the Ides of March, 44 B.C. in a conspiracy led by Brutus ("et tu Brute") and Cassius.

Roman Empire

The birth of the Roman Empire coincided roughly with the beginning of the A.D. era. During the first century A.D., the Emperor Nero committed suicide. Jewish zealots also committed suicide at Masada following the destruction of their temple by the Romans. The empire reached its greatest size during this century. A code of law was established. Scientists Ptomely and Pliny the Elder were active, and the Colosseum was constructed.

Following the death of Emperor Marcus Aurelius, the Roman Empire began its decline. Civil war raged in the 200s A.D. and there were defeats of provinces by the Persians and the Goths. Constantine's attempts to stop the empire's decline were ultimately fruitless, and the Visigoths looted Rome in about 400 A.D.

Octavius defeated Antony and Cleopatra at the Battle of Acton around 38 B.C. Following this, Octavius was crowned the first "God-Emperor." The 500 years of peace that followed, called the Pax Romana, is the longest period of peace in the Western World.

DEVELOPMENT OF WORLD RELIGIONS

MAJOR WORLD RELIGIONS

Most of the world's religions emerged in Africa and Asia. There are about six billion people alive today. About two billion follow some Christian religion, and one billion Christians are Roman Catholics. There are about one billion Muslims, 800 million Hindus and 350 million Buddhists. There are fewer who follow tribal religions or who are Sikhs, Jews, Shamanists, Confucians, and followers of other religions. About one billion people are nonreligious and about 250 million people are atheists.

Judaism

Judaism developed from the beliefs of the Hebrew tribes located in and around Israel before 1300 B.C. From about 1000 B.C. to 150 B.C. a number of different authors wrote a series of books describing the religion, laws, and customs which are now known as the Old Testament of the Bible. The Old Testament describes a single just God. Judaism is an important world religion because elements of Judaism can be found in both Islam and Christianity.

Hebrews trace their ancestry to Abraham and his grandson Jacob, whose 12 sons are said to have founded the 12 tribes of Israel. About 1000 B.C. David is believed to have united these 12 tribes into a single religious state. Modern Jews refer to the Talmud, a book of Jewish law and tradition written around 400 A.D.

Christianity

Jesus was probably born about 5 B.C. He acquired a small following of Jews who believed he was the Messiah. Later this belief was developed into a worldwide religion known as Christianity. Christianity was generally tolerated in Rome, although there were periods of persecution. The Emperor Constantine converted to Christianity about 300 A.D. In the mid 300s Christianity was decreed the state religion of Rome. Augustine (St. Augustine) converted to Christianity in the late 300s.

In the Byzantine Era, starting after the Visigoths looted Rome, there was an Eastern and Western emperor. Constantinople was the capital in the East. This division led in 1054 to the great schism of the Catholic church, which survives to this day. The Crusaders captured Constantinople and defeated the Eastern Byzantines in 1204. In 1453 Constantinople was captured by the Turks and renamed Istanbul.

Islam

Mohammed was born in 570 A.D. and went into Mecca in 630 and founded Islam. The Koran contains the 114 chapters of Islamic religion and law. Around 640 A.D. the Omar, religious leader, established an Islamic empire with Damascus as the capital. The capital was eventually moved to Baghdad. The Muslims enjoyed a prosperous economy, and in the late days of the empire Omar Khayyam wrote the *Rubaiyat*.

Muslim armies conquered Spain and much of France by about 730. A series of Caliphs ruled from 750 until 1250 when an army originally led by Ghengis Kahn sacked Baghdad and killed the last caliph.

Buddhism

Buddhism was founded around 525 B.C. in India. The religion was founded by Buddha, Gautama Siddhartha, who lived from about 560 B.C. to about 480 B.C. The Triptika contains Buddha's teachings. A large number of *Sutras* contains a great body of Buddhist beliefs and teachings. Monastic life provides the main organizational and administrative structure for modern-day Buddhism.

It is said that Buddha achieved his enlightenment through meditation, and meditation is an important Buddhist practice. Buddhism holds that life is essentially meaningless and without reality. Buddhists seek to achieve Nirvana, a great void of perfection, through meditation and just acts.

Hinduism

Hinduism emerged in India about 25 years after Buddhism. Hindu beliefs are a mixture of the religious beliefs of invaders of India and the religious beliefs of native Indians. Hinduism embraces a caste system with religious services conducted by members of the priestly caste. Most Hindus worship one of the gods Vishnu and Shiva, and the goddess Shakti.

Hindus believe that a person's *karma*, the purity or impurity of past deeds, determines a person's ultimate fate. A karma can be improved through pure acts, deeds, and devotion.

FEUDALISM IN JAPAN AND EUROPE

Japan

The Japanese Islands had an early civilization by 3000 B.C. Throughout the whole B.C. period Japan remained a primitive society overrun by successive invasions by Mongols and Malays. Around the beginning of the A.D. period, Chinese writers referred to Japan as a backward nation.

The first religion in Japan was Shinto, a cult of nature and ancestor worship. Around 550 A.D., Buddhism was introduced in Japan and quickly spread throughout the country. Throughout this period Japan existed in the shadow of China. Chinese words are still found today in the Japanese language.

Shoguns

Japanese emperors had always been powerful, godlike figures. But around 1150 A.D., Shoguns were installed as the permanent leaders of Japan, leaving the emperor with only ceremonial duties. Until that time Shoguns had been only military leaders. In the following years a succession of Shoguns were ultimately unsuccessful in unifying Japan. Japan was reduced to a group of warring states.

Around 1600 the strong Tokugawa Shogunate was formed. This Shogunate ruled Japan until 1868. Japan was at peace for most of this period. Under this Shogunate, Christians were persecuted, and in 1639 foreign ships were forbidden in Japanese waters. This period of isolation lasted until American Commodore Perry forced Japan to sign a treaty in 1853, opening limited trade with the West.

Menji Period

The Menji period of Japan lasted from 1868 until 1912. Feudalism established under the Shogunates was outlawed, and Japan started to develop an industrial economy. As lords lost their feudal manors, the importance of the samurai (a lord's private soldiers) declined. In 1876 samurai were forbidden to wear their swords. Some 250,000 samurai rebelled in 1876 but were easily defeated by soldiers bearing modern weapons.

Buddhism declined, and Shintoism enjoyed a rebirth during this period. Japan actively sought contact with Western nations and adopted a number of Western customs and institutions. In 1889 the first Diet or parliament was established.

Wars

In 1894 Japan entered into war with China (Sino-Japanese War) over a dispute about Korea. Japan defeated China, establishing Japan as a military power. In 1904 Japan entered into war with Russia (The Russo-Japanese War). Japan also emerged victorious in this war and established a new balance of power between East and West. This new balance of power set the stage for conflicts yet to come.

Europe

Charlemagne

Charles Martel, a Frankish palace mayor who became known as Charlemagne, halted the Muslims in what is now France. Later he ruled the Frankish kingdom from about 770–815 A.D. He was named emperor of the Holy Roman Empire in 800 A.D. by Pope Leo III. Charlemagne's authority was also accepted in the East. After much fighting in Europe, the Normans, under William the Conqueror, defeated England at the Battle of Hastings in 1066.

The High Middle Ages lasted from the Battle of Hastings until about 1300. During this time the Roman road system was rebuilt, and Europe grew larger than the Muslim and Byzantine Empires.

In England a long series of battles with the Danes and Danish occupation preceded the Battle of Hastings. Henry II arranged for Archbishop Thomas Becket's murder in the late 1100s followed by the reign of Richard the Lionhearted and the signing of the Magna Carta in 1215.

Crusades

There were at least seven crusades from 1100 and 1300 to dislodge "infidels" from the Holy Land. The third crusade was led by Richard the Lionhearted. Ultimately, these crusades were unsuccessful, and many Muslims and Jews were massacred. Jews were persecuted throughout Europe beginning with the first crusade. Hundreds of Jewish communities were destroyed in the area of present-day Germany alone.

Scholasticism, an attempt to bring together the Christian faith and logic, was active during this period with leaders such as St. Anselm, Thomas Aquinas, Albertus Magnus, and Peter Abelard.

THE MIDDLE AND LATE AGES (1300–1500)

Hundred Years War

For much of this period, England and France were engaged in the Hundred Years War (actually about 120 years long). Most of the war was fought in France. Joan of Arc led the French army to a number of victories. She was burned at the stake at age 19. England was ultimately defeated. During this time, Chaucer wrote the *Canterbury Tales*.

Black Death

The bubonic plague, carried by rats' fleas, was epidemic in Europe by 1350. According to some estimates, almost half of the European population was killed by the plague.

CHINESE AND INDIAN EMPIRES

CHINA TO 1900

Early civilization developed near the Yellow River in ancient times. It appears that cities developed in China after they appeared in Egypt. The Shang Dynasty emerged in China about 1500 B.C. and lasted until about 1100 B.C. This dynasty is known for its works of art, particularly its fine bronze castings and walled cities. Life in this dynasty did not emphasize religion, a trait noted also in modern China.

The Chou Dynasty ruled from about 1100 to 250 B.C. Jade carvings and Chinese calligraphy were developed during this time.

Confucius

Confucius was born near the end of this dynasty around 550 B.C. He was a philosopher who was concerned with the way people acted. He emphasized regard for authority, self-control, conformity, and respectful behavior. Confucius had little impact during his lifetime. His disciples carried his thoughts and ideas throughout China. Eventually he came to be revered, and his ideas and sayings give a distinct shape and form to Chinese thought.

250 B.C.–220 A.D.

Following the Chou Dynasty were the Ch'in rulers, including the first emperor of China. During this time the Great Wall of China was expanded and built along the northern Chinese border. Confucian writings were destroyed by these leaders.

A successor in this period founded the Han Dynasty, which ruled China from about 200 B.C. to 220 A.D. During this period Confucius became a revered figure, and his writings were the objects of careful study.

Invaders

Invaders from the north attacked China around 315 A.D. and controlled north China until about 560 A.D. The Chinese maintained their independence in the south, but China was divided into a number of states. Influence from India established Buddhism in China during this time.

580 A.D.–1279 A.D.

China was reunited under the Sui Dynasty about 580 A.D. In 618 the Sui Dynasty was overthrown. The T'ang Dynasty that followed lasted until about 906 A.D. During this time Turkish incursions were halted, and Chinese influence grew to include Korea and northern Indochina. The T'angs developed a civil service testing apparatus, and the Chinese economy improved during this time.

During the Sung Dynasty (960–1279 A.D.) gunpowder was used for weapons. The nation prospered during this time, and the standard of living rose to new heights.

Mongols

The Mongols, under Genghis Kahn, invaded and controlled much of northern China by 1215. Kublai Khan followed, and his successors ruled China until 1368. During this time the Chinese launched a fleet to attack Japan. The fleet was destroyed in a typhoon. The Japanese refer to this typhoon as the divine wind—*kamikaze*.

Ming Dynasty

In 1368 Peking was captured, the Khan was overthrown, and the Ming Dynasty was born. The Mings reigned until 1644. Rulers of the Ming Dynasty launched a campaign to stamp out any remnants of the Mongol occupation. Even though there were some contacts with the West, the rulers of this dynasty forbade sea travel to foreign lands. Beginning in 1433 Chinese isolation and suspicion of foreigners grew.

Western Contacts

Contacts with the West increased under the Manchu Dynasty. However, in 1757 the Chinese government became offended by some Western traders. They allowed trade only through the port of Canton and under very strict regulations. At that time, opium was one of the few Chinese imports. The Chinese government objected to these imports, and this led to the Opium War of 1839, won by the British. Western intervention in China continued through 1900.

India to 1900

Early, advanced civilizations developed in the Indus Valley. The inhabitants were called Dravidians. Around 2500 B.C., a series of floods and foreign invasions appears to have all but destroyed these civilizations. Between 2500 and 1500 B.C. the Dravidians were forced into southern India by a nomadic band with Greek and Persian roots.

The conquerors brought a less sophisticated civilization to India. It was this latter group that formed the Indian civilization. An early caste system was established with the Dravidians serving as slaves.

After a time the society developed around religious, nonsecular concerns. The Mahabarata became a verbal tradition around 1000 B.C. It describes a war hero Krishna. The Mahabarata's most significant impact was the frequent descriptions of correct conduct and belief. The Mahabarata also describes how the soul remains immortal through transmigration—the successive occupation of many bodies.

Castes

From about 1000 to 500 B.C. the caste system became fixed and it was almost impossible for people to move out of their caste. The priests, or Brahmans, were at the top of the caste system. Next were rulers and warriors and then farmers and tradesmen. Near the bottom were workers. Finally, there were those who had no caste at all—outcastes—who could not participate in society.

Buddha

Buddha was born in India about 580 B.C. His teachings developed the Buddhist religion. Buddha preached nirvana—a rejection of worldly and material concerns and a surrender of individual consciousness. During his lifetime his ideas spread throughout India.

Maurya Empire

The Maurya Empire ruled India from about 320 to 185 B.C. During this time Buddhism was spread throughout Asia, China, and Southeast Asia. The Andrhan Dynasty ruled India proper to 220 A.D. Buddhism became less popular in India during this period while Brahmans gained more prominence.

Gupta Dynasty

After disorder following the collapse of the Andhran Dynasty, the Gupta Dynasty ruled from about 320 to 500 A.D. Arts, literature, and mathematics flourished during this period. Indian mathematicians used the decimal system and probably introduced the concept of zero. Hinduism developed from earlier religions and became the dominant religion in India. Most people in India worshipped many gods including Brahma (creator), Vishnu (preserver), and Shiva (destroyer).

The Gupta Dynasty declined with the invasion of the Huns in the fifth century A.D. Successors of these invaders, called Rajputs, intermarried, joined Hindu society, and dominated northern India until 1200 A.D. Other kingdoms were established in central and southern India.

By this time the caste system and the power of Brahman priests were dominant throughout India.

Muslims

Around 1200 A.D. Muslims (Turks and Afghans) invaded India from the north. The invaders controlled all but the southern part of India by about 1320. The Delhi Sultanate lasted in a state of intrigue until about 1530. Muslim sultans oppressed Hindus while their supporters killed or converted many Hindus. Remnants of this strife between Muslims and Hindus can be seen to this day.

In 1530 the Mongols, also Muslims, invaded India and by 1600 controlled most of India. The Mongol leader Akbar assumed the throne about 1560. His reign featured religious tolerance, the development of arts and literature, and a massive building campaign. In 1756 the Mongol Dynasty was overthrown by internal strife and Hindu resistance. India became a divided state.

Britain

Into this void stepped the European powers, particularly England. The East India Company of England virtually ruled India through 1857. In 1857, sepoys, Indian soldiers in the British army, mutinied. The British government began to rule Indian directly. This form of British rule was superior to that provided by the East India Company. Indian troops fought with Britain in World War I.

SUB-SAHARAN KINGDOMS AND CULTURES

EARLY AFRICA

Humans (*Homo sapiens*) are believed to have developed in Africa about 250,000 years ago. Humans formed nomadic bands that spread throughout Africa about 30,000 years ago. The first "towns" were founded in the Nile River Valley about 4500 B.C.

By about 3000 B.C. sophisticated civilizations developed throughout Egypt, which occupied a swath of land along the Nile River and extending to the Mediterranean. Pharaohs ruled with godlike powers, and there was a sophisticated bureaucracy. The Egyptians had writing (hieroglyphics) and invented a calendar still in use today. Pyramids were built during the Old Kingdom of Egypt from 2700 to 2150 B.C.

PHARAOHS

Beginning around 2150 B.C., a century of weak pharaohs, civil wars, and famines weakened and fragmented Egypt. From about 2050 to 1650 B.C., Egypt came together in the Middle Kingdom. In 1650 B.C., foreign armies invaded and conquered Egypt. In about 1550 B.C. the Egyptians overthrew the foreign leaders and the New Kingdom (1550–1100 B.C.).

In the beginning of the New Kingdom, Egypt stretched along the Nile and occupied the coast of the Mediterranean out of Africa and in Palestine and Syria. By 1250 B.C., the Egyptian Empire was in decline. Egypt ceased to be the dominant force in the area about 750 B.C.

SUB-SAHARAN AFRICA

The Sudan, south of Egypt, developed a culture patterned after Egypt in about 1000 B.C. The Cush civilization of Sudan flourished in middle Africa and was dominant until about 250 A.D. The A.D. period marks the conquest of North Africa by the Roman Empire. Christian European influence was dominant until about 640 A.D.

ISLAM

Islam spread throughout Africa in the seventh century A.D. During this time Muslims conquered the area occupied by Egypt and the rest of North Africa, including Morocco and Libya. By about 1050 A.D. most of northern Africa was an Islamic land.

WEST AFRICA

The earliest state in West Africa was probably Ghana (established about 700 A.D.). By 1050 Ghana was also a Muslim state. In about 1100 A.D., the Mali evolved from tribes near the headwaters of the Senegal and Niger Rivers. Around 1300 Mali became a Muslim state. Songhai emerged as the dominant state in West Africa about 1400 A.D. Islam became the dominant faith in Songhai around 1500 and the capital, Timbuktu, became a major center for trade and learning. Songhai was overrun by Morocco in 1591.

EAST AFRICA

East African civilizations had an early exposure to Asian peoples. Most towns were established by Arab and Indonesian settlers. There was a great deal of intermarriage among natives and settlers. Mogadishu and Mombassa were among a number of smaller states, which emerged around 1250 A.D.

CENTRAL AFRICA

Civilizations in central Africa are shrouded in mystery. Bantu-speaking people apparently settled there around 700 A.D. In the fourteenth century the Kongo Kingdom was formed. The area around Lake Tanganyika was formed in the Luba Empire about the time Columbus made his first voyage. South Africa is best known for the Zulu people. They conquered most of South Africa between 1816 and 1850.

Slaves

European conquest and domination of Africa began in the late fifteenth century. Slave trade began at this time. Most slaves were supplied by African kingdoms, which grew rich on the slave trade.

CIVILIZATIONS OF THE AMERICAS

EARLY CULTURES

Before 1500 the inhabitants of the Americas were related to the Native Americans. This group had migrated over the land bridge from Siberia about 30,000 years before. About 90 percent of the tens of millions of ancestors of this migratory tribe were found in Latin America in 1500.

By 7000 B.C., primitive cultures existed throughout the Americas. Cultures developed more slowly in the jungle areas of South America. Primitive cultures still exist there today. Agriculture seems to have been widespread by about 2500 B.C.

MAYAN CULTURE

The dominant civilization in Mexico until about 900 A.D. were the Mayans. They began to occupy the Yucatan peninsula of Mexico and surrounding areas about 1700 B.C. The Mayans probably developed the most sophisticated indigenous American culture. The Mayan civilization ended suddenly with the mysterious desertion of Mayan cities and migration of the Mayan population.

Striking Mayan cities, plazas, and pyramids survive to this day. Mayans had a written language and wrote books about astronomy. Their calendar was the most accurate in the world at that time. Many Mayan descendants live as peasants in Mexico and speak dialects of their ancient language.

From about 1500 to 500 B.C., the Olmec civilization was a sophisticated culture in northern Mexico. About this time a culture centered in Teotihuacan also grew in prominence. This culture was to dominate northern Mexico until about 900 A.D.

AZTEC CULTURE

In about 900 A.D. the Aztecs began their rise to power in northern Mexico. Aztecs referred to themselves as Mexica. Aztecs were warlike and sacrificed humans. By about 1300 A.D. they established a capital city in a marsh, which is now the site of Mexico City.

The Spaniards, under Cortez, duped the Aztec Emperor Montezuma II and easily defeated the Aztec confederation in 1521. Over a million descendants of the Aztecs still live in Mexico, mainly living a subsistence existence and speaking their ancient language.

INCAN CULTURE

The Incas were the dominant pre-Columbian civilization in South America. This culture existed in Peru by about 500 A.D. From about 1100 to about 1500 A.D. the Incas expanded their empire to most of the western coast of South America including parts of Argentina.

The Incas had the best developed system of government in the Americas. They built extensive systems of stone roads and huge stone structures such as the Temple of the Sun. The Incas also built the fortress Machu Picchu high in the Andes. Machu Picchu may have been the last stronghold of the Incas after the Spaniard Pizzaro overcame the Incan empire in 1532 with about 200 troops and palace intrigue.

RISE AND EXPANSION OF EUROPE

RENAISSANCE (1300–1600)

The Renaissance, which means the rebirth, arose in Italy and particularly in Florence. It was a time for the discovery and rediscovery of literature and art. Humanism, reading, and the ideas of Classical Greece were dominant during this period. Dante wrote the *Inferno* and the *Divine Comedy* early in the Renaissance and Machiavelli wrote *The Prince* near the end of the period. Leonardo DiVinci painted the Mona Lisa and designed many workable mechanical devices. Michelangelo painted the ceiling of the Sistine Chapel, among other accomplishments.

LUTHER AND THE REFORMATION (1500–1600)

The abuses of the Catholic church, then monolithic in Europe, drew much criticism. The practice of selling indulgences (relief from punishment in purgatory) was considered particularly repugnant. Martin Luther drew particular attention these abuses when, on October 31, 1517, he nailed his *95 Theses* to the Wittenburg Church door. Luther authored many books and wrote the most popular hymn of the time, *A Mighty Fortress Is Our God.* Since Luther's teachings *protested* church practice, his followers were called Protestants.

The reform movement spread beyond Luther in Germany to England and other parts of Europe. Henry VIII in England broke with the pope and formed the Church of England. Protestantism was effectively blocked in Spain and Italy and was the subject of warfare in France.

RELIGIOUS WARFARE

Most national boundaries were fixed at the end of the Reformation in 1560. The 90 years that followed were marked by religious strife. Gunpowder, available since the 1300s, was now used in cannons. Warfare became more regimented and more deadly. There were no fewer than seven civil wars in France. The St. Bartholomew's Day Massacre occurred in 1572, when Catherine DeMedici arranged the death of about 20,000 French Huguenots (Calvinist Protestants).

Mary I (Bloody Mary) of England killed many Protestants in her brief five-year reign (1553–1558). Her successor, Elizabeth I, was a Protestant and achieved some degree of religious peace in England. Later attempts were made to force England back to Catholicism.

By 1575 governments were in shambles, and many religious groups were discriminated against. In England the Puritans objected to what they saw as a pro-Catholic shift in the Church of England. Many Puritans escaped to the New World.

AGE OF EXPLORATION (1500–1650)

Countries sponsored exploration throughout the world toward the end of the Renaissance. These countries were seeking new trade and easily accessible trade routes.

The New World had already been visited when Columbus sailed from Spain in 1492. His voyage followed on other explorations by Prince Henry the Navigator and Vasco De Gama. Many other explorers traveled to the New World and circumnavigated the world during this period. Cortes conquered the Aztecs, in Mexico, and Pizarro, in Peru, conquered the Incas.

The effect of exploration on the Native Indian population of the Americas was disastrous. Some estimates indicate that 80 percent of the native population was wiped out by disease in one of the greatest epidemics on earth. Gold and food were shipped back to Europe. A large number of English settled in North America. Small numbers of Spanish settlers went to South and Central America. Still smaller numbers of French settled in Canada following the explorations of Champlain.

Europeans, with the complicity of some African kingdoms, began transporting slaves from Africa to the Americas. The first African slaves arrived in Jamestown, Virginia, about 1620. By the early 1800s there were about 1 million slaves in the United States. By 1860 there were more than four million slaves in the United States.

We will return later to the development of the New World following this period of exploration.

SCIENTIFIC REVOLUTION (1550–1650)

The scientific revolution took place toward the end of the Renaissance and spilled over into the age of exploration. Copernicus showed that the sun was at the center of the solar system. Kepler discovered the orbits of the planets. Galileo made significant discoveries in astronomy, mechanics, and surveying. He proved that all falling bodies fall at the same rate.

Francis Bacon championed inductive investigations in which data are gathered and used to form hypotheses. Rene Decartes (Cartesian coordinates) provided leadership in mathematics and championed the deductive, step-by-step method of proof.

ENLIGHTENMENT (C. 1650–1790)

In 1650 Europe consisted of 300–500 smaller states and a Germany devastated by the Thirty Years War. A series of treaties and wars brought a kind of order out of this chaos.

Peace of Westphalia (1648)—Holland and Switzerland officially formed.

First Dutch War (1667–1668)—Warfare between France and Spain led to the Triple Alliance (England, Holland, and Sweden).

War of the League of Augsburg (1688–1697)—France fought England and Holland. The conflict between England and France continued on and off for about 125 years.

The Grand Alliance (1701)—A coalition of Spain and France against England led to the formation of the Grand Coalition (Holy Roman Empire, England, Holland, and Prussia).

Treaty of Utrecht (1742)—The Spanish Empire was partitioned. England received Gibraltar, Newfoundland, Hudson Bay, and Nova Scotia.

King William's War (1744–1748)—Prussia emerged as a world power.

Seven Years War (1756–1763)—Prussia fought Austria, France, and Russia. With help from England and the withdrawal of Russia from the conflict, Prussia held onto its lands.

Treaty of Paris (1763)—France, which had already given Spain all its western American lands, lost the rest of its North American possessions to England. England traded Cuba to Spain for the Floridas.

Treaty of Paris (1783)—Britain recognized the United States following the Revolutionary War, but no lands were given to France, even though France (Lafayette, Rochambeau) had aided the United States in the Revolutionary War.

Life was still difficult in the 1700s. In the early 1700s the average life expectancy was 30, and almost no one lived to see their grandchildren. Famine and disease (including smallpox, bubonic plague, and typhus) were rampant. But, slowly, the economies and social institutions of Europe began to change for the better.

Mercantilism, an emphasis on material wealth, became a leading force in Europe. In Holland and England productivity became important. As a result, these countries became leading economic powers.

TECHNOLOGY, ART, AND LITERATURE

In the early 18th century, technology provided a means for further economic development. Watt refined and developed the steam engine, while other inventors devised power-driven textile equipment.

The Enlightenment established intellect as distinct from God and sought to establish a rational basis for life. Descartes paused in his scientific work to proclaim, "I think; therefore, I am."

This period included the Baroque art movement. Baroque art featured grandeur and included the works of Michelangelo. Rubens, Bach, and Handel were great Baroque artists and composers.

The impact of the Enlightenment can be seen in the theories of Jean Jacques Rousseau who believed that common people should have a wider role in their own government. The centralized mercantilist theory was attacked by economist Adam Smith and others, who believed in free trade and the law of supply and demand.

ROMANOV RUSSIA

The Romanovs ruled Russia from about 1613 until 1917. From 1682 until 1725 the giant (7 feet tall), driven, and cruel Peter the Great ruled Russia. He used secret police to identify and punish those who opposed him. Despite his bizarre behavior, he spent time among the common people. He modernized and westernized Russia. He built St. Petersburg as a modern western city. Many of the companies begun during his reign were controlled by the state. After six short-lived emperors, Catherine the Great (1762–1796) continued the modernization of Russia.

FRENCH REVOLUTION

King Louis XVI was on the throne as France became bankrupt in the late 1780s. Food was in short supply and food prices were inflated as the Third Estate (commoners) asserted themselves and took over the national assembly. They forced recognition by the king.

Galvanized by food shortages, repression, and unemployment, Parisian workers armed themselves and stormed the fortress Bastille on July 14, 1789. The French Revolution was born. After two years of fighting and intrigue, the newly formed national assembly condemned and executed Louis XVI and Marie "let them eat cake" Antoinette in 1792.

Robespierre emerged to direct a Committee of Public Safety, which conducted the Reign of Terror from 1793–1794. The Reign led to the deaths of over 20,000 who were summarily found guilty of real or imagined wrongs. Robespierre was executed under orders from the National Convention on July 27, 1794.

NAPOLEON

Napoleon was born in 1769, and while in Paris in 1795, he helped put down a royalist uprising. He was also there to lead the overthrow of the government in 1799 and soon become the dictator (Consul for Life in 1801) of France. Napoleon was a brilliant, charismatic man and a true military genius. He led France on a 10-year quest for an expanded empire from 1805 to 1815.

However, he was unable to complete his militaristic expansion successfully. He was deposed and exiled to Elba only to return to "meet his Waterloo" at the battle of that name. He was exiled again and died on the island of St. Helena in 1821.

The Quadruple Alliance (Austria, England, Prussia, and Russia), who had defeated Napoleon, reached a settlement that encircled France. This settlement maintained a balance of power in Europe until Germany was unified 60 years later.

INDUSTRIAL REVOLUTION (1750–1850)

Increased population, cheap labor, available capital, raw materials, and industrial skill led to the beginning of the Industrial Revolution in England about 1750. Textiles and metal industries were the first to develop. These industries were helped along by the steamboat and the locomotive. During the early 1800s this industrialism moved to the continent.

The Industrial Revolution produced a new class of factory workers. These workers did not benefit from the Industrial Revolution until late in the 1800s. Until then, work had centered around the family, but all that changed. Generally speaking, men worked outside the home, and women worked in the home.

ROMANTICISM (1790–1850)

Romanticism had its biggest impact from the late 1700s through 1850. This movement stressed personal freedom and humanitarianism. The names of many Romantic writers, painters, and composers are familiar to us. Some writers were Balzac, Burns, Browning, Byron, Coleridge, Cooper, Dostoyevsky, Dumas, Emerson, Longfellow, Poe and Thoreau. Painters included Goya and Delacorte. Composers of the era were Brahms, Chopin, and Schubert.

Romanticism broadened thought and led to a number of different philosophies and approaches to living. Liberalism celebrated the individual and proclaimed that individuals have certain natural rights. Conservatism proposed that some people were better prepared to rule and lead than others. Nationalism stressed loyalty to a group or country rather than the individual. Socialism expressed the view that all should receive their share of a nation's wealth. Marxism developed by Marx and Engels was a popular form of socialism. Marxism is described in *Das Kapital* and *Communist Manifesto*.

A series of revolutions swept Europe in 1820, 1825, and 1830, culminating in 1848. Italy and Germany were unified as an aftermath of these revolutions.

EUROPEAN DEVELOPMENTS

CRIMEAN WAR

The year 1854 found Great Britain and France allied with the Turks against Russia in the Crimean War. It was this war that sparked the writing of "The Charge of the Light Brigade" and featured the nursing work of Florence Nightingale and her disciples. The war ended in 1856 with the Peace of Paris.

CAPITALISM, MARXISM, AND ANARCHISM

Following the revolutions of 1848, capitalism and communism competed for economic supremacy in Europe. Anarchists believed that there should be no authority. They used violent means to further their ends.

NEW IMPERIALISM

Beginning about 1870, Europe was producing more goods than it could consume. So European powers began to vie for colonies. Much of the early activity focused on Africa. By 1914 Belgium, Britain, France, Germany, Italy, Portugal, and Spain controlled about 90 percent of Africa, with Britain and then France controlling the most territory.

During this time the German Empire developed under Bismarck. Great Britain's move to democratic government ended in 1911 when the House of Commons usurped the power of the House of Lords. The Third French Republic survived infighting and socialist challenges and solidified support of the majority of the French populace.

This period also saw the emergence of new and revolutionary ideas. Freud established psychoanalytic psychology, Einstein presented his theory of relativity, and Darwin wrote the *Origin of the Species*.

OTHER SOCIAL STUDIES TOPICS

Other social studies topics are also the subject of test questions. These topics, which include anthropology, government/politics, geography, and graph interpretation, are discussed next.

ANTHROPOLOGY

Anthropology is a holistic study of humans. Anthropologists study the biology, culture, and development of human species and communities. Anthropologists rely on field work, fossils, and observation in their work.

Physical Anthropology

Physical anthropology is concerned with the evolution of primates and humans. Physical anthropologists are seeking to trace the evolution of humans through human fossils. Louis Leakey is probably the most famous physical anthropologist. He discovered the three-million-year-old remains of "Lucy" at the Olduvai gorge in Africa.

Biological Anthropologists

Human biology is another focus of anthropologists. Biological anthropologists study the genetic development of primates and humans. They seek to identify the cause of human diseases such as high blood pressure. Other biological anthropologists such as Jane Goodall study the behavior of apes and other primates. These anthropologists have found that primates can use tools and communicate.

Cultural Anthropologists

Cultural anthropology is concerned with the social systems, customs, languages, and religion of existing cultures. Cultural anthropologists classify cultures as patrilineal, matrilineal, or bilateral depending on whether the family roots are traced through the father, mother, or both father and mother.

Anthropological Development

The simplest cultures are associated with nomadic hunter-gatherers. About 13,000 years ago, humans began domesticating livestock and raising crops. More stable communities developed as cultures became more stationary. Then these communities became linked together to form tribes with a shared tradition (religion). Political systems developed, and leaders or chiefs of these tribes appeared. Some of these tribes developed unevenly into kingdoms with a shared language. Occasionally a kingdom would develop into a civilization with different hierarchies of individuals.

More advanced cultures featured complex religious systems, important priests, and codified religious rules. Early cultures typically had a single religious system. Until recently there was a close relationship between religion and government.

Most cultural anthropologists agree that the primary determinants of culture are the material conditions of life—food, energy sources, and technology. Geography and climate have a tremendous influence on these factors. Ideas, movements, and personalities also have a significant impact on a culture.

GOVERNMENT AND POLITICAL SCIENCE

Government and political science are studies of the ways governments are organized and how governments function.

There are a number of ways to classify governments. Aristotle placed governments in one of three categories:

Democracy—government by the populace

Aristocracy—government by a few

Monarchy—government by one

Current classifications of government include the following.

Parliamentary, or Cabinet (England)—The executive branch is subordinate to the legislative branch.

Presidential (United States)—The executive branch is independent of the legislative branch, although some executive actions require legislative action.

Federal States (United States)—The power of the central government is limited by rights of the states.

Unitary (England)—The states are subordinate to the central government.

Dictatorship (Nazi Germany)—Rule by a single individual or a small group in which the needs of the state are generally more important than the needs of the people.

Democracy (United States)—Rule through the will of the people within which the needs of the people are generally more important than the needs of the state.

UNITED STATES GOVERNMENT

The United States government is based on the Constitution of the United States. The Constitution can be amended by a two-thirds vote of Congress with concurrence of three-fourths of the state legislatures. The first ten amendments to the Constitution are called the Bill of Rights. Other important amendments provided protection by due process of law, abolished slavery, and gave women the right to vote.

The Constitution established a federal form of government. States have rights and hold all power not expressly granted to the federal government.

The federal government of the United States has three branches: legislative, executive, and judicial. The framers of the Constitution established these as three complementary, overlapping branches to provide checks and balances in the governmental process.

Legislative

The Congress of the United States consists of the Senate and the House of Representatives. The 100 senators, two from each state, serve for six years with one-third standing for election every two years. The 435 representatives in the House are partitioned among the states according to population. Every state must have at least one representative. All representatives stand for election every two years.

Measures passed by a majority of Congress present and voting are sent to the president as a bill. The president may sign the bill into law or veto it. If the bill is vetoed, the Congress may still make the bill law by a two-thirds vote of each body.

Executive

The president and the vice president are the elected heads of the federal government. Their election takes place through a cumbersome process in which electors are chosen from each state by popular vote. These electors then gather in an Electoral College to cast votes for the president and vice president.

The president is Commander-in-Chief of the Armed Forces, but only Congress has the power to declare war. The president also has the right to negotiate treaties. Two-thirds of the Senate must vote to ratify any treaties. Treaties are null and void without this ratification.

Judicial

The Constitution established the Supreme Court as the final arbiter of whether a law adhered to the Constitution. Other federal courts established by Congress can also rule on a law's constitutionality.

Supreme Court justices are nominated by the president. A majority of the Senate must consent to any Supreme Court nomination.

Checks and Balances

The three branches of government provide adequate checks and balances. There are ways to remove presidents, legislators, and judges from office.

SPECIAL STRATEGY FOR ANSWERING HISTORY AND SOCIAL STUDIES ITEMS

MAPS

The items below are the sorts of map questions you might find on the MSAT.

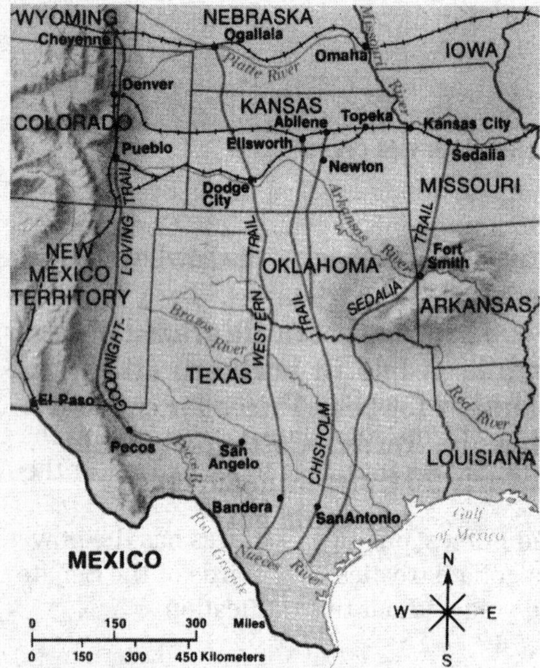

Western cattle trails and railroads about 1875

1. Which cattle trail goes from San Antonio to Abilene?
   (A) Chisholm
   (B) Sedalia
   (C) Goodnight-Loving
   (D) Western Trail

2. Which cattle trail crosses the Pecos River?
   (A) Chisholm
   (B) Sedalia
   (C) Goodnight-Loving
   (D) Western Trail

3. Which cattle trail passes through the fewest states?
   (A) Chisholm
   (B) Sedalia
   (C) Goodnight-Loving
   (D) Western Trail

4. About how far is it by train from Sedalia to Abilene?
   (A) 150 miles
   (B) 300 miles
   (C) 450 miles
   (D) 600 miles

5. The Goodnight-Loving trail turns north after Pecos because
   (A) that's the way to Denver
   (B) cattle drovers did not want to go into Mexico
   (C) of the mountains
   (D) of the Rio Grande River

6. Which state contains the final railhead for the largest number of cattle trails?
   (A) Texas
   (B) Kansas
   (C) Oklahoma
   (D) Nebraska

7. If drovers move a herd of cattle about 25 kilometers per day, about how many days would it take to move a herd from Fort Smith to Sedalia on the Sedalia Trail?
   (A) 8
   (B) 16
   (C) 24
   (D) 32

Answers

1. **A**	5. **C**
2. **C**	6. **B**
3. **A**	7. **B**
4. **B**	

HISTORY AND SOCIAL STUDIES MSAT PRACTICE ITEMS

These items will help you practice for the real MSAT. These items have the same form and test the same material as the MSAT items and test material. The items you encounter on the MSAT may have a different emphasis and may be more complete.

Instructions

Mark your answers on the sheet provided below. Complete the items in 20 minutes or less. Correct your answer sheet using the answers on page 200.

1	Ⓐ Ⓑ Ⓒ Ⓓ	5	Ⓐ Ⓑ Ⓒ Ⓓ	9	Ⓐ Ⓑ Ⓒ Ⓓ	13	Ⓐ Ⓑ Ⓒ Ⓓ	17	Ⓐ Ⓑ Ⓒ Ⓓ
2	Ⓐ Ⓑ Ⓒ Ⓓ	6	Ⓐ Ⓑ Ⓒ Ⓓ	10	Ⓐ Ⓑ Ⓒ Ⓓ	14	Ⓐ Ⓑ Ⓒ Ⓓ	18	Ⓐ Ⓑ Ⓒ Ⓓ
3	Ⓐ Ⓑ Ⓒ Ⓓ	7	Ⓐ Ⓑ Ⓒ Ⓓ	11	Ⓐ Ⓑ Ⓒ Ⓓ	15	Ⓐ Ⓑ Ⓒ Ⓓ	19	Ⓐ Ⓑ Ⓒ Ⓓ
4	Ⓐ Ⓑ Ⓒ Ⓓ	8	Ⓐ Ⓑ Ⓒ Ⓓ	12	Ⓐ Ⓑ Ⓒ Ⓓ	16	Ⓐ Ⓑ Ⓒ Ⓓ	20	Ⓐ Ⓑ Ⓒ Ⓓ

1. Which of the following has the least significant impact on the culture of a group?
(A) material conditions of life
(B) geography
(C) climate
(D) physical appearance

2. Which of the following forms of government is least used in the countries of today's world?
(A) democracy
(B) aristocracy
(C) monarchy
(D) federal states

3. In the United States, the power to declare war is given to the
(A) president.
(B) Congress.
(C) Supreme Court.
(D) Senate.

4. Which of the following limits the powers of the federal government?
(A) judicial branch
(B) the Bill of Rights
(C) Constitution
(D) executive branch

5. Social psychologists study
(A) people as individuals.
(B) animals in interactive settings.
(C) children at play.
(D) people's behavior in groups.

6. The Ming, Chou, Sung, and Manchu Dynasties were
(A) Indian.
(B) Taiwanese.
(C) Japanese.
(D) Chinese.

7. Sigmund Freud's psychosexual stages of development listed below are organized into which sequence?
(A) oral, genital, anal, latency
(B) genital, anal, oral, latency
(C) oral, anal, genital, latency
(D) oral, anal, latency, genital

8. All the following would be considered the job of an anthropologist EXCEPT:
(A) studying the genetic make up of a fossil.
(B) living with a community of Aborigines.
(C) testing a rock sample with carbon 14.
(D) organizing a dig at a burial site.

9. Who coined the term "iron curtain"?
(A) Churchill
(B) Truman
(C) Lenin
(D) Stalin

10. A U.S. Army officer describes any victory over Native American groups as a triumph, but any defeat as a massacre. What is this an example of?
(A) authoritarianism
(B) ethnocentrism
(C) righteousness
(D) an inferiority complex

11. Which invention revolutionized the South's economy and breathed new life into slavery?
(A) the steam engine
(B) the cotton gin
(C) standard parts
(D) the conveyor belt

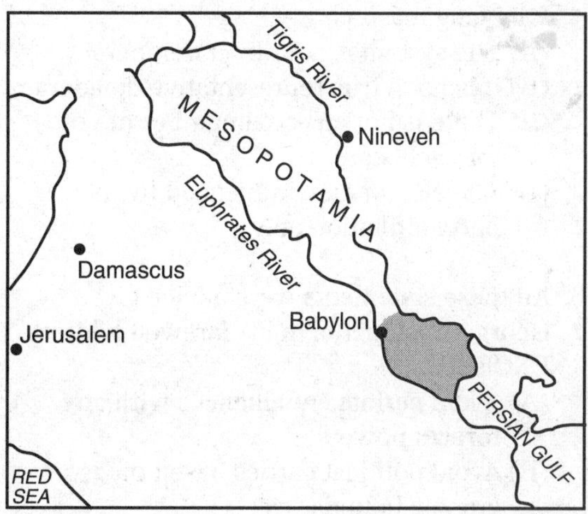

12. Which of the following is not a reason why early civilization began in these shaded areas?
(A) comfortable climate
(B) fertile land
(C) fresh water supply
(D) potential commerce opportunities

13. Why do multinational corporations produce goods in countries such as Mexico and the Philippines?
(A) to increase cash flow in these countries
(B) to widen the marketing area
(C) to lower the cost of labor
(D) to lower the price of the product

14. During one of the Lincoln-Douglas debates, Abraham Lincoln acknowledged that the Southern people were no more responsible for the existence of slavery than those in the North. He went on to say that he understood and appreciated the position of those in the South who said that it was very difficult to get rid of the institution of slavery in an acceptable way. He concluded, however, that these arguments were no more a basis for extending slavery into the free territories of the United States, than they were a basis for legalizing the importation of African slaves.
    During this debate, Lincoln conveyed the notion
    (A) existence doesn't justify expansion.
    (B) hate the sin but not the sinner.
    (C) do unto others as they would do unto you.
    (D) let sleeping dogs lie.

15. Those who validly criticize the workings of the electoral college do so for which of the following reasons?
    (A) The system is not direct democracy.
    (B) It is not a true representative democracy.
    (C) There is not an equal number of votes for each state.
    (D) The electors are influenced by their party affiliation only.

16. All these statements were advice given by George Washington in his farewell address EXCEPT:
    (A) Avoid permanent alliances with any foreign powers.
    (B) Avoid political parties based on geographic boundaries.
    (C) The ability of America to pay its national debts must be safeguarded.
    (D) Avoid supplying monetary aid to foreign countries.

17. Karl Marx's *Communist Manifesto* wished for what result for an economic revolution?
    (A) a society where the proletariat ruled
    (B) a democratic society
    (C) authoritarian society
    (D) a classless society

18. What reason was given to Japanese Americans when they were put in internment camps during World War II?
    (A) They were told that their lives were in danger.
    (B) They were thought to be plotting a sneak attack on home soil.
    (C) They were considered a threat to national security.
    (D) They were being shipped back to Japan as soon as possible.

Use this map to answer questions 19 and 20.

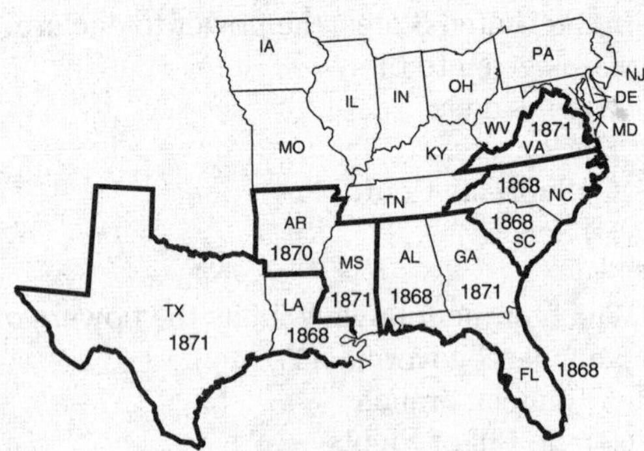

Military Districts During Reconstruction
Date State Readmitted to the Union

19. Which of the states listed below was under federal rule for the longest period of time?
    (A) Texas
    (B) Arkansas
    (C) Alabama
    (D) South Carolina

20. Florida was part of a military district with which two other states?
    (A) Mississippi and Arkansas
    (B) Texas and Louisiana
    (C) North Carolina and South Carolina
    (D) Georgia and Alabama

Answers

1. **D**	5. **D**	9. **A**	13. **C**	17. **D**
2. **D**	6. **D**	10. **B**	14. **A**	18. **A**
3. **B**	7. **D**	11. **B**	15. **C**	19. **A**
4. **C**	8. **C**	12. **D**	16. **D**	20. **D**

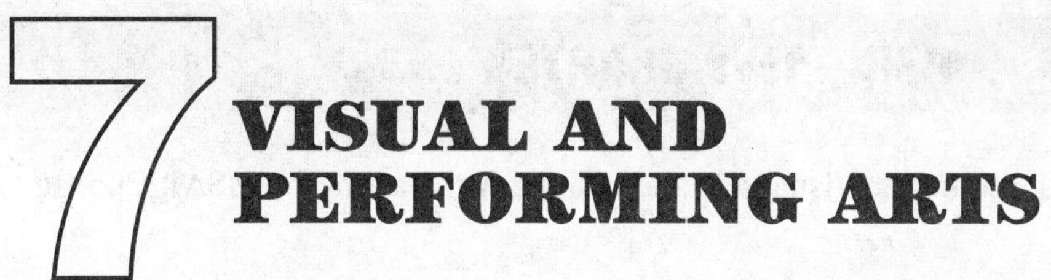

7 VISUAL AND PERFORMING ARTS

TEST INFO BOX

12 of 120 Multiple Choice items — 10% of Content Knowledge items
2 of 18 Short Answer items — 11% of Content Area Exercise items

VISUAL AND PERFORMING ARTS ITEMS

Visual and Performing Arts multiple choice items look like this.

If you see a fresco, it is almost certainly

(A) on a canvas.
(B) in a church.
(C) on a board.
(D) on a wall.

Visual and Performing Arts short answer items look like this.

Describe the different roles of the melody and bass notes in a song.

USING THIS CHAPTER

This chapter prepares you to take the Visual and Performing Arts part of the MSAT. Choose one of these approaches.

I want a Visual and Performing Arts review.

❑ Read the Visual and Performing Arts review.
❑ Complete the Visual and Performing Arts MSAT Practice Questions on page 215.

I want to practice Visual and Performing Arts questions.

❑ Complete the Visual and Performing Arts MSAT Practice Questions on page 215.

I don't need any Visual and Performing Arts review.

❑ OK. If you're sure, skip this chapter.

VISUAL AND PERFORMING ARTS REVIEW

The visual and performing arts items are the most difficult to review for. There is no clear, agreed-on body of knowledge for the test. Each of the four fields that comprise visual and performing arts is as extensive as history or science. This chapter gives a good overview of the types of material and the types of questions you will encounter on the MSAT.

The visual and performing arts include dance, drama/theater, music, and visual art. Three themes provide the focus for the visual and performing arts items on the MSAT: aesthetic perception, cultural heritage, and aesthetic valuing.

Aesthetic Perception (40 percent of questions)

Aesthetic perception is an intrinsic valuing of any art form. Questions in this category ask about the following:

- Essential arts elements and vocabulary
- Arts principles and fundamentals

Cultural Heritage (40 percent of questions)

Cultural heritage means relating artworks to their setting. Questions in this category ask about the following:

Relating artworks to

- each other
- their historical, artistic, cultural, or social period
- their geographic setting

Aesthetic Valuing (20 percent)

Aesthetic valuing means understanding how art works are interpreted or judged. Questions in this category ask about the following:

- Interpreting the meaning of an artwork
- Deciding on and using criteria for judging an artwork

DANCE

Dance is closely related to physical education. Many of the terms and concepts in physical education also apply to dance.

Dance means an intentional movement designed to express a thought, image, feeling, or reality. *A dance* is a sequential, rhythmic movement in two or three dimensional space. A dance has a beginning, a middle, and an end.

Dance medium refers to the types of movement used during dance, including space, shape, force, and time. *Space* refers to the outer space or sphere immediately around the body, and inner space, the real or imaginary space inside the body. *Shape* is the deliberate positioning of the body to create a particular appearance. *Force* is release of energy. Force is the energy that produces a dance. *Time* refers to tempo, beat, and accent during a dance.

Creative movement refers to children's dance movement, which is more exploratory and less purposeful than adult dance. Body movements during a dance may be locomotor or non-locomotor.

Kinesthetic perception describes the body's ability to sense movement. It refers to the muscles' retention of the movement and effort required to produce a dance.

Dancing means to move in a dance-like way. *Choreography* refers to the art of composing dances. A dance style describes the kind of dance associated with a particular style, location, or time period.

There are several types of dance including ballet, tap, jazz, and modern. Improvisation refers to an unplanned dance.

DANCE OBJECTIVES

The following text summarizes drama/theater objectives under the categories Aesthetic Perception, Cultural Heritage, and Aesthetic Valuing.

Aesthetic Perception

Motor Efficiency and Control
Explain the principles of kinesiology.

Space
Describe when actors are using personal or general stage space.

Time
Identify time concepts found in a dance.

Force
Explain internal force (tensions within physical structure of body) during a dance.
Explain external force (tensions created by gravitational pull on body) during a dance.
Explain range of movement qualities (sustained, percussive, vibratory, swing) during a dance.

Cultural Heritage

Historical and Cultural Context of Dance
Identify dance styles from a variety of cultures.
Describe dance styles from historical and cultural perspectives.
Describe dance in various periods of history.
Identify major dance innovators and their innovations.
Explain the place of dance and movement in social contexts in selected cultures.
Discuss the dance that evolved into ballet, jazz, tap, and social forms.

Aesthetic Valuing

Aesthetic Perception
Explain the movements, motifs, and phrases of dance.

Creative Expression
Discuss dance form, noting relationship and manipulation of movement materials.
Interpret dance meaning.

Dance Heritage
Discuss dance history, its roles in society, its variety as related to cultural context, and its numerous contemporary styles and forms.

Viewing and Reviewing
Describe theatrical performances using the terminology of evaluation: intent, structure, effectiveness, and worth.
Discuss the character, theme, and meaning of a performance.

DRAMA AND THEATER

PARTICIPATION

As used here, *drama* means the reenactment of life situations. Drama emphasizes the participant and does not require an audience. *Theater* involves an audience. Theater is a more formal presentation that may include a script, sets, acting, directing, and producing.

A *script* is a written description of a play or other performance. The script tells actors what to say, where to stand, and how to enter and leave a stage. *Actors* are the participants in a play or presentation. *Playmaking* means creating an original story and structuring, performing, and evaluating the presentation without a formal audience.

Acting includes the skills of speaking, movement, and sensory awareness. Acting requires preparation and rehearsal before presentation to the audience. Acting may also involve *improvisation* in which actors create their own spontaneous presentation in response to a problem or some other stimulus.

Production means to arrange for a theater performance. Producers coordinate all the technical aspects of the theater presentation. Producers may be concerned with the overall presentation or with technical aspects within a presentation. *Direction* means to coordinate the on-stage activities. Directors help actors practice and are concerned with the actual on-stage presentation.

EVALUATING DRAMATIC WORKS

Drama and theater provides a natural basis for reflection and evaluation. The following criteria can be used to reflect on and evaluate a dramatic work.

Intent is the reason for a drama or theater work. The intent reflects the objective or purpose for presenting the work.

Structure is the relationship among the different components of a dramatic work. These components include, but are not limited to, balance, coherence, conflict, contrast, emphasis, harmony, rhythm, stress, and transition.

Effectiveness refers to the impact of the dramatic work on the audience. An audience may be affected in many ways by a work including being amused, elated, informed, interested, or moved.

Worth refers to the value of the work itself. That is, it refers to the amount of insight, knowledge, or wisdom found in a work.

DRAMA AND THEATER OBJECTIVES

The following text summarizes drama/theater objectives under the categories Cultural Heritage and Aesthetic Valuing.

Cultural Heritage

Literature and History
Describe the theater including storytelling, improvisation, fairy tales, folklore, and myths.
Discuss theatrical history and the literature of the theater.

Culture
Discuss theater from many cultures and countries.
Discuss the social, psychological, and cultural impact of theater productions on contemporary culture.

Aesthetic Valuing

Function
Categorize music by function and purpose.

Underlying Structures
Observe the details of design principles (e.g., repetition, rhythm, balance, and variation on a theme).
Recognize and compare the three-dimensional composition details of forms from various viewpoints and angles.
Categorize and analyze the three-dimensional qualities of forms.
Discriminate visual characteristics.
Observe that things look different due to varying light, position, and motion.
Identify effects on visual impressions from changes in light, distance, atmosphere, position, recurring motion, lasers, and holograms.

Respond Aesthetically to Visual and Tactile Characteristics
Use various descriptors, analogies, similes, and metaphors to describe unique visual and tactile characteristics observed in works.

MUSIC

Music can be thought of as organized sounds. Our culture has many different types of music, and there are various types of music from cultures all over the world. We usually classify our music in three categories.

1. Popular music is professionally composed, recorded, or performed live and represents the type of music of most current interest to the public.
2. Classical music was composed in the past and, while it is also recorded for sale, is usually performed by large orchestras in “symphony” halls.

3. Folk music usually has a rural origin, is usually not composed professionally, and is often transmitted by oral tradition.

Music consists of pitch, the actual frequency or sound of a note, and duration. A tone has a specific pitch and duration. Different tones occurring simultaneously are called chords.

Harmony is chords with a duration. A melody is the tones that produce the distinctive sound of the music.

Rhythm in our music refers primarily to the regularity of beats or meter. The most common meter in our music has four beats with an emphasis on the first beat.

Pitches separated by specific intervals are called a scale. Most music is based on the diatonic *scale* found on the piano white keys (C, D, E, F, G, A, B). The chromatic scale includes the seven notes of the diatonic scale with the five sharps and flats corresponding to the white and black keys on the piano.

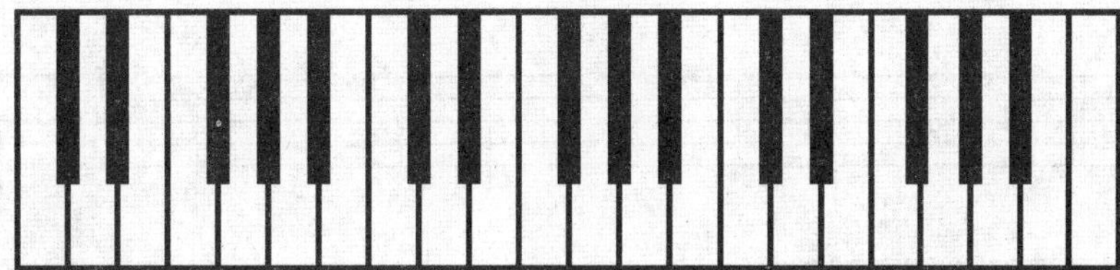

Think of the piano. The piano represents the chromatic scale with groups of seven white keys and five black keys. Music is played using tones from this scale for varying durations.

Usually the melody consists of one note at a time and is played with the right hand. Harmony usually consists of chords and is played with the left hand. The rhythm of the music reflects the meter, and the arrangements and duration of notes.

Form refers to the overall structure of music. Patterns or sections of a musical may repeat or all parts of the pieces may be unique. Phrases or sections in a musical piece may complement one another or they may contrast.

Dynamics describes how loud or how soft the music is. The dynamic aspects of a musical work add to its expressive qualities. Terms such as *pianissimo* (play very softly) are used to refer to musical dynamics.

Tempo refers to the speed of a musical work. The tempo of a piece may vary in different sections of the piece to provide contrast and alert the listener to the various meanings that sections are meant to convey.

Texture refers to the "feel" the musical work imparts. Terms such as *staccato* (choppy) are used to describe the texture of a musical work.

Timbre describes the unique sound produced by different instruments, instrumental combinations and by the human voice. Families of instruments such as woodwinds (clarinet, saxophone) and horns (trumpet, trombone) have similar timbres.

MUSICAL NOTATION

Our musical notation uses a staff to represent notes. The clef placed at the beginning of the staff determines the pitches for each line and space on the staff.

Notes are written on the staff using the following notation. A flat (♭) lowers the note a half tone while a sharp (♯) raises the note a half tone. The natural (♮) cancels a flat or sharp. Rests indicate a time when no music is played. A note followed by a dot is increased in value by half.

Whole-note	Dotted quarter-note
Half-note	Whole-rest
Quarter-note	Half-rest
Eighth-note	Quarter-rest
Sixteenth-note	Eighth-rest

The staff is partitioned into measures. The sum of the values of the notes in any measure equals 1. A key signature of sharps and/or flats can be written at the beginning of a staff to change these notes throughout the piece.

A time signature is written at the beginning of each staff. The top number shows how many beats per measure and the bottom number shows which note gets a beat. A typical staff showing the G clef is shown here.

MUSICAL INSTRUMENTS

Until recently, music was created by the human voice or by instruments. One typical classification of instruments follows.

Percussion instruments are played by being struck. Bell, drum, gong, piano, symbol, and xylophone are examples.

Brass instruments have traditionally been made from "brass" or some other metal and are played by vibrating the lips against the mouthpiece. French horn, trombone, trumpet, and tuba are examples.

Woodwinds are played by blowing. Most woodwinds have reeds while a few, such as the flute, do not. Bassoon, clarinet, flute, oboe, and saxophone are examples.

Stringed instruments are played by plucking or drawing a bow across the strings. Notes are formed by holding the strings down while plucking or bowing. Cello, guitar, viola, and violin are examples.

In this century, music began to be produced electronically. In the past few decades, computers and other devices have been able to replicate exactly the sounds of almost every instrument. Today, a person can compose a musical piece on a computer and have the computer play that music using a full array of musical sounds without ever picking up an instrument. The full impact of this electronic music is yet to be realized.

GLOSSARY OF MUSICAL TERMS

acoustics The science of sound or the sound property of a room or auditorium.

allegro Cheerful or happy music.

aria A song set off from the rest of the opera.

bass The lower notes in a musical piece; the lowest voice in a choir.

cadence Several notes that signal the ending of a musical piece or phrase.

chamber music Music played by a small group of eight or fewer musicians.

chorale German Protestant hymns.

concerto A musical piece that juxtaposes an orchestra with a soloist or small group of soloists.

movement One part of a piece of music consisting of several large parts.

orchestra A large group of musicians playing many different types of instruments.

overture A musical, orchestral introduction.

MUSIC OBJECTIVES

The following text summarizes music objectives under the categories Aesthetic Perception and Cultural Heritage.

Aesthetic Perception

Sound Generation and Modification
Group sounds according to how they were produced.
Identify ways of changing the sound of a voice or an instrument.

Musical Elements
Identify *pitch* and pitch relationships.
Identify *rhythm* and discriminate among the rhythmic forms of musical works.
Describe and identify polyphonic, homophonic, and monophonic *harmonies.*
Describe the *form* of a musical work.
Describe and identify polyphonic, homophonic, and monophonic *texture.*
Identify the *tempo* of a musical work.
Describe how musical works combine elements to produce a particular timbre.

Notation Symbols
Identify a musical piece from its written form.

Cultural Heritage

Cultural Musical Contributions
Describe how composers have drawn inspiration from regional and national cultures.
Explain the similarities and differences in styles, performance media, and tone colors in various cultures.
Describe how music is determined by the performance media.
Describe how the social and environmental influences of a cultural group determine the character of the music.
Explain how the function of music dictates the style and form.

VISUAL ARTS

Visual art includes paintings, photographs, prints, carvings, sculpture, and architecture. *Representational* art presents a recognizable representation of real people, places, or things. *Abstract* art presents nonrecognizable representations of real things or thoughts, perhaps using geometric shapes or designs. *Nonrepresentational* art is unrelated to real things or thoughts and represents only itself.

Visual arts are built around certain visual elements.

Points are represented by dots and are the simplest visual element. **Lines** are created when points move and may be horizontal, vertical, diagonal, straight, jagged, or wavy. Lines come in many thicknesses and lengths. Lines in a painting or drawing may suggest three-dimensional images or outline a shape.

Shapes are bounded forms in two-dimensional art. The boundary of a shape is usually a line, but it may also be created by color, shading, and texture. A shape may be geometric or fluid.

Space refers to the area occupied by the art. Paintings occupy two-dimensional space, while sculpture occupies three-dimensional space. Sculptors manipulate three-dimensional space and forms to create the desired effect, while painters often manipulate two-dimensional space to create the illusion of three-dimensional space.

Color: The colors of the spectrum are red, orange, yellow, green, blue, indigo, and violet. White is actually the combination of all the spectral colors, and black is an absence of color. Colors communicate mood (blue is cold, yellow is warm). Warm colors appear to expand a work's size while cold colors appear to contract its size. Color has three properties.

1. **Hue** is the color itself. It describes a color's placement in the color spectrum.
2. **Value** refers to the amount of lightness or darkness in a color. Low value shades are dark, while high value shades are light. You can raise the value of a color by adding white, and lower the value by adding black.
3. **Saturation** (also called chroma or intensity) describes the brightness or dullness of a color.

Perspective refers to methods of manipulating two-dimensional space to create the illusion of three-dimensional space. *Foreshortening* means exaggerating linear perspective by drawing the near parts of an object in close proximity to the far parts of the same object. *Linear perspective* means drawing objects smaller as they get further away. Still photographs naturally employ linear perspective.

PRINCIPLES OF DESIGN

These elements of design are frequently used to analyze and describe an artwork.

Balance refers to the equilibrium of elements that create a work. Balance can be achieved through both symmetrical and asymmetrical arrangements.

Symmetry is achieved when one half of an artwork more or less reflects the other half. Symmetrical works tend to create a sense of formality.

Asymmetry is achieved when color and the lightness of different parts of a work create a sense of balance. For example, a lighter area may balance a darker area. Asymmetrical works tend to create a sense of informality.

Rhythm refers to the repetition of elements in an artwork. Effective repetition of design elements tends to create a more dynamic work.

Dominance means to use color or positioning to draw the attention of the viewer to the most important element or elements in a work.

PAINTING

Painting techniques include oil, watercolor, gouache, and fresco. The paint for all of these techniques consists of a pigment (color), binder (e.g., egg, oil, wax), which holds the pigment together, and solvents (water, turpentine), which permit the paint to spread on a surface.

Oil is the primary painting form. The oil can be applied as thinly or thickly as desired and dries slowly so that the artist can rework it until the desired result is obtained.

Watercolor presents a thin wispy appearance and is widely used for landscape painting. Gouache is an opaque watercolor that is often applied to a board. Acrylic paints combine most of the advantages of oil paint with easy clean up. Acrylics are often applied with an airbrush.

ART OBJECTIVES

The following text summarizes art objectives under the categories Aesthetic Perception, Cultural Heritage, and Aesthetic Valuing.

Aesthetic Perception

Recognize Design Elements
Recognize and distinguish among the elements of line, color, value, shape, and texture. Recognize and discriminate between the impact of light and shadow on the other design elements.

Cultural Heritage

Recognize Varying Cultural Themes
Name, compare, and contrast themes in selected works of art from various cultures.

Analyze the Creative Process
Identify that artists make art by conceiving an idea, developing and refining it, and giving form to the idea with art media.
Describe ways that historians, curators, critics, and anthropologists describe particular works.

Recognize the Artist's Role
Identify how artists who have achieved national and international recognition have influenced thinking.

Recognize Varying Cultural Styles
Identify the general style and period of major works of art and relate social, political, and economic factors that influenced the works.

Discriminate National Cultural Styles
Identify contemporary style trends in American art as reflections of diverse developments in our culture.

Recognize Visual Arts from World Cultures
Identify works of art from a variety of world cultures and recognize differences in media used by various cultures. Relate these differences to visual arts achievements.

Aesthetic Valuing

Analyze Design Elements
Use design elements (line, color, value, shape, and texture) to describe works of art.
Identify the interaction among design elements that give the work of art a particular emphasis.

Recognize Use of Design Elements
Describe art based on the way design principles are organized.
Explain how design principles contribute to the qualities of a work of art.
Recognize art media and processes.
Understand the use of specific media (oil, watercolor, clay, wood, stone, metal) that are used to create works of art and other art forms.
Explain a process related to a medium, such as watercolor, clay, or weaving, and how it is used in producing a work of art.

Recognize Artistic Mood
Explain the meaning of works of art in terms of mood, such as selected ideals (e.g., courage and wisdom).
Describe aesthetic characteristics.
Employ descriptors, metaphors, and analogies to describe works of art.

Discriminate Artistic Style
Identify those qualities that indicate that two pieces of art have the same style.

ANALYZING ART

Art appears in many incarnations, including paintings, photographs, prints, carvings, sculpture, and architecture. When asked to analyze any work of art, you can comment on the content, the form, the style, and the method used by the artist.

The *content* is what actually appears in a work of art. It is the subject matter of the art. Don't take the obvious subject matter for granted when considering your analysis. Choose descriptive words as you search for ways to capture the content of the image in front of you. For example, a landscape may contain peaceful blue skies, a raging river, cows and horses grazing, or seemingly endless grassy fields. A portrait may show a happy person or someone filled with concern or worry. A sculpture may show a smoothly muscled athlete. A building may have cascading stairs or a series of columns that thrust upward to the ceiling.

The *form* of a work of art is the order imposed by the artist. Form is the design of the work regardless of the content. A painting or photograph may show strong horizontal or vertical orientation. Perhaps the work is symmetrical, with one part a mirror image of the other. Some works may be tilted or asymmetrical.

The *style* refers to the artist's way of expressing ideas including formal styles such as gothic, high renaissance, baroque, or impressionist. In a painting or picture you can notice how the artist uses color. The colors may blend or clash. There may be an overall dark tone to the picture, or it may be light and airy. Perhaps the artist used dots of paint to produce the image.

The *method* is the medium used by the artist to create the work. It may be an oil painting or a watercolor. Perhaps the artist created prints or an etching. A three-dimensional work of art may have been sculpted, cast, carved, molded, or turned on a potter's wheel.

Keep these elements of content, form, style, and method in mind as you respond to the questions on the MSAT.

GLOSSARY OF ART TERMS

allegory Art that represents or symbolizes some idea or quality.
amphora An egg-shaped Grecian urn.
ankh An Egyptian hieroglyph that represents life. See illustration.

Ankh

annealing Softening by heating glass or metal that has become hardened.
arebesque Very intricate designs based on plant forms.
arch A curved span. See illustration.

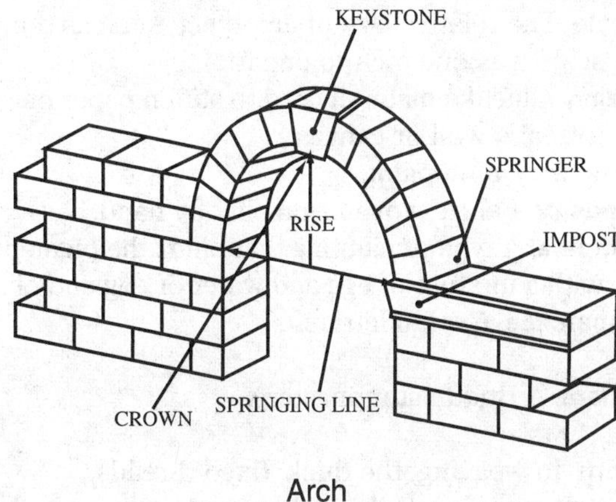

Arch

atrium An open rectangular-shaped court, often in front of a church.
avant-garde Art considered ahead of its time.

baluster A small curved post or pillar.
balustrade A railing usually supported by balusters.
batten Strips of wood used as a base for plastering or for attaching tile.
belfry The top floor of a tower usually containing bells.
bevel To round off a sharp edge.
biscuit Unglazed porcelain.
bust A sculpture showing the head and shoulders.

calligraphy Decorative writing.
canopy A fabric covering.
casement A vertically hinged window frame.
ceramics All porcelain and pottery.
chalice An ornamental cup often used in religious services.
chancel The part of a church reserved for clergy.
collage Art created by pasting together many media including newspaper, fabric, and wood. A collage may also include paintings or drawings.
colors Many colors can be created by combining the primary colors. See illustration.

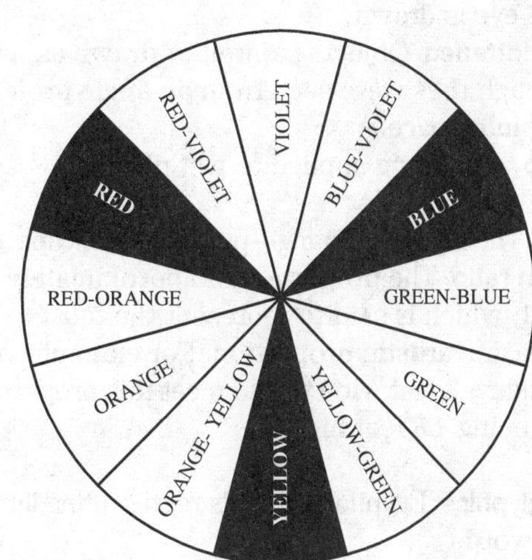

Color Wheel

column A free-standing, circular pillar. Several different styles exist. See illustration.

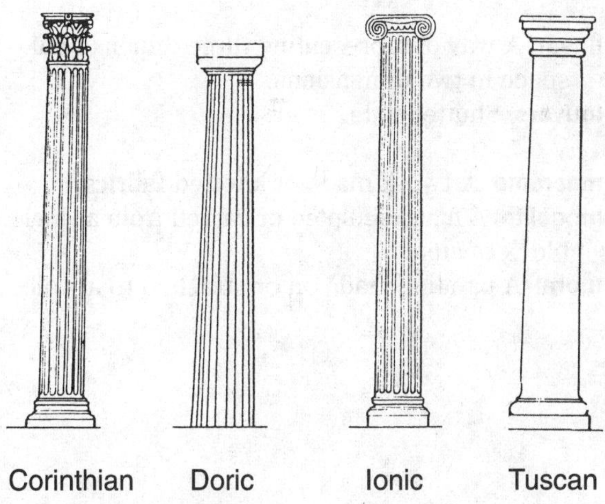

Corinthian Doric Ionic Tuscan

course A row of bricks or stones.
cuneiform Wedge-shaped writing associated with Babylonians and Sumerians.

decoupage Cutting out designs to be used in a collage.

eclectic Drawing on many styles.
enamel Powdered glass bonded to a metal surface by firing.

engraving Inscribing a design on glass, metal, or some other hard surface.
etching Designs created on metal plates by applying acid to initial scratchings and the prints made from these plates.

filigree Gold or silver soldered to create elaborate, delicate patterns.
focal point The place on a work of art to which the eye is drawn.
foreshortened Objects painted or drawn as though they were seen from an angle projecting into space.
fresco A painting applied to wet plaster.

genre The type of painting—portrait, landscape, etc.
golden ratio The proportion of approximately 1.6 to 1, which is said to represent the most pleasing artistic proportion. For example, a window 3 feet wide would meet this proportion by being 4.8 feet high.

hieroglyphics Egyptian symbols representing letters or words.

illustration An idea or scene represented in art.

jamb The sides of a window or door.

kiosk A small booth with a roof and open sides.

linear A way of representing three-dimensional space in two dimensions.
louvers Shutter slats.

macrame Artwork made of knotted fabrics.
monolith A figure sculpted or carved from a single block of stone.
mural A painting made on or attached to a wall.

niche A wall recess.

obelisk A rectangular block of stone, often with a pyramidal top.

papier maché Paper (newspaper) soaked with water and flour and shaped into figures.
parquet A floor made of wooden tile.
perspective Representing three dimensions on a flat surface.
pigment The material used to color paint.
plaster Limestone and sand or gypsum mixed with water, which can be shaped and then hardened. Plaster can also be carved and is often used to finish walls and ceilings.
projection The techniques of representing buildings on a flat surface.
quarry tile Unglazed tile.

relief Carved or molded art in which the art projects from the background.
sarcophagus A stone coffin.
scale The relative size of an object, such as the scale was one inch to one foot.
sizing Gluelike material used to stiffen paper or to seal a wall or canvas.
stipple Dab on paint.
tapestry Fabric woven from silk by hand.
tempera A type of painting that binds the pigment with a mixture of egg and water or egg and oil.
uppercase Capital letters.

vihara A Buddhist monastery.

warp In weaving, the thick, fixed threads.
weft In weaving, the thin threads that are actually woven.

VISUAL AND PERFORMING ARTS MSAT PRACTICE ITEMS

These items will help you practice for the real MSAT. These items have the same form and test the same material as the MSAT items. The items you encounter on the real MSAT may have a different emphasis and may be more complete.

Instructions

Mark your answers on the sheet provided below. Complete the items in 20 minutes or less. Correct your answer sheet using the answers on page 219.

1 Ⓐ Ⓑ Ⓒ Ⓓ	5 Ⓐ Ⓑ Ⓒ Ⓓ	9 Ⓐ Ⓑ Ⓒ Ⓓ	13 Ⓐ Ⓑ Ⓒ Ⓓ	17 Ⓐ Ⓑ Ⓒ Ⓓ
2 Ⓐ Ⓑ Ⓒ Ⓓ	6 Ⓐ Ⓑ Ⓒ Ⓓ	10 Ⓐ Ⓑ Ⓒ Ⓓ	14 Ⓐ Ⓑ Ⓒ Ⓓ	18 Ⓐ Ⓑ Ⓒ Ⓓ
3 Ⓐ Ⓑ Ⓒ Ⓓ	7 Ⓐ Ⓑ Ⓒ Ⓓ	11 Ⓐ Ⓑ Ⓒ Ⓓ	15 Ⓐ Ⓑ Ⓒ Ⓓ	19 Ⓐ Ⓑ Ⓒ Ⓓ
4 Ⓐ Ⓑ Ⓒ Ⓓ	8 Ⓐ Ⓑ Ⓒ Ⓓ	12 Ⓐ Ⓑ Ⓒ Ⓓ	16 Ⓐ Ⓑ Ⓒ Ⓓ	20 Ⓐ Ⓑ Ⓒ Ⓓ

A.

The Metropolitan Museum of Art, Gift of Mrs. Charles Stewart Smith, Charles Stewart Smith Jr. and Howard Casell Smith, in memory of Charles Stewart Smith, 1914. (14.76.37)

B.

The Metropolitan Museum of Art, Rogers & Fletcher Funds, Erving & Joyce Wolf Fund, Raymond J. Horowitz Gift, Bequest of Richard De Wolfe Brixey, by Exchange, & John Osgood & Elizabeth Amis Cameron Blanchard Memorial Fund, 1978. (1978.203)

C.

The Metropolitan Museum of Art, Gift of Mr. and Mrs. Joseph G. Blum, 1970. (1970.527.1)

1. Picture A expresses
   (A) anger.
   (B) pensiveness.
   (C) distraction.
   (D) assertiveness.

2. Picture A could be best described as
   (A) an abstract work whose primary meaning is the work itself.
   (B) a central figure surrounded by rectangular border.
   (C) an impressionistic work in which the figure represents an animal.
   (D) an 18th century American work.

3. Picture A is distinctive because
   (A) the border is decorated.
   (B) the figure is horned.
   (C) The sword has a carved, ornamental handle.
   (D) The figure is thrust forward.

4. Picture B depicts a
   (A) rocky shore.
   (B) seaport.
   (C) sloping shore.
   (D) turgid sea.

5. Picture B could be best described as
   (A) a bucolic scene.
   (B) an active scene.
   (C) a morning scene.
   (D) a languid scene.

6. Which of the following best describes Picture B?
   (A) A scene with people talking
   (B) A scene with children playing
   (C) A commercial scene
   (D) A scene dominated by the sky

7. Picture C primarily depicts
   (A) geometric contrasts.
   (B) a swirling sky.
   (C) a skyward needle.
   (D) a supported walkway.

8. Which of the following best describes Picture C?
   (A) A brick plaza sweeping by open latticed rectangles
   (B) A surreal world visited by real people
   (C) A visitors center at a spaceport
   (D) A central spire framed by sphere, semi-circle, and sky.

9. Picture C is most likely
   (A) an artist's rendering of buildings to be constructed.
   (B) a set for a futuristic movies.
   (C) a three-dimensional model of a NASA visitors center.
   (D) a picture of an actual structure.

10. Which picture best depicts determination?
    (A)
    (B)
    (C)

11. Which picture does not include a semicircular shape?
    (A)
    (B)
    (C)

12. Which picture shows multiple events?
    (A)
    (B)
    (C)

13. Which of the following is the name for the process of applying watercolors to a freshly plastered surface?
    (A) fresco
    (B) watercolor
    (C) mosaic
    (D) mural

14. When a mason refers to a course, he or she usually means
    (A) time spent as an apprentice.
    (B) a row of bricks.
    (C) a layer of plaster.
    (D) a stretch of lawn.

15. The songs "Frankie and Johnny," and "John Henry" are American examples of
    (A) blues.
    (B) jazz.
    (C) protest.
    (D) ballads.

16. The impressionist art movement, which included artists such as Monet and Renoir, was founded as a reaction against more classical styles and featured
    (A) abstract, linear works.
    (B) undetailed, but recognizable works.
    (C) blue and rose hues.
    (D) realistic, precise works.

17. Masks were worn regularly in Greek and Roman plays. A character wore the mask from the very beginning of the play
    (A) to conceal the actor's identity.
    (B) until the very last act, when it was removed.
    (C) enabling the actor to show a range of emotions.
    (D) removing any doubt about the characters eventual fate.

18. What form of dance do you associate with Alvin Ailey?
    (A) ballet
    (B) modern
    (C) rock
    (D) tap

19. In the key of C, which of these chords is a minor chord?
    (A) C E G
    (B) G B D
    (C) A C E
    (D) F A C

20. The Dutch artist Mondrian is best known for what art form?
    (A) abstract art
    (B) architecture
    (C) non-representational art
    (D) representational art

Answers

1. **D**	5. **D**	9. **D**	13. **A**	17. **D**
2. **B**	6. **D**	10. **A**	14. **B**	18. **A**
3. **D**	7. **A**	11. **A**	15. **D**	19. **C**
4. **A**	8. **D**	12. **B**	16. **B**	20. **C**

HUMAN DEVELOPMENT

TEST INFO BOX

8 of 120 Multiple Choice items — **7% of Content Knowledge items**
2 of 18 Short Answer items — **11% of Content Area Exercise items**

HUMAN DEVELOPMENT ITEMS

Human Development multiple choice items look like this.

A child in the eighth grade is developing normally. According to Eriksen's theory of psychosocial development, what primary emotional crisis is the child going through?

(A) Intimacy vs. isolation
(B) Initiative vs. guilt
(C) Industry vs. inferiority
(D) Identity vs. identity confusion

Human Development short answer items look like this.

The Swiss psychologist Jean Piaget believed that children learn through a process called equilibration. Briefly explain what Piaget meant and include an example.

USING THIS CHAPTER

This chapter prepares you to take the Human Development part of the MSAT. Choose one of these approaches.

I want all the Human Development review I can get.

- ❑ Skip the Review Quiz and read the entire review section.
- ❑ Take the Human Development Review Quiz on page 222.
- ❑ Correct the Review Quiz and reread the indicated parts of the review.
- ❑ Complete the Human Development MSAT Practice Questions on page 243.

I want a thorough Human Development review.

- ❑ Take the Human Development Review Quiz on page 222.
- ❑ Correct the Review Quiz and reread the indicated parts of the review.
- ❑ Complete the Human Development MSAT Practice Questions on page 243.

I want a quick Human Development review.

- ❑ Take and correct the Human Development Review Quiz on page 222.
- ❑ Complete the Human Development MSAT Practice Questions on page 243.

I want to practice Human Development questions.

- ❑ Complete the Human Development MSAT Practice Questions on page 243.

I don't need any Human Development review.

- ❑ OK. If you're sure, skip this chapter.

HUMAN DEVELOPMENT REVIEW QUIZ

This quiz uses a short answer format to help you find out what you know about the Human Development topics reviewed in this chapter. The quiz results direct you to the portions of the chapter you should read.

This quiz will also help focus your thinking about Human Development, and these questions and answers are a good review in themselves. It's not important to answer all these questions correctly, and don't be concerned if you miss many of them.

The answers are found immediately after the quiz. It's to your advantage not to look at them until you have completed the quiz. Once you have completed and corrected this review quiz, use the answer checklist to decide which sections of the review to study.

Write the answers in the space provided or on a separate sheet of paper.

1. Who provided an experimental basis for behaviorism?

2. Give Piaget's four stages of cognitive development along with the approximate ages and one characteristic of each stage.

3. According to Eriksen, what is the primary emotional crisis experienced by children in grades 6–9?

4. What do social learning theorists mean when they talk about modeling?

5. About what percent of American families have children, a mother at home, and a father at work?

6. Where do most seventh and eighth graders turn for leadership?

7. Do students learn more when they are being taught or when they are working independently?

8. What is extrinsic motivation?

9. Generally speaking, what moral behavior do children exhibit in Kohlberg's stage of Preconventional Morality?

10. About what percent of those who commit serious crimes are caught?

11. What is the most used and abused drug?

12. How is the HIV virus transmitted?

13. At about what age do boys and girls enter adolescence? Boys ______Girls ______

14. Lectures and explanations are most effective when they begin with what first step?

15. Using Bloom's Taxonomy, what level of questions should be asked in classrooms?

16. About how long should a teacher wait for a student to respond to a question?

17. What types of questions do teachers ask in a student-centered classroom?

18. What important aspects characterize active learning?

19. What is the last step in inquiry learning?

20. Which has the most significant impact on human development, nature or nurture?

21. How can modeling change student behavior?

22. How can negative reinforcement change student behavior?

23. Describe formative evaluation.

24. What is the most common error made when reading standardized test reports?

25. What is content validity?

26. What is authentic assessment?

27. What factor correlates most highly with normed scores?

28. What types of diversity might require modification of objectives?

29. How would you adapt instruction for learning-disabled students?

30. Overall, what factor correlates most highly with school achievement?

31. About when would we expect the school population in America to be evenly divided between Caucasian and minority students?

32. To what country do most Hispanic Americans trace their origin?

33. Which ethnic group in America has the highest suicide rate and alcoholism rate?

ANSWER CHECKLIST

The answers are organized by review sections. Check your answers. If you miss any questions in a section, check the box and review that section.

❑ **Implications and Applications of Theory,** *page 225*

1. Pavlov with his experiments on dogs.

2. Piaget's four stages of cognitive development:

- Sensorimotor (Birth to 18 months)—Children develop the idea of object permanence (out of sight not out of mind) during this stage.
- Preoperational (18 months to 7 years)—Children develop language and are able to solve some problems. Students' thinking is egocentric, and they have difficulty developing concepts such as the conservation of number task.
- Concrete operational (7-12 years)—students' thinking becomes operational. This means that concepts become organized and logical, as long as they are working with or around concrete materials or images. Students master the conservation tasks.
- Formal operational (12+ years)—Children develop and demonstrate concepts without concrete materials or images. Students think fully in symbolic terms about concepts. Children become able to reason effectively, abstractly, and theoretically.

3. Identity vs. identity confusion

4. acting in a way you want others to act

5. about 10 percent

6. They turn to their peer group.

❑ **Implications and Applications of Research,** *page 228*

7. Students learn more when they are being taught.

8. external rewards to improve student performance

9. no conscience, no clear morality

10. about 30 percent

11. alcohol

12. exchange of blood and bodily fluids (Intravenous drug users can acquire AIDS when they share needles and inject small quantities of infected blood.)

13. boys about 12, girls about 10

14. motivation

❑ *Major Developmental Perspectives, page 232*

15. Questions should be asked at all levels.

16. 4 to 5 seconds.

17. more open-ended questions.

18. group work, active learning, full participation, and democratic structure

19. metacognition—that is, students analyze their thought processes.

20. The issue remains unresolved.

21. Students who observe a person behaving in a particular way often emulate that person.

22. Negative reinforcement can change behavior when it is used to show students how to avoid undesirable consequences by doing acceptable work.

❑ *Gathering and Using Information, page 236*

23. Formative information is used to plan instruction.

24. looking at a single score instead of a range of scores

25. Content validity describes the extent to which a test measures the material being taught.

26. Students are evaluated as they demonstrate knowledge or a skill in a real life setting.

27. socioeconomic status (SES)

❑ *Human Diversity, page 238*

28. academic, cultural, and linguistic

29. Provide structured brief assignments, manipulative activities, and auditory learning

30. socioeconomic status (SES)

31. by about 2020 (Count your answer correct if you were within 10 years.)

32. Mexico

33. Native Americans

HUMAN DEVELOPMENT REVIEW

IMPLICATIONS AND APPLICATIONS OF THEORY

This section describes theories of learning and development.

Behavioral Development

Behaviorism was the first significant theory of development. Behaviorism is concerned with observable, measurable behavior and with those events that stimulate or reinforce the behavior.

Watson

John Watson originated the behaviorist movement during the early 1900s. His theoretical ideas centered around conditioned responses in children. Conditioned response means that a child was "taught" to respond in a particular way to a stimulus that would not naturally elicit that response. Watson's experiment to condition a child to fear a white rat that the child initially liked is most quoted in texts. Many claim that the success of the experiment was overstated.

Pavlov

Many trace the experimental basis for behaviorism to the Russian psychologist Pavlov who, in the 1920s, conducted classical conditioning experiments with dogs. Dogs naturally salivate in an unconditioned response to the unconditioned stimulus of food. Pavlov showed that dogs would salivate in response to any neutral stimulus. The neutral stimulus is called a conditioned stimulus, and the salivation that occurs is called a conditioned response.

Thorndike

Also in the early 1900s Edward Thorndike developed his own form of behaviorism called instrumental conditioning. Thorndike's work with animals led him to two significant conclusions.

- The law of exercise—a conditioned response can be strengthened by repeating the response (practice).
- The law of effect—rewarded responses are strengthened while punished responses are weakened.

Skinner

Skinner was the most influential behaviorist. Skinner referred to his approach as operant conditioning, which studied how voluntary behavior could be shaped. Operant conditioning relies on these basic mechanisms.

- Reward or positive reinforcement—Students are rewarded for repeating desired responses.
- Negative reinforcement—Students escape punishment by repeating desired responses.
- Extinction—Undesired responses are not reinforced.
- Punishment—Undesired responses are punished.

Skinner showed that he could condition very complex behaviors in animals. He believed that students learned when teachers gave immediate positive feedback for a desired behavior and used extinction or punishment for undesirable behaviors.

Cognitive Development

Jean Piaget

Jean Piaget is the most prominent of cognitive psychologists, who believe that students develop concepts through a series of stages. Stage theory is currently the most popular form of child development.

According to Piaget, children proceed through a fixed but uneven series of stages of cognitive development. His stages help us understand the general way in which students learn and develop concepts.

Action and logic versus perception are at the center of Piaget's theory. He believed that children learn through an active involvement with their environment. He also believed that students have developed a concept when their logical understanding overcomes their perceptual misunderstanding of the concept.

His conservation experiments explain this last point. In conservation of number, students are shown two matched rows of checkers. The child confirms that there are the same number of checkers in each row. Then one row of checkers is spread out and the child is asked if there are still the same number of checkers. Children who believe there are more checkers in one of

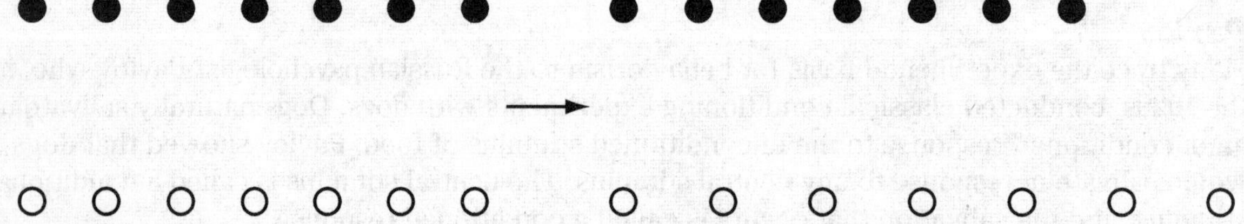

the rows do not understand the concept of number because their perception holds sway over their logic.

Piaget presents these four stages of cognitive development.

- Sensorimotor (birth to 18 months)—Children exhibit poor verbal and cognitive development. Children develop the idea of object permanence (out of sight not out of mind) during this stage.
- Preoperational (18 months to 7 years)—Children develop language and are able to solve some problems. Students' thinking is egocentric, and they have difficulty developing concepts. For example, students in this stage may not be able to complete the conservation of number task shown above.
- Concrete operational (7–12 years)—Students' thinking becomes operational. This means that concepts become organized and logical, as long as they are working with or around concrete materials or images. During this stage, students master the number conservation and other conservation tasks, but most students do not understand symbolic concepts.
- Formal operational (12+ years)—Children develop and demonstrate concepts without concrete materials or images. In this stage, students think fully in symbolic terms about concepts. Children become able to reason effectively, abstractly, and theoretically. Full development of this stage may depend on the extent to which children have had a full range of active manipulative experiences in the concrete operational stage.

Social Learning

Social learning theory is a fairly new field. Social learning theorists seek to combine behavioral and cognitive learning theories along with other types of learning.

Albert Bandura is the leading social learning theorist. He believes that a great deal of learning can take place through modeling. That is, students often act the way they see others act, or they learn vicariously by observing others. Bandura believes that verbal explanations and reinforcement are also important and that students become socialized through systematic modeling of appropriate behavior. Students can also develop cognitive skills by observing a problem-solving process and learn procedures by observing these procedures in action.

Psychosocial Development

Eriksen built on Freud's work and partitioned the life span into eight psychosocial stages. An emotional crisis at each stage can lead to a positive or negative result. The result achieved at each stage determines the development pattern for the next stage. Four of these stages fall within the school years.

Stage	Characteristic	Description
Kindergarten	Initiative vs. Guilt	Children accepted and treated warmly tend to feel more comfortable about trying out new ideas. Rejected children tend to become inhibited and guilty.
Elementary grades	Industry vs. Inferiority	Students who are accepted by their peer group and who do well in school and students who just feel that the above is true are more successful than those who do not feel good about themselves.
Grade 6–9	Identity vs. Identity Confusion	Students who establish an identity and a sense of direction and who develop gender, social, and occupational roles experience an easier transition into adulthood than those students who do not establish these roles.
Grades 10–12	Intimacy vs. Isolation	Students who have passed successfully through the other stages will find it easier to establish a relationship with a member of the opposite sex. Those students who are unsuccessful at this stage may face an extremely difficult transition into adult life.

IMPLICATIONS AND APPLICATIONS OF RESEARCH

This section summarizes research findings on how children learn and develop.

The Family

The family remains the predominant influence in the early lives of children. However, the nature of the American family has changed, and for the worse.

Divorce rates are very high and some say that a majority of Americans under 40 will be divorced. American families are fragmented with about 30 percent of children living with a step-parent. About one-quarter of children are raised in one-parent families, and about two-thirds of these children live below the poverty level.

An increasing number of children, called latchkey children, return from school with no parents at home. School programs developed for these students cannot replace effective parenting.

In many respects, the school, social or religious institutions, peer groups, and gangs have replaced parents. This means that parents and families have less influence on children's values and beliefs.

The pressures of economic needs have drastically changed the American family. Less than 10 percent of American families have children, a mother at home, and a father at work. Over 30 percent of married couples have no children, and over 70 percent of mothers with children are working mothers.

Characteristics of Students

We can make some general statements about the students in a class. We know that 3–7 percent of girls and 12–18 percent of boys will have some substantial adjustment problems. Prepare yourself for these predictable sex differences.

Boys are more physically active and younger children have shorter attention spans. Respond to this situation by scheduling activities when students are more likely to be able to complete them.

A teacher's management role is different at different grade levels. Prepare for these predictable differences in student reaction to teacher authority.

In the primary grades, students see teachers as authority figures and respond well to instruction and directions about how they should act in school. In the middle grades, students have learned how to act in school and still react well to the teacher's instruction.

In seventh through tenth grade, students turn to their peer group for leadership and resist the teacher's authority. The teacher must spend more time fostering appropriate behavior among students. By the last two years of high school, students are somewhat less resistant and the teacher's role is more academic.

We know that many adolescents resent being touched and that teachers may anger adolescents by taking something from them. Avoid this problem by not confronting adolescent students.

We know that there will be cultural differences among students. Many minority students, and other students, may be accustomed to harsh, authoritarian treatment. Respond to these students with warmth and acceptance. Many minority students will feel completely out of place in school. These students also need to be treated warmly and also with the positive expectation that they will succeed in school.

Many other students may be too distracted to study effectively in school. These students may need quiet places to work and the opportunity to schedule some of their own work time.

Other factors, such as low self esteem, anxiety, and tension, can also cause students to have difficulty in school.

Crime and Violence

The number of serious crimes in the United States is at the highest level in memory. Students bring guns to school, and large urban areas report dozens of deaths each year from violent acts in school. Murder is the leading cause of death among African American teens. More than 70 percent of those who commit serious crimes are never caught. We live in a society where crime is rampant and crime pays.

Crime in school presents a particular problem for teachers. Some estimate that 3–7 percent of all students bring a gun with them to school. Students attack teachers every day in America. While this behavior is not defensible, attention to the principles of classroom management mentioned earlier can help in averting some of these incidents.

Substance Abuse

Alcohol is the most used and abused drug. Even though it is legal, there are serious short- and long-term consequences of alcohol use. Alcoholism is the most widespread drug addiction and untreated alcoholism can lead to death.

Tobacco is the next most widely used and abused substance. Some efforts are being made to declare tobacco a drug. Irrefutable evidence shows that tobacco use is a causative factor in hundreds of thousands of deaths each year.

Other drugs including marijuana, cocaine, heroin, and various drugs in pill form carry with them serious health, addiction, and emotional problems. The widespread illicit availability of these drugs creates additional problems. Many students engage in crimes to get money to pay for drugs. Others may commit crimes while under the influence of drugs. Still others may commit crimes by selling drugs to make money.

More than 90 percent of students have used alcohol by the time they leave high school. About 70 percent of high school graduates have used other illegal drugs. Awareness programs that focus on drug use can have some positive effects. However, most drug and alcohol abuse and addiction has other underlying causes. These causes must be addressed for any program to be effective.

Substance abuse has a devastating effect on the unborn child. Children born to substance-abusing mothers are addicted themselves. These babies frequently have low body weight and brain damage. These babies may be doomed to a life of physical and intellectual problems.

Sex

Many teens, and preteens, are sexually active. While many of these children profess to know about sex, they do not. It is in this environment that we find increases in teenage pregnancies, abortions, dropouts, and ruined lives. Sex spreads disease. So we also note increases in syphilis, gonorrhea, and other sexually transmitted diseases.

About 10 percent of teenage girls will become pregnant. Teenage pregnancy is the primary reason why girls drop out of high school. These girls seldom receive appropriate help from the child's father and are often destined for a life of poverty and dependence.

AIDS

AIDS stands for Acquired Immune Deficiency Syndrome. AIDS is a breakdown in the body's immune system caused by a virus called HIV. This virus can be detected with blood tests. People with HIV may take 10 years or longer to develop AIDS. Those who develop AIDS die.

The HIV virus is transmitted by infected blood and other bodily fluids. Sexual relations and contact with infected blood, including blood injected with shared hypodermic needles, are all examples of ways that AIDS can be transmitted. Some 2 to 5 percent of the teens in some urban areas may be HIV positive.

Students can try to avoid becoming HIV positive by reducing their risk factors. Abstinence from sex and never injecting drugs will virtually eliminate the likelihood that a teenager will become HIV positive. Less effective measures can be taken to help sexually active students reduce the likelihood of becoming HIV positive. Girls run a higher risk than boys of becoming HIV positive through sexual activity.

Acquiring the HIV virus is associated with drug and alcohol use. Even when students know the risks, and how to avoid them, alcohol and drug use can lower inhibitions and lead to unsafe practices.

Dropouts

About 10 percent of white students, 15 percent of African American students, and 30 percent of Hispanic students drop out of school. Dropout rates are worst in urban areas, with over half the students dropping out of some schools. High school dropouts are usually headed for a life of lower wages and poorer living conditions.

Many of these students feel alienated from society or school and need support or alternative learning environments. Intervention, counseling, and alternative programs such as therapeutic high school, vocational high schools, and other special learning arrangements can help prevent a student from dropping out.

Child Abuse

Child abuse is the secret destroyer of children's lives. Some estimate that between two and three million children are abused each year. Child abuse is a primary cause of violent youth, runaways, and drug abusers.

Physical and sexual abuse are the most destructive of the abuses heaped upon children. Contrary to popular belief, most child abuse is perpetrated by family members, relatives, and friends. Younger children are often incapable of talking about their abuse and may not reveal it even when asked.

In many states, teachers are required to report suspected child abuse. When child abuse is suspected, a teacher should follow the guidelines given by the school, the district, or the state.

MAJOR DEVELOPMENTAL PERSPECTIVES

This section reviews different ways of helping children learn and develop.

CHILDHOOD DEVELOPMENT

Adequate nutrition in mothers is essential for proper fetal development. Adequate nutrition and exercise are essential for a child's physical growth. Inadequate nutrition can hamper growth and lead to inattentiveness and other problems that interfere with learning.

Alcohol and drug abuse by mothers can cause irreparable brain damage to unborn children. Children of drug-and-alcohol-abusing mothers tend to have lower birth weights. Low birth weight is associated with health, emotional, and learning problems. Alcohol and drug addiction, smoking, stress, and adverse environmental factors are among the other causes of abnormal physical and emotional development.

During the first 12 months after birth, the body weight of infants triples and brain size doubles. Infants crawl by about 7 months, eat with their hands at about 8 months, sit up by about 9 months, stand up by about 11 months, and walk by about 1 year.

From 12–15 months to 2.5 years, children are called toddlers. During this period, children become expert walkers, feed themselves, evidence self control, and spend a great deal of their time playing. This period is characterized by the word *no* and is also when children begin bowel training.

The preschool years span the time from the end of toddlerhood to entry into kindergarten. Children start to look more like adults with longer legs and a shorter torso. Play continues but becomes more sophisticated.

The elementary school years refer to ages 6–10 in girls but 6–12 in boys. During this period children enter a period of steady growth. Most children double their body weight and increase their height by one-half. Play continues but involves more sophisticated games and physical activities, often involving groups or teams of other children.

Adolescence begins at about age 10 for girls but at about age 12 for boys. The growth rate spurt begins during this time. Because this period begins earlier for girls than for boys, girls are more mature than boys for a number of years. Sexual and secondary sex characteristics appear during this time. Most adolescents rely heavily on peer group approval and respond to peer pressure.

LEARNING APPROACHES

Effective learning is characterized by a variety of approaches. The approaches should be tailored to the ability of the learner and the lesson objectives.

Adult-Centered Approaches

Adult-centered approaches are characterized by teacher presentation, a factual question, and a knowledge-based response from the student.

Lecture or Explanation

You can present material through a lecture or an explanation. A lecture is a fairly long verbal presentation of material. Explanation refers to a shorter presentation. Lecture and explanation are efficient ways to present information. However, lecture and explanation may place learners in too passive a role.

Lecture and explanation work best under the following circumstances: (1) the lesson begins with a motivation, (2) the teacher maintains eye contact, (3) the teacher supplies accentuating gestures but without extraneous movements, (4) the presentation is limited to about 5–40 minutes depending on the age of the student, and (5) the objective is clear and the presentation is easy to follow and at an appropriate level.

Demonstrations

Demonstrations are lectures or explanations in which you model what you want students to learn. That is, you exhibit a behavior, show a technique, or demonstrate a skill to help students reach the objective. Demonstrations should follow the same general rules as lectures and the actual demonstration should be clear and easy to follow.

Teacher Questions

Teachers frequently ask questions during class. The following guidelines describe successful questions.

- Formulate questions so that they are clear, purposeful, brief, and at an appropriate level for the class.

- Address the vast majority of questions to the entire class. Individually addressed questions are appropriate to prepare "shy" students to answer the question.
- Avoid rhetorical questions.
- Use both higher and lower level questions on Bloom's taxonomy (knowledge, comprehension, application, analysis, synthesis, evaluation). All types of questions have their place.
- Avoid question-and-answer drills. A consistent pattern of teacher questions that call for responses at the first level of Bloom's Taxonomy is too limiting for most classrooms.
- Pause before you call on a student to answer the question, giving students an opportunity to formulate their responses.
- Call on a wide range of students to answer. Do not pick students just because they are either likely or unlikely to respond correctly.
- Wait 4 or 5 seconds for an answer. Don't cut off students who are struggling with an answer.
- Rephrase a question if it seems unclear or vague.
- Set a target for about 70 percent or so of questions to be answered correctly.

Child-Centered Approaches—Active Learning

In a child-centered or active learning environment, the teacher ceases to be the prime presenter of information. The teacher's questions are more open ended and indirect. Students will be encouraged to be more active participants in the class. This type of instruction is characterized by student-initiated comments, praise from the teacher, and the teacher's use of students' ideas.

Just because there is student involvement does not mean that the teacher is using a student-centered or active approach. For example, the pattern of questions and answers referred to as drill is not a student-centered approach.

Cooperative Learning

Students involved in cooperative learning work together in groups to learn a concept or skill or to complete a project. Students, in groups of two to six, are assigned or choose a specific learning task or project presented by the teacher. The group consults with the teacher and devises a plan for working together.

Students use many resources, including the teacher, to help and teach one another and to accept responsibilities for tasks as they complete their work. The students summarize their efforts and, typically, make a presentation to the entire class or the teacher.

Cooperative learning is characterized by active learning, full participation, and democracy within a clearly established structure. Cooperative learning also engages students in learning how to establish personal relationships and a cooperative working style.

Inquiry Learning

Inquiry learning uses students' own thought processes to help them learn a concept, solve a problem, or discover a relationship. This kind of instruction has also been referred to as Socratic. Inquiry learning often requires the most structure and preparation by the teacher. The teacher must know that the situation under study will yield useful results.

The teacher begins by explaining inquiry procedures to students, usually through examples. Next the teacher presents the problem to be solved or the situation that will lead to the concept or relationship. Students gather information and ask questions of the teacher to gain additional

A test result shows that a student falls into a range of scores and not just the single reported score. Focusing on a single score and ignoring the score range is among the most serious of score-reporting errors.

- Reliability—A reliable test is consistent. That is, a reliable test will give similar results when given to the same person in a short time span. You can't count on unreliable tests to give you useful scores. Use only very reliable standardized tests and be very aware of how important reliability is when you make up your own tests.
- Validity—Valid tests measure what they are supposed to measure. There are two important types of validity: content validity and criterion validity.

  A test with high content validity measures the material covered in the curriculum or unit being tested. Tests that lack high content validity are unfair. When you make up a test it should have complete content validity. This does not mean that the test has to be unchallenging. It does mean that the questions should refer to the subject matter covered.

  A test with high criterion validity successfully predicts the ability to do other work. For example a test to be an automobile mechanic with high criterion validity will successfully predict who will be a good mechanic.

Norm-Referenced and Criterion-Referenced Tests

Norm-referenced tests are designed to compare students. Intelligence tests are probably the best-known norm-referenced tests. These tests yield a number that purports to show how one person's intelligence compares to everyone else's. The average IQ score is 100.

Standardized achievement tests yield grade-level equivalent scores. These tests purport to show how student achievement compares to the achievement of all other students of the same grade level.

A fifth grader who earns a grade level equivalent of 5.5 might be thought of as average. A second-grade student with the same grade equivalent score would be thought of as above average. About half of all the students taking these test will be below average.

Standardized tests also yield percentile scores. Percentile scores are reported as a number from 0 through 100. A percentile of 50 indicates that the student did as well as or better than 50 percent of the students at that grade level who took the test. The higher the percentile, the better the relative performance.

Criterion-referenced tests are designed to determine the degree to which an objective has been reached. Teacher-made tests and tests found in teachers' editions of texts are usually criterion referenced tests. Criterion referenced tests have very high content validity.

Authentic Assessment

Standardized and teacher-made tests have significant drawbacks. These types of tests do not evaluate a student's ability to perform a task or demonstrate a skill in a real-life situation. These tests do not evaluate a student's ability to work cooperatively or consistently.

In authentic assessment, students are asked to demonstrate the skill or knowledge in a real-life setting. The teacher and students collaborate in the learning assessment process and discuss how learning is progressing and how to facilitate that learning. The idea is to get an authentic picture of the student's work and progress.

The student has an opportunity to demonstrate what they know or can do in a variety of settings. Students can also demonstrate their ability to work independently or as part of a group.

Portfolio assessment is another name for authentic assessment. Students evaluated through a system of authentic assessment frequently keep a portfolio of their work.

Authentic assessment might include the following approaches.

- The student might be observed by the teacher, or occasionally by other students. The observer takes notes and discusses the observation later with the students.
- Students establish portfolios that contain samples of their work. Students are told which work samples they must include in their portfolios. The students place their best work for each requirement in the portfolio. Portfolios are evaluated periodically during a conference between the teacher and the student.
- Students maintain journals and logs containing written descriptions, sketches, and other notes that chronicle their work and the process they went through while learning. The journals and logs are reviewed periodically during a conference between the teacher and the student.

Grading and Interpreting Test Scores

The grade level at which you are teaching determines the approach you will take to grading. In the primary grades, you are often asked to check off a list of criteria to show how a student is progressing. Starting in intermediate grades, you will usually issue letter grades.

You should develop a consistent, fair, and varied approach to grading. Students should understand the basis for their grades. You should give students an opportunity to demonstrate what they have learned in a variety of ways.

It is not necessary to adopt a rigid grading system in the elementary grades. Remember, the purpose of a grading system should be to help students learn better, not just to compare them to other students.

Beginning about sixth or seventh grade, the grade should reflect how students are doing relative to other students in the class. By this age, students need to be exposed to the grading system they will experience through high school and college. The grading system should always be fair, consistent, and offer students a variety of ways to demonstrate their mastery.

You will need to interpret normed scores. These scores may be reported as grade equivalents or as percentiles. You may receive these results normed for different groups. For example, one normed score may show performance relative to all students who took the test. Another normed score may show performance relative to students from school districts that have the same Socioeconomic Status (SES) as your school district.

When interpreting normed scores for parents, point out that the student's performance falls into a range of scores. A student's score that varies significantly from the average score from schools with a similar SES requires attention followed by remediation or enriched instruction.

When interpreting district-wide normed scores, remember that these scores correlate highly with SES.

HUMAN DIVERSITY

This section discusses human diversity and the implications of diversity for learning. Teachers should adapt instruction for the following factors, types of learners, and students.

> Age—Primary students should have more structure, shorter lessons, less explanation, more public praise, more small group and individual instruction, and more experiences with manipulatives and pictures. Older students should have less structure, increasingly longer lessons, more explanation, less public praise, more whole-class instruction, more independent work, and less work with manipulatives.

Many African Americans have achieved middle class status. However, the overwhelming proportion of poor in urban areas are African Americans. The unemployment rate of young African Americans can be near 50 percent in some areas.

Native Americans

Groups of Eskimos and other Native Americans have lived on the North American continent for over 25,000 years. Most Native Americans living today are ancestors of tribes conquered and put on reservations about 100 years ago.

During this time of conquest, treaties made with tribes were frequently broken. Native Americans lost their lands and their way of life. They were made dependent on the federal government for subsidies and were not able to develop the education, experience, or self-sufficiency needed for upward mobility.

Native Americans have the largest family size and fastest growth rate of any ethnic group. They also have among the highest suicide and alcoholism rates of any ethnic group.

Native Americans are disproportionally poor and disenfranchised. They live in poverty on reservations and are often alienated when they move off reservations to metropolitan areas.

Asian Americans

Asian Americans are predominately Chinese and Japanese together with recent immigrants from Korea and Southeast Asia. Asian Americans represent a countertrend among American minorities. Their achievement and success tend to be above the national average.

Many recent immigrants do not have the educational background of other Asian Americans. They tend to be more ghettoized and to attain a lower SES than other Asian Americans.

However, overall, Asian students perform better on American standardized tests than non-Asian students. This finding holds also for those Asian Americans who immigrated to this country unable to speak, read, or understand English.

Some researchers have said that a particular work ethic currently found in Asian countries together with a strong family structure are responsible for these trends.

HUMAN DEVELOPMENT MSAT PRACTICE ITEMS

These items will help you practice for the real MSAT. These items have the same form and test the same material as the MSAT items and test material. The items you encounter on the real MSAT may have a different emphasis and may be more complete.

Instructions

Mark your answers on the sheet provided below. Complete the items in 20 minutes or less. Correct your answer sheet using the answers on page 247.

1 Ⓐ Ⓑ Ⓒ Ⓓ	5 Ⓐ Ⓑ Ⓒ Ⓓ	9 Ⓐ Ⓑ Ⓒ Ⓓ	13 Ⓐ Ⓑ Ⓒ Ⓓ	17 Ⓐ Ⓑ Ⓒ Ⓓ
2 Ⓐ Ⓑ Ⓒ Ⓓ	6 Ⓐ Ⓑ Ⓒ Ⓓ	10 Ⓐ Ⓑ Ⓒ Ⓓ	14 Ⓐ Ⓑ Ⓒ Ⓓ	18 Ⓐ Ⓑ Ⓒ Ⓓ
3 Ⓐ Ⓑ Ⓒ Ⓓ	7 Ⓐ Ⓑ Ⓒ Ⓓ	11 Ⓐ Ⓑ Ⓒ Ⓓ	15 Ⓐ Ⓑ Ⓒ Ⓓ	19 Ⓐ Ⓑ Ⓒ Ⓓ
4 Ⓐ Ⓑ Ⓒ Ⓓ	8 Ⓐ Ⓑ Ⓒ Ⓓ	12 Ⓐ Ⓑ Ⓒ Ⓓ	16 Ⓐ Ⓑ Ⓒ Ⓓ	20 Ⓐ Ⓑ Ⓒ Ⓓ

1. Which of the following best describes the current state of the American family?
   (A) Most families don't have a working father, a mother at home, and children in school.
   (B) Most families today consist of two full-time working parents with children in day care.
   (C) Single parent families are headed by fathers.
   (D) Married people are choosing to start careers before they start families.

2. Research shows that modeling is an appropriate way of modifying behavior. Which of the following is an example of a good modeling technique?
   (A) Show students how to construct replicas of historic buildings.
   (B) Respond courteously to students' questions.
   (C) Demonstrate students' inappropriate behavior.
   (D) Stress the importance of appearance and show students how to dress.

3. Which of the following is an appropriate reinforcement of student behavior?
   (A) Grading on the basis of performance
   (B) Praising appropriate behavior
   (C) Explaining that students will lose privileges
   (D) Ignoring inappropriate behavior

4. Which of the following educational practices best reflects B.F. Skinner's model of learning?
   (A) Active involvement of students in learning
   (B) Token reinforcement of student's success
   (C) Problem solving as the central focus of instruction
   (D) Manipulative materials to help students learn

5. An adult honestly discusses her or his sexual abuse as a child. The adult does not say who the abuser was, but health professionals know that the abuser is most likely
   (A) a teacher or coach.
   (B) a relative or family member.
   (C) a convicted sexual abuser.
   (D) an intruder or thief.

6. Which of the following best depicts the way in which schools have reacted to America's multiethnic and multicultural society?
   (A) The academic atmosphere of our schools is not affected by the ethnic and cultural backgrounds of the students.
   (B) Recent immigrant groups are accustomed to the academic atmosphere of American schools.
   (C) There is no longer a need for schools to deal with the cultural differences of students.
   (D) The schools have noted a shift toward cultural pluralism.

7. Which of the following activities would engage the student at the highest level of *Taxonomy of Educational Objectives: Cognitive Domain*?
   (A) Evaluate a book
   (B) Understand a reading passage
   (C) Analyze a written paragraph
   (D) Apply a mathematics formula to a real situation

8. Repeated testing of a fourth grade student reveals an IQ in the range of 110–115 and two or more years of standardized achievement test scores are below grade level. Which of the following is the most appropriate interpretation of these test scores?
   (A) The student's achievement and potential match.
   (B) The student is mildly retarded.
   (C) The student is gifted.
   (D) The student has a learning disability.

9. When it comes to the general characteristics of elementary school students,
   (A) all ethnic groups adapt equally well to school.
   (B) boys have more adjustment problems than girls.
   (C) girls are more physically active than boys of the same age.
   (D) primary students rebel against the teacher's authority.

10. Maintaining discipline in seventh through tenth grade is particularly difficult because
    (A) students are reaching puberty.
    (B) students are peer oriented.
    (C) teachers are subject oriented.
    (D) teachers are authority figures.

11. According to researchers, which of the following is the most powerful overall motivation for students?
    (A) grades
    (B) privileges
    (C) learning
    (D) personal satisfaction

12. Behaviorism was the first significant theory of learning. Which of the following methods would be supported most strongly by behaviorists?
    (A) cooperative learning
    (B) inductive teaching
    (C) activism
    (D) inquiry learning

13. Piaget wrote that children learn through a process of equilibration. Which of the following classroom practices is most likely to promote this process in children?
    (A) Teachers teach skills while using manipulative techniques.
    (B) Students learn a concept through the repeat-practice method.
    (C) Students learn concepts vicariously.
    (D) Students actively learn concepts through their own experiences.

14. Which of the following summarizes Glasser's Reality Therapy approach to classroom management?
    (A) Students are left on their own to discover the harsh reality of their own mistakes.
    (B) The teacher establishes clear rules and the rewards or punishment that accompany acceptable and unacceptable behavior.
    (C) The teacher explains all positive and negative outcomes in terms of the real world.
    (D) Students help develop and then accept the consequences of any rule breaking.

15. Eriksen's stages of psychosocial development describe
    (A) the emotional crisis which, when resolved, leads to further development.
    (B) Freud's stages of development in more detail.
    (C) stages of cognitive development for males and for females.
    (D) the social skills needed to be successful at each level of schooling.

16. Which of the following does NOT describe the impact of physical and mental health on school learning?
    (A) Inadequate nutrition can lead to inattentiveness and other problems that interfere with learning.
    (B) Alcohol and drug addiction are causes of abnormal physical and emotional development.
    (C) Most adolescents rely heavily on peer group approval and respond to peer pressure.
    (D) Alcohol abuse by expectant mothers does little if any damage to the unborn child.

17. When a learning theorist says that children can learn vicariously this means that
    (A) children can learn by doing.
    (B) children can learn through a wide variety of activities.
    (C) children can learn if there is a clear structure.
    (D) children can learn from others' experiences.

18. All the following teacher actions are examples of cueing EXCEPT
    (A) flickering the lights quickly.
    (B) glancing directly at a student.
    (C) holding up an arm.
    (D) snapping fingers before asking a question.

19. Which of the following does NOT describe the American family?
    (A) A majority of families have mothers who work.
    (B) An increasing number of children are latchkey children.
    (C) Families are groups of people living together who are related to one another.
    (D) Less than 10 percent of American families have a mother (as a homemaker), a father (as the breadwinner), and the children.

20. Punishment can be an effective way to change students' behavior when
(A) the whole class is involved.
(B) it involves pertinent extra work.
(C) it is used for limited and specific reasons.
(D) it makes the teacher feel better.

Answers

1. **A**	5. **B**	9. **B**	13. **D**	17. **D**
2. **B**	6. **D**	10. **B**	14. **D**	18. **A**
3. **D**	7. **D**	11. **A**	15. **A**	19. **D**
4. **B**	8. **D**	12. **C**	16. **D**	20. **C**

PHYSICAL EDUCATION

TEST INFO BOX

8 of 120 Multiple Choice items — 7% of Content Knowledge items
2 of 18 Short Answer items — 11% of Content Area Exercise items

PHYSICAL EDUCATION ITEMS

Physical Education multiple choice items look like this.

Which of the following would be an appropriate way to practice a nonlocomotor skill?

(A) Hop in place.
(B) Leap over obstacles.
(C) Run around a circular path and stop in your original position.
(D) Hang from a bar or ring and then swing.

Physical Education short answer items look like this.

Choose one locomotor skill. Briefly describe three primary-grade learning activities for the skill.

USING THIS CHAPTER

This chapter prepares you to take the Physical Education part of the MSAT. Choose one of these approaches.

I want all the Physical Education review I can get.

- ❑ Skip the Review Quiz and read the entire review section.
- ❑ Take the Physical Education Review Quiz on page 250.
- ❑ Correct the Review Quiz and reread the indicated parts of the review.
- ❑ Complete the Physical Education MSAT Practice Questions on page 265.

I want a thorough Physical Education review.

- ❑ Take the Physical Education Review Quiz on page 250.
- ❑ Correct the Review Quiz and reread the indicated parts of the review.
- ❑ Complete the Physical Education MSAT Practice Questions on page 265.

I want a quick Physical Education review.

- ❑ Take and correct the Physical Education Review Quiz on page 250.
- ❑ Complete the Physical Education MSAT Practice Questions on page 265.

I want to practice Physical Education questions.

- ❑ Complete the Physical Education MSAT Practice Questions on page 265.

I don't need any Physical Education review.

- ❑ OK. If you're sure, skip this chapter.

PHYSICAL EDUCATION REVIEW QUIZ

This quiz uses a short answer format to help you find out what you know about the Physical Education topics reviewed in this chapter. The quiz results direct you to the portions of the chapter you should read.

This quiz will also help focus your thinking about Physical Education, and these questions and answers are a good review in themselves. It's not important to answer all these questions correctly, and don't be concerned if you miss many of them.

The answers are found immediately after the quiz. It's to your advantage not to look at them until you have completed the quiz. Once you have completed and corrected this review quiz, use the answer checklist to decide which sections of the review to study.

Write the answers in the space provided or on a separate sheet of paper.

1. According to the NASPE, what reaction to new skills indicates that a person is a physically fit person?

2. Briefly describe the movement concept of flow.

3. What kinds of space does a child use while jumping rope?

4. Describe the slide in terms of some other locomotor skill.

5. What is the name for an a-rhythmic skip?

6. What is the difference between a turn and a twist?

7. Which manipulative skill does not use the arms?

8. What is the difference between aerobic and anaerobic exercises?

9. What four categories are used to categorize sport games?

10. Rolling is an example of what type of gymnastic activity?

11. What are the three gross motor areas of the body?

12. Describe how the field of motor development is concerned with the nature/nurture controversy.

13. What holds bone joints together?

14. What three different types of muscles make up the muscular system?

15. What part of the blood carries oxygen?

16. What is the most effective measurement for assessing the impact of exercise on a person?

17. What is the most abused drug?

18. What attaches muscles to bone?

19. What is the primary way to avoid tendinitis?

20. Briefly describe the ecological integration approach to teaching physical education.

ANSWER CHECKLIST

Answers are organized by review sections. Check your answers, and if you miss any questions in a section, review that section.

❑ *Overview, page 252*

1. A physically fit person is able to learn new skills.

❑ *Movement Concepts, page 252*

2. Flow describes the continuity of movement (e.g., free flow and bound flow).
3. High space and personal space.

❑ *Locomotor Skills, page 253*

4. The slide is a sideways gallop.
5. An a-rhythmic skip is called hop and step.

❑ *Nonlocomotor Activities, page 254*

6. A turn rotates the body or part of the body around the body's *vertical* axis. A twist rotates part of the body around *any* axis.

❑ *Manipulative Skills, page 254*

7. Kicking is a manipulative skill that does not use the arms.

❑ *Fitness Education, page 255*

8. Aerobic exercise uses oxygen in the blood. Anaerobic exercise does not use oxygen in the blood.

❑ *Sports, page 257*

9. The four categories are court, field, target, and territory.

❑ *Tumbling and Gymnastics, page 257*

10. The roll is a weight transfer activity.

❑ *Growth and Development, page 258*

11. The gross motor areas are the neck, the arms, and the legs.
12. Motor development addresses how motor performance is related to heredity as opposed to learning and the environment.

❑ *Anatomy, page 258*

13. Bones are held together by ligaments.
14. The three types of muscle are skeletal, smooth, and cardiac.
15. Red blood cells carry oxygen.

❑ *Exercise Physiology, page 262*

16. Heart rate is the most effective measure of the impact of exercise.
17. Alcohol is the most abused drug.

❑ *Kinesiology, page 263*

18. Muscles are attached to bones by tendons.
19. A person avoids tendinitis by avoiding overuse of a tendon.

❑ *Social Science Foundations, page 263*

20. The ecological responsibility approach emphasizes learning physical education skills to enable students to participate successfully with groups in the future.

PHYSICAL EDUCATION REVIEW

OVERVIEW

The National Association for Sport and Physical Education (NASPE)

The NASPE Outcomes Project sets the stage for physical education into the next century. The following list of 20 outcomes from this project describes the characteristics of a physically fit person.

Possesses Skills

1. has movement skills including space awareness, body awareness, and relationships
2. is competent in a number of locomotor, nonlocomotor, and manipulative activities
3. is competent in combinations of these activities individually and cooperatively
4. is competent in many forms of physical activity
5. is proficient in a few forms of physical activity
6. can learn new skills

Stays Physically Fit

7. achieves, assesses, and maintains physical fitness
8. designs safe personal fitness programs using the principles of physical fitness

Regularly Participates

9. in health enhancing activity three times a week
10. in lifetime physical activities

Is Aware of the Implications and Benefits of Physical Education Involvement

11. identifies benefits, costs, and obligations of regular physical activity
12. recognizes risk and safety factors of regular participation in physical activity
13. applies concepts and principles to the development of motor skills
14. understands wellness is more than physical fitness
15. knows rules, strategies, and appropriate behavior for selected physical activities
16. recognizes that participation in physical activity can lead to multicultural, international understanding
17. knows that physical activity provides the opportunity for self-expression and communication

Values Physical Activity and Its Contributions

18. appreciates relationship with others that results from participation in physical activity
19. respects the role of physical activity in lifelong health
20. cherishes the feelings that result from regular participation in physical activity

MOVEMENT CONCEPTS AND FORMS

Physical education has shifted from an emphasis on sports to an emphasis on movement and motor activities. Those who favor movement education place a greater emphasis on the aesthetic aspect of physical education than on the competitive aspect of physical education. Movement education is now the most important factor in most primary grade physical education programs and this influence is having an increased impact on physical education programs for the upper elementary grades.

The fundamental concepts and terms of a movement education program are quite different from those used to describe a traditional or sports based physical education program. These concepts and terms are presented below.

Movement Concepts

All movement can be described using these concepts or terms.

Space describes the place where the movement is performed. High space movements are performed in the air, or standing on tiptoe. Middle space movements are performed standing upright. Low space activities are performed when bending, crouching, kneeling, crawling, and so on.

Space can be partitioned into general space and personal space. Personal space is everything a child can touch without moving from his or her position. General space refers to all the other space. Personal space activities are necessarily confined to the area immediately around the child. General space activities that involve moving along a path will either be straight, curved, or zigzag.

A child crawling directly from one place to another is performing a low space, straight movement in general space.

Shape describes the relative position of different parts of the body. A body can assume a very large number of shapes. Children can try to make themselves square, tall, or round. Children trying to make their bodies look like a letter are exploring shape.

Time describes the speed at which a movement is performed. Time is often described in terms of other things or events. Children moving as slowly as a bird walking or as quickly as a bird flying are exploring time. Children clapping in a particular pattern are exploring the time concept of rhythm. In rhythmical movements each component has the same time value. In arhythmical movements each component has a different time value.

Force describes the body tension used with a movement. Children moving as softly as a gentle breeze or as strong as a thunderstorm are exploring force.

Flow describes the continuity of movement. *Free flow* movement is continuous, while *bound flow* is halting. Skipping from one place to another is an example of free flow, while the pattern skipping-halting from one point to another is an example of bound flow.

LOCOMOTOR, NONLOCOMOTOR, AND MANIPULATIVE SKILLS

Locomotor skills describe the movements that convey the body from one location to another. Nonlocomotor skills describe movements done in place in which the objective is body movement. Manipulative skills describe movements that have some effect on (manipulate) other things.

Locomotor Skills

Important locomotor skills are listed below. The skills are listed in the approximate order that they are acquired by children, although the age at which children develop these skills varies widely from child to child.

Crawl means a child is lying on his stomach but the upper part of his body is held aloft by his elbows, and he moves through space using his hips and elbows. The hands are not used when crawling.

Creep means using the hands along with either the knees or feet to move through space. *Cross-pattern* creeping or crawling means using opposite extremities (e.g., left knee, right hand.).

Homolateral creeping or crawling means using the extremities on the same side of the body (e.g., right elbow, right knee).

Walk means moving through space by transferring weight from one foot to the other foot. The feet move heel-ball-toes. At least one foot is always in contact with the surface while walking.

Run means moving through space by transferring weight (ball = toes) of one foot to (ball = toes) of the other foot. Both feet are frequently off the surface during a run. Arms swing in opposition (e.g., right leg forward, left arm forward) to the legs, and the arms are usually slightly bent.

Jump means to push the body upward (heel-ball-toes) from one or two feet until both feet are entirely off the surface. The knees are usually bent at landing, which usually occurs toe-ball-heel.

Leap is like an exaggerated run in which one foot pushes off then trails behind as the knee of the other leg leads forward. The foot of the leading leg lands and the action is repeated.

Gallop is an a-rhythmic combination of walking and running in which one leg remains in front and the other leg lags behind following the front leg.

Hop means to push the body upward (heel-ball-toe) from one foot and to land on the same foot (toe-ball-heel). The other foot does not touch the ground. Balance may be better maintained if the weight is shifted toward the leg that makes contact with the surface.

Slide is a sideward gallop. This movement skill does not refer to actions such as sliding across ice or down a slide.

Skip is an a-rhythmic combination of a hop and a step with the primary stress on the step. The leading foot alternates and both feet are briefly off the surface.

Nonlocomotor Activities

Important nonlocomotor skills are listed below. The skills are listed in the approximate order that they are acquired by children, although the age at which children develop these skills varies widely from child to child.

Stretch means to stretch muscles and extend a body part or parts away from the center of the body. A child standing in place and reaching upward with his or her arms is stretching.

Bend means that ball-and-socket or hinge joints are used to bring parts of the body together.

Turn means to rotate the entire body or a body part clockwise or counterclockwise around the body's vertical axis. A turn often, but not necessarily, involves turning the feet.

Twist rotates just a part of the body around some axis. For example, arms can be twisted but not turned. The neck can be twisted and turned.

Manipulative Skills

Important manipulative skills are listed below. The skills are listed in the approximate order that they are acquired by children, although the age at which children develop these skills varies widely from child to child.

Pull means to move something, usually with the arms and sometimes while walking, from one place to another toward the person doing the pulling.

Push means to move something, usually with the arms and sometimes while walking, from one place to another away from the person doing the pulling.

Lift means to move something, usually with the arms, from a lower to a higher position somewhat parallel to the person doing the lifting. *Carrying* is a locomotor activity that combines lifting and walking.

Strike is a strong movement from a bent arm position with the intent of hitting something or, when used with an implement such as a bat or a racquet, with the intent of hitting something with the bat or racquet.

Throw means to use a hand or hands to propel an object away from the body so that the object leaves the hands. A throw can be two-hand, one-hand, overhand, or underhand.

Kick means to use the instep of a foot to propel an object away from the body.

Bounce means to use one or both hands to strike a ball down toward the surface. Continuous bouncing is often referred to as *dribbling. Dribbling* can also refer to moving a ball with one or both feet.

FITNESS EDUCATION

Physical fitness has always been a focus of physical education programs. The emphasis on fitness has increased in recent years and there has been a corresponding increased emphasis on fitness in physical education programs. Fitness is an important component of almost every physical education program.

Tests on elementary age children, secondary age children, and adults reveal low levels of cardiovascular performance, high levels of body fat, and an overly sedentary population. The main objective of the fitness approach to physical education is to improve cardiovascular performance through cardiovascular endurance. Cardiovascular endurance is the ability of the respiratory and circulatory systems to supply oxygen to the body through the bloodstream during prolonged exercise.

Cardiovascular endurance improves with *aerobic exercise* (exercise such as running, which uses oxygen in the blood). A person must usually reach and hold a threshold of training for about 20 minutes, a minimum of three times a week to maintain and improve fitness.

Fitness experts frequently emphasize the coronary problems, which occur later in life, that may be diminished by participation in a regular program of physical fitness. These coronary problems include *arteriosclerosis* in which plaque is deposited on artery walls, *congestive heart failure* in which the heart is too weak to supply sufficient blood to the body, and *coronary thrombosis* in which blood clots form that block a coronary artery.

These experts also point out that improved cardiovascular fitness has many positive benefits, including those listed below.

Benefits of Cardiovascular Fitness

- Lower heart rate and lower blood pressure
- Lower LDL (bad) cholesterol levels
- Higher HDL (good) cholesterol levels
- Reduced risk of heart attack
- Better chance of heart attack survival

Body composition, the ratio of body fat to overall body mass, is another important measure of fitness. A high percentage of body fat is also a risk factor for disease. Body composition can be determined by taking skin-fold measurements at various places on the body. More accurate measures of body composition are taken with hydrostatic weighing, which determines body weight normally and then underwater to get a very accurate measure of the percent of body fat.

But the fitness approach also seeks to improve the strength, endurance, and flexibility of participants. Fitness program proponents also point out that these programs create a leaner body with increased flexibility, strength, and endurance.

Flexibility means the range of motion at a joint. *Endurance* means a muscle's ability to contract repeatedly and efficiently. *Strength* is the amount of force that a muscle can exert. The compound ATP transfers and stores energy in the muscle cells. This compound is produced by aerobic exercise, anaerobic exercise (exercise such as pull-ups of maximum effort for short periods) and by the lactic acid produced during muscle contraction in anaerobic exercise.

These other attributes that are improved by fitness education also have many positive benefits, some of which are listed here.

Other Benefits of Fitness Education

- Reduced stress
- Reduced likelihood of heart attack
- Reduced likelihood of injury and disease
- Reduced likelihood of lower back problems
- Increased ability to work and perform motor skills.

Fitness programs also increase *agility* (the ability to quickly change bodily position), *balance* (the ability to maintain equilibrium), *coordination* (the ability to perform motor activities quickly when needed), and *power* (the ability to generate force quickly).

PLAY, GAMES, SPORTS

Play

Games begin as spontaneous, unstructured play. Games and sports develop from play. A child's participation in games and sports is frequently motivated by their early play experiences. But children frequently go off to "play" a game that is not particularly playful.

Children progress from watching others play to active and cooperative participation. Children's play is unbounded and frequently involves more creativity and imagination than actual physical activity. Children learn about their world as they play. Their experiences in early play both shape and reveal the types of social interactions they will evidence in life.

Games

Gradually as children play they develop their own rules and organization, and play develops into games. Most experts agree that the group of activities called games involve some form of competition using physical or mental prowess. The competition may be against a goal, and not between individuals or teams, but competition is always involved.

These experts say that noncompetitive games don't exist. They say there can be cooperation in a game, but there must be competition.

Competition is one of the most controversial aspects of games. To compete, to achieve competence, is a part of life. Accepting success and failure is a part of life. Competition fosters cooperation and respect. Those who learn how to compete effectively can have enjoyable, successful lives. Of course, competing successfully does not mean a person will win.

Children usually compete very constructively. But those not directly involved in the game may take competition too far. How many times have we all seen a parent or spectator press their child for performance even during informal games.

Games are not always the formalized games we are accustomed to. They are frequently unique to a group of children, or to a geographic area. However, every game has rules. The "appropriate" way to play the game is understood and adhered to by most participants. At the same time, rules for play are transmitted from older or more experienced children to their younger, less experienced friends.

Sports

Sports refers to organized, formalized games. Many of the rule-bound games that children play are not sport games. Children often participate in sport games such as basketball, field hockey, and soccer as a part of their social development.

The *primary rules* that define these games are well known and are usually written. Striking the ball with a bat is a primary rule of baseball. *Secondary rules* refer to the changes in the way these games are played to compensate for the age, varying skill, or varying number of participants and local playing conditions. Hitting a baseball off a stationary tee is a secondary rule of baseball to accommodate the developmental limitations of younger players.

Leagues in towns or in schools and professional leagues are examples of sports. A group of overseers regulates the league, umpires or referees officiate the games, and there are often special arrangements for spectators. There is usually some pre-game and/or post-game ritual.

Sport games require physical exertion and strategic thinking. Sport games are not games such as chess that involve only strategy or such as a state lotto that involve only chance. Experts use four categories to classify sport games: court, field, target, and territory.

Court games include the *divided court* games of tennis and badminton and the *shared court* games of handball or jai-lai. The basic idea in these games is to hit a ball or other objects so that the opponent(s) can't successfully return it.

Field games include baseball and softball. The basic idea in these games is to hit a ball so that defenders can't effectively retrieve it.

Target games include games such as golf and bowling in which the players are not direct opponents and games such as croquet and horseshoe in which the players are direct opponents.

Territory games include games such as football, soccer, basketball, and water polo.

TUMBLING AND GYMNASTICS

An elementary school gymnastics program should be different from the competitive gymnastics we associate with older students and adults. Elementary school gymnastics fosters the development of the individual child. That is, the program is child oriented. Children do not compete with other children. Children do try to improve their skills, and their rewards are the progress they make.

In an elementary school gymnastics program, children make appropriate use of mats, low balance beams, slides, and low bars for hanging and swinging. Some elementary school gymnastics skills are described below.

Weight transfer means moving weight from one body part to another. Walking is a weight transfer activity, as is moving from a lying to a kneeling position.

Roll means to roll the body, first lying down around the body's vertical axis; then roll while in a compact egg shape; then a backward roll; and finally a forward roll. The roll is a weight transfer activity.

Balance means that a person's center of gravity is directly over the support base. The wider the base the easier it is to maintain balance. *Dynamic balance* refers to moving balance activities, while *static balance* refers to balance activities while stationary. The low balance beam is an excellent apparatus for balance activities.

Climb means pushing and pulling to a higher or lower position while maintaining balance. A jungle gym apparatus with sufficient underprotection is an excellent apparatus for climbing.

Hang and swing is usually performed on a bar no more than twice a child's height so that injury will not result from a fall.

PHYSICAL AND BIOLOGICAL SCIENCE FOUNDATIONS

Growth and Development

See pages 234–235 in the Human Development section for a complete review of the stages of growth and development and sensory-perceptual maturation.

Motor development in children follows some predictable patterns. Motor skills develop from the head down to the toes, from the waist out to the extremities and from the gross motor area (neck, arms, legs) to the fine motor areas (fingers, toes).

Motor Learning

Motor learning, and its subspecialties of motor control and motor development, are the basis for how children develop motor skills. Motor skills are the physical skills that children use for motor activities and other physical education and sports skills.

Motor learning describes *how* motor performance can be affected by attention and interest on the part of the child, and on the type of feedback and practice that the child receives. In particular, motor learning is about how the type, the frequency, and the timing of feedback influence the acquisition and maintenance of motor skills. Motor learning also addresses how factors such as aging and fatigue interfere with motor performance.

Motor development addresses *what* motor skills look like. That is, motor learning describes the essential qualities of motor skills. Motor development addresses how motor performance is related to heredity as opposed to learning and the environment. Motor development formulates the age or developmental stage at which a child is ready for particular motor activities.

Motor control addresses the *relationship* between the nervous system and muscular control, and how cognitive development and cognitive activities are related to motor skill development. Motor control formulates the schema that enables children to use motor skills once they have been learned. Motor control also establishes a relationship between the cognitive development, verbal instructions, and a child's ability to perform the motor skill.

Anatomy

The human body has a number of systems essential to the body's functioning. The most important anatomical systems are described in the following sections.

Skeletal System

The body gets its shape from a system of bones as shown in the accompanying illustration. The bones consist of a living marrow, blood vessels, and nerves surrounded by a hard calcium exterior.

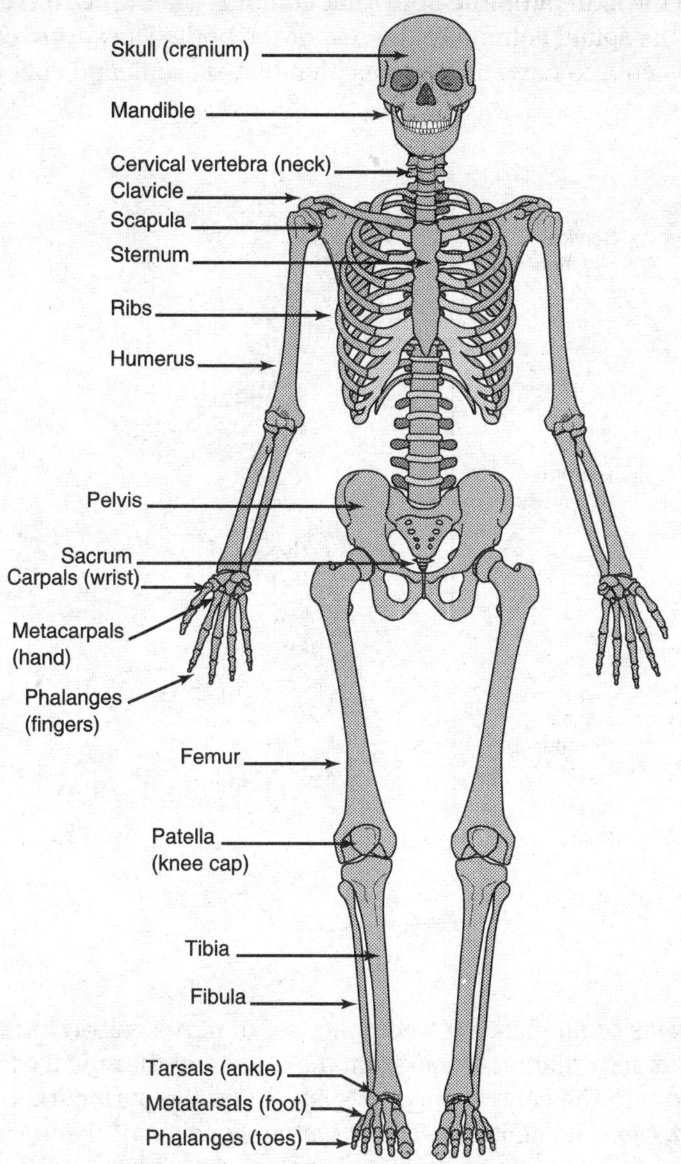

The *thorax* consists of the ribs and the sternum. The *pelvis* consists of the hip bones and the sacrum. The *femur* refers to the thighbone, the *patella* refers to the kneecap, and the *tibia* refers to the shinbone. *Tarsal* refers to the seven anklebones. Five *metatarsals* form the sole and instep of the foot.

The *clavicle* is the shoulder bone and the *scapula* is the shoulder blade. The *humerus* refers to the upper arm bone. The *radius* and *ulna* refer to the two bones that form the forearm. *Carpal* refers to the eight wrist bones and *metacarpal* refers to the five bones that form the palm.

A *joint* is where two or more bones meet. Joints are typically held together by ligaments. In most joints, cartilage between the bones absorbs the shock of the bones moving against one another.

The *cranium* refers to the skull atop the body that contains the brain. Nerves extend from within the skull, through the spinal column to the rest of the body. The *spinal column* consists of vertebra and is partitioned into cervical, thoracic, lumbar, sacrum, and coccyx sections as shown below.

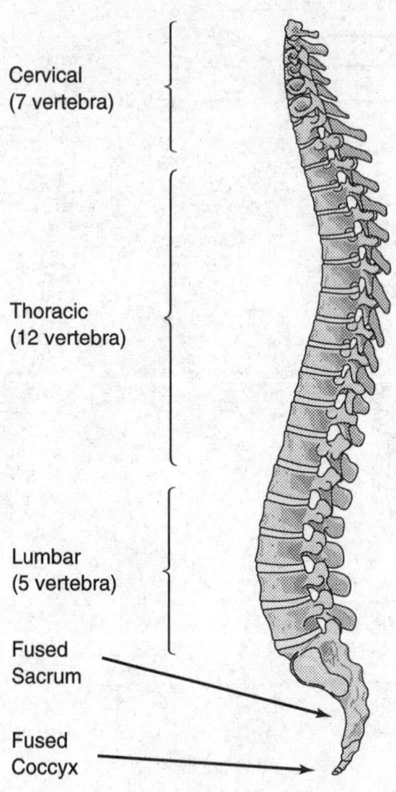

Nervous System

The nervous system consists of an incredibly complex set of nerve cells (*neurons*). Neurons receive stimuli and transmit information to and from the brain and the spinal cord. The nervous system can be partitioned into the central nervous system and the peripheral nervous system.

Central nervous system—The central nervous system consists of the *brain* and the *spinal cord*. The brain permits humans to reason and enables the human body to perform its functions. The brain's *cerebrum* takes up about three quarters of the brain's mass and is partitioned into left and right hemispheres. The temporal lobe of the cerebrum controls hearing and smell; the occipital lobe controls sight. Each side of the brain controls sensations and reactions on the other side of the body.

The *cerebral cortex* surrounds the cerebrum. The *cerebellum* controls muscle activity and is located below the cerebrum. The brain stem extends from the base of the brain to the spinal cord. The spinal cord carries impulses to and from the brain and nerves along the cord to control functions in various parts of the body.

Peripheral nervous system—The peripheral nervous system consists of *nerve cells* that exit the spinal cord and extend to all parts of the body. This system is partitioned into voluntary and involuntary (autonomic) systems. The voluntary system controls the senses and motor activity. The autonomic system controls activities not consciously controlled such as heartbeat and digestion.

Respiratory System

The respiratory system introduces oxygen into the body from the air. Air moves in the nose, down the throat (*pharynx*), down the windpipe (*trachea*), through one of two bronchial tubes and into the *lungs*. The lungs filter out oxygen and transfer oxygen to the bloodstream. Carbon dioxide is removed from the blood and is exhaled along with other gases.

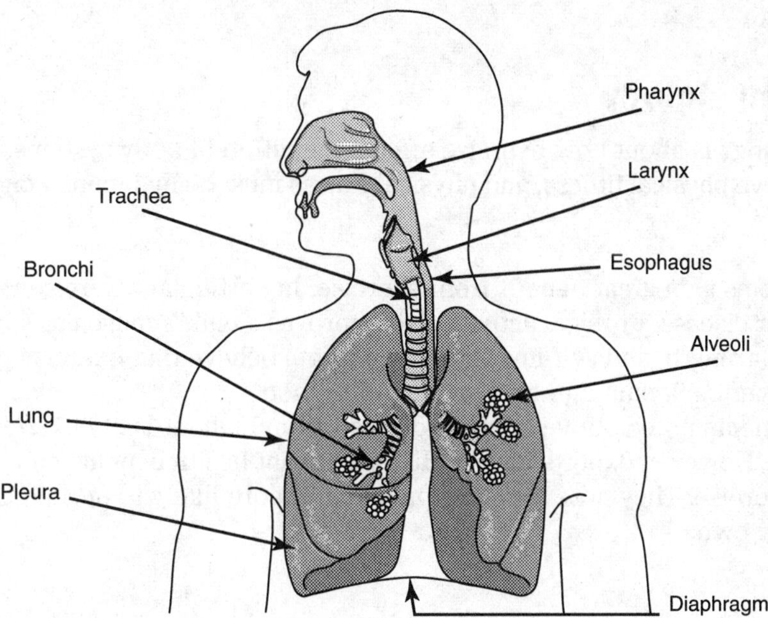

Circulatory System

The circulatory system is a vast array of blood vessels that deliver oxygen-rich blood to the body's cells and carry waste-filled blood away from these cells. A powerful heart drives this system.

The heart (a heart diagram is on page 120 in the science section.)—The heart has a left and right side. Each side has an upper portion (atrium) and lower portion (ventricle). The heart contracts and relaxes.

> **Heart contracts.**
> Oxygen-poor blood goes from the right ventricle, through the lungs to the left atrium.
> Oxygen-rich blood goes from the left ventricle, through the body and back to the right atrium.
>
> **Heart relaxes.**
> Oxygen-rich blood enters the left atrium from the lungs.
> Oxygen-poor blood enters the right atrium from the body.

Blood vessels—*Arteries* are strong tubes that carry blood away from the heart. Arteries branch into increasingly smaller and smaller vessels and finally into very tiny *capillaries* that deliver oxygen to individual cells. At the cell level, the other capillaries start to carry oxygen-poor carbon dioxide rich blood away from the cells. These capillaries join into larger and larger *veins* and finally back to the heart.

Blood—The plasma in blood transports the red blood cells, white blood cells, and platelets throughout the body. Red blood cells carry oxygen. White blood cells are a part of the immune system. Platelets aid clotting.

Muscular System

The muscular system consists of dense fibers. There are three types of muscles: skeletal muscles, smooth muscles, and cardiac muscles. Skeletal muscles control voluntary acts such as chewing, jumping, and turning the head. Smooth muscles control involuntary activities and are found in blood vessels and the urinary tract. Cardiac muscles are highly specialized and are found only in the heart.

Exercise Physiology

Exercise physiology is about how exercise affects the different body systems. The body must exercise to achieve physical fitness, and physical fitness must be maintained once it is achieved.

Exercise

Many body systems gain great benefit from exercise. In particular, exercise reduces the risk of cardiovascular disease. Physical activity also improves a child's muscular strength, muscular flexibility, bone strength, and self-image. Many experts believe that exercise can reduce the likelihood of lower back pain and fractures in adulthood.

The improvements noted above are best derived from high intensity exercise performed at regular intervals. However, experts believe that significant health benefits can be achieved from low intensity exercise. They note also that people are more likely to engage in low intensity exercise on their own.

Assessment

There are many sophisticated ways to effectively assess the impact of exercise. Heart rate, which can be assessed through pulse readings, is the most effective. Other involved observational systems also exist. Determining pulse should probably not be taught to elementary school students. Experts recommend that elementary school teachers use the amount of sweating or when students start hard breathing as general indicators of physical fitness.

Nutrition

Appropriate nutrition is required for a person to be physically fit. Inappropriate diets that increase HDL, cholesterol, sugar, or fat in blood have a devastating impact on body systems. Poor nutrition can devastate the circulatory system. Clogged hearts and blood vessels are the likely result, along with increased risk of diabetes and other diseases.

Drug and Alcohol Use

Inappropriate drug and alcohol use is devastating to body systems. Tobacco abuse and alcohol abuse represents the single largest health problem in this country. Tobacco devastates the respiratory system and results in cancer, emphysema, and other diseases.

Alcohol is the most abused drug and the most lethal drug. Alcohol disables the nervous system and is a factor in about 50 percent of traffic deaths and innumerable other accidental deaths in the country. Alcohol abuse creates many health problems that lead to premature death.

Abuse of other drugs is a factor in many other diseases. These drugs also disable the nervous system and are a factor in heart attacks, traffic deaths, and other accidental and premature deaths. Most nonprescription drugs are not monitored or controlled and there is no assurance of their contents. The devastating impact of drug abuse combined with uncertainty about the drug's contents makes nonprescription drug abuse particularly dangerous.

Kinesiology

Kinesiology is about how the body's muscles move the skeleton. The body moves itself through work performed by muscles.

Muscles are attached to bones by tough cords called tendons. A synovial membrane lines the area where bone and muscle meet and secretes synovial fluid to lubricate the area making it easier for tendons to move.

Injuries

Many injuries can be successfully prevented. Physical fitness, including muscle strength and flexibility, prevents injuries. A thorough warm-up and stretch and appropriate taping will help prevent most sprains (stretched or torn ligament) and strains (stretched or torn muscle). Bone strength developed through exercise and appropriate nutrition can help reduce the likelihood of a fracture (broken bone). Avoiding overuse can prevent tendinitis (inflammation of a tendon).

Safety Equipment

Appropriate safety equipment can help prevent many injuries. In particular, helmets and other headgear can help avoid skull fractures, concussions (swollen brain), and contusions (bruised brain). Mats and climbing equipment of the appropriate height can help avoid falls that can lead to fractures, loss of feeling, or paralysis (damage to the nervous system).

SOCIAL SCIENCE FOUNDATIONS

Physical education is a significant socializing agent and a powerful psychological force. Children learn to interact and develop psychologically through their play participation with other children. Play and games fill the days of most young children.

Social Status

A child's status in a school and community is frequently a function of his or her perceived athletic ability. Physical ability, and particularly the ability to participate in sports, is among the most valued attributes in our society. Children who show ability can receive favorable treatment combined with pressure to excel.

Children from lower socioeconomic levels are less fit than their higher socioeconomic counterparts. Children from more affluent families are more likely to participate in physical activity and sport.

Sex Related Differences

On average, boys are more physically fit and less sedentary that girls. Furthermore, girls tend to loose some of their fitness levels as they progress through the elementary school years, while boys tend to maintain their fitness level.

Social Approaches

There are several social approaches to teaching physical education. The *self-actualization* approach emphasizes matching the curriculum to the interests and motivation of students. The *ecological integration* approach emphasizes learning physical education to enable students to participate successfully with groups in the future. The *social responsibility* approach emphasizes establishing strong interpersonal relationships among students and learning to work together.

Responsibility Level

Sociologists have studied the responsibility level of physical education participants. They suggest five levels starting at irresponsibility (uncooperative) and progressing through self-control (cooperative nonparticipation), involvement (playing cooperatively), and self-responsibility (independent participation) to caring (helping others participate).

PHYSICAL EDUCATION MSAT PRACTICE ITEMS

These items will help you practice for the real MSAT. These items have the same form and test the same material as the MSAT items and test material. The items you encounter on the real MSAT may have a different emphasis and may be more complete.

Instructions

Mark your answers on the sheet provided below. Complete the items in 20 minutes or less. Correct your answer sheet using the answers on page 268.

1 Ⓐ Ⓑ Ⓒ Ⓓ	5 Ⓐ Ⓑ Ⓒ Ⓓ	9 Ⓐ Ⓑ Ⓒ Ⓓ	13 Ⓐ Ⓑ Ⓒ Ⓓ	17 Ⓐ Ⓑ Ⓒ Ⓓ
2 Ⓐ Ⓑ Ⓒ Ⓓ	6 Ⓐ Ⓑ Ⓒ Ⓓ	10 Ⓐ Ⓑ Ⓒ Ⓓ	14 Ⓐ Ⓑ Ⓒ Ⓓ	18 Ⓐ Ⓑ Ⓒ Ⓓ
3 Ⓐ Ⓑ Ⓒ Ⓓ	7 Ⓐ Ⓑ Ⓒ Ⓓ	11 Ⓐ Ⓑ Ⓒ Ⓓ	15 Ⓐ Ⓑ Ⓒ Ⓓ	19 Ⓐ Ⓑ Ⓒ Ⓓ
4 Ⓐ Ⓑ Ⓒ Ⓓ	8 Ⓐ Ⓑ Ⓒ Ⓓ	12 Ⓐ Ⓑ Ⓒ Ⓓ	16 Ⓐ Ⓑ Ⓒ Ⓓ	20 Ⓐ Ⓑ Ⓒ Ⓓ

1. Which of the following is the most accurate description of a fact about the movement concept of force?
   (A) Objects should be pushed away from the center of weight.
   (B) More muscle contraction leads to more force.
   (C) The sequence of body movements affects the amount of force.
   (D) The more contracted the arm, the more force it produces.

2. The NASPE physical fitness test of sit-ups is used to assess
   (A) the number of repetitions
   (B) lower back flexibility
   (C) abdominal strength
   (D) cardiovascular fitness

3. Which of the following is NOT an appropriate objective for a soccer lesson?
   (A) play soccer
   (B) chest trap a ball
   (C) kick a ball with the instep
   (D) foot trap a ball

4. Which of the following is most likely to result in maximum learning?
   (A) all time on task at a child's level of development
   (B) most time on task above the child's level of ability
   (C) all time on task above the child's level of ability
   (D) some time on task below the child's level of ability

5. The locomotor skill of jumping can involve which of the following?

   I. weight transfer from one foot to the other
   II. weight transfer from one foot to the same foot
   III. weight transfer from both feet to both feet

   (A) I only
   (B) I and III only
   (C) I, II, and III
   (D) Neither I, nor II, nor III

6. Which of the following nonlocomotor skills involves rotating the body parts around the body's vertical axis?
   (A) swinging
   (B) turning
   (C) twisting
   (D) bending

7. Which of the following is the most appropriate way to determine the fatness of a child?
   (A) overall weight
   (B) ration of weight to body type
   (C) sum of skinfold measurements
   (D) ratio of weight to height

8. Which muscle type is most prevalent?
   (A) tendons
   (B) skeletal muscles
   (C) smooth muscles
   (D) cardiac muscles

9. Which of the following does NOT affect body stability?
   (A) line of gravity
   (B) inertia
   (C) support base
   (D) center of gravity

10. Which of the following describes the body tension used with a movement?
    (A) strength
    (B) agility
    (C) force
    (D) contraction

11. Which of the following is a nonlocomotor skill?
    (A) bend
    (B) slide
    (C) push
    (D) kick

12. Which of the following is a benefit of cardiovascular fitness?
    (A) lower HDL cholesterol levels
    (B) higher LDL cholesterol levels
    (C) lower blood pressure
    (D) higher alcohol tolerance

13. Which of the following coronary problems means depositing plaque on artery walls?
    (A) coronary thrombosis
    (B) arteriosclerosis
    (C) congestive heart failure
    (D) angina

14. Which of the following is NOT a category used to classify sport games?
    (A) court games
    (B) field games
    (C) target games
    (D) water games

15. Which of the following terms refers to moving balance activities in gymnastics?
    (A) flowing balance
    (B) dynamic balance
    (C) static balance
    (D) progressive balance

16. The roll is which of the following types of motion activities?
    (A) locomotor activity
    (B) nonlocomotor activity
    (C) weight transfer activity
    (D) dynamic balance activity

17. Motor development in children follows predictable patterns, including all of the following EXCEPT:
    (A) head to toes
    (B) waist out to extremities
    (C) gross motor area to fine motor area
    (D) fingers to shoulders

18. The patella refers to what skeletal part?
    (A) kneecap
    (B) thighbone
    (C) shinbone
    (D) hipbone

19. Joints are held together by
    (A) muscles
    (B) ligaments
    (C) tendons
    (D) membranes

20. Manipulative skills include all of the following EXCEPT:
    (A) bounce
    (B) kick
    (C) strike
    (D) twist

Answers

1. **C**	5. **D**	9. **B**	13. **B**	17. **D**
2. **C**	6. **B**	10. **C**	14. **D**	18. **A**
3. **A**	7. **C**	11. **A**	15. **B**	19. **B**
4. **A**	8. **B**	12. **C**	16. **C**	20. **D**

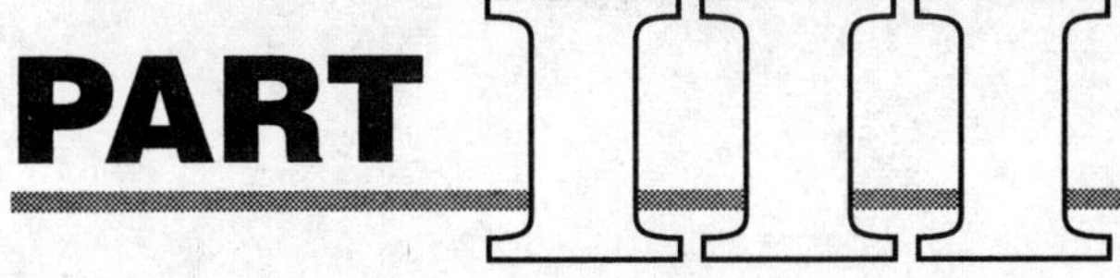

PART III

Two Complete MSATs with Explained Answers

10 PRACTICE MSAT I

CONTENT KNOWLEDGE

Take this test in a realistic, timed setting. You should not take this practice test until you have completed the appropriate review and practice questions.

The setting will be most realistic if another person times the test and ensures that the test rules are followed exactly. If another person is acting as test supervisor, he or she should review these instructions with you and say "Start" when you should begin a section and "Stop" when time has expired.

You have 2 hours to complete the 120 multiple choice questions in areas of Literature and Language Studies, Mathematics, History and Social Studies, Science, Visual and Performing Arts, Human Development, and Physical Education.

Keep the time limit in mind as you work. Answer the easier questions first. Be sure you answer all the questions. There is no penalty for guessing. You may write on the test booklet and mark up the questions.

Each multiple choice question or statement in the test has four answer choices. Exactly one of these choices is correct. Mark your choice on the answer sheet provided for this test.

Your score is based on the spaces you fill in on the answer sheet. Make sure that you mark your answer on the answer sheet in the correct space next to the correct question number.

Use a pencil to mark the answer sheet. The actual test will be machine scored so completely darken in the answer space.

Once the test is complete, review the answers and explanations for each item, as you correct the answer sheet.

When instructed, turn the page and begin.

Each item on this test includes four answer choices. Select the best choice for each item and mark that letter on the answer sheet.

LITERATURE AND LANGUAGE STUDIES

1. The speaker described her teen years and spoke about the arguments she had with her brothers and sisters. Then the speaker told the audience that she and her siblings were now the best of friends.

   This account of the speaker's presentation best characterizes
   (A) argumentation.
   (B) exposition.
   (C) narration.
   (D) propaganda.

2. Class A had an average grade equivalent of 5.6 on a reading test while Class B had an average grade equivalent of 5.4 on the same test. The research report concluded that Class A had performed better than Class B.

   What is the basis for the main criticism for this conclusion?
   (A) The research report should have used medians not averages.
   (B) The research report should have reported a range of scores.
   (C) The research report should have reported earlier average scores for these classes.
   (D) The research report should have taken into account any learning or home problems among students in the classes.

Questions 3 and 4 refer to the following passage.

In response to my opponent's question about my record on environmental issues, I want to say that the real problem in this election is not my record. Rather the problem is the influence of my opponent's rich friends in the record industry. I hope you will turn your back on his rich supporters and vote for me.

3. What type of rhetorical argument does this passage reflect?
   (A) narration
   (B) reflection
   (C) argumentation
   (D) exposition

4. What type of fallacious reasoning is found in the passage?
   (A) begging the question
   (B) non sequitur
   (C) false analogy
   (D) bandwagon

---

5. Which of the following is the most accurate statement about children's literature?
   (A) The *Wizard of Oz* was among the first books written specifically for children.
   (B) *Robinson Crusoe* was really written for adults, not children.
   (C) Most children's literature through about 1890 conveyed a religious or moral theme.
   (D) Washington Irving wrote *Last of the Mohicans.*

6. The stories of *King Arthur and the Knights of the Round Table* originated between about 1000 A.D. and 1200 A.D. To which genre of literature do these stories belong?
   (A) poetry
   (B) epic
   (C) lyric
   (D) romance

Questions 7–10 refer to the following poem by R. Derek

The Sullen Sky

I see the sullen sky;
Dark, foreboding sky.
Swept by dank and dripping clouds;
Like ominous shrouds.

A sky should be bright,
Or clear and crisp at night.
But it hasn't been that way;
Oh, a dungenous day.

That has been my life,
And that has been my strife.
I wish the clouds would leave;
Ah, a sweet reprieve.

7. Which of the following best describes the author's message?
   (A) The author doesn't like rainy, cloudy weather.
   (B) The author wants people to be free of worry.
   (C) The author is hoping his life will get better.
   (D) The author lives in an area where it is often cloudy and rainy.

8. The last two lines in the first stanza reflect which of the following?
   (A) simile
   (B) hyperbole
   (C) metaphor
   (D) euphemism

9. What main literary technique does the author use to convey the poem's message?
   (A) morphology
   (B) alliteration
   (C) allegory
   (D) personification

10. The author wants to use a line that reflects onomatopoeia. Which of the following lines could be used?
    (A) Soggy, slippery, sad
    (B) Drip, drip, drip
    (C) Like being at the bottom of a lake
    (D) The rain, the pain, explain

---

11. Everyone who finished a test in under 2 hours correctly answered 70 percent or more of the questions. Because Arum did not finish the test in under 2 hours, we know that he got less than 70 percent of the questions correct.

    What type of fallacious reasoning does this statement reveal?
    (A) false analogy
    (B) non sequitur
    (C) using the inverse
    (D) stereotyping

12. The research report noted a significant difference between two tested groups with $p < 0.05$. What does this mean?
    (A) The probability that each group was drawn from the same population is less than 5 percent.
    (B) The probability that this significant difference would occur again is less than 5 percent.
    (C) The probability that the test was inaccurately measuring important data is less than 5 percent.
    (D) The probability that the same test results would not occur again is less than 5 percent.

13. You ain't going to no party.

    Which of the following statements most accurately describes this quote?
    (A) The quote effectively communicates in function and structure.
    (B) The quote effectively communicates in function but not structure.
    (C) The quote effectively communicates in structure but not function.
    (D) The quote effectively communicates in neither function nor structure.

14. Which of the following could NOT be used to access information randomly?
    (A) a hard disk
    (B) a floppy disk
    (C) a videotape
    (D) a videodisk

15. The novels *The Jungle* by Sinclair Lewis and the *Grapes of Wrath* by John Steinbeck share what main common theme?
    (A) They exposed American social problems.
    (B) They focused on overpricing in the food industry.
    (C) They exposed the plight of California migrant workers.
    (D) They exposed the dangers of imported meat and produce.

16. Which of the following examples does NOT point out the difficulty of using the 26-letter alphabet to represent spoken English?
   (A) "Live and on stage, the rock group Phish"
   (B) "The new tuf truck line from Tough Trucks"
   (C) "'I' before 'e' except after 'c' and when sounded as 'a' in neighbor and weigh."
   (D) "It's a terrrr-iffic day here at the car wash."

17. The Newbery Award and Caldecott Medal are given annually to the best American books for young people. Which type of book receives which recognition?
   (A) Newbery, elementary grade book; Caldecott, young adult book
   (B) Newbery, young adult book; Caldecott, elementary grade book
   (C) Newbery, children's book; Caldecott, picture book
   (D) Newbery, picture book; Caldecott, children's book

18. About how many English words are there?
   (A) 2,000,000
   (B) 1,000,000
   (C) 500,000
   (D) 250,000

19. Which sentence below is incorrect?
   (A) The dinner tastes good.
   (B) The dinner tastes badly.
   (C) The chef cooked badly.
   (D) The chef cooked well.

20. Which of the following would be a primary source for papers and research about education?
   (A) LEXIS
   (B) ERIC
   (C) CAD/CAM
   (D) NSF

21. Which alphabet does the English language use?
   (A) French
   (B) Greek
   (C) Latin
   (D) Persian

22. Which sentence below is correct?
   (A) The cowboy reigned in his horse to accept a cup of water.
   (B) The cowboy led his horse and spoke of times passed.
   (C) The cowboy gave his assent to their request for a ride.
   (D) The cowboy only wanted peace on they're section of the plains.

23. What does *ante* in the word *antebellum* mean?
   (A) Before
   (B) Against
   (C) After
   (D) During

24. What statement best characterizes how poems have developed since ancient times?
   (A) From figurative meaning to literal meaning
   (B) From rhymed to unrhymed verse
   (C) From high regard to ill repute
   (D) From the rhythm of music to a linguistic cadence

MATHEMATICS

25. It is Monday at 6 P.M. near the coast of California when you call your friend who lives near the coast of New Jersey. It takes you 5 ½ hours to get through. What time is it in New Jersey when you get through?
   (A) 8:30 P.M. Monday
   (B) 9:30 P.M. Monday
   (C) 2:30 A.M. Tuesday
   (D) 3:30 A.M. Tuesday

26. The science section of the newspaper reports that new planets have been found. One planet is within 100,000 miles of Venus and the other planet is within 100,000 miles of Neptune. If this report were true, what would be Earth's new position from the sun?
   (A) Third
   (B) Fourth
   (C) Fifth
   (D) Sixth

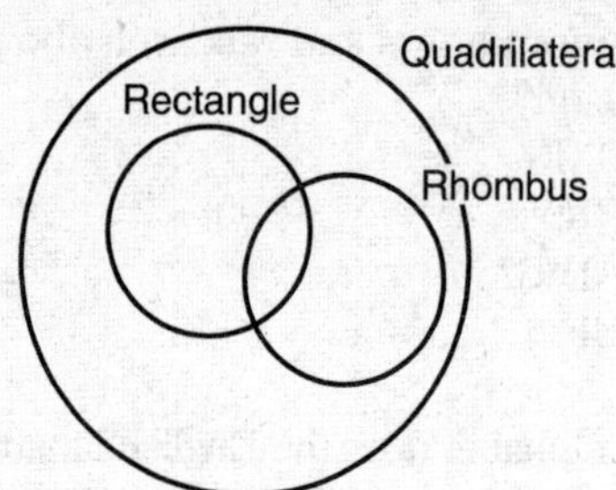

27. The above diagram shows the relationship among quadrilaterals, rectangles, and rhombuses. What conclusion can we draw from this diagram?
(A) All quadrilaterals are rhombuses.
(B) All quadrilaterals are rectangles.
(C) All rectangles are not rhombuses.
(D) Some rhombuses are not rectangles.

28. The sum of the measures of two angles is 90°. What do we know about these two angles?
(A) They are right angles.
(B) The are supplementary angles.
(C) They are acute angles.
(D) The are obtuse angles.

29. Three very bright light beams go out into space from the same spot on earth. None of the beams are parallel and none point in the same direction. What conclusion can we reach?
(A) All three beams will cross at the same point.
(B) Exactly two of the beams will cross.
(C) At least two of the beams will cross.
(D) At least two of the beams may be skewed.

30. The points (– 4, +3) and (+4, – 3) are plotted on the Cartesian plane. If you draw a line connecting the two points, where would it cross through the y axis?
(A) (+1, 0)
(B) (0, 0)
(C) (0, –1)
(D) (–1, 0)

31. Bob walked about 2,750 meters to school every day. About how many kilometers is that?
(A) 2.750
(B) 27.50
(C) 275
(D) 275,000

32. You buy 20 shares of stock on March 10 for 17 $^7/_8$ a share. You sell the 20 shares stock on May 5 for 19 $^5/_8$ a share. How much in dollars and cents did you make on the stock?
(A) \$75.00
(B) \$4.50
(C) \$37.50
(D) \$35.00

33. You add the first 5 odd numbers (1, 3, 5, 7, 9) and find that the answer is 25. What is the sum of the first 90 odd numbers?
(A) 450
(B) 8,100
(C) 179
(D) 4,500

34. Alpha Centauri is about 4 light years from earth. Light travels about 186,000 miles in a second. About how far is it from Alpha Centauri to earth?
(A) 23 quintillion miles
(B) 23 quadrillion miles
(C) 23 trillion miles
(D) 23 billion miles

35. An unusual plant is 10 feet tall when planted and then, starting the next day, grows 20 percent of each the previous day's final height. About how tall is the tree at the end of the fourth day after planting?
(A) 19.4 feet
(B) 20.7 feet
(C) 18 feet
(D) 16 feet

36. A block of stone is 9 feet wide by 12 feet long by 8 feet high. A stone mason cuts the stone to form the biggest cube possible. What is the volume of the cube?
(A) 864 cubic feet
(B) 144 cubic feet
(C) 81 cubic feet
(D) 512 cubic feet

Use this information for questions 37 and 38.

An archaeologist was investigating the books of an old civilization. She found the following table, which showed the number of hunters on top and the number of people they could feed on the bottom. For example, 3 hunters could feed 12 people. The archaeologist found a pattern in the table.

Hunters	1	2	3	4	5	6	7
Eaters	2	6	12	20	30		

37. Look for the pattern. How many eaters can 6 hunters feed?
(A) 42
(B) 40
(C) 30
(D) 36

38. What is the formula for the pattern:
H stands for hunters and
E stands for eaters?
(A) $E = 3 \times H$
(B) $E = 4 \times H$
(C) $E = H^2 + H$
(D) $E = 3 \times (H + 1)$

39. A couple owes $1,000 on a credit card. Each month they pay 1.5% interest on the outstanding balance, and then they pay off $50 each month. Rounding all answers to the nearest cent, how much do they owe after 3 months?
(A) $895.00
(B) $893.42
(C) $891.13
(D) $892.75

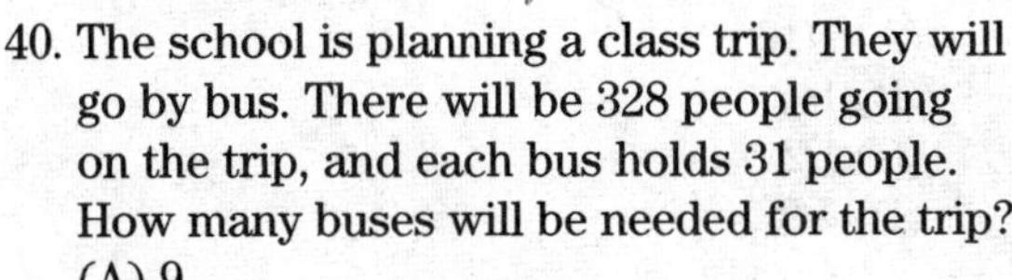

40. The school is planning a class trip. They will go by bus. There will be 328 people going on the trip, and each bus holds 31 people. How many buses will be needed for the trip?
(A) 9
(B) 10
(C) 11
(D) 18

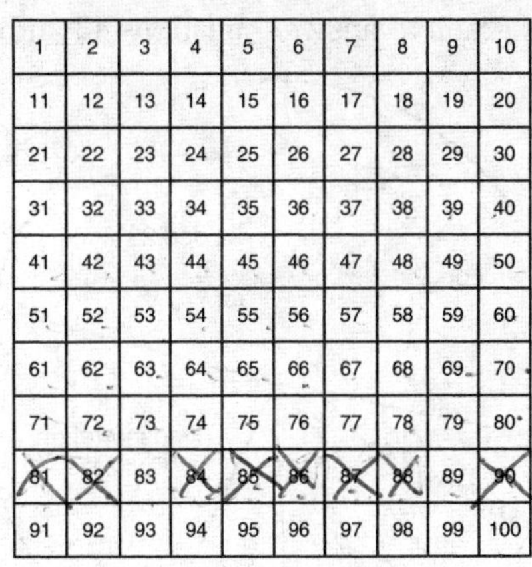

1	2	3	4	5	6	7	8	9	10
11	12	13	14	15	16	17	18	19	20
21	22	23	24	25	26	27	28	29	30
31	32	33	34	35	36	37	38	39	40
41	42	43	44	45	46	47	48	49	50
51	52	53	54	55	56	57	58	59	60
61	62	63	64	65	66	67	68	69	70
71	72	73	74	75	76	77	78	79	80
81	82	83	84	85	86	87	88	89	90
91	92	93	94	95	96	97	98	99	100

41. Cross off the multiples of 2, 3, 4, 5, 6, 7, and 8 in the above hundreds square. Which numbers in the 80s are not crossed off?
(A) 83, 87
(B) 81, 89
(C) 83, 89
(D) 81, 83, 89

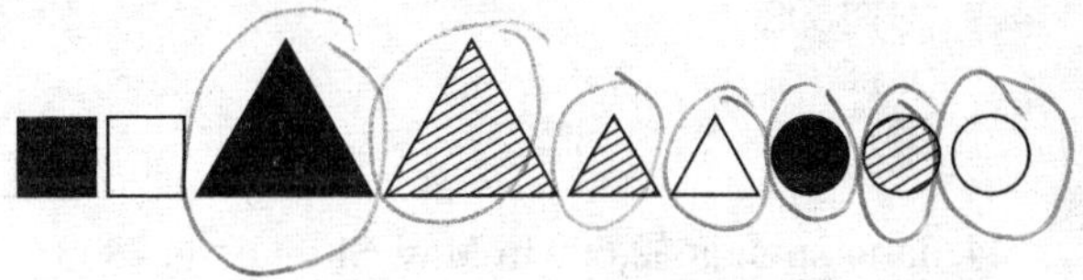

42. Study the above shapes, and select A, B, C, or D, according to the rule:
(small or striped) and large.
Which pieces are selected?

(A) 

(B) 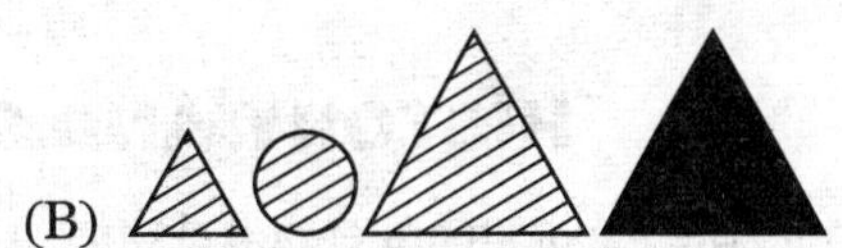

(C) 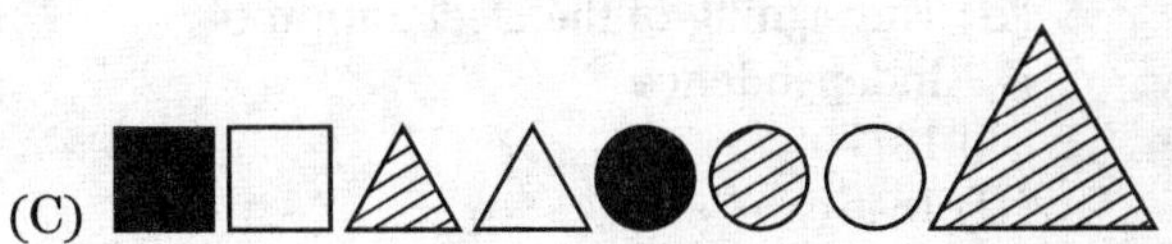

(D) 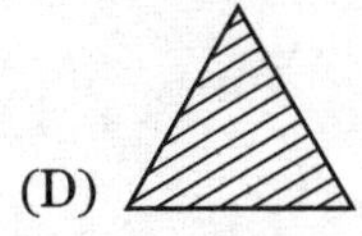

Use this graph to answer questions 43 and 44.

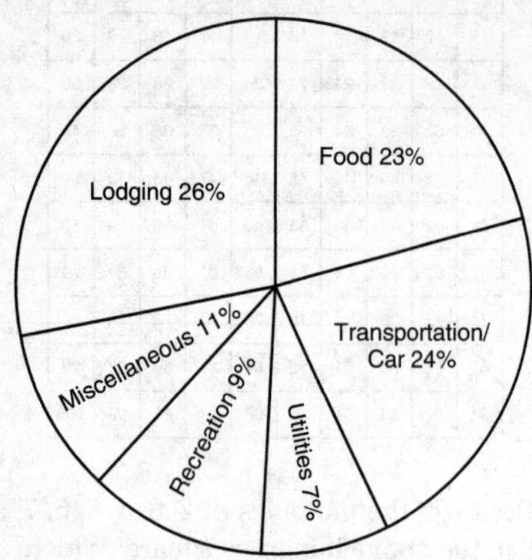

Jane's Monthly Budget

43. Jane spends $2,600 in the month of March. How much did she spend on food?
(A) $624
(B) $598
(C) $312
(D) $400

44. Jane spends $2,600 in May. She needs $858 that month for transportation/car expenses, which is more than the budget allows. Any needed money will come from miscellaneous. When she recalculates her budget chart, what percent is left for miscellaneous?
(A) 2 percent
(B) 6 percent
(C) 9 percent
(D) 11 percent

45. The bakers make brownies and cookies in a ratio of 2 : 9. Today the bakers made 1,350 cookies. How many brownies did the bakers make?
(A) 150
(B) 300
(C) 675
(D) 2750

46. A candy manufacturer will make and ship 2,026,214,229,962,952 pounds of jelly beans this year. The manufacturer wants to ship the jelly beans in a single size package with no jelly beans left over. The package could hold either 1, 2, 3, 4, 5, 6, 7, 8, 9, or 10 pounds. Which answer below lists ALL the manufacturer's choices?
(A) 1, 2, 3, 4
(B) 1, 2, 3, 4, 6
(C) 1, 2, 3, 4, 6, 8
(D) 1, 2, 3, 4, 6, 8, 9

47. A tent standing on level ground is 40 feet high. A taut rope extends from the top of the tent to the ground 30 feet from the bottom of the tent. About how long is the rope?
(A) 26.455 feet
(B) 50 feet
(C) 63.255 feet
(D) 70 feet

48. You flip a fair coin three times and it comes up heads each time. What is the probability that the fourth flip will be a head?
(A) 1/16
(B) 1/4
(C) 1/2
(D) 1/3

HISTORY AND SOCIAL STUDIES

49. In California, the Mexican era ended about what date?
(A) The battle of the Alamo
(B) The signing of the Declaration of Independence
(C) 1877
(D) 1846

50. The primary impact of early colonization on the North American continent was that
(A) more than half of the indigenous population died from disease.
(B) trade goods were available for shipment back to Europe.
(C) religiously oppressed minorities came in large numbers to North America.
(D) England expanded the British Empire to include North America.

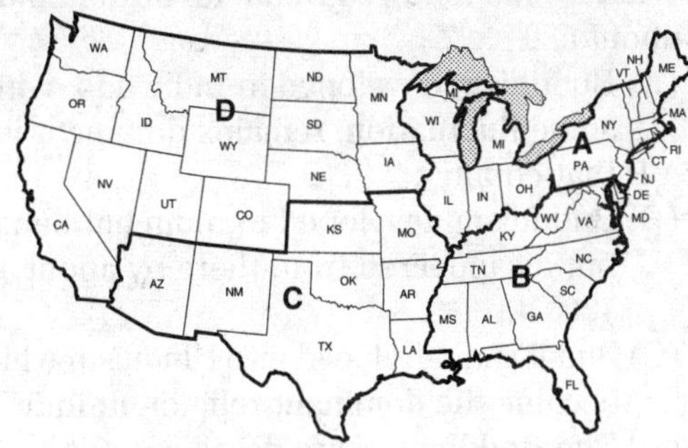

51. In which region of the United States did Algonquin-speaking people live?

52. Which quotation is attributed to the Nez Percé Indian Chief Joseph?
   (A) "The white man covers the land like the buffalo."
   (B) "We wanted only food—not war."
   (C) "I will fight no more—forever."
   (D) "Your prison can hold my body but not my spirit."

53. Who was the first European to explore what is now California?
   (A) Juan Rodriguez Cabillero
   (B) Sir Francis Drake
   (C) Antonio de Mendoza
   (D) Herman Cortes

54. What impact did the Russian Revolution have on World War I?
   (A) The Russian Revolution had no impact because it occurred much earlier than World War I.
   (B) The Russian Revolution had no impact because the fighting was in Europe.
   (C) The Russian Revolution had an impact because Russia left the war.
   (D) The Russian Revolution had an impact because it was a cause of World War I.

55. President Hoover's approach to the Depression can best be characterized in the following way.
   (A) He acted immediately to establish work and relief programs.
   (B) He acted immediately by making loan programs available to the unemployed.
   (C) He acted slowly but imposed strict rules that stabilized the stock market.
   (D) He acted slowly but established a program that loaned money to employers.

56. Which of the following most accurately describes what happened following Japan's bombing of Pearl Harbor?
   (A) The United States declared war on Japan.
   (B) The United States declared war on Japan and Germany.
   (C) The United States continued the war already underway with Japan.
   (D) The United States continued the ongoing war with Germany and declared war on Japan.

57. What was the intent of Lincoln's Emancipation Proclamation?
   (A) To free all slaves
   (B) To free slaves, but not in Washington D.C.
   (C) To free slaves in the confederate states
   (D) To free immediately all slaves who fought for the North and all other slaves at war's end.

58. What was the federal government's reaction to management and unions during the Pullman and Anthracite strikes in the late 1800s and early 1900s?
   (A) The government was even handed in the Pullman and Anthracite strikes.
   (B) The government favored management in both the Pullman strike and the Anthracite strike.
   (C) The government favored the unions in the Pullman strike and management in the Anthracite strike.
   (D) The government favored management in the Pullman strike and unions in the Anthracite strike.

59. *An iron curtain has fallen across the continent.*

   Winston Churchill

   What does this quote from Churchill refer to?
   (A) The establishment of the French Maginot Line
   (B) Germany's occupation of Western Europe
   (C) Postwar Eastern Europe secretiveness and isolation
   (D) The establishment of flying bomb launching ramps across Europe

60. What does this picture show?
    (A) Egyptian pyramids built about the time Rome was founded
    (B) Egyptian pyramids built about 2500 B.C.
    (C) Mayan pyramids built about 1800 B.C.
    (D) Mayan American pyramids built about 3000 B.C.

61. What happened to the English soldiers who fired on colonial protesters, killing five including Crispus Attucks, during the Boston Massacre?
    (A) They returned to England before they could be tried for the crime.
    (B) They were defended by colonial patriots including John Adams.
    (C) They were found guilty but were freed by English soldiers dressed as colonials.
    (D) They were acquitted primarily because Crispus Attucks was African American.

62. In the debate during the late 1700s over a stronger versus a weaker federal government, which group took the position for a weaker federal government?
    (A) The Federalists
    (B) The Jeffersonians
    (C) The Whigs
    (D) The Hamiltonians

63. Which of the following denotes the activity that separates prehistoric from historic times?
    (A) Use of tools
    (B) Use of fire
    (C) Writing on clay tablets
    (D) Use of the wheel

64. What events followed Buddha's birth in India about 580 B.C.?
    (A) Buddhism developed in India and, with some fluctuation, remains dominant in that country.
    (B) Buddhism developed in India but had all but disappeared from there by about 1200 A.D.
    (C) Buddhism developed into Hinduism which became the dominant religion in India.
    (D) The Buddhists were dominant until about 1530 when they were defeated by Moslem armies.

65. Which South American civilization featured human sacrifice?
    (A) Aztec
    (B) Incan
    (C) Manchu
    (D) Mayan

66. What was Robespierre's role during the French Revolution?
    (A) He was an advisor to Marie Antoinette and a defender of the throne who opposed the Reign of Terror.
    (B) He headed the Committee of Public Safety which conducted the Reign of Terror.
    (C) He was an advisor to Napoleon and in this role reported to Napoleon about the Reign of Terror.
    (D) He headed the storming of the Bastille but later opposed the excesses of the Reign of Terror.

67. How were the negotiations about the Common Market concluded?
    (A) The United States was accepted as a provisional member of the Common Market.
    (B) Britain and Western Europe agreed to form a Common Market.
    (C) A Common Market including England, Western Europe, China and Russia was established.
    (D) The Common Market was denied most favored nation status by the United States.

68. What people conquered most of South Africa between 1816 and 1850?
    (A) The British
    (B) The Dutch
    (C) The Bantu
    (D) The Zulu

69. Which Allied leaders met at Potsdam in 1945?
    (A) Churchill, de Gaulle, Roosevelt, Stalin
    (B) Churchill, de Gaulle, Truman, Stalin
    (C) Churchill, Truman, Stalin
    (D) Churchill, Roosevelt, Stalin

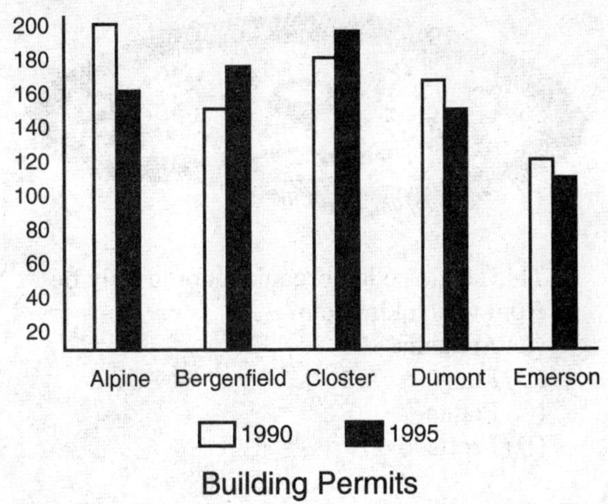

Building Permits

70. This graph best demonstrates which of the following?
    (A) The town with the most building permits every year is Closter.
    (B) Alpine has the biggest difference in permits between 1990 and 1995.
    (C) The town with the least permits every year is Emerson.
    (D) Bergenfield had more building permits in 1990 than Dumont had in 1995.

SCIENCE

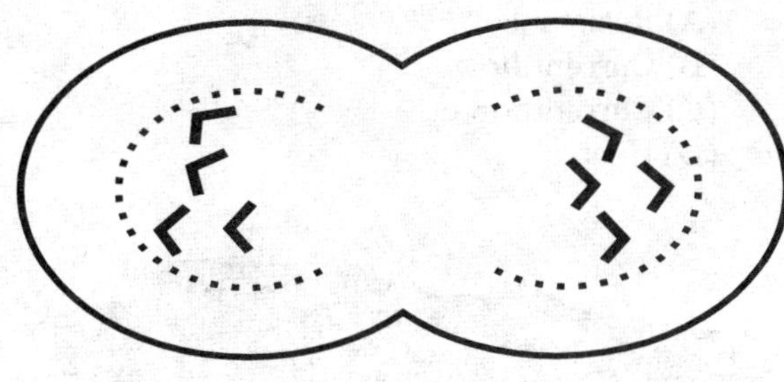

71. This illustration shows a stage of which cell reproduction method?
    (A) Mitosis
    (B) Meiosis
    (C) Photosynthesis
    (D) Chromosomal

72. Which of the following is an accurate statement about DNA and RNA?
    (A) DNA and RNA are found on chromosomes, which are found on genes.
    (B) All the DNA and RNA in a cell affects the makeup of that cell.
    (C) The DNA in a cell creates RNA.
    (D) RNA stays in the nucleus; DNA carries the genetic code throughout the cell.

73. Which is not an option for subdominant individuals in a species?
    (A) Migrate
    (B) Perish
    (C) Assert their dominance
    (D) Give up resources

74. The word *ecology* refers to what area of scientific endeavor?
    (A) The methods for keeping the environment clean
    (B) The relationship between organisms and their habitat
    (C) The effect of industrial and residential pollution on water resources
    (D) The methods for determining the quality of water and the atmosphere

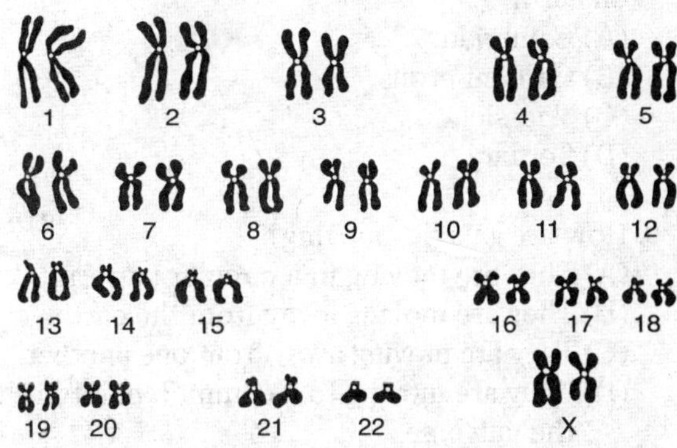

75. What conclusion could you reach about the person whose chromosomes are shown here?
    (A) The person is a man.
    (B) The person is a woman.
    (C) The person has an abnormal gene.
    (D) The person has more genes than usually found in humans.

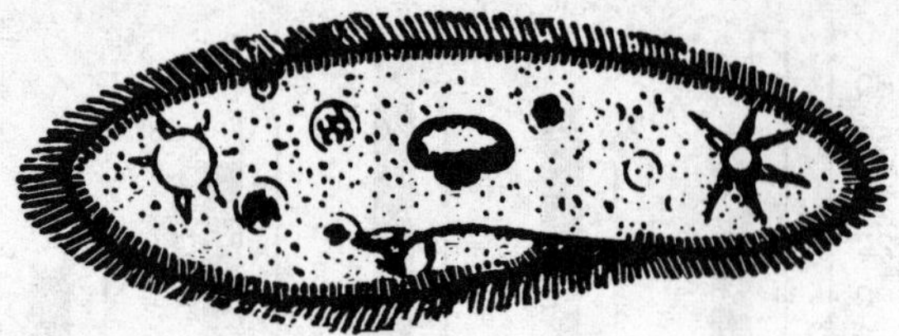

76. This single-celled organism could only be from which kingdom?
(A) Animalia
(B) Fungi
(C) Plantae
(D) Protista

77. About how long does it take for light to travel from Polaris, the North Star, to the earth?
(A) 300 days
(B) 300 years
(C) 3 months
(D) 3 years

78. A scientist discovers evidence of the very first cells. The scientist would describe them as
(A) Algae
(B) Bacteria
(C) Mold
(D) Protozoa

79. During which period did dinosaurs appear on earth?
(A) Cambrian
(B) Carboniferous
(C) Triassic
(D) Tertiary

80. How are galaxies moving?
(A) They are moving in a circular pattern.
(B) They are moving away from the earth.
(C) They are moving away from one another.
(D) They are moving to a common point in the universe.

81. Which of the following most correctly shows the make-up of earth's atmosphere?
(A) Oxygen 78 percent, nitrogen 21 percent
(B) Oxygen 58 percent, nitrogen 41 percent
(C) Oxygen 41 percent, nitrogen 58 percent
(D) Oxygen 21 percent, nitrogen 78 percent

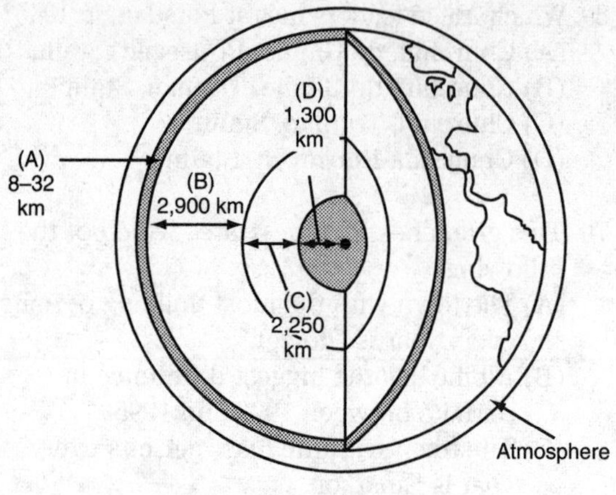

The Earth

82. In the diagram, what letter labels the mantle?

83. In electricity, what does the ohm measure?
(A) Resistance
(B) Current flow
(C) Current force
(D) Heat

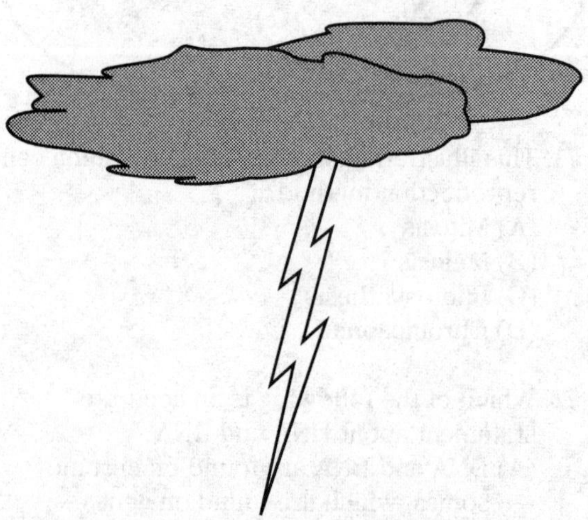

84. You hear the thunderbolt 14 seconds after you see the lightning bolt. About how far away is the lightning bolt?
(A) 7 miles
(B) 5 miles
(C) 3 miles
(D) 1 mile

85. About what percent of ocean water is salt?
(A) 0.5 percent
(B) 3.5 percent
(C) 6.5 percent
(D) 9.5 percent

86. Which of the following choices is a part of the carbon cycle?
(A) Respiration
(B) Evaporation
(C) Condensation
(D) Excretion

87. Which of the following is not a subatomic particle?
(A) Neutron
(B) Electron
(C) Proton
(D) Nucleus

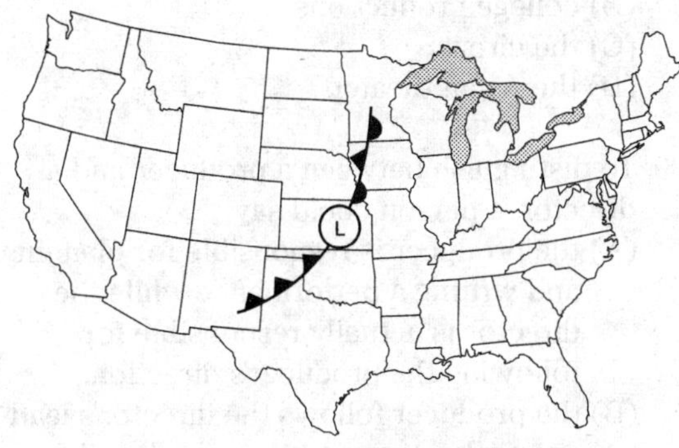

88. What is the pattern of air circulation in the pressure system on this weather map?
(A) Around it to the right
(B) Around it to the left
(C) Through it to the north
(D) Through it to the east

89. Which type of rock is usually found near the surface of the earth?
(A) Sedimentary
(B) Metamorphic
(C) Igneous
(D) Cretaceous

90. Which of the following is a correct statement about matter?
(A) Matter cannot be created, nor destroyed, nor converted into energy.
(B) The mass of an object on the moon is the same as the mass on earth.
(C) The weight of matter is the sum of its atomic numbers.
(D) Once established, the form of matter cannot change.

91. What is produced when a base is dissolved in water?
(A) Oxygen
(B) Hydrogen
(C) Hydroxide
(D) Salt

92. What does heat measure?
(A) The amount of reflection of energy off a surface
(B) The ratio of friction to air temperature
(C) The speed of moving molecules
(D) The rate of connective activity

VISUAL AND PERFORMING ARTS

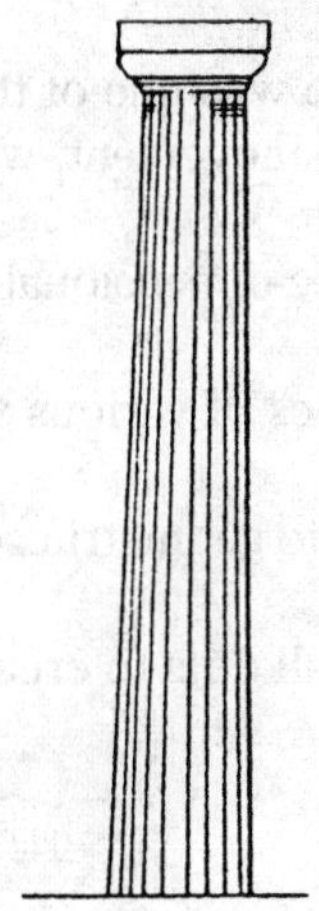

93. What style of column is shown here?
(A) Corinthian
(B) Doric
(C) Ionic
(D) Tuscan

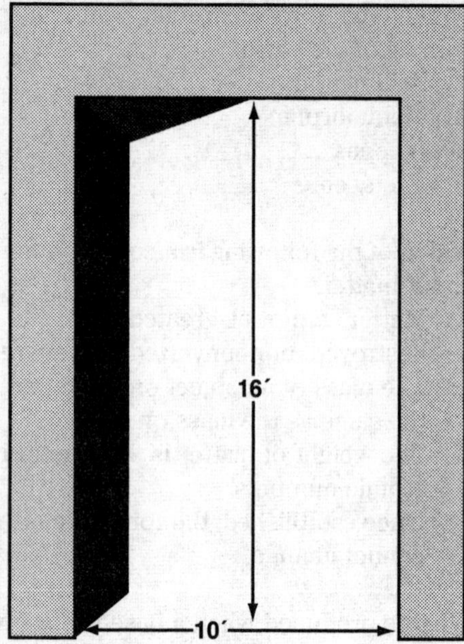

94. What artistic principle is shown in this drawing?
(A) golden ratio
(B) foreshortening
(C) etching
(D) allegory

95. Which scale corresponds to the white and black keys on the piano?
(A) Chromatic
(B) Diatonic
(C) Harmonic
(D) Piano

96. If you see a fresco, it is almost certainly
(A) on a canvas.
(B) in a church.
(C) on a board.
(D) on a wall.

97. What color results from mixing two complementary colors?
(A) A supplementary color
(B) Reddish brown
(C) Gray
(D) A primary color

98. What sequence of notes does the staff show?
(A) A, B, G, B flat
(B) A, B flat, G, B flat
(C) A, B, G, B
(D) A, B flat, G, B

99. The arena stage, completely surrounded by the audience, is most commonly used in
(A) small theaters.
(B) college productions.
(C) the circus.
(D) the Asian theater.

100. To distinguish between a producer and a director, a person could say
(A) the producer is responsible for planning and writing a performance while the director is actually responsible for following the producer's direction.
(B) the producer follows the director's lead and makes arrangements for locations and props.
(C) the producer is responsible once the performance begins or the movie is finished while the director is responsible for everything leading up to this final phase.
(D) the producer has overall administrative responsibility while the director has creative responsibility.

101. Pablo Picasso was one of the founders of the cubist art movement, which is characterized by
(A) using three-dimensional objects to create images.
(B) using cubes of various sizes to create images.
(C) using basic geometric solids to create images.
(D) using small dots to create images.

102. Jazz music, developed by African-American musicians about 100 years ago, is characterized by
   (A) chaotic sounds interspersed with individual solos.
   (B) a "battle" between musicians to create the most pleasing sound.
   (C) standard, if unfamiliar songs, interspersed with individual solos.
   (D) improvisation accompanied by repetition of chords from a popular song.

103. Modern dance was developed about 100 years ago and differs from ballet in that
   (A) music is often developed after movement.
   (B) the dancer usually faces the audience.
   (C) movement is often developed after music.
   (D) the dancer usually wears leotards.

104. A libretto is
   (A) a script of a play detailing characters movements.
   (B) a small drama library.
   (C) the musical score of an opera.
   (D) the text of a popular musical.

PHYSICAL EDUCATION

105. Which of the following groups of locomotor skills should be mastered first?
   (A) Walking, leaping, sliding, skipping, and hopping
   (B) Walking, running, leaping, jumping, and hopping
   (C) Walking, skipping, hopping, running, and jumping
   (D) Walking, skipping, running, jumping, and sliding

106. Which of the following would be an appropriate way to practice a nonlocomotor skill?
   (A) Hop in place
   (B) Leap over obstacles
   (C) Run around a circular path and stop in your original position
   (D) Hang from a bar ring then swing

107. Which of the following is the most appropriate way to help a first grader learn to skip?
   (A) Show the child how to maintain balance by holding out the arms.
   (B) Ask the child to hop around the room.
   (C) Ensure that the child doesn't lean forward too much.
   (D) Ask the child to take short skips.

108. Which of the following could be used to screen a child for scoliosis?
   (A) A treadmill
   (B) A plumb line
   (C) A chinning bar
   (D) A stethoscope

109. All the following skills are important in volleyball EXCEPT
   (A) dink.
   (B) serve.
   (C) spike.
   (D) lay-up.

110. Which of the following would be most appropriate to improve the eye-hand coordination of a primary student?
   (A) Provide numerous highly organized team activities.
   (B) Provide for numerous pyramid-building activities.
   (C) Provide many different sized articles for them to juggle.
   (D) Provide many different sized balls for them to throw, catch, and kick.

111. A proven method for leading a child to a healthy, nutritional life-style is to
   (A) have the child listen to a nurse or other health professional discuss nutrition.
   (B) have the child weigh in weekly.
   (C) measure each child's body fat with skinfold calipers.
   (D) forbid the child to eat sweets while in school.

112. All the following are sound recommendations for running a safe playground area EXCEPT
   (A) provide competent supervision within the playground at all times.
   (B) inspect all equipment regularly.
   (C) establish a list of safety rules and make sure each child follows them.
   (D) choose equipment on the basis of proven safety and practical value.

HUMAN DEVELOPMENT

113. Authentic assessment is best characterized by which of the following?
(A) Portfolio assessment
(B) Using valid and reliable tests
(C) Using only nationally authenticated tests
(D) Ensuring that test results are reported honestly

114. Which of the following best describes an effective approach to teaching learning-disabled students?
(A) Use large print books.
(B) Apply highly relevant skills with a lot of practice.
(C) Provide brief assignments and auditory learning.
(D) Permit them to test out of requirements.

115. What single factor correlates most significantly with achievement?
(A) Socioeconomic status
(B) Intelligence
(C) Cooperativeness
(D) Motivation

116. Which of the following statements best characterizes Kohlberg's theory of moral development?
(A) All humans move through stages of human development culminating in post-conventional morality.
(B) Even the youngest child displays a clear sense of conscience and morality.
(C) As they near the last stage of moral development, people distinguish between legality and morality.
(D) In the middle stages of moral development, the principle of justice takes precedence over social acceptability.

117. A child is standing outside a room and looks in to see all the students gathered around the teacher's desk. The child looks away for a minute and then looks back to see all the students sitting at their desks. The child knows that no one came in or out of the room but wonders why there are more children now than before. This child is most likely at which of Piaget's developmental stages?
(A) Sensorimotor
(B) Preoperational
(C) Concrete operational
(D) Formal operational

118. A child developing within normal parameters is in the eighth grade. According to Erikson's theory of psychosocial development, what primary emotional crisis is the child experiencing?
(A) Intimacy vs. isolation
(B) Initiative vs. guilt
(C) Industry vs. inferiority
(D) Identity vs. identity confusion

119. Which of the following choices is not a typical symptom in children born to drug-abusing mothers?
(A) Low birth weight
(B) Brain damage
(C) Down's syndrome
(D) Emotional problems

120. Which of the following ensures that student-centered instruction is taking place?
(A) Student involvement
(B) Students arranged in groups
(C) Cooperative learning
(D) Teacher answering student questions

CONTENT AREA EXERCISES I

Take these content area exercises in a realistic, timed setting. You should not work on this part of the test until you have completed the appropriate review and practice tests in the book.

The setting will be most realistic if another person times you and ensures that the test rules are followed exactly. If another person is acting as supervisor, he or she should review these instructions with you and say "Start" when you should begin a section and "Stop" when time has expired.

You have 2 hours to complete these 12 short-answer questions in the areas of Literature and Language Studies (3), Mathematics (3), Visual and Performing Arts (2), Human Development (2), and Physical Education (2). You may use a nonprogrammable calculator.

Keep the time limit in mind as you work. You may answer the easier questions first, but be sure to answer all the questions. Write your answers in the space provided.

When you are finished, show your responses to a professor, teacher, or some other person who is able to evaluate them.

When instructed, turn the page and begin.

LITERATURE AND LANGUAGE STUDIES

1. Discuss two main differences between literature for children before the late 1700s and children's literature after that date.

2. Discuss two main differences between how the model-repeat-reinforce approach and Chomsky's transformational grammar explain the development of language in children.

3. Discuss the meaning and importance of morphology in language.

MATHEMATICS

4. An artist has a portrait, landscape, urban scene, and watercolor to display and four spaces set aside at the art gallery. In how many different ways can the artist arrange the works?

5. You have a 1-inch hollow paper cube and a pair of scissors. Display the different flat designs you can make by cutting the cube along the edges.

6. The contractor is painting a room in a house with paint that costs $28.03 a gallon including tax. One gallon of paint covers about 400 square feet with one coat. A gallon can put a second coat on about 600 square feet. Use the following plan to estimate the cost of the gallons of paint to put two coats of paint on all the walls. Ceilings are 10 feet high, doors are 8 feet high, and windows are 4 feet high. Doors and windows are 3 feet wide.

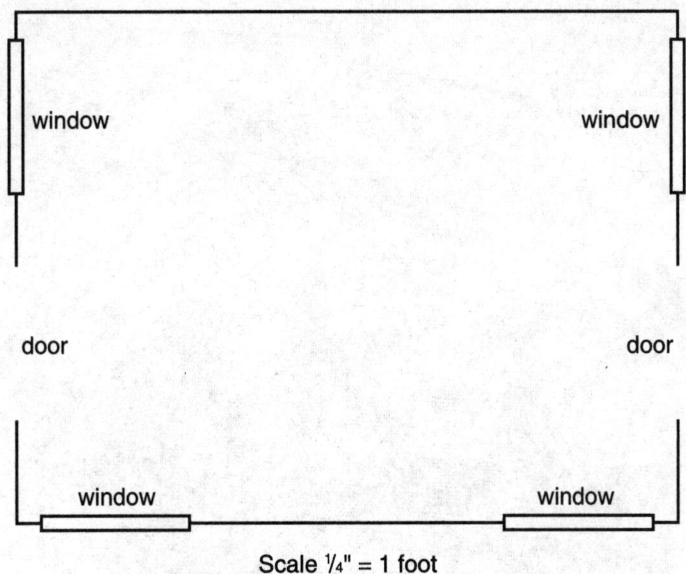

VISUAL AND PERFORMING ARTS

<u>Questions 7 and 8</u> relate to this painting.

"The Fishbowl" by Pavel Tcehelitchew. The Metropolitan Museum of Art, Gift of Constance Atwood Askew in Memory of R. Kirk Askew, Jr., 1974. (1974.37)

7. This painting was created with gouache on board. Describe this process and how the artist used artistic principles to create the work.

8. Interpret the image shown in "The Fishbowl." Explain what the artist was trying to convey and how the images in the painting further this goal.

HUMAN DEVELOPMENT

9. The late psychologist Jean Piaget believed that children learn through a process of equilibration. Explain briefly what Piaget meant and give an example of how a child would learn through this process.

10. Children who are physically abused do more poorly in school and may themselves become abusers. Briefly describe this phenomenon and present a school/family intervention program that might help such a child.

PHYSICAL EDUCATION

11. Locomotor skills include walking, running, and hopping. Choose one locomotor skill. Briefly describe three appropriate primary-grade learning activities for the chosen skill.

12. A fifth grade child with perceptual-motor difficulties participates in physical education. Describe three sports this child might be encouraged to participate in and three sports the child should be encouraged to avoid. Give reasons for your choices.

CONTENT AREA EXERCISES II

Take these content area exercises in a realistic, timed setting. You should not work on this part of the test until you have completed the appropriate review and practice tests in the book.

The setting will be most realistic if another person times you and ensures that the test rules are followed exactly. If another person is acting as test supervisor, he or she should review these instructions with you and say “Start” when you should begin a section and “Stop” when time has expired.

You have 1 hour to complete these six short-answer questions in the areas of History and Social Studies (3) and Science (3). You may use a nonprogrammable calculator.

Keep the time limit in mind as you work. You may answer the easier questions first, but be sure to answer all the questions. Write your answers in the space provided.

When you are finished, show your responses to a professor, teacher, or some other person who is able to evaluate them.

When instructed, turn the page and begin.

HISTORY AND SOCIAL STUDIES

1. Describe the view supported by the Federalist Papers and the impact of the debate between the Jeffersonians and the Federalists on the American political system.

2. Briefly describe the plight of the British armies shown in this map and the military and political aftermath of this event.

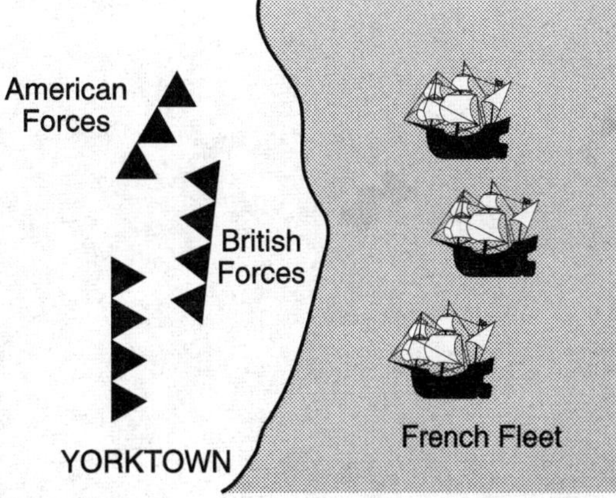

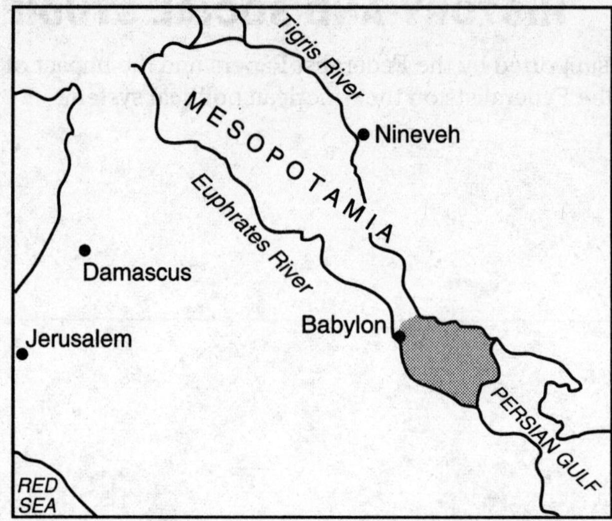

3. Briefly describe the advantages of this region for supporting civilizations and the culture and people that developed in this area.

SCIENCE

4. The endocrine system consists of glands that secrete hormones. Choose either the adrenal gland or the thyroid gland. Describe how the human body would be affected if the chosen gland were missing.

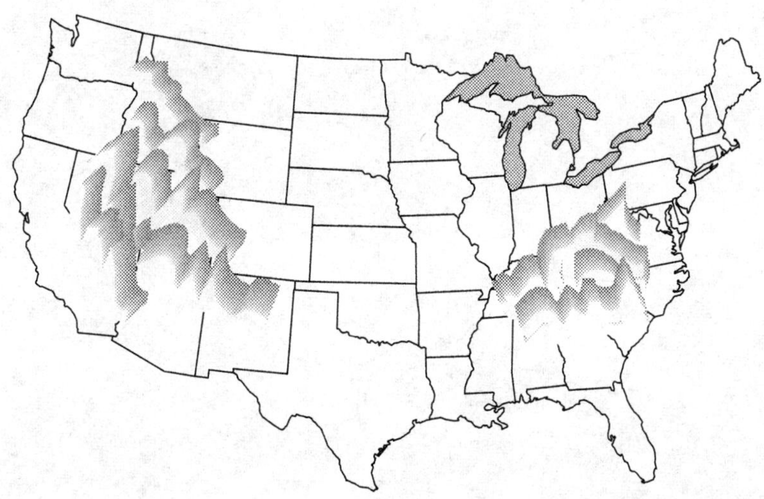

5. What geologic processes could account for the differing heights of these mountains in the United States?

6. Sophisticated technological processes permit a very precise DNA typing for organic material, including blood. Describe three uses of this process.

ANSWER KEY

CONTENT KNOWLEDGE

Literature and Language Studies

1. **C**	4. **A**	7. **C**	10. **B**	13. **B**	16. **D**	19. **B**	22. **C**
2. **B**	5. **B**	8. **A**	11. **C**	14. **C**	17. **C**	20. **B**	23. **A**
3. **C**	6. **D**	9. **C**	12. **A**	15. **A**	18. **B**	21. **C**	24. **D**

Mathematics

25. **C**	28. **C**	31. **A**	34. **C**	37. **A**	40. **C**	43. **B**	46. **D**
26. **B**	29. **D**	32. **D**	35. **B**	38. **C**	41. **C**	44. **A**	47. **B**
27. **D**	30. **B**	33. **B**	36. **D**	39. **B**	42. **D**	45. **B**	48. **C**

History/Social Studies

49. **D**	52. **C**	55. **D**	58. **D**	61. **B**	64. **B**	67. **B**	70. **B**
50. **A**	53. **A**	56. **B**	59. **C**	62. **B**	65. **A**	68. **D**	
51. **A**	54. **C**	57. **C**	60. **B**	63. **C**	66. **B**	69. **C**	

Science

71. **A**	74. **B**	77. **B**	80. **C**	83. **A**	86. **A**	89. **A**	92. **C**
72. **C**	75. **B**	78. **B**	81. **D**	84. **C**	87. **D**	90. **B**	
73. **C**	76. **D**	79. **C**	82. **B**	85. **B**	88. **B**	91. **C**	

Visual and Performing Arts

93. **B**	95. **A**	97. **C**	99. **C**	101. **C**	103. **A**
94. **A**	96. **D**	98. **D**	100. **D**	102. **D**	104. **C**

Physical Education

105. **B**	106. **D**	107. **B**	108. **B**	109. **D**	110. **D**	111. **C**	112. **A**

Human Development

113. **A**	114. **C**	115. **A**	116. **C**	117. **B**	118. **D**	119. **C**	120. **C**

EXPLAINED ANSWERS

CONTENT KNOWLEDGE

Literature and Language Studies

Detailed explanations for the concepts covered in these questions are given in the review sections.

1. **C** The speaker is telling a story about her life.
2. **B** The report treated the grade equivalent scores as though it were a single number instead of a range of scores. This practice makes it appear that there are real differences between the classes when this is probably not the case.
3. **C** The speaker is clearly trying to convince the audience of his or her position and uses several rhetorical devices to that end.
4. **A** The speaker is begging the question because he or she does not respond to the original question and raises other issues completely unrelated to the question asked.
5. **B** *Robinson Crusoe* was written for adults. The *Wizard of Oz* was written in this century. Most children's literature conveyed a religious or moral theme through about the 1600s, and James Fenimore Cooper wrote the *Last of the Mohicans*.
6. **D** The King Arthur legends showing brave men, defenseless women, and stories of love are the classic romance. The epic and the lyric appeared much earlier.
7. **C** This poem is not to be taken literally. The poet is talking about his or her life and is hoping that his or her own life will get better.
8. **A** The last two lines in the first stanza compare clouds to shrouds. We know that the figure of speech must be a metaphor or simile. The poem uses the word *like*, and the figure of speech must be a simile.
9. **C** Allegory means that a work represents some other idea and is not to be taken literally.
10. **B** Onomatopoeia uses words to represent sounds.
11. **C** Using the inverse means turning the premise (finished under 2 hours) and the conclusion (70 percent or more correct) around. Getting more than 70 percent correct does not mean that a person finished in under 2 hours.
12. **A** Answer A is literally what the statement in the question means. In order to say that the difference between two groups or samples is significant, we must be able to show that the groups or samples were drawn from different populations.
13. **B** Language has two main aspects—function and structure. Language function refers to the ability to communicate. Language structure refers to the way words are used in a language. The structure of the quote is inappropriate; however, we know what it means.
14. **C** A videotape has serial access. That is, you have to go through one part of the tape to get to another. The others listed all have random access. That is, you can jump right to the part of the disk you need.
15. **A** Both of these novels exposed American social ills. *The Jungle* described the problems with the meat and meat-packing industry, while *Grapes of Wrath* described the plight of migrant workers in the Depression.
16. **D** Choices A, B, and C point out the kind of spelling difficulties regularly encountered in the English language. Choice D does not have such a problem but emphasizes the *r* sound by repeating the letters a number of times.
17. **C** Choice C is correct.
18. **B** Most experts agree that there are about 1,000,000 English words.
19. **B** This sentence uses the adverb *badly* to modify the noun *dinner*. Choice A correctly uses the adjective *good*. Choices C and D correctly use the adverbs *badly* and *well*.

20. **B** ERIC is an extensive file of education materials on microfiche. LEXIS is primarily for lawyers; CAD/CAM describes a computer drawing program, and NSF stands for National Science Foundation.
21. **C** Choice C is correct.
22. **C** Other choices contain "classic" word usage errors. These errors: (A) *reigned* instead of *reined* (B) *passed* instead of *past*, and (D) *they're* instead of *their*.
23. **A** *Ante* means before. *Anti* means against, and *post* means after.
24. **D** Poems were originally sung. Over time, the melody of the song was replaced with a word cadence.

Mathematics

25. **C** There is a 3-hour time difference between coasts, and the time is later on the east coast.
26. **B** Earth is the third planet from the sun. Mars and Venus are between Earth and the sun. A third planet near Venus would make Earth the fourth planet. A planet near Neptune would not affect Earth's position from the sun.
27. **D** The overlap of the rhombus and rectangle rings shows that some rhombuses are rectangles, which means that some rhombuses are not rectangles.
28. **C** Each angle must measure less than 90° to total 90°. Acute angles have measures less than 90°.
29. **D** We can't draw any conclusions about whether the light beams will cross or not. We just know that since they are not parallel and don't point in the same direction, at least two of them may be skewed (not touch).
30. **B** The points are symmetrical and so the line passes through the origin. A sketch confirms the answer.
31. **A** There are 1,000 meters in a kilometer. So, divide 2,750 by 1,000 to find the answer.
32. **D** The difference in the two stock prices ($19\frac{5}{8}$–$17\frac{7}{8}$) is $1\frac{3}{4}$ dollars or $1.75. Multiply $1.75 by 20 to find the answer.
33. **B** Investigate a pattern to find that the sum of the first n odd numbers is n^2. The sum of the first 90 odd numbers is 90^2 or 8,100.
34. **C** There are about (60) × (60) × (24) or 86,400 seconds in a day. There are about (365) × (86,400) or 31,536,000 seconds in a year. There are about (4) × (31,536,000) or 126,144,000 seconds in 4 years. Light travels about (186,000) × (126,144,000) or about 23,000,000,000,0000 (23 trillion) miles in 4 years.
35. **B** 10 feet + 20% (first) = 12 feet + 20% (second) = 14.4 feet+ 20% (third) = 17.28 feet + 20% (fourth) = 20.736 or about 20.7 feet.
36. **D** The maximum length of the side of the cube is the shortest of the three dimensions. The volume of the cube is 8^3 or 512.
37. **A** The correct answer is 42. The pattern increases by 4, 6, 8, 10, and then 12.
38. **C** This formula gives the correct answer. The formula $H \times (H + 1)$ is equivalent to this formula.
39. **B**

Month 1	$1,000 + 1.5% = $1,015–$50.00 = $965.00
Month 2	$965 + 1.5% = $979.48–$50.00 = $929.48
Month 3	$929.48 + 1.5% = $943.42–$50.00 = $893.42

40. **C** Round the quotient (10) to 11 to have room for all the people to go on the class trip.
41. **C** This process crosses off all numbers but the prime numbers. The numbers in answer C are all the prime numbers in the 80s.
42. **D** The process yields the one piece that is both (small or striped) and large.
43. **B** Multiply 0.23 and $2,600.
44. **A** Divide $858 by $2,600 to find the percent (33 percent) needed for transportation. Subtract the current transportation percentage from 33 percent to find the percent to be taken from miscellaneous (33% – 24% = 9%). Subtract 11% – 9% = 2% to find the percent left for miscellaneous.
45. **B** Solve a proportion. $\frac{2}{9} = \frac{x}{1,350}$
$9x = 2,700$ $x = 300$
46. **D** This question asks which of the first ten numbers evenly divides the large number in the question. Choice D contains those numbers.

47. **B** This question asks you to apply the Pythagorean theorem $a^2 = b^2 = c^2$.

$$300^2 + 400^2 = 500^2$$

(300, 400, 500 is a Pythagorean triple.)

48. **C** The probability is always 1/2 regardless of what happens on previous flips.

History/Social Studies

49. **D** American settlement in California preceded the Civil War. This settlement brought an end to the Mexican era.
50. **A** The mass death of indigenous Americans began as soon as the first colonists arrived.
51. **A** The Algonquin-speaking tribes included the Iroquois Federation and other Northeast Indians.
52. **C** Choice C is correct.
53. **A** Cabillero explored southern California. Sir Frances Drake came later. Mendoza and Cortes never explored California.
54. **C** Withdrawal from the war had been a revolutionary promise. Russia left the war and gave up vast expanses of land and resources.
55. **D** Hoover adopted a hands off policy and only attempted a "trickle down" approach by making money available to employers.
56. **B** Japan and Germany were allies. So when the United States declared war on Japan, it also declared war on Germany.
57. **C** The Emancipation Proclamation applied only to slaves in confederate states.
58. **D** The United States government had been pro business until Roosevelt came into office and sided with the strikers in the Anthracite strike.
59. **C** This famous quote from Churchill referred to the isolation of Communist bloc European countries.
60. **B** These are Egyptian pyramids, and almost all major Egyptian pyramids were built during a 200-year period about 2500 B.C.
61. **B** They were successfully defended by patriots, including John Adams, on the grounds that they acted in self defense.
62. **B** The Jeffersonians favored a weaker federal government, and they were opposed by the Federalists (Hamiltonians) who favored a stronger federal government.
63. **C** Introduction of writing separates prehistoric from historic times, and the first symbols were cuneiform symbols.
64. **B** Buddhism had a more lasting impact on China and the rest of the world than in India.
65. **A** The Aztecs who inhabited the area around Mexico City featured human sacrifice.
66. **B** Robespierre was executed for his role as head of the Committee on Public Safety, which arranged the deaths of over 20,000 people.
67. **B** The Common Market includes only England and European countries.
68. **D** The Zulu were dominant in South Africa in the early 1800s.
69. **C** Roosevelt died just months before. De Gaulle never participated in this conference.
70. **B** Choices A and C cannot be inferred from the information given. Choice D is incorrect.

Science

71. **A** Mitosis involves cell division, meiosis does not. The other choices are not reproductive methods.
72. **C** The DNA creates RNA to carry information outside the nucleus.
73. **C** Subdominant individuals have no dominance to assert. They must migrate, perish, or give up resources.
74. **B** Choice B is the definition of ecology.
75. **B** Women typically have 23 sets of chromosomes with two x chromosomes. Men typically have 23 sets of chromosomes with an x and y chromosome.
76. **D** All other choices are multicelled organisms.
77. **B** It takes light about 300 years to travel from Polaris to earth.
78. **B** Bacteria were the very first cells to develop on earth.
79. **C** The Triassic period about 225,000,000 years ago saw the appearance of dinosaurs on earth.
80. **C** Computations that show all galaxies are moving away from each other are used as a basis for the big bang theory.
81. **D** Most of the earth's atmosphere is nitrogen. Oxygen makes up about 21 percent of the atmosphere. The remaining 1 percent of earth's atmosphere is partitioned among trace elements and gases.

82. **B** The earth's mantle is the first part of the earth beneath the surface.
83. **A** The amp measures the current flow, and the volt measures the current force.
84. **C** Sound travels about 1,100 feet per second. 14 × 1,100 feet = 15,400 feet or about 3 miles.
85. **B** Seawater is about 3.5 percent salt.
86. **A** Choices B and C are part of the water cycle.
87. **D** The nucleus is the central part of the atom. The subatomic particles revolve around the nucleus.
88. **B** Air circulates counterclockwise around a low and clockwise around a high in the Northern Hemisphere. This pattern is reversed in the Southern Hemisphere.
89. **A** Sedimentary rocks are found near the surface. Igneous and metamorphic rocks are found beneath the surface. The term Cretaceous refers to a time period, not a rock type.
90. **B** Mass is the amount of an object and it does not vary. Weight is the force of gravity on mass, and weight does vary with gravity.
91. **C** Acids dissolved in water produce hydrogen. Acids and bases combined chemically form salt.
92. **C** Answers A and D might play a role in the speed of molecules. However, heat measures the speed of moving molecules.

Visual and Performing Arts

93. **B** The column shown is of Doric design.
94. **A** The golden ratio is 1.6 to 1. Many believe that this is the most pleasing artistic and architectural proportion.
95. **A** The diatonic scale refers to the piano's white keys only.
96. **D** A fresco is paint applied to wet plaster. Frescoes almost always appear on walls.
97. **C** Mixing complementary colors, opposing colors on the color wheel, produces gray.
98. **D** The flat at the beginning of the staff means that all B's are played flat. However, the natural before the second B means it is played as just a B.
99. **C** The arena stage is most commonly encountered in a circus. The circus has been considered a performing art since ancient times.
100. **D** Generally speaking the producer has business responsibilities while the director has creative responsibilities.
101. **C** Cubist art work employs many geometric solids not just the cube.
102. **D** Jazz consists of improvisation of popular songs.
103. **A** In ballet, movement followed music, but this is not always the case in modern dance.
104. **C** A libretto shows the musical score of an opera.

Physical Education

105. **B** These are the five simple locomotor movements that lead to the development of more complex movement skill. Galloping and sliding and skipping combine several of these first five skills.
106. **D** Nonlocomotor skills are performed from a relatively stable support base. Usually no distance is covered.
107. **B** Skipping involves a step and a hop.
108. **B** Scoliosis is a lateral curvature of the spine; any common plumb line can help in initial screening.
109. **D** Lay-up is a basketball shot that is taken close to the backboard.
110. **D** Eye-hand coordination is not fully developed in young children. These activities will help develop this skill.
111. **C** Research has shown that this method is effective.
112. **A** It is impossible to provide constant supervision of playgrounds.

Human Development

113. **A** Authentic assessment means evaluating work that students have completed. Portfolio assessment is one form of authentic assessment.
114. **C** Learning-disabled students benefit most from brief, structured assignments and auditory opportunities for learning.
115. **A** This one factor consistently correlates highest with achievement.
116. **C** Choice C is correct. Choice A is wrong because all humans do not move through all the stages, choice B is incorrect because young children have no such sense, and choice D is wrong because this characteristic identifies people at the final stage of development.

117. **B** Preoperational children can't conserve number.
118. **D** Identity crisis typifies these junior high school and early high school years.
119. **C** All the other choices are symptoms found in children born to drug-abusing mothers.
120. **C** Cooperative learning is truly student-centered. All the other activities could take place in a teacher-centered classroom.

CONTENT AREA EXERCISES I AND II

Show your short-answer question responses to an appropriate teacher or college professor. Ask the reader to evaluate your responses using the following scoring standards.

3 This response shows that the writer clearly understood the question and responded effectively to all parts of the question or assignment. All explanations are clear, show an understanding of the subject matter, and are supported by appropriate details and facts.

2 This response shows that the writer understood most of the question and responded effectively to most parts of the question or assignment. Explanations show an adequate knowledge of the subject matter and are usually supported by appropriate details and facts.

1 This response shows that the writer did not understand much of the question and did not respond effectively to most parts of the question or assignment. Explanations are usually unclear and are usually not well supported.

0 The response was completely wrong, just restates the question, or was completely off the topic.

MSAT PRACTICE TEST I SCORING

CONTENT KNOWLEDGE

		Number Correct
Literature and Language Studies	24 questions	______
Mathematics	24 questions	______
History/Social Studies	22 questions	______
Science	22 questions	______
Visual and Performing Arts	12 questions	______
Physical Education	8 questions	______
Human Development	8 questions	______
	RAW SCORE	______

CONTENT AREA EXERCISES I

Question	Points
1	______
2	______
3	______
4	______
5	______
6	______
7	______
8	______
9	______
10	______
11	______
12	______
TOTAL	______

CONTENT AREA EXERCISES II

Question	Points
1	______
2	______
3	______
4	______
5	______
6	______
TOTAL	______

FINAL SCORING

CONTENT KNOWLEDGE RAW SCORE [ ]

CONTENT AREA EXERCISES RAW SCORE [ ]

Compare your scores to the passing scores that follow.

CALIFORNIA PASSING AND MINIMUM SCALE SCORES

Overall Passing Score	311
Content Knowledge Minimum Score	148
Content Area Exercises Minimum Score	147

As long as you get the minimum scale score on each test, there are a large number of passing score combinations. You can make up for a lower score on one test with a higher score on the other test.

ESTIMATED RAW SCORES NEEDED FOR CALIFORNIA MINIMUM SCORES

Content Knowledge	72–74 correct out of 120 items
Content Area Exercises	26–27 points out of a possible 54 points

CALIFORNIA ESTIMATED PASSING RAW SCORE COMBINATIONS

Combination	Content Knowledge	Content Area Exercises
Passing Combination with the Content Knowledge Minimum Score	72–74 correct (60%–62%)	33–34 points (60%–63%)
Passing Combination with the Content Area Exercises Minimum Score	88–90 correct (73%–75%)	26–27 points (48%–50%)
Passing Combination with Half the Scale Points from each Test	80–82 correct (67%–68%)	30–31 points (56%–58%)

OREGON PASSING SCALE SCORE AND ESTIMATED RAW SCORE NEEDED TO PASS

	Passing Scale Score	Estimated Passing Raw Scores
Content Knowledge	147	71–73 correct of 120 items
Content Area Exercises	Submit any score	

PRACTICE MSAT II

CONTENT KNOWLEDGE

Take this test in a realistic, timed setting. You should not take this practice test until you have completed the appropriate review, the practice questions, and MSAT Practice Test I.

The setting will be most realistic if another person times the test and ensures that the test rules are followed exactly. If another person is acting as test supervisor, he or she should review these instructions with you and say "Start" when you should begin a section and "Stop" when time has expired.

You have 2 hours to complete the 120 multiple choice questions in areas of Literature and Language Studies, Mathematics, History and Social Studies, Science, Visual and Performing Arts, Human Development, and Physical Education.

Keep the time limit in mind as you work. Answer the easier questions first. Be sure you answer all the questions. There is no penalty for guessing. You may write on the test booklet and mark up the questions.

Each multiple choice question or statement in the test has four answer choices. Exactly one of these choices is correct. Mark your choice on the answer sheet provided for this test.

Your score is based on the spaces you fill in on the answer sheet. Make sure that you mark your answer on the answer sheet in the correct space next to the correct question number.

Use a pencil to mark the answer sheet. The actual test will be machine scored so completely darken in the answer space.

Once the test is complete, review the answers and explanations for each item, as you correct the answer sheet.

When instructed, turn the page and begin.

Each item on this test includes four answer choices. Select the best choice for each item and mark that letter on the answer sheet.

LITERATURE AND LANGUAGE STUDIES

Questions 1–3 refer to the following poem.

My love falls on silence nigh
I am alone in knowing the good-bye
For while a lost love has its day
A love unknown is a sadder way

1. The word *nigh* in line 1 means
   (A) clear.
   (B) complete.
   (C) near.
   (D) not.

2. This passage describes
   (A) loving someone and being rebuffed.
   (B) being loved by someone you do not love.
   (C) loving someone who loves another person.
   (D) loving someone without acknowledgment.

3. The subject and the verb in line 2 are
   (A) I . . . am.
   (B) I . . . alone.
   (C) I . . . knowing.
   (D) alone . . . knowing.

---

4. Literature written specifically for children did not appear until the
   (A) 1500s.
   (B) 1600s.
   (C) 1700s.
   (D) 1800s.

5. *Peter Piper picked a peck of pickled peppers.*

   The sentence above is an example of
   (A) alliteration.
   (B) euphemism.
   (C) hyperbole.
   (D) metaphor.

6. *The Odyssey* is best categorized as
   (A) an epic.
   (B) a lyric.
   (C) a novel.
   (D) a romance.

7. I grew up in Kearny, New Jersey, now known as Soccer Town, USA. I played football in high school and barely knew that the soccer team existed. However, a look back at my high school yearbook revealed that the soccer team won the state championship. We had a 0.500 season.

   Which of these techniques is used by the author of this passage?
   (A) exposition
   (B) reflection
   (C) argumentation
   (D) narration

8. [1] Their heads were filled with thoughts of laughing children and whirling rides. [2] Finally they were on their way. [3] Now every school day seemed like a month. [4] The children had been waiting for months to visit their favorite amusement park.

   Which of the following choices represents the most logical way to order the sentences from the paragraph above?
   (A) 3, 1, 4, 2
   (B) 3, 4, 1, 2
   (C) 4, 3, 1, 2
   (D) 4, 2, 3, 1

9. To search for information on the World Wide Web you would most likely use which of the following?
   (A) Excite
   (B) Norton Utilities
   (C) Windows
   (D) WordPerfect

10. Which of the following words or word pairs would NOT be used to coordinate sentence elements?
    (A) and
    (B) either or
    (C) but
    (D) when

11.

ah autumn coolness
hand in hand paring away

Which of the following could be the third line in the haiku poem above?
(A) in the wetness
(B) branches and leaves
(C) eggplants cucumbers
(D) til the end of day

12. The word *paring* in the poem above means
(A) putting together.
(B) doubling up.
(C) cutting off.
(D) planting fruit.

13. How is haiku different from a cinquain?
(A) The cinquain has a 5-5-5 scheme instead of 5-7-5.
(B) Lines can rhyme in haiku but not in a cinquain.
(C) A cinquain has five lines instead of three.
(D) A cinquain is of Spanish origin, and haiku originated in Japan.

14. The root *frac* in the word *fraction* means
(A) break.
(B) eighths.
(C) part.
(D) piece.

15. [1] All of my visits came before the series of fires that burned the park. [2] I have some very happy memories about Yellowstone National Park. [3] The United States National Park system is extensive. [4] Although most land dedicated to the park system is in western states.

Which of the following choices represents the most logical way to order the sentences from the paragraph above?
(A) 4, 3, 2, 1
(B) 4, 3, 1, 2
(C) 3, 4, 1, 2
(D) 3, 4, 2, 1

16. In which sentence is the underlined word used correctly?
(A) The rider grabbed the horse's reign.
(B) The teacher had just begun her lessen.
(C) The dog's collar showed its address.
(D) The road offered a steep assent to the plateau.

17. Which of the following shows the correct syllables for *simultaneous*?
(A) simul ta neous
(B) sim ul ta neous
(C) si mul ta ne ous
(D) sim ul ta ne ous

18. Which of the following would most likely appear in concrete poetry?
(A) dlrow drawkcab a ni evil ew
(B) the world is backward and it's tough
(C) the world's a wall–that's all
(D) hard, tough, backward rancid world

19. The infomercial hostess announces that "every person who participated in our skin care program now has beautiful skin." She then goes on to say that "This shows that if you want to have beautiful skin, you need to participate in our program."

Which of the following fallacious arguments does this passage represent?
(A) using the converse
(B) begging the question
(C) non sequitur
(D) false analogy

20. Remove the jack from the trunk. Set the jack under the car. Use the jack to raise the car. Remove the lug nuts. Remove the tire and replace it with the doughnut. Reset the lug nuts loosely and use the jack to lower the chassis to the ground. Tighten the lug nuts once the tire is touching the ground.

The organization pattern used by the author to develop this passage could be best described as
(A) time order.
(B) simple listing.
(C) cause and effect.
(D) definition.

21. Japanese students have always been considered to be well prepared for life in the world's business and engineering communities. The mathematics and science curricula of Japanese schools are considered to be superior to those in American schools. With the daily advancement of Japanese technological prowess, how can American children ever hope to compete with their Japanese counterparts?

    Which of the following is the best descriptor of the author's tone in this passage?
    (A) disbelief
    (B) anger
    (C) pride
    (D) concern

22. Empty halls and silent walls greeted me. A summer day seemed like a good time for me to take a look at the school in which I would student teach. I tiptoed from classroom door to classroom door—looking. Suddenly the custodian appeared behind me and said, "Help you?" "No sir," I said. At that moment she may have been Plato or Homer for all I knew.

    Which of the following best describes the main character in the paragraph above?
    (A) timid and afraid
    (C) confident and optimistic
    (C) pessimistic and unsure
    (D) curious and respectful

23. Homer, mentioned in the last line of this passage, is a
    (A) general.
    (B) painter.
    (C) poet.
    (D) religious leader.

24. The storm moved slowly through the day
    Like a huge car wash for the earth

    What figure of speech is represented in the second line of this passage?
    (A) simile
    (B) metaphor
    (C) euphemism
    (D) onomatopoeia

MATHEMATICS

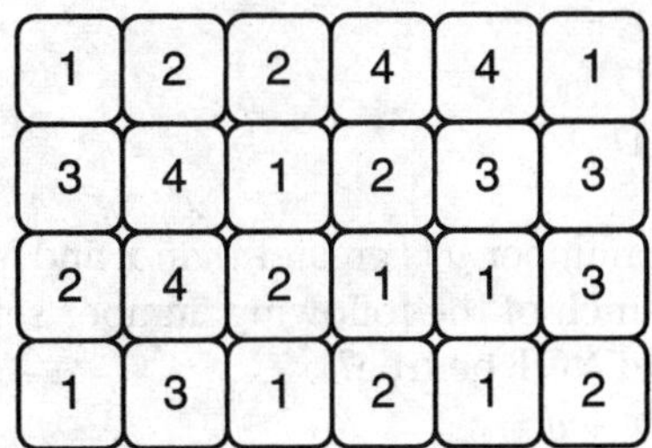

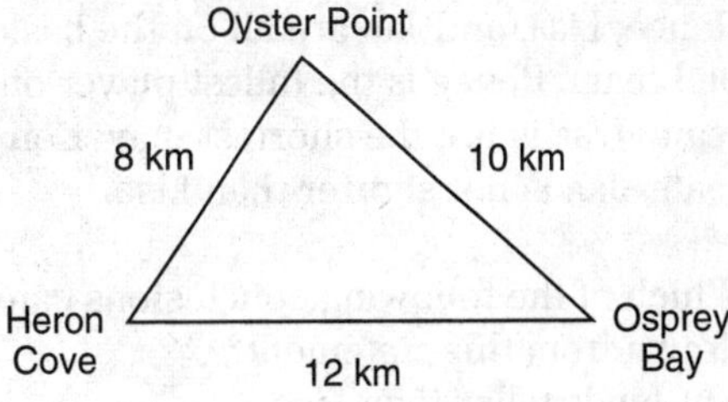

25. A ball is dropped randomly into the container shown above. What is the probability that the ball will land in a hole labeled "1"?
    (A) 8/12
    (B) 1/2
    (C) 1/3
    (D) 1/4

26. The diagram shows three towns, the roads connecting them, and the distance between each town. Which of the following is the shortest distance?
    (A) Osprey Bay to Heron Cove to Oyster Point and then half-way to Osprey Bay
    (B) Halfway between Oyster Point and Heron Cove, to Heron Cove to Osprey Bay to Oyster Point
    (C) Quarter-way from Heron Cove to Osprey Bay, to Osprey Bay to Oyster Point to Heron Cove
    (D) Heron Cove to Oyster Point to Osprey Bay, then halfway to Heron Cove

27. The first (F) person in a line is the same height or smaller than the second (S) person and the third person in line. The third (T) person in line is taller than the first person. Using the letters F, S, and T, which of the following choices correctly represents the height order of these three people?
(A) F > S > T
(B) F ≥ S > T
(C) T > S ≥ F
(D) T > F ≤ S

28. Which of the following ratios is NOT equivalent to 3 : 8?
(A) 3/8
(B) 24 to 9
(C) 6 to 16
(D) 12 : 32

29. (123 + 186 + 177) ÷ (3) =

Which of the following statements could result in the number sentence given above?
(A) The athlete wanted to find the median of the three jumps.
(B) The athlete wanted to find the average of the three jumps.
(C) The athlete wanted to find the quotient of the product of three jumps.
(D) The athlete wanted to find the sum of the quotients of the three jumps.

30. Renee, Lisa, and Jan are all on the basketball team. Renee is the tallest player on the team. Lisa is not the shortest player on the team. Jan is not shorter than Lisa.

Which of the following conclusions can be drawn from this statement?
(A) Jan is taller than Lisa.
(B) Jan is the second-tallest player on the team.
(C) Jan is not the shortest player on the team.
(D) Either Jan or Lisa is the second tallest player on the team.

31. If $x = 5/6$, which of the following inequalities is correct?
(A) $5/9 < x < 7/9$
(B) $5/8 < x < 3/4$
(C) $3/4 < x < 7/8$
(D) $7/8 < x < 15/16$

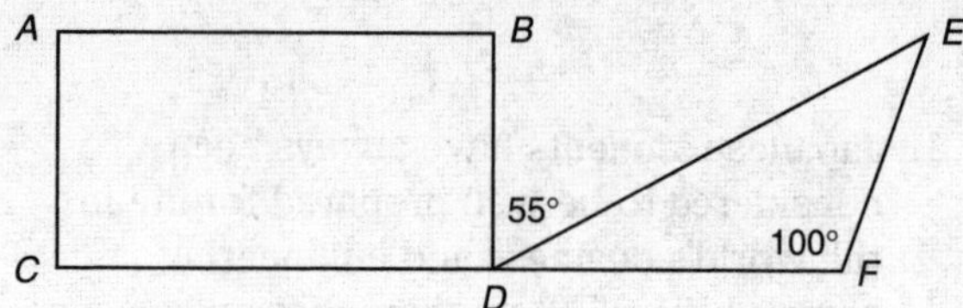

32. Given that *ABCD* is a rectangle and *DEF* is a triangle, what is the measure ∠*E*?
(A) 25°
(B) 35°
(C) 45°
(D) 55°

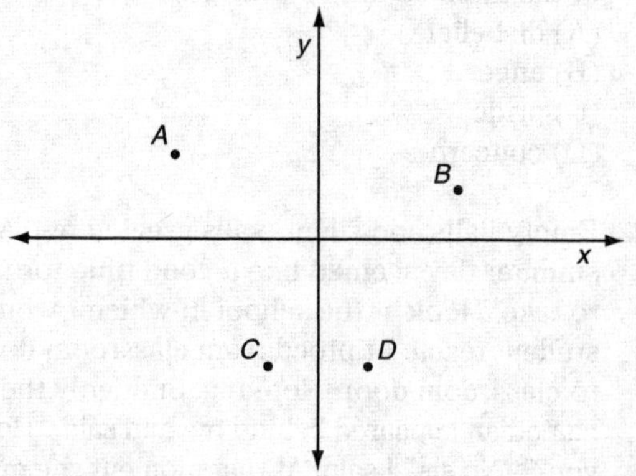

33. Which letter on the coordinate grid above could represent the point (2, –5)?
(A) A
(B) B
(C) C
(D) D

34. One number y is greater than x and less than z. Which of the following number sentences could NOT be true?
(A) $x + y = z$
(B) $z - x = y$
(C) $z - y = x$
(D) $y - x = z$

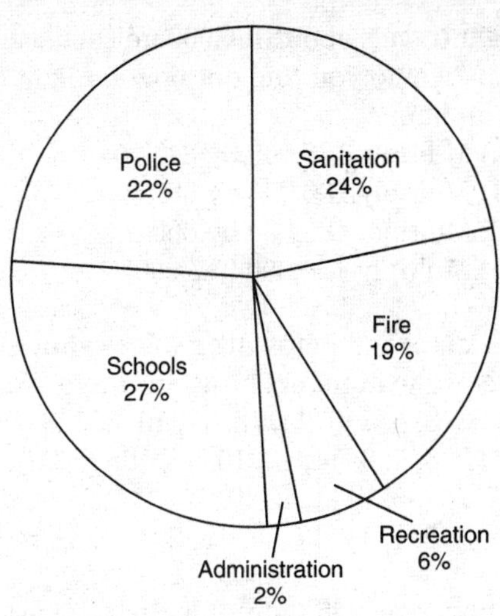

Tax money spent on town services.

35. A town collects $2,600,000 in taxes. The town needs $624,000 for police. Any needed money will come from sanitation. The percents in the circle graph are recalculated. What percent is left for sanitation?
(A) 22%
(B) 20%
(C) 19%
(D) 18%

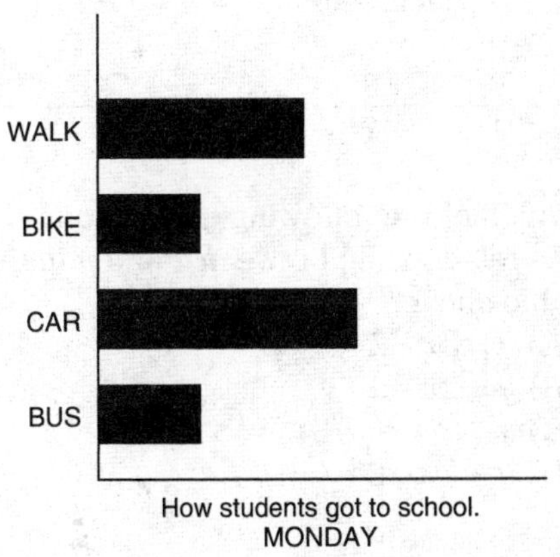

How students got to school.
MONDAY

Students took a survey to find out how students got to school one Monday morning. The results of the survey are shown on the bar graph above. The survey was taken again on the next day, Tuesday. The results for car and bus stayed the same. But the graphs for walking and biking were reversed.

36. Which of the following statements accurately describes the graph on that Tuesday?
(A) There were about twice as many walkers as bikers.
(B) There were about three times as many car riders as bus riders.
(C) There were about three times as many car riders as bikers.
(D) There were about half as many car riders as bike riders.

37. The disaster relief specialist found that 289, or 85%, of the houses on the beach had been damaged by the storm. How many houses were on the beach?
(A) 294
(B) 332
(C) 340
(D) 400

38. A person flips a fair penny twice and it lands heads up each time. What is the probability that the penny will land heads up on the next flip?
(A) 1
(B) 1/2
(C) 1/4
(D) 1/8

39. What power of 10 would you multiply times 3.74 to get 374,000,000?
(A) 10^6
(B) 10^7
(C) 10^8
(D) 10^9

40. Which of the following number sentences is an example of the associative property?
(A) $3 [(5 + 6) + 7] = 15 + 18 + 21$
(B) $3 [(5 + 6) + 7] = 3 [(6 + 5) + 7]$
(C) $3 [(5 + 6) + 7] = [(5 + 6) + 7] 3$
(D) $3 [(5 + 6) + 7] = 3 [5 + (6 + 7)]$

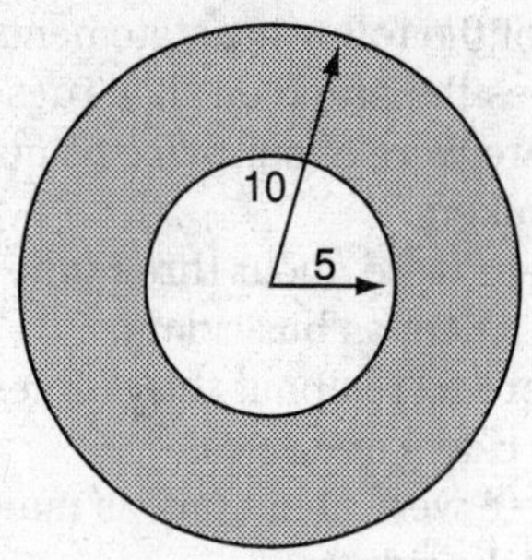

41. Two circles share the same center. What is the approximate area of the shaded part of the outer circle?
(A) 100π
(B) 75π
(C) $25\pi^2$
(D) 10π

42. Beth's front walk is 58 feet long. If y stands for yards, which of the following number statements best represents this distance?
(A) $19y + .1y$
(B) $19y + 1/3y$
(C) $19y$
(D) $19.1y$

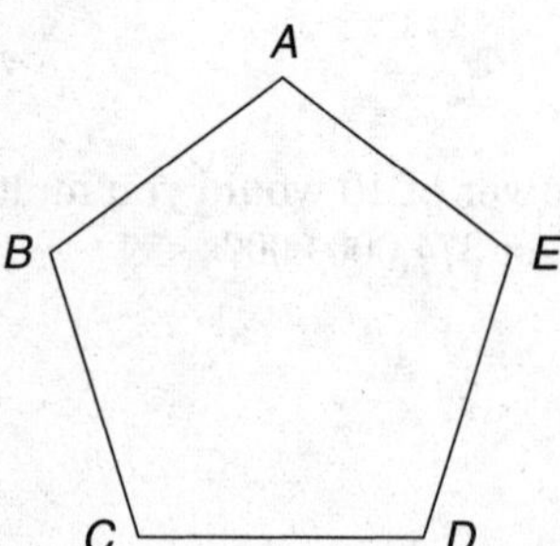

43. The figure shown above is a regular pentagon. What is the total of measurements of all the angles A through E.
(A) 360°
(B) 450°
(C) 540°
(D) 630°

44. Light travels about 186,000 miles in a second. How would you find out how far light travels in an hour?
(A) Multiply 186,000 by 24.
(B) Multiply 186,000 by 60.
(C) Multiply 186,000 by 360.
(D) Multiply 186,000 by 3600.

45. Which of the following choices shows all the prime numbers between 1 and 25?
(A) 2, 3, 5, 7, 9, 11, 13, 17, 19, 21, 23
(B) 3, 5, 7, 9, 11, 13, 15, 17, 19, 21, 23
(C) 2, 3, 5, 7, 11, 13, 17, 19, 23
(D) 3, 5, 7, 11, 13, 17, 19, 23

46. A boat costs $5 more than half the price of a canoe. Which of the following expressions shows this relationship?
(A) B + $5 = C/2
(B) B = 1/2C + $5
(C) B + $5 = 2C
(D) B + $5 > B/2

47. Which of the following could be the length of a couch in a person's living room?
(A) 75 cm
(B) 4 meters
(C) 150 mm
(D) 1.2 decimeters

x	0	3	6	7	9
y	1	7	13	15	19

48. Which of the following expressions shows the relationship between x and y in the table above?
(A) $y = 3x - 2$
(B) $y = 2x + 1$
(C) $y = x + 3$
(D) $y = 2x - 2$

HISTORY AND SOCIAL STUDIES

49. *The Jungle*, written by Upton Sinclair in the early 1900s, described
    (A) an expedition into central Africa.
    (B) abuses in the meat-packing industry.
    (C) the plight of immigrants in New York.
    (D) a man's struggle for business success.

50. The words "let them eat cake" were uttered by
    (A) Marie Antoinette during the French Revolution.
    (B) King Louis XVI during the French Revolution.
    (C) Robespierre during the Reign of Terror.
    (D) Napoleon before the Battle of Waterloo.

51. For religious guidance a person of Islamic faith is most likely to turn to
    (A) the Bible.
    (B) the Koran.
    (C) the Rubaiyat.
    (D) the Mahabarata.

52. Which of the following led to the great schism of the Catholic church?
    (A) establishment of Constantinople as the Eastern capital of the Roman Empire
    (B) establishment by Queen Elizabeth I of the Protestant Church of England
    (C) conversion of the Emperor Constantine and (St.) Augustine to Catholicism
    (D) nailing by Martin Luther of his *95 Theses* to the Wittenberg Church door

53. What conclusion can reasonably be drawn from the information on this map?
    (A) Were it not for Texas and California, Fremont would have won the election.
    (B) Buchanan was a strong supporter of the rebel cause.
    (C) Fremont was favored by those living in the northernmost states.
    (D) Fremont was favored by the states that fought on the Union side in the Civil War.

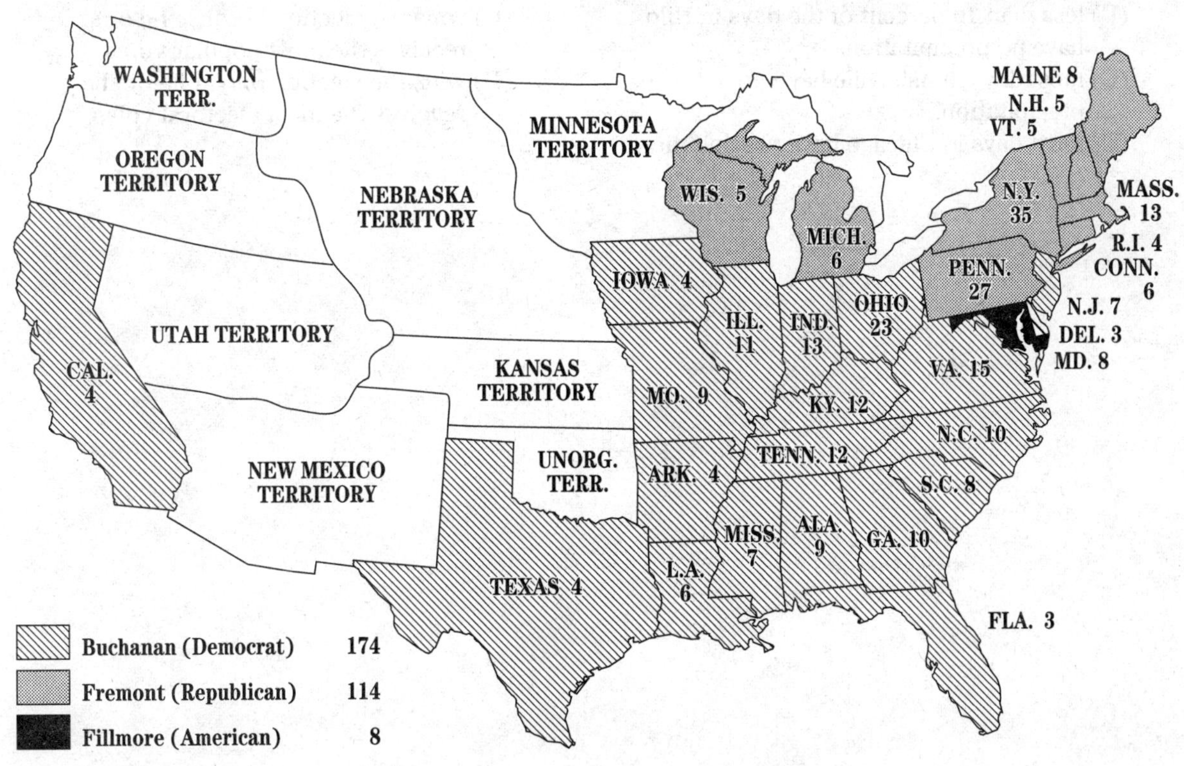

54. During which of the following conflicts involving England did the nursing efforts of Florence Nightingale become famous?
    (A) American Revolutionary War
    (B) Crimean War
    (C) World War I
    (D) World War II

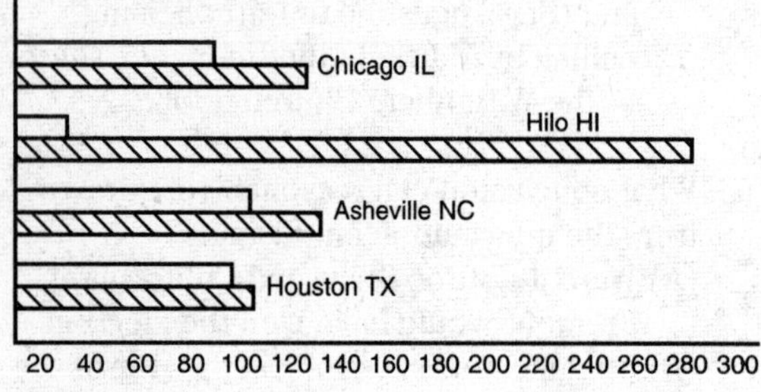

55. The correct interpretation of the double line graph above is, on average,
    (A) most days in Houston have precipitation.
    (B) less than 10 percent of the days in Hilo have no precipitation.
    (C) most days in Asheville have no precipitation.
    (D) most days in Chicago have precipitation.

56. The manifest destiny of the United States refers primarily to acquiring lands
    (A) north of the Mason-Dixon line.
    (B) south of the Mason-Dixon line.
    (C) east of the Mississippi.
    (D) west of the Mississippi.

57. The main effect of the Treaty of Utrecht in 1742 was that
    (A) France lost North American possessions to England.
    (B) Spanish Empire was partitioned.
    (C) Britain recognized the United States after the Revolutionary War.
    (D) Holland and Switzerland were officially formed.

58. In an election of the president of the United States, a candidate who receives the most popular votes for the entire country
    (A) wins the election because he or she receives the most electoral votes.
    (B) wins the election even if he or she does not receive the most electoral votes.
    (C) wins the election because he or she receives the most popular votes.
    (D) wins the election only if he or she receives the most electoral votes.

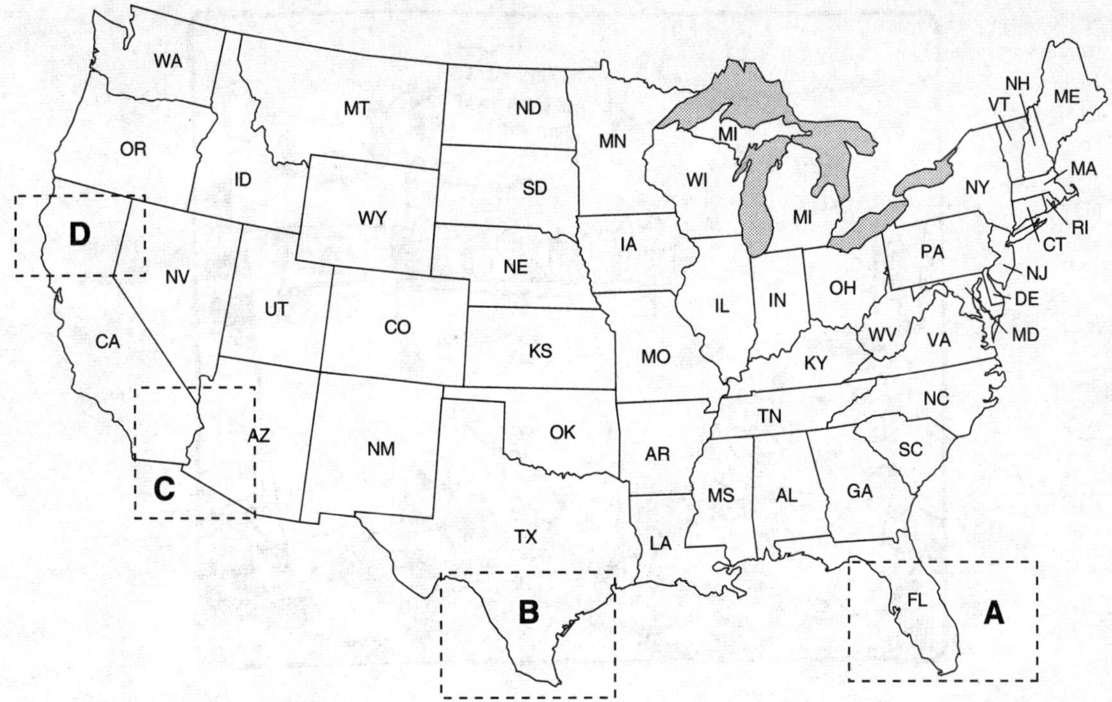

59. Which of the four lettered areas on the map above of the United States has the highest daily temperatures?
    (A) A
    (B) B
    (C) C
    (D) D

60. Which of the following shows the correct order of the listed events in United States history?

    I. Reconstruction
    II. Sherman's March to the Sea
    III. the Gettysburg Address
    IV. approval of the XIII Amendment

    (A) I, II, III, IV
    (B) II, III, I, IV
    (C) II, I, III, IV
    (D) IV, II, III, I

61. Say that Company A and Company B try to raise money by selling bonds to the public. Which of the following could cause the interest rate for Company A's bonds to be much higher than the rates for Company B's bonds?
    (A) The bonds for Company A have a higher risk.
    (B) The bonds for Company B have a higher risk.
    (C) The management of Company A wants to reward its investors.
    (D) The management of company B wants to reward its investors.

62. When Julius Caesar uttered the words "et tu Brute,"
    (A) he was talking to his collaborator, Brutus.
    (B) he was talking to his assassin, Brutus.
    (C) he was preparing Brutus to become his second in command.
    (D) he was preparing Brutus for fateful days to come in the Ides of May.

63. "The cause of liberty becomes a mockery if the price to be paid is the wholesale destruction of those who are to enjoy it."

    The quote above from Mohandas Gandhi is best reflected in which of the following statements about the American civil rights movement?

    (A) Bus boycotts are not effective because boycotters are punished.
    (B) Nonviolence and civil disobedience are the best approach to protest.
    (C) Desegregation laws were a direct result of freedom marches.
    (D) America will never be free as long as minorities are oppressed.

64. The main idea of the cartoon by Toles shown above is

    (A) alliances among neighboring countries in Europe have broken down the barriers between them.
    (B) those in East Germany are working hard, while workers in other countries are running away from their duties.
    (C) some countries are gaining freedom from the USSR, while other countries remain under Soviet control.
    (D) a break in the prison wall is letting citizens from some countries escape while citizens from other countries remain captive.

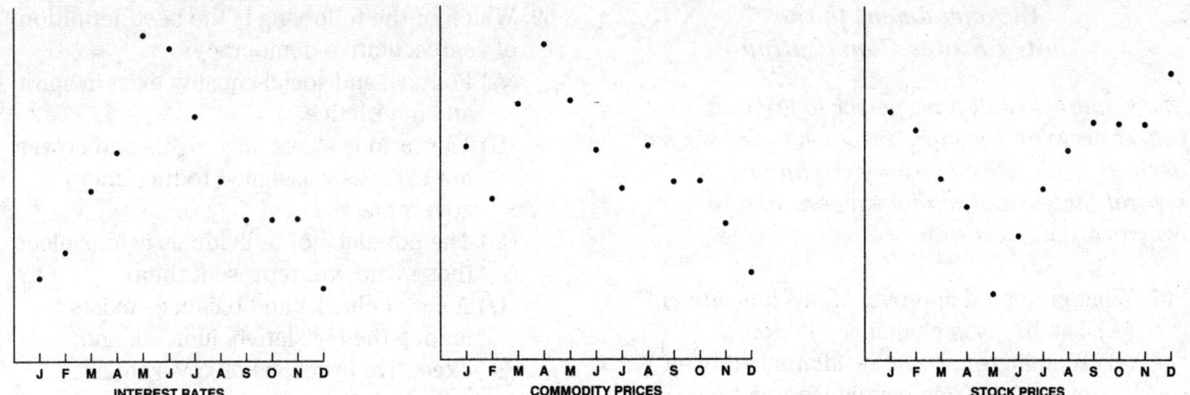

Graphs of Three Economic Indicators for the Same 12-month Period

65. Which of the following conclusions can be drawn from the information on the three graphs shown above?
   (A) Higher interest rates cause lower stock prices.
   (B) Interest rates and stock prices are inversely related.
   (C) Commodity prices and interest rates are not related to one another.
   (D) Commodity prices and stock prices are directly related.

66. The non-Spanish languages spoken in western South America result from
   (A) early Mayan influence.
   (B) early Incan influence.
   (C) early Aztec influence.
   (D) early Anasazi influence.

Official Languages of South American Countries

An Amendment to the United States Constitution

The Congress shall have power to lay and collect taxes on incomes, from whatever source derived, without apportionment among the several States, and without regard to any census or enumeration.

67. What prompted approval of this amendment?
    (A) The IRS was challenged in court.
    (B) Washington, D. C., residents had been exempted from paying income taxes.
    (C) Southern states objected to paying taxes to the federal government.
    (D) The Supreme Court ruled the income tax unconstitutional.

68. Anthropology is a holistic study of human beings. Which of the following types of anthropology is concerned with tracing the evolution of primates?
    (A) Biological Anthropology
    (B) Cultural Anthropology
    (C) Physical Anthropology
    (D) Political Anthropology

69. Which of the following is the best definition of representative democracy?
    (A) Political and social equality exist in spirit and in practice.
    (B) The various states have rights and power not expressly assigned to the federal government.
    (C) The populace of individual regions elect those who will represent them.
    (D) A set of checks and balances exists among the legislative, judicial, and executive branches of government.

70. During the Spanish-American War in the late 1890, the battleship *Maine* was sunk in the harbor at
    (A) Boston.
    (B) Havana.
    (C) New York.
    (D) Madrid.

SCIENCE

71. The first cells to develop on earth were most likely
    (A) algae.
    (B) bacteria.
    (C) DNA.
    (D) protozoa.

72. Through which of the media listed below will sound travel the fastest?
    (A) air
    (B) stone
    (C) water
    (D) vacuum

73. Geologists are reasonably certain that earth's continents are moving. In that case, in which order would the following events have occurred?

    I. The Atlantic Ocean is formed.
    II. Earth's land mass forms a single continent.
    III. Glaciers cover most of North America.
    IV. The bridge between North America and Europe disappears.

    (A) II, I, III, IV
    (B) II, IV, I, III
    (C) II, I, IV, III
    (D) III, II, IV, I

74. Which diagram shows object • to have the most potential energy?

(A)
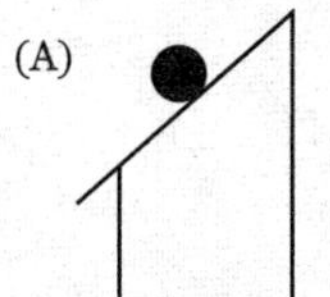
(B)
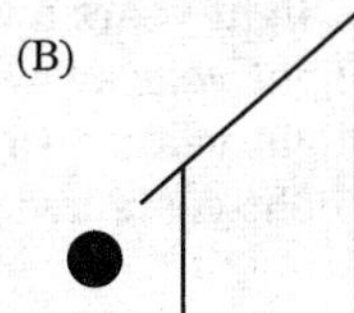
(C)
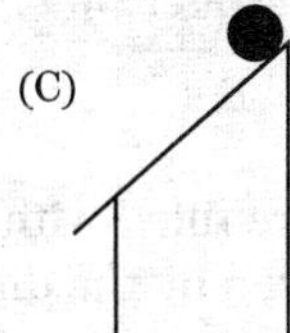
(D)
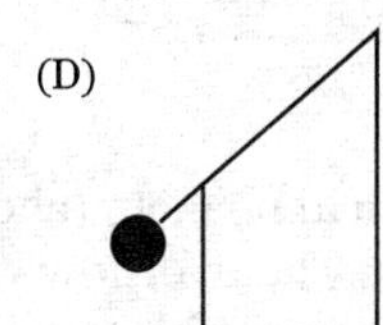

75. Which of the following represents the correct sequence of events that occurs during photosynthesis?

I. CO_2 and water are broken down
II. Carbohydrates are formed
III. Sunlight is absorbed by chlorophyll
IV. The plant emits O_2

(A) I, III, II, IV
(B) I, II, III, IV
(C) III, I, II, IV
(D) II, IV, I, III

76. Which of the following best describes the subject matter of an ecology course?
(A) the impact of earth's topography on plant growth
(B) the relationship between earth's atmosphere and living things
(C) the impact of earth's biosphere on plants and animals
(D) the relationship of organisms and their habitat

77. What type of rock, millions of years from now, would most likely contain current animal remains?
(A) conglomerate
(B) sedimentary
(C) igneous
(D) metamorphic

78. The two cats are the parents of these three kittens. Which of the following would explain this situation?
(A) Both parents have recessive white genes.
(B) One parent has a dominant white gene.
(C) The female parent has a recessive white gene.
(D) One parent has a dominant black gene.

79. The destruction of a South American rain forest directly influences all of the following EXCEPT:
(A) animal habitats
(B) climate shifts
(C) reproduction of natural resources
(D) production of world oxygen

80. Which of the following diagrams represents a situation that could result in a solar eclipse?

(A)

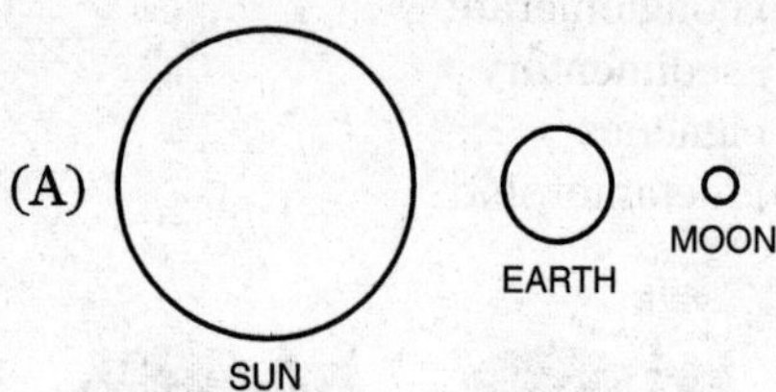

(B)

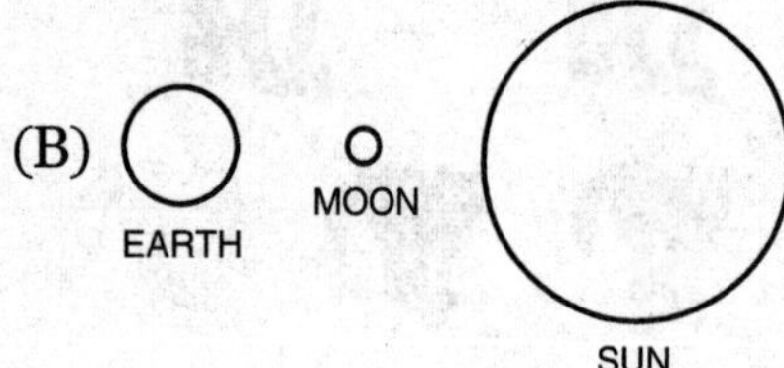

(C)

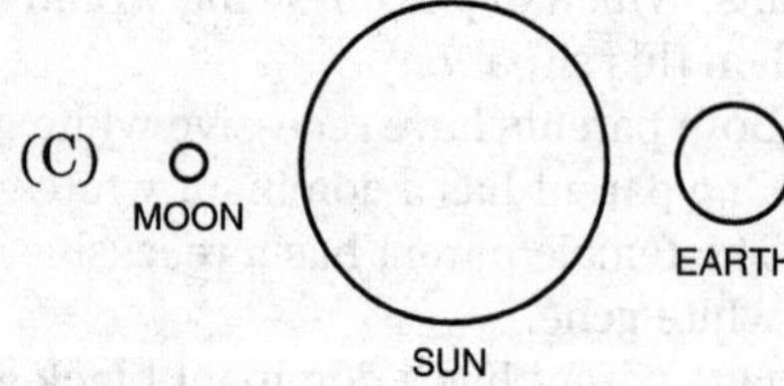

(D)

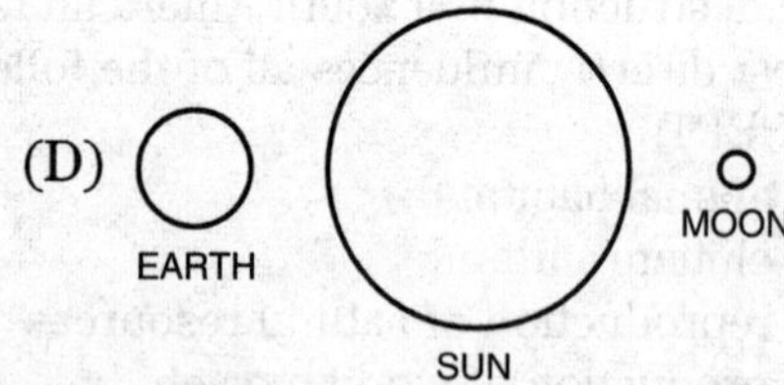

81. You are standing in an open field in the Northern Hemisphere facing north. You feel the wind coming from the front of your right side. It is most likely that
   (A) a low pressure system is to your right.
   (B) a low pressure system is to your left.
   (C) a high pressure system is to your right.
   (D) a high pressure system is to your left.

82. Meiosis always involves
   (A) cells making carbon copies of themselves.
   (B) the formation of zygotes.
   (C) the formation of gametes.
   (D) chromosomes that duplicate.

83. Light travels about 12,000,000,000 (12 billion) miles a year. The closest star to earth, other than our sun, is about
   (A) 0.5 light years away.
   (B) 1 light year away.
   (C) 2 light years away.
   (D) 4 light years away.

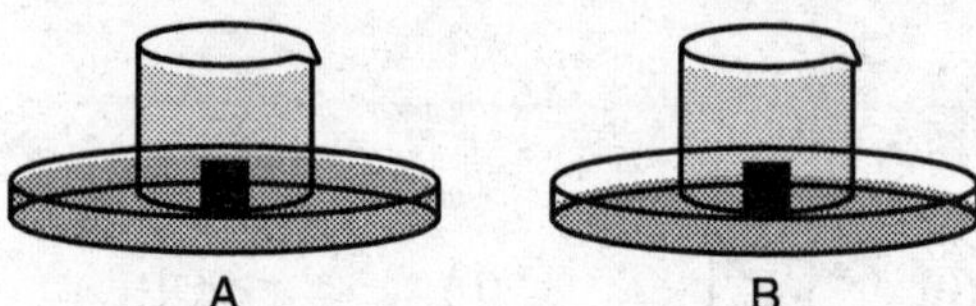

84. Identical beakers (above) were filled with water. The overflow was caused by the different solid objects placed in the beakers. The size of the objects cannot be determined. What is the most likely explanation of the differing amounts of overflow?
   (A) The object in beaker A is heavier.
   (B) The object in beaker B is heavier.
   (C) The object in beaker A has more mass.
   (D) The object in beaker B has more mass.

85. A glass rod that does not attract bits of paper does attract the paper after it has been rubbed with a piece of silk. The best scientific explanation for this phenomenon is that
   (A) the rod was charged with static electricity.
   (B) electrons were removed from the rod.
   (C) neutrons were removed from the rod.
   (D) protons were removed from the rod.

86. Which of the following contributes to the notion that DDT is NOT biodegradable?
   (A) Insects and animals other than pests are poisoned by DDT.
   (B) DDT is found in the carcasses of life forms.
   (C) DDT has been found in river banks.
   (D) Many pests have developed a resistance to DDT.

87. A scientist cuts in half a just fallen hail stone and finds a series of rings much like tree rings. What could be found from counting the approximate number of rings?
    (A) how long the hail stone was in the atmosphere before falling to earth
    (B) how far from the surface the hail stone was before it started falling
    (C) how much precipitation fell during the hail storm
    (D) how many times the hail stone was blown above the freezing level

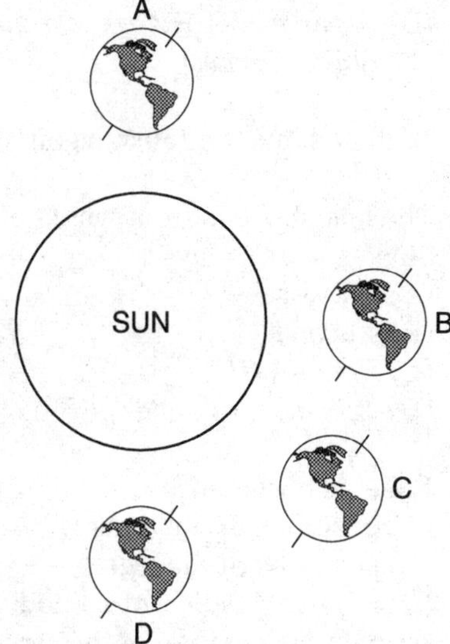

88. Which diagram shows earth's position at the beginning of summer in the Southern Hemisphere?
    (A) A
    (B) B
    (C) C
    (D) D

89. A person puts a black cloth over a pile of snow to make the snow melt faster. Why is that?
    (A) The black material absorbs more sunlight and more heat.
    (B) The black material holds the heat in close to the snow.
    (C) The black material reflects more light and so it gets hotter.
    (D) The black cloth is the opposite color of the white snow.

90. When ironing clothes, heat is transferred from the iron to the clothes by
    (A) convection.
    (B) radiation.
    (C) conduction.
    (D) attraction.

AVERAGE OUNCES GAINED PER ANIMAL

Week #	HF1	HF2
1	4	9
2	3	4
3	2	3
4	1	2
5	1	2
6	1	1

91. An experiment is set up to determine the effects of a new hamster food HF2 as compared to the effects of a current hamster food HF1. Each group receives the same quantity of food and the same attention. From the above data choose the best conclusion for the experiment.
    (A) HF2 group gained more weight.
    (B) HF1 group lived longer.
    (C) HF2 group got more protein.
    (D) HF1 group got better nutrition.

92. What appropriate criticism might a scientist have of the experiment in the previous question?
    (A) Averages should not be used in this type of experiment.
    (B) The null hypothesis is not stated in the appropriate form.
    (C) Hamsters are not found as pets in enough homes for the experiment to be widely applicable.
    (D) The experiment does not describe sufficient controls to be valid.

VISUAL AND PERFORMING ARTS

93. Which of the following songs begins with the four bars shown above?
    (A) "My Country 'Tis of Thee"
    (B) "Appalachian Spring"
    (C) "I Fall to Pieces"
    (D) "Star Spangled Banner"

94. Which of the following would NOT be associated with an opera?
    (A) aria
    (B) chorus
    (C) libretto
    (D) sonata

95. The impressionist French composer Ravel is most closely associated with what work?
    (A) "American in Paris"
    (B) "Bolero"
    (C) "Pictures on Exhibition"
    (D) "Scheherazade"

96. Secondary colors refer to
    (A) all the colors found in the spectrum.
    (B) colors formed by mixing two primaries.
    (C) colors that cannot be formed by mixing other colors.
    (D) colors opposite primary colors on the color wheel.

97. Andy Warhol is most closely associated with which of the following art movements?
    (A) Abstract Expressionism
    (B) Dada
    (C) Op
    (D) Pop

98. Which type of perspective is typically represented in still photographs?
    (A) aerial perspective
    (B) foreshortening
    (C) linear perspective
    (D) two-point perspective

99. Which of the following shows a correct association between a play and its theme?
    (A) *The Glass Menagerie:* mental illness
    (B) *Arsenic and Old Lace:* a destructive child
    (C) *All My Sons:* poisoning
    (D) *Children's Hour:* irresponsibility

100. Which of the following incorrectly matches playwright and play?
    (A) George Bernard Shaw: *Pygmalion*
    (B) Noel Coward: *The Vortex*
    (C) T. S. Eliot: *The Shadowy Waters*
    (D) Oscar Wilde: *The Importance of Being Earnest*

101. "Full of sound and fury, signifying nothing"

    The line above is from which of Shakespeare's plays?
    (A) *Hamlet*
    (B) *Macbeth*
    (C) *Henry VIII*
    (D) *Tristan and Isolde*

102. Ballet is based on
    (A) positions of the arms.
    (B) positions of the legs.
    (C) relative position of all body parts.
    (D) relative position of the torso and legs.

103. Which famous composer wrote the score for the ballet *Swan Lake*?
    (A) Copland
    (B) Lennon
    (C) Mozart
    (D) Tchaikovsky

104. Which of the following shows a correct association between a dance and its country of origin?
    (A) Italy: flamenco
    (B) Spain: tarantella
    (C) Japan: kubuki
    (D) France: waltz

PHYSICAL EDUCATION

105. Which of the following soccer skills should NOT be introduced to primary students (K–3)?
(A) foot trap
(B) heading
(C) instep kick
(D) chest trap

106. Which of the following describes the most effective way to overcome inertia when beginning to run?
(A) shorten arm swing
(B) begin from crouch position
(C) touch heel to ground before toe
(D) throw head upward

107. When it comes to fatigue, 5- to 7-year-olds
(A) fatigue quickly and recover rapidly.
(B) fatigue quickly and recover slowly.
(C) fatigue slowly and recover rapidly.
(D) fatigue slowly and recover slowly.

108. Which of the following is the most appropriate way to determine how obese a child is?
(A) ratio of weight to body type
(B) overall weight
(C) sum of skinfold measurements
(D) ratio of weight to height

109. Which of the following is NOT a symptom of a perceptual-motor deficiency?
(A) The child is not able to name a body part cited by the teacher.
(B) The child is not able to imitate the movements of others.
(C) The child is not able to distinguish right from left.
(D) The child is not able to kick a ball.

110. Which of the following nonlocomotor skills involves rotating body parts around the body's axis?
(A) swinging
(B) turning
(C) twisting
(D) bending

111. Which of the following most accurately describes a fact about the movement concept of force?
(A) Objects should be pushed away from the center of weight.
(B) More muscle contraction leads to more force.
(C) The sequence of body movements affects the amount of force.
(D) The more contracted the arm, the greater the force it produces.

112. Which of the following does NOT affect body stability?
(A) line of gravity
(B) inertia
(C) support base
(D) center of gravity

HUMAN DEVELOPMENT

113. According to researchers, which of the following is the most powerful overall motivation for students to do schoolwork?
   (A) praise
   (B) grades
   (C) privileges
   (D) personal satisfaction

114. Modeling by the teacher is an effective way to modify children's behavior. Which of the following is an example of a good modeling technique?
   (A) Show students how to construct replicas of historic buildings.
   (B) Respond courteously to students questions.
   (C) Demonstrate students' inappropriate behavior.
   (D) Correct mispronounced words.

115. Kohlberg described stages of moral development. Which of the following stages best describes most fifth- and sixth-grade students?
   (A) children who are very egocentric and have no conscience
   (B) children who have no clear morality
   (C) children who associate with authority figures and show concern for others
   (D) children who place personal motivation before moral concerns

116. Which of the following is NOT a true statement about the nature vs. nuture controversy?
   (A) The nature part refers to heredity.
   (B) The nurture part refers to environment and experience.
   (C) Studying twins split at birth have cleared up this controversy.
   (D) It is difficult to isolate interaction between these two factors.

117. Which of the following summarizes Glasser's Reality Therapy approach to classroom management?
   (A) Students are left on their own to discover the harsh reality of their own mistakes.
   (B) The teacher establishes clear rules and the rewards or punishments that accompany acceptable and unacceptable behavior.
   (C) The teacher explains the real world positive and negative outcomes of behavior.
   (D) Students help develop and then accept the consequences of any rule breaking.

118. Eriksen's stages of psychosocial development describe
   (A) the emotional crises that, when resolved, lead to further development.
   (B) Freud's stages of development in more detail.
   (C) stages of cognitive development for males and for females.
   (D) the psychological awareness and social skill needed for successful development.

119. Piaget wrote that children learn through a process of equilibration. Which of the following classroom practices is most likely to promote this process in children?
   (A) Teachers actively teach skills while using manipulative techniques.
   (B) Children actively learn concepts through their own experiences.
   (C) Children learn by modeling others.
   (D) Children learn concepts vicariously.

120. A child thinks that, when one of two matched rows of buttons is spread out, the number of buttons has changed. According to Piaget, that child
   (A) is in the sensorimotor stage.
   (B) has not experienced equilibration.
   (C) does not comprehend seriation.
   (D) does not conserve number.

CONTENT AREA EXERCISES I

Take these content area exercises in a realistic, timed setting. You should not work on this part of the test until you have completed the other tests in the book.

The setting will be most realistic if another person times you and ensures that the test rules are followed exactly. If someone else is acting as test supervisor, that person should review these instructions with you and say "Start" when you should begin a section and "Stop" when time has expired.

You have two hours to complete these 12 short-answer questions in the areas of Literature and Language Studies (3), Mathematics (3), Visual and Performing Arts (2), Human Development (2), and Physical Education (2). You may use a nonprogrammable calculator.

Keep the time limit in mind as you work. You may answer the easier questions first, but be sure to answer all the questions. Write your answers in the space provided.

When you are finished, show your responses to a professor, teacher, or some other person who is able to evaluate them.

When instructed, turn the page and begin.

LITERATURE AND LANGUAGE STUDIES

1. There was a time in the United States when a married woman was expected to take her husband's last name. Most women still follow this practice, but things are changing. In fact, Hawaii has been the only state with a law requiring a woman to take her husband's last name when she marries.

   Many women look forward to taking their husband's surname. They may enjoy the bond it establishes with their husband, or want to be identified with their husband's professional status. Other women want to keep their own last name. They may prefer their original last name, or want to maintain their professional identity.

   Some women resolve this problem by choosing a last name that hyphenates their surname and their husband's surname. This practice of adopting elements of both surnames is common in other cultures. As the modern American woman increases her social standing, she will no longer need the pseudo support of her husband's surname. The future generations of women will offer their surnames to their new husbands at the nuptial table.

Discuss the bias in the passage above and the kind of language the author uses to express the bias.

2. Discuss the meaning and importance of morphology in language.

3. How are reliability and validity important when interpreting written reports of research?

MATHEMATICS

4. If you have a set with two elements A and B, you can make 4 subsets A, B, A&B and the null set (the set with nothing in it). Show how many subsets you would have for 3, 4 elements.

5. About how tall is the above tree?

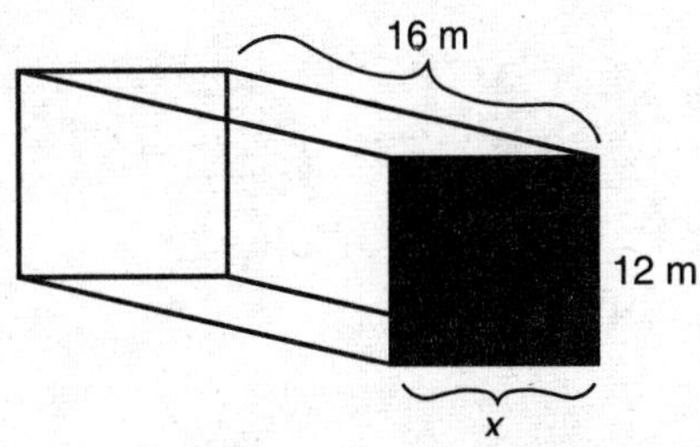

6. The rectangular solid shown here has a volume of 1920 m^3. What is the area of the shaded side?

VISUAL AND PERFORMING ARTS

7. Describe two different ways an artist can create perspective in a painting.

8. Describe one fundamental difference between popular, classical, and folk music.

HUMAN DEVELOPMENT

9. Describe one aspect of social learning theory as proposed by Albert Bandura.

10. Give an example of authentic assessment in an elementary school setting.

PHYSICAL EDUCATION

11. Discuss the difference between nonlocomotor and manipulative skills.

12. Describe two beneficial outcomes of fitness education.

CONTENT AREA EXERCISES II

Take these content area exercises in a realistic, timed setting. You should not work on this part of the test until you have completed the other tests in the book.

The setting will be most realistic if another person times you and ensures that the test rules are followed exactly. If someone else is acting as supervisor, that person should review these instructions with you and say "Start" when you should begin a section and "Stop" when time has expired.

You have one hour to complete these six short-answer questions in the areas of History and Social Studies (3) and Science (3). You may use a nonprogrammable calculator.

Keep the time limit in mind as you work. You may answer the easier questions first, but be sure you answer all the questions. Write your answers in the space provided.

When you are finished, show your responses to a professor, teacher, or some other person who is able to evaluate them.

When instructed, turn the page and begin.

HISTORY/SOCIAL STUDIES

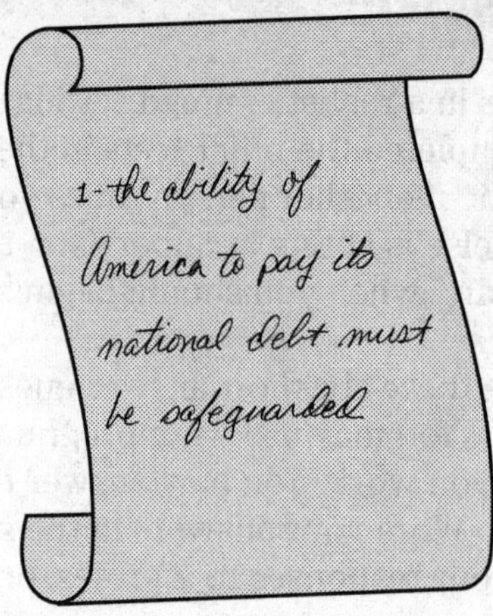

1. Briefly describe what Washington meant by this statement and describe two means for attaining his goal.

2. Discuss the differences between the British and the American forms of national government.

3. Discuss the interaction among the federal government, the management of large companies, and the labor unions during the industrialization of America.

SCIENCE

4. Sophisticated technological processes permit a very precise DNA typing for organic material, including blood. Describe two uses of this process.

5. Describe what a scientist means when he or she says that the earth has a secondary atmosphere.

6. The universe we live in is a vast and mysterious place. We have developed telescopes that can detect a large number of galaxies. But this is not very helpful. How can we decipher anything about our world through looking at stars so very far away? Can we tell anything even from the stars we can see in our own galaxy, the Milky Way? I would say that these distant galaxies and solar systems can give us few clues to our own planet.

How would you respond to this comment? Discuss what is uninformed or incorrect, using appropriate examples.

ANSWER KEY

CONTENT KNOWLEDGE

Literature and Language Studies

1. **C**	4. **C**	7. **D**	10. **D**	13. **C**	16. **C**	19. **A**	22. **D**
2. **D**	5. **A**	8. **C**	11. **C**	14. **A**	17. **C**	20. **A**	23. **C**
3. **A**	6. **A**	9. **A**	12. **C**	15. **D**	18. **A**	21. **D**	24. **A**

Mathematics

25. **C**	28. **B**	31. **C**	34. **D**	37. **C**	40. **D**	43. **C**	46. **B**
26. **D**	29. **B**	32. **C**	35. **A**	38. **B**	41. **B**	44. **D**	47. **B**
27. **D**	30. **C**	33. **D**	36. **B**	39. **C**	42. **B**	45. **C**	48. **B**

History/Social Studies

49. **B**	52. **A**	55. **C**	58. **D**	61. **A**	64. **C**	67. **D**	70. **B**
50. **A**	53. **C**	56. **D**	59. **C**	62. **B**	65. **B**	68. **C**	
51. **B**	54. **B**	57. **B**	60. **B**	63. **B**	66. **B**	69. **C**	

Science

71. **B**	74. **C**	77. **B**	80. **B**	83. **D**	86. **B**	89. **A**	92. **D**
72. **B**	75. **A**	78. **A**	81. **D**	84. **D**	87. **D**	90. **C**	
73. **C**	76. **D**	79. **B**	82. **B**	85. **B**	88. **B**	91. **A**	

Visual and Performing Arts

93. **A**	95. **B**	97. **D**	99. **A**	101. **A**	103. **D**
94. **D**	96. **B**	98. **C**	100. **C**	102. **B**	104. **C**

Physical Education

105. **B** 106. **B** 107. **A** 108. **C** 109. **C** 110. **B** 111. **C** 112. **B**

Human Development

113. **B** 114. **B** 115. **C** 116. **C** 117. **D** 118. **A** 119. **B** 120. **D**

EXPLAINED ANSWERS

CONTENT KNOWLEDGE

Language and Literature Studies

1. **C** The word *nigh* means near in space or time.
2. **D** The passage tells us that love falls on silence and that love unknown is sad, leading to the conclusion that the passage is about loving without acknowledgment.
3. **A** I is the subject; am is the verb. Alone is not a verb, and knowing is a part of the prepositional phrase.
4. **C** The first books written for children appeared during this time. Books such as *Robinson Crusoe* and *Gulliver's Travels* were adult books that appealed to some children.
5. **A** Alliteration refers to the repetition of an initial consonant in nearby words.
6. **A** *The Odyssey* is an epic, a very long narrative with great scope.
7. **D** The author is narrating, or telling a story, about a part of his life.
8. **C** Sentence 4 is the opening sentence followed in order by sentences, 3, 1, and 2. Some other arrangements not listed could also be logical.
9. **A** Excite is among the most popular search utilities on line. It is used to search for information on the World Wide Web.
10. **D** The word *when* is used to subordinate sentence elements. All of the other choices are used to coordinate sentence elements.
11. **C** Haiku follows a 5-7-5 syllabic scheme with no rhyming. Choice C alone meets these criteria.
12. **C** The word *paring* means to cut off. Do not confuse this word with its homonym *pairing*.
13. **C** A cinquain is a five-line poem with no particular rhyming scheme. The cinquain originated in France.
14. **A** The word *fraction* developed from the root *frac*, which means breaking something into pieces.
15. **D** Sentence 4 only makes sense after reading sentence 3. Sentence 1 only makes sense after reading sentence 2. Choice D, alone, shows this arrangement.
16. **C** This sentence correctly uses the possessive form of *its*. The other underlined words are homonyms (words that sound the same but are spelled differently) of the correct word.
17. **C** This is the correct syllabication for *simultaneous*.
18. **A** The "backward writing" concretely reflects the backward world that this answer choice refers to.
19. **A** This hostess is using the converse. Her premise is this: participation in our program means beautiful skin. Her conclusion is beautiful skin means participating in our program. She is arguing backwards, which is a fallacious form of argument.
20. **A** Each of the steps must be followed in chronological order. Time order is the only logical answer.
21. **D** The author is concerned that American children will have limited opportunities.
22. **D** The character visited the school and is certainly curious. The character's response to the custodian shows respect.
23. **C** Homer is a Greek poet from the 9th century B.C. Historians believe that he wrote *The Odyssey* and *The Iliad*.
24. **A** A simile compares to different things, usually using the words *like* or *as*. A metaphor does not use the words *like* or *as*.

Mathematics

25. **C** There are 24 holes all together and 8 of them are labeled "1." So the probability of landing on a "1" is 8/24 or 1/3.
26. **D** Use your calculator to find the distances. The totals for each answer choice are A: 25, B: 26, C: 27, D: 24. D is the shortest.
27. **D** Use F, S, and T for the first, second, and third person. The third person is taller than the first person, so put T first. The first person's height is less than or equal the second persons height so use the symbol $\leq$. Then, $T > F \leq S$.

28. **B** The ratio 9 to 24 is equivalent to the ratio 3 : 8, but the ratio 24 to 9 reverses the order of the terms. All of the other ratios are correct ways to write a ratio equivalent to 3 : 8.
29. **B** The number sentence corresponds to finding an average. To find an average, you add the terms and divide by the number of terms.
30. **C** Jan is either the same height as Lisa or she is taller than Lisa. Because Lisa is not the shortest player, Jan cannot be the shortest player.
31. **C** You can cross multiply to find that $5/6 > 3/4$, but that $5/6 < 7/8$. You can also use a calculator to find that $5/6 = 0.833$, and see that this decimal comes between $3/4 = 0.75$ and $7/8 = 0.875$
32. **C** The three angles that meet at point D form a straight line, and so the sum of the measures of these angles must be 180°. The angle in the rectangle is 90°. The angle between the rectangle and the triangle is 55°, so the angle in the triangle must be 35°. The sum of the angles in any triangle is 180°. The sum of the two known angles is 135°, so the measure of ∠E must be 45°.
33. **D** Only points in this quadrant of the graph have a positive x value and a negative y value.
34. **D** Think of an example. 5 is greater than 4 and less than 9.
    A. 5 + 4 = 9
    B. 9 – 4 = 5
    C. 9 – 5 = 4
    D. 5 – 4 = 9
    D is the only choice that could not be true.
35. **A** Use your calculator to find this answer. Divide to find what percent $624,000 is of $2,600,000. 624,000 ÷ 2,600,000 = 0.24 = 24% The town needs 24% for police, 2% more than in the pie chart. Take the 2% from sanitation leaving 22% for sanitation.
36. **B** The graphs for walkers and bikers remained unchanged from Monday to Tuesday, so this statement is true for both Monday's graph and Tuesday's graph. Choice (A) is true only for Monday's graph. The other statements are false.
37. **C** This is another calculator problem. Think of the percent equation.
    85% × □ = 289
    So, □ = 289 ÷ 0.85
    Divide 289 by 0.85 to find how many houses there were altogether.
    289 ÷ 0.85 = 340
38. **B** The probability that a "fair" penny will land heads up is always 1/2 regardless of what has occurred on previous flips.
39. **C** You have to move the decimal point eight places to the right to get from 3.74 to 374,000,000. To do this multiply by 10^8.
40. **D** The associative property asserts that the sum or product of three numbers is the same no matter how you group them.
    $(a + b) + c = a + (b + c)$
    $(a \times b) \times c = a \times (b \times c)$
41. **B** The formula for the area of a circle is πr^2.
    Area of the smaller circle = $\pi 5^2 = 25\pi$
    Area of the larger circle = $\pi 10^2 = 100\pi$
    $100\pi - 25\pi = 75\pi$
42. **B** There are 3 feet in a yard, so 58 is $19\frac{1}{3}y$, which can also be written $19y + \frac{1}{3}y$
43. **C** You can draw three triangles inside the pentagon from the vertices of the pentagon. The total angle measures of each triangle is 180°, so the total angle measure of the pentagon must be 3 × 180° = 540°. By the way, the answer would be the same even if the pentagon was not a regular figure.
44. **D** There are 60 seconds in a minute and 60 minutes in an hour. So there are 60 × 60 = 3600 seconds in an hour. 186,000 × 3600 is about how far light travels in an hour.
45. **C** This is the correct list of numbers between 1 and 25 that are evenly divisible only by 1 and by themselves. The number 2 is the only even prime.
46. **B** This expression correctly shows the relationship.

Boat	costs	$5	more than	half the price	of	a canoe
B	=	$5	+	½	×	C

or B = ½C + $5

47. **B** This length comes out to a little over 12 feet. This is the only measurement that could be the length of a couch. Choices (A) and (C) are too short and choice (D) is too long.
48. **B** Multiply x by 2 and then add 1. Some of the other choices work for individual values of x, but only this choice works for all the values of x.

History/Social Studies

49. **B** *The Jungle* is famous for exposing abuses in the meat-packing industry.
50. **A** This was Marie Antoinette's response upon hearing that there was not enough bread for the people of Paris.
51. **B** Those of the Islamic faith consider the Koran to be the direct word of God.
52. **A** The great schism of the Catholic church refers to the division of the church into eastern and western churches. This schism was the direct result of the establishment of an eastern capital of the Roman Empire.
53. **C** The map clearly shows that Fremont won in the northernmost states.
(A) is false because the electoral votes from Texas and California would not have been enough to elect Fremont.
(B) is false because Buchanan won elections in many states that did not join the Confederacy.
(D) is false because Fremont did not win elections in many states that joined the Union.
54. **B** It was during the Crimean War, which pitted Great Britain, France, and Turkey as allies against Russia, that Florence Nightingale became famous.
55. **C** On average, Asheville has 235 days without precipitation. Note that the graph does not show days that are cloudy but have no precipitation.
56. **D** The manifest destiny of the United States referred to a country that spread from the Atlantic Ocean to Pacific Ocean. Most eastern lands were under American control, so lands west of the Mississippi had to be acquired for this country to realize its manifest destiny.
57. **B** As a result of the Treaty of Utrecht the Spanish Empire was partitioned.
58. **D** In presidential elections, each state has a certain number of electoral votes based on that state's population. The candidate who wins the popular vote for each state gets those electors. So it is possible for a candidate to win the national popular vote and not win the election.
59. **C** This section of the Southwest, which includes Death Valley, is a desert region. The highest temperatures are recorded here.
60. **B** Sherman's March to the Sea occurred during the Civil War followed by the Gettysburg Address. Reconstruction and then the XIII Amendment followed the war.
61. **A** Companies only pay higher rates to attract investors. The main reason one company pays a higher rate than another company is that their bonds are riskier.
62. **B** Julius Caesar supposedly spoke the words "and you, Brutus" to his "friend" Brutus who had joined others in assassinating Julius Caesar during the Ides (middle days) of March.
63. **B** The quote supports the nonviolent, nondestructive approach to protest supported by Gandhi.
64. **C** The liberty bells in some countries are freeing them from Soviet dominance.
65. **B** The charts show that stock prices and interest rates go in the opposite direction. (A) is false because the charts do not show a cause and effect relationship. (C) is false because the charts do show some relationship between commodity prices and stock prices, but not the direct relationship mentioned in (D).
66. **B** The Inca Indians originally inhabited this region of South America.
67. **D** The Amendment was passed by Congress and ratified by the states because the United States Supreme Court ruled that the income tax was unconstitutional.
68. **C** Physical anthropologists study the evolution of human beings. Louis and Mary Leakey are probably the most famous physical anthropologists.
69. **C** In a representative democracy people elect others to represent them. States' rights and checks and balances are a part of the unique system in the United States.
70. **B** The Spanish American War was fought in Cuba and the Philippines.

Science

71. **B** The earliest cells on earth were most likely bacteria (prokaryotes). Algae and protozoa developed later. DNA developed before these other organisms, but DNA is not a cell.
72. **B** Sound travels through stone a little less than 20 times faster than it travels through air and about 4 times faster than it travels through water. Sound does not travel through a vacuum.

73. **C** Earth's land started out as a single continent and then separated until the Atlantic Ocean was formed. It then separated more until the land bridge disappeared, and much later North America was covered by glaciers.
74. **C** The ball at the top of the ramp has the most potential to create energy.
75. **A** This is the correct sequence.
76. **D** Ecology is about the relationship of organisms and their habitat.
77. **B** Current sedimentary rocks are most likely to contain the remains of animals from millions of years ago. It is most likely that current animal remains would also be found in sedimentary rocks millions of years from now.
78. **A** The effects of a recessive gene may not appear in a parent, but may appear in their offspring if parents share the recessive gene.
79. **B** Even the vastness of the rainforest cannot directly influence climatic shifts.
80. **B** In a solar eclipse, the moon blocks the sun's light from reaching earth. The moon must be between the sun and the earth for a solar eclipse to occur.
81. **D** In the Northern Hemisphere, winds circulate counterclockwise around a low. If you were facing north a low pressure system to your right would blow winds in from the front of your right side. The wind directions for other choices are shown below.
(B) low pressure left - winds back left
(C) high pressure right - winds back right
(D) high pressure left - winds front left
82. **B** Zygote formation is a fundamental step in meiosis.
83. **D** The nearest star to earth, other than our sun, Alpha Centuri, is about 4.2 light years away, or about 50 billion miles away. The light from this star reaches earth in a little over four years.
84. **D** More mass means that there is more of the object, that it takes up more space. A heavier object would not necessarily take up more space.
85. **B** Rubbing the rod with silk removes electrons (negative charges) and creates a positively charged rod. The rod is not charged with static electricity as stated in choice (A).
86. **B** Something is NOT biodegradable if it cannot be broken down by living things. The presence of DDT in carcasses shows that even living animals were not able to biodegrade DDT.
87. **D** A new layer of water is added below the freezing level in the atmosphere and then that layer of water is frozen when the hail stone is blown above the freezing level.
88. **B** The sun is directly over the Southern Hemisphere at the beginning of summer. This position is best shown in choice B.
89. **A** Dark colored material absorbs more sunlight and more heat than lighter colored material. Lighter colored material reflects more sunlight than darker colored material.
90. **C** Conduction means heat transfer by physical contact.
91. **A** This conclusion is clear and is the only one supported by the data.
92. **D** The experiment does not describe how the experimenters ensured that group HF2 did not receive any special attention, nor does it describe any other controls.

Visual and Performing Arts

93. **A** These notes show the distinctive beginning of "My Country Tis of Thee."
94. **D** The sonata is instrumental chamber music. Sonatas do not feature the singing or story line found in operas.
95. **B** Ravel is most closely associated with his work *Bolero*. This work, composed in the early 1900s, remains popular today.
96. **B** The secondary colors (orange, green, and violet) are made by mixing two primary colors.
97. **D** Warhol was the most famous pop artist. He often painted repetitious forms of common commercial objects.
98. **C** In linear perspective, more distant objects appear smaller. The camera represents distance in precisely this way.
99. **A** *The Glass Menagerie* by Tennessee Williams is about his mentally ill sister. The correct associations for the others are
(B) *Arsenic and Old Lace:* poisoning
(C) *All My Sons:* irresponsibility
(D) *Children's Hour:* a destructive child
100. **C** *The Shadowy Waters* was written by William Butler Yeats. (This is a very difficult item, but you'll run into some like this.)

101. **A** This famous line comes from *Hamlet.*

102. **B** Ballet is based on five formal positions of the feet.

103. **D** Tchaikovsky wrote the score for *Swan Lake.* None of the other composers wrote music for ballet.

104. **C** Kubuki is a popular folk dance in Japan; The flamenco is from Spain; the tarantella is from Italy; the waltz is from Austria and Germany.

Physical Education

105. **B** Primary students are not developed enough to use their heads to direct or propel the soccer ball.

106. **B** The spring up from a crouch position is the choice to overcome the body's tendency to stay at rest.

107. **A** Choice A best describes how young children fatigue and recover from fatigue.

108. **C** The skinfold measurements from a child's body give the best indication of how obese the child is.

109. **C** The ability to distinguish right from left is not related to a motor deficiency.

110. **B** The body's axis starts at the top middle of the head and goes straight down through the center of the body.

111. **C** The movement concept of force describes forces as a function of body movements.

112. **B** The inertia in a body is the same for all body positions.

Human Development

113. **B** Research indicates that grades are clearly the most powerful motivation for students to work in school.

114. **B** Modeling means the teacher acts as he or she wants the students to act. Students often emulate the behavior they see in the teacher.

115. **C** According to Kohlberg, students in late elementary school are most like the characteristics described in this choice.

116. **C** Research on identical twins separated at birth and studied later has shed some light on this controversy, but it has not cleared up the controversy.

117. **D** Glasser's approach features consequences for students for breaking rules that the students themselves helped formulate.

118. **A** Eriksen describes stages as emotional crises that can have a positive or negative result.

119. **B** The dynamic process of equilibration is best supported when children learn through their own experiences.

120. **D** If a child can conserve number he or she understands that the number of elements in one of the rows is unchanged when one of the rows is lengthened.

CONTENT AREA EXERCISES I AND II

Show your short-answer question responses to an appropriate teacher or college professor. Ask the reader to evaluate your responses using the following scoring standards.

3 This response shows that the writer clearly understood the question and responded effectively to all parts of the question or assignment. All explanations are clear, show an understanding of the subject matter, and are supported by appropriate details and facts.

2 This response shows that the writer understood most of the question and responded effectively to most parts of the question or assignment. Explanations show an adequate knowledge of the subject matter and are usually supported by appropriate details and facts.

1 This response shows that the writer did not understand much of the question and did not respond effectively to most parts of the question or assignment. Explanations are usually unclear and are usually not well supported.

0 The response was completely wrong, just restates the question, or was completely off the topic.

MSAT PRACTICE TEST II SCORING

CONTENT KNOWLEDGE

		Number Correct
Literature and Language Studies	24 questions	_______
Mathematics	24 questions	_______
History/Social Studies	22 questions	_______
Science	22 questions	_______
Visual and Performing Arts	12 questions	_______
Physical Education	8 questions	_______
Human Development	8 questions	_______
	RAW SCORE	_______

CONTENT AREA EXERCISES I

Question	Points
1	_______
2	_______
3	_______
4	_______
5	_______
6	_______
7	_______
8	_______
9	_______
10	_______
11	_______
12	_______
TOTAL	_______

CONTENT AREA EXERCISES II

Question	Points
1	_______
2	_______
3	_______
4	_______
5	_______
6	_______
TOTAL	_______

FINAL SCORING

CONTENT KNOWLEDGE RAW SCORE [ ]

CONTENT AREA EXERCISES RAW SCORE [ ]

Compare your scores to the passing scores that follow.

CALIFORNIA PASSING AND MINIMUM SCALE SCORES

Overall Passing Score	311
Content Knowledge Minimum Score	148
Content Area Exercises Minimum Score	147

As long as you get the minimum scale score on each test, there are a large number of passing score combinations. You can make up for a lower score on one test with a higher score on the other test.

ESTIMATED RAW SCORES NEEDED FOR CALIFORNIA MINIMUM SCORES

Content Knowledge	72–74 correct out of 120 items
Content Area Exercises	26–27 points out of a possible 54 points

CALIFORNIA ESTIMATED PASSING RAW SCORE COMBINATIONS

Combination	**Content Knowledge**	**Content Area Exercises**
Passing Combination with the Content Knowledge Minimum Score	72–74 correct (60%–62%)	33–34 points (60%–63%)
Passing Combination with the Content Area Exercises Minimum Score	88–90 correct (73%–75%)	26–27 points (48%–50%)
Passing Combination with Half the Scale Points from each Test	80–82 correct (67%–68%)	30–31 points (56%–58%)

OREGON PASSING SCALE SCORE AND ESTIMATED RAW SCORE NEEDED TO PASS

	Passing Scale Score	**Estimated Passing Raw Scores**
Content Knowledge	147	71–73 correct of 120 items
Content Area Exercises	Submit any score	

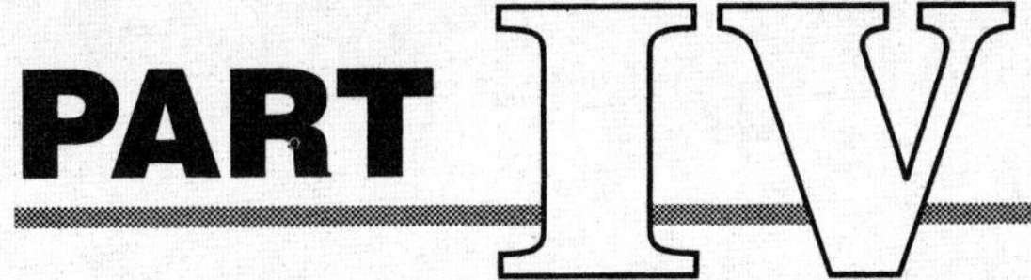

PART IV

Beginning a Career in Teaching

12 GETTING CERTIFIED IN CALIFORNIA AND OREGON

TEST INFO BOX

This chapter shows you how to get certified in California and Oregon.

It explains the certification requirements and the steps to follow for certification in each state.

The section also includes the colleges in California and Oregon with approved teacher-certification programs.

You may be able to teach for a year while you complete the MSAT.

INTRODUCTION

The certification section for each state begins with the address and phone number for the teacher certification office, followed by the required certification tests. Next comes the certification requirements and the steps to follow for certification. Finally, each section lists the address and phone number of each college in the state offering teacher certification programs.

Teacher certification requirements and procedures change frequently. Check with the state certification office for up-to-date information.

CALIFORNIA

California Commission on Teacher Credentialing
1812 Ninth Street
Sacramento, CA 94244-7000
(916) 445-7254

CERTIFICATION TESTS

CORE BATTERY
- ☐ General Knowledge
- ☐ Communication Skills
- ☐ Professional Knowledge

MSAT
- ■ Content Knowledge
- ■ Content Essays

PRAXIS I: ACADEMIC SKILLS
- ☐ PPST—Mathematics
- ☐ PPST—Reading
- ☐ PPST—Writing
- ☐ CBT—Mathematics
- ☐ CBT—Reading
- ☐ CBT—Writing

■ STATE TEST
Refer to Barron's *How to Prepare for the CBEST*

☐ NO REQUIRED TEST

Refer to Barron's *How to Prepare for Praxis* for other Praxis tests.

PRAXIS II: SUBJECT ASSESSMENTS AND NTE SPECIALTY AREA TESTS

Art & Music
- ☐ 10130 Art Education (NTE)
- ■ 20131 Art Making
- ■ 20132 Content, Trad., Aesthet. Crit.

- ☐ 10110 Music Education (NTE)
- ■ 20112 Music: Analysis
- ■ 30111 Music: Concepts & Processes

Elementary Education
- ☐ 20010 Ed. in the Elem. School (NTE)
- ☐ 20011 Elem. Ed. Curric., Inst. & Asses.
- ☐ 20012 Elem. Ed. Content Area Exer.

English
- ☐ 10040 English Language & Lit. (NTE)
- ☐ 10041 Lang., Lit., & Comp.: Cont.
- ■ 20042 Lang., Lit. & Comp.: Essays
- ☐ 30043 Eng. Lang., Lit., & Comp.: Ped.

Foreign Language
- ☐ 10170 French (NTE)
- ■ 20171 French: Productive Lang. Skills
- ■ 30172 French: Ling., Lit., & Cult. Anal.

- ☐ 10190 Spanish (NTE)
- ☐ 10191 Spanish: Content Knowledge
- ■ 20192 Spanish: Productive Lang. Skills
- ■ 30193 Spanish: Ling., Lit. & Cult. Anal.
- ☐ 30194 Spanish: Pedagogy

Mathematics
- ☐ 10060 Mathematics (NTE)
- ☐ 10061 Mathematics: Content Knowledge
- ■ 20063 Math.: Proof, Model & Prob.—1
- ■ 30064 Math.: Proof, Model & Prob.—2
- ☐ 20065 Mathematics: Pedagogy

Physical Education
- ☐ 10090 Phys. Ed. (NTE)
- ☐ 10091 Phys. Ed. Content Knowledge
- ■ 30092 Phys. Ed. Move. Form Anal. & Des.
- ■ 20093 Phys. Ed. Move. Form Vid. Eval.
- ☐ 30094 Phys. Ed. Pedagogy

Science
- ☐ 10030 Biology & Gen. Science (NTE)
- ☐ 10230 Biology (NTE)
- ☐ 20232 Biology: Content Knowledge II
- ■ 30233 Biology: Content Essays
- ☐ 30234 Biology: Pedagogy

- ☐ 10240 Chemistry (NTE)
- ☐ 20241 Chemistry: Content Knowledge
- ■ 30242 Chemistry: Content Essays

- ☐ 10430 General Science (NTE)
- ☐ 10431 General Science: Cont. Know.—1
- ☐ 10432 General Science: Cont. Know.—2

Science (Cont.)

- ■ 30433 General Science: Cont. Essays
- □ 20481 Physical Science: Content Know.
- ■ 20482 Physical Science: Content Essays
- □ 30483 Physical Science: Pedagogy

Science (Cont.)

- □ 10260 Physics (NTE)
- □ 10261 Physics: Content Knowledge
- ■ 30262 Physics: Content Essays

Social Studies

- □ 10080 Social Studies (NTE)
- □ 10081 Social Studies: Content Know.

Social Studies (Cont.)

- □ 20082 Social Studies: Analytical Essays
- □ 20083 Social Studies: Interpret. of Mat.
- □ 30084 Social Studies: Pedagogy

Special Education

- □ 10350 Special Education (NTE)

CALIFORNIA REQUIREMENTS AND PROCEDURES

MULTIPLE SUBJECT TEACHING CREDENTIAL

A Multiple Subject Teaching Credential authorizes the holder to teach in a self-contained classroom such as the classrooms in most elementary schools. **Candidates for the Multiple Subject Credential who complete their teacher preparation through a Commission-approved program in California must be recommended for the credential through their college or university credentials office.** Elementary school teachers who completed their professional preparation **outside of California** may apply directly to the Commission for their initial credentials. The credentialing process in California is made up of a sequence of requirements that may take as long as six years to complete. The teacher receiving his or her preliminary credential is making a commitment to complete the process and obtain the professional clear credential. The sequence of requirements is diagrammed below, then each requirement is explained in detail. Please contact the Commission, your employer, or a Commission-approved college or university for application materials.

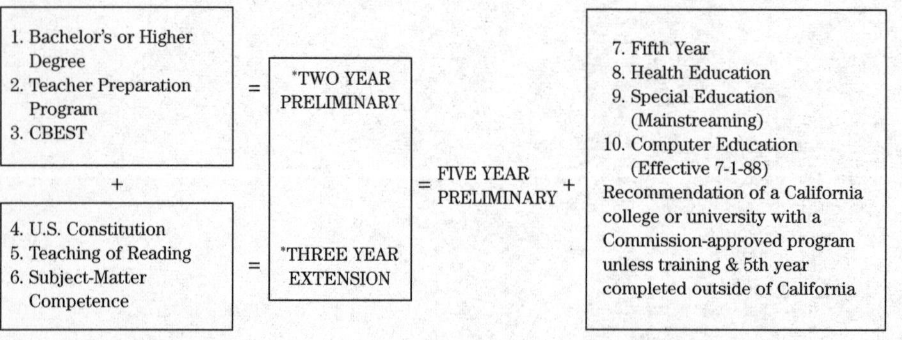

* Only available to candidates who have completed a full teacher preparation program outside of California.

Diagram of Credential Requirements

REQUIREMENTS FOR THE PRELIMINARY CREDENTIAL

1. **Education:** Completion of a baccalaureate or higher degree, except in professional education, from a regionally accredited college or university. A degree in education may be acceptable if (1) the degree was completed *outside* of California, **OR** (2) the applicant verifies the completion of two years of successful teaching on the basis of a standard credential in the state in which the service was rendered, **OR** (3) the degree in education contains no less subject-matter course work than would be required for a subject other than education.

2. **Professional Teacher Preparation:** Completion of a multiple subject professional teacher preparation program, including student teaching with a minimum grade of C on a five-point scale, taken at a regionally accredited institution approved by the Commission or by the state certification agency of the state in which the program was completed. If no professional preparation program was completed or if the grade in student teaching was less than a C, the applicant may qualify for the credential if he or she can verify the completion of three years of successful full-time multiple subject (self-contained classroom) teaching within the

last ten years. *This experience must have been completed while the applicant held or was eligible for a full professional certificate based on a baccalaureate or higher degree from the state in which the experience was obtained.* If the grade in student teaching was a pass or credit, the applicant is assumed to have completed student teaching at the C grade level or better. Applicants who meet the requirements of the *Interstate Agreement* (see below) are considered to have successfully completed the teacher preparation program requirement.

3. **CBEST:** Passage of the California Basic Educational Skills Test (CBEST). To pass CBEST one must obtain a minimum scaled score of 41 in each of the three sections (reading, mathematics, and writing). However, a section score as low as 37 is acceptable if the total scaled score is at least 123. Out-of-state applicants who have not yet passed the CBEST may wish to contact their California employers about the possibility of getting a One-Year Non-Renewable (OYNR) Credential pending the passage of CBEST. See the CBEST leaflet (*CL-667*) for more details.

4. **Provisions and Principles of the U.S. Constitution:** Completion of a course (two semester units or three quarter units) in the provisions and principles of the United States Constitution **OR** passage of an examination in the subject given by a regionally accredited junior college, college, or university, **OR** verification of meeting the Interstate Agreement requirements described below.

5. **Methods of Teaching Reading:** Completion of a course in the methods of teaching reading **OR** passage (with a minimum score of 680) of the Praxis Series Subject Assessment entitled "Introduction to Teaching of Reading."

6. **Subject-Matter Competence:** Verification of subject-matter competency by one of two methods: (1) completing a Commission-approved liberal arts subject-matter program or its equivalent and obtaining a subject-matter statement from the authorized person in the education department of a California college or university with an approved program (California colleges and universities may have recency requirements that have to be met before a subject-matter statement can be granted), **OR** (2) achieving a passing score on the appropriate subject-matter examination. Information about the appropriate subject-matter examination, including passing scores and registration, are on the Verifying Subject Matter Competence leaflet, which may be obtained from the Commission.

REQUIREMENTS FOR THE PROFESSIONAL CLEAR

Formal Recommendation from a California College or University: In order to obtain the professional clear credential, the applicant must secure the recommendation of a California teacher preparation institution with a Commission-approved program. The preliminary credential is issued for a maximum of five years. If requirements for the professional clear credential are not completed before the expiration date of the preliminary, the holder will be unable to teach in the public schools of California on that credential. When the requirements are complete, if the responsible authorities at the institution are unable or refuse to recommend the applicant, he or she is entitled to have the specific reasons for such refusal given in writing. He or she may then use that information in support of an application for a direct appeal to the Commission. Applicants prepared outside of California who have already completed their fifth year of study will be given a complete evaluation by the Commission so they may apply directly to the Commission for the professional clear credential without going through the institution for a formal recommendation.

7. **Fifth Year of Study:** Completion of a fifth year of study after the bachelor's degree. A fifth year of study consists of 30 semester units in a defined field of study designed to improve the teacher's competence and skills. Those applicants who have not completed a fifth year must do so within five years of the receipt of the preliminary credential. This fifth year course of study should be approved by a California teacher preparation institution and may be used for one or more of the following purposes:

   (a) additional subject-matter preparation including, but not limited to, pursuit of a master's or higher degree,
   (b) completion of an approved program for an advanced or specialized credential,
   (c) in-service training for which college or university credit is given, or
   (d) study undertaken to complete an approved program of professional preparation.

8. **Health Education:** Completion of a unit requirement in health education, including, but not limited to, nutrition, the physiological and sociological effects of abuse of alcohol, narcotics, and drugs, and the use of tobacco. This requirement must include verification of training in cardiopulmonary resuscitation (CPR), which covers *infant* and *child* to *adult* CPR skills, plus rescue breathing and choke rescue, education risk factors, sudden cardiac arrest, and may include causes of respiratory arrest, healthy heart concept, and emphasis on recognizing the symptoms of heart attack and taking action before CPR becomes necessary. CPR certification must be completed while in a teacher preparation program or while teaching on a valid credential based on a teacher education program.

9. **Special Education:** Completion of a requirement in the needs of, and methods of providing educational opportunities to, individuals with exceptional needs (mainstreaming).

10. **Computer Education:** Satisfactory completion of computer education course work that includes general and specialized skills in the use of computers in educational settings.

COURSE WORK SUBMITTED FOR A CREDENTIAL

An applicant must have an overall grade point average of C or better on a five-point scale, or the approved institution's required GPA, whichever is higher, in all course work offered toward fulfillment of credential requirements. Continuing education units (CEU's) are not acceptable to fulfill credential requirements. If it is not clear from the entry on college transcripts that a particular course fulfills one of the specific credential requirements, a course description or a letter from the appropriate department chairperson verifying the content of the course work should be enclosed with the credential application.

INTERSTATE AGREEMENT

Applicants who meet the Interstate Agreement are considered to have successfully completed their professional teacher prepartion program requirement (#2 above) and the U.S. Constitution requirement (#4 above). The Interstate Agreement does not clear any of the other requirements. The Interstate Agreement applies to applicants for the Multiple Subject Teaching Credential who hold or are eligible for a comparable credential (for teaching in an elementary or self-contained, not special education, classroom) from outside of California and who:

1. have completed a state-approved baccalaureate or post-baccalaureate level elementary teacher preparation program *since September 30, 1986* at a regionally accredited institution in a state with which California has an agreement, OR

2. hold a regular or advanced certificate for elementary or self-contained classroom teaching issued by a state with which California has an agreement AND have taught in an elementary classroom in that state 27 months within the past seven years. At least 18 months of this experience must be under the certificate. If no state certificate was required for the experience, the applicant must have taught the subjects to which the certificate applies in a school where student attendance satisfies the state compulsory attendance law.

STATES HAVING INTERSTATE AGREEMENTS WITH CALIFORNIA AS OF JANUARY 1, 1995:

Alabama
Arkansas
Colorado
Connecticut
Delaware
District of Columbia
Florida
Georgia
Hawaii
Idaho
Illinois
Indiana
Kentucky
Maine
Maryland
Massachusetts
Michigan
Montana
Nevada
New Hampshire
New Jersey
New York
North Carolina
Ohio
Oregon
Pennsylvania
Rhode Island
South Carolina
Tennessee
Texas
Utah
Vermont
Virginia
Washington
West Virginia

AUTHORIZATION FOR SERVICE

A teacher authorized for multiple subject instruction may be assigned to teach in any self-contained classroom (preschool, kindergarten, and grades 1 through 12 inclusive, or in classes organized primarily for adults); or to teach any subject in departmentalized classes to a given class or group of students in grade 8 and below, provided that the teacher has completed at least 12 semester units or six upper division or graduate units or course work at an accredited institution in each subject to be taught. Governing boards determine the authorization needed for a teaching assignment.

COLLEGES AND UNIVERSITIES IN CALIFORNIA WITH APPROVED TEACHER CERTIFICATION PROGRAMS

Institution	Address	Telephone
California State University		
California Polytechnic State University, San Luis Obispo	San Luis Obispo, CA 93407	(805) 756-2126
California State Polytechnic University, Pomona	3801 W Temple Ave Pomona, CA 91768	(909) 869-2303
California State University, Bakersfield	9001 Stockdale Hwy Bakersfield, CA 93309	(805) 664-3074
California State University, Chico	First & Normal Streets Chico, CA 95929-0222	(916) 898-6455
California State University, Dominguez Hills	1000 E. Victoria Street Carson, CA 90747	(310) 243-3521
California State University, Fresno	5241 N Maple Avenue Fresno, CA 93740	(209) 278-0300
California State University, Fullerton	800 N. State College Blvd. Fullerton, CA 92831	(714) 773-3205
California State University, Hayward	25800 Hillary Street Hayward, CA 94542	(510) 881-3031
California State University, Long Beach	1250 Bellflower Blvd Long Beach, CA 90840	(310) 985-5710
California State University, Los Angeles	5151 State University Drive Los Angeles, CA 90032	(213) 343-4340
California State University, Monterey Bay	100 Campus Center Seaside, CA 93955-8001	(408) 582-3638
California State University, Northridge	18111 Nordhoff St Northridge, CA 91330	(818) 677-2586
California State University, Sacramento	6000 J Street Sacramento, CA 95819-6079	(916) 278-4567
California State University, San Bernardino	5500 University Pkwy San Bernardino, CA 92407	(909) 880-5609
California State University, San Marcos	San Marcos, CA 92069	(619) 750-4279
California State University, Stanislaus	801 W Monte Vista Turlock, CA 95382	(209) 667-3534
Humboldt State University	Arcata, CA 95521	(707) 826-3752

San Diego State University, San Diego	5300 Campanile Drive San Diego, CA 92182-1100	(619) 594-5964
San Diego State University, Imperial Valley	720 Heber Ave Calexico, CA 92231	(619) 357-5511
San Francisco State University	1600 Holloway Ave San Francisco, CA 94132	(415) 338-1758
San Jose State University	1 Washington Square San Jose, CA 95192-0071	(408) 924-3608
Sonoma State University	1801 East Cotati Ave Rohnert Park, CA 94928	(707) 664-2593

University of California

University of California, Berkeley	1603 Tolman Hall Berkeley, CA 94720	(510) 642-0836
University of California, Davis	Davis, CA 95616	(916) 752-0758
University of California, Irvine	2001 Berkeley Place Irvine, CA 92697-5500	(714) 824-6673
University of California, Los Angeles	405 Hilgard Ave Los Angeles, CA 90024	(310) 825-8328
University of California, Riverside	Riverside, CA 92521-0128	(909) 787-5227
University of California, San Diego	9500 Gilman Drive LaJolla, CA 92093	(619) 534-2958
University of California, San Francisco	513 Parnassus Avenue San Francisco, CA 94143	(415) 476-4668
University of California, Santa Barbara	Santa Barbara, CA 93106	(805) 893-2036
University of California, Santa Cruz	1156 High Street Santa Cruz, CA 95064	(408) 459-3712

Independent Colleges and Universities

Azusa Pacific University	901 E Alosta Azusa, CA 91702	(818) 815-5366
Bethany College of the Assemblies of God	800 Bethany Dr Scotts Valley, CA 95066	(408) 438-3800 x 1503
Biola University	13800 Biola Ave LaMirada, CA 90639	(310) 903-6000 x 5679
California Baptist College	8432 Magnolia Ave Riverside, CA 92504	(909) 689-5771 x 313
California Lutheran University	60 Olsen Rd Thousand Oaks, CA 91360-2787	(805) 493-3425
Chapman University - Orange	333 N Glassell Street Orange, CA 92666	(714) 997- 6781

Christian Heritage College	2100 Greenfield Drive El Cajon, CA 92021	(619) 440-3043
Claremont Graduate School	160 E 10th Street Claremont, CA 91711	(909) 621-8076
College of Notre Dame	1500 Ralson Avenue Belmont, CA 94002	(415) 593-1601 x 304
Concordia University	1530 Concordia West Irvine, CA 92715	(714) 854-8002 x 353
Dominican College of San Rafael	50 Acacia Street San Rafael, CA 94901	(415) 457-4440 x 287
Dominican College of San Rafael, Ukiah Campus	Mendocino Office of Education 2240 Eastside Road Ukiah, CA 95482	(707) 463-4801
Fresno Pacific College	1717 S Chestnut Ave Fresno, CA 93702	(209) 453-2053
Holy Names College	3500 Mountain Blvd Oakland, CA 94619	(510) 436-1063
John F. Kennedy University	12 Altarinda Road Orinda, CA 94563	(510) 253-2232
La Sierra University	4700 Pierce Street Riverside, CA 92515-8247	(909) 785-2203
Loma Linda University	Loma Linda, CA 92350	(909) 824-4998
Loyola Marymount University	7900 Loyola Blvd Los Angeles, CA 90045	(310) 338-2863
Masters College, The	21726 W Placerita Canyon Road Santa Ana, CA 91321	(805) 259-3540 x 215
Mills College	5000 MacArthur Blvd Oakland, CA 94613	(510) 430-2118
Mount Saint Mary's College	10 Chester Place Los Angeles, CA 90007	(213) 746-0450 x 2224
National Hispanic University	14271 Story Road San Jose, CA 95127	(408) 254-6900 x 13
National University - Sacramento	9320 Tech Center Drive Sacramento, CA 95826	(916) 855-4304
National University - San Diego	11255 N Torrey Pines Road La Jolla, CA 92037	(619) 642-8648
National University - Vista	2022 University Dr Vista, CA 92083	(619) 945-6363
New College of California	777 Valencia Street San Francisco, CA 94110	(415) 437-3430
Occidental College	1600 Campus Road Los Angeles, CA 90041	(213) 259-2781

Pacific Christian College	2500 E Nutwood Ave Fullerton, CA 92361	(714) 879-3901
Pacific Oaks College	5 Westmoreland Place Pasadena, CA 91103	(818) 397-1331
Pacific Union College	One Angwin Ave Angwin, CA 94508	(707) 965-6643
Patten College	2433 Coolidge Oakland, CA 94601	(510) 533-8300 x 232
Pepperdine - Los Angeles	400 Corporate Pointe Culver City, CA 90230	(310) 568-5608
Pepperdine - Malibu	24255 Pacific Coast Hwy Malibu, CA 90265	(310) 456-4341
Point Loma Nazarene College	3900 Lomaland Drive San Diego, CA 92106-2899	(619) 221-2371
Point Loma Nazarene College - Pasadena	1530 E Elizabeth Pasadena, CA 91104	(818) 798-0541
Saint Mary's College	1928 St. Mary's Road Moraga, CA 94575	(510) 631-4727
Santa Clara University	Santa Clara, CA 95053	(408) 554-4434
Simpson College	2211 College View Drive Redding, CA 96003	(916) 224-5600
Southern California College	55 Fair Dr Costa Mesa, CA 92626	(714) 556-3610 x 252
Stanford University	Stanford, CA 94305	(415) 723-2110
United States International University	10455 Pomerado Road San Diego, CA 92131	(619) 635-4824
University of LaVerne	1950 Third Street LaVerne, CA 91750	(909) 593-3511 x 4631
University of the Pacific	3601 Pacific Ave Stockton, CA 95211	(209) 946-2277
University of Redlands	1200 E Colton Redlands, CA 92373	(909) 793-2121 x 6011
University of San Diego	5998 Alcala Park San Diego, CA 92110-2492	(619) 260-4821
University of San Francisco	2130 Fulton Street San Francisco, CA 94117	(415) 666-6525
University of Southern California	University Park Los Angeles, CA 90089-0031	(213) 740-3467
Westmont College	955 LaPaz Road Santa Barbara, CA 93108	(805) 565-6165
Whittier College	13406 E Philadelphia Street Whittier, CA 90608	(310) 693-0771 x 322

OREGON

Oregon Teacher Standards and Practices Commission
630 Center Street NE, Suite 200
Salem, OR 97310
(503) 378-3586

CERTIFICATION TESTS

CORE BATTERY
- □ General Knowledge
- □ Communication Skills
- ■ Professional Knowledge

MSAT
- ■ Content Knowledge
- ■ Content Essays

PRAXIS I: ACADEMIC SKILLS
- ■ PPST—Mathematics
- ■ PPST—Reading
- ■ PPST—Writing
- ■ CBT—Mathematics
- ■ CBT—Reading
- ■ CBT—Writing

■ STATE TEST
CBEST may be taken in place of the PPST

Refer to Barron's *How to Prepare for the Praxis* for other Praxis tests.

PRAXIS II: SUBJECT ASSESSMENTS AND NTE SPECIALTY AREA TESTS

Art & Music
- ■ 10130 Art Education (NTE)
- □ 20131 Art Making
- □ 20132 Content, Trad., Aesthet. Crit.

- ■ 10110 Music Education (NTE)
- □ 20112 Music: Analysis
- □ 30111 Music: Concepts & Processes

Elementary Education
- □ 20010 Ed. in the Elem. School (NTE)
- □ 20011 Elem. Ed. Curric., Inst. & Asses.
- □ 20012 Elem. Ed. Content Area Exer.

English
- □ 10040 English Language & Lit. (NTE)
- ■ 10041 Lang., Lit., & Comp.: Cont.
- ■ 20042 Lang., Lit. & Comp.: Essays
- □ 30043 Eng. Lang., Lit., & Comp.: Ped.

Foreign Language
- ■ 10170 French (NTE)
- □ 20171 French: Productive Lang. Skills
- □ 30172 French: Ling., Lit., & Cult. Anal.

- □ 10190 Spanish (NTE)
- ■ 10191 Spanish: Content Knowledge
- ■ 20192 Spanish: Productive Lang. Skills
- □ 30193 Spanish: Ling., Lit. & Cult. Anal.
- □ 30194 Spanish: Pedagogy

Mathematics
- □ 10060 Mathematics (NTE)
- ■ 10061 Mathematics: Content Knowledge
- ■ 20063 Math.: Proof, Model & Prob.—1
- ■ 30064 Math.: Proof, Model & Prob.—2
- ■ 20065 Mathematics: Pedagogy

Physical Education
- □ 10090 Phys. Ed. (NTE)
- ■ 10091 Phys. Ed. Content Knowledge
- ■ 30092 Phys. Ed. Move. Form Anal. & Des.
- ■ 20093 Phys. Ed. Move. Form Vid. Eval.
- □ 30094 Phys. Ed. Pedagogy

Science
- □ 10030 Biology & Gen. Science (NTE)
- □ 10230 Biology (NTE)
- ■ 20232 Biology: Content Knowledge I
- ■ 20232 Biology: Content Knowledge II
- ■ 30233 Biology: Content Essays
- □ 30234 Biology: Pedagogy

- □ 10240 Chemistry (NTE)
- ■ 20241 Chemistry: Content Knowledge
- ■ 30242 Chemistry: Content Essays

- □ 10430 General Science (NTE)
- ■ 10431 General Science: Cont. Know.—1
- ■ 10432 General Science: Cont. Know.—2

Science (Cont.)

- ■ 30433 General Science: Cont. Essays
- □ 20481 Physical Science: Content Know.
- □ 20482 Physical Science: Content Essays
- □ 30483 Physical Science: Pedagogy

Science (Cont.)

- □ 10260 Physics (NTE)
- ■ 10261 Physics: Content Knowledge
- ■ 30262 Physics: Content Essays

Social Studies

- ■ 10080 Social Studies (NTE)
- ■ 10081 Social Studies: Content Know.

Social Studies (Cont.)

- ■ 20082 Social Studies: Analytical Essays
- ■ 20083 Social Studies: Interpret. of Mat.
- □ 30084 Social Studies: Pedagogy

Special Education

- ■ 10350 Special Education (NTE)

CERTIFICATION REQUIREMENTS AND PROCEDURES

INSTRUCTIONS FOR APPLYING FOR A BASIC TEACHING LICENSE

STEP 1—DO YOU HAVE THE CORRECT INSTRUCTIONS?

These instructions are for your first Oregon Basic Teaching License. If you are renewing or reinstating any Oregon license, or if you are applying for your first counselor, school psychologist, or administrator license, contact TSPC at the address on the previous page for the correct instructions.

STEP 2—DETERMINE YOUR BASIS FOR APPLICATION

Oregon recognizes two bases for evaluation for a Basic Teaching License:

A. You hold a license in another state that is currently valid for the subject(s) requested, **OR**

B. You completed a teacher education program in Oregon or another state that made you eligible for a teaching license.

If you do not meet A or B above, or if your teacher preparation was taken outside of the United States, contact an approved teacher education institution for advice on qualifying for licensure.

STEP 3—PROVIDE EVIDENCE OF ACADEMIC COMPETENCE

Oregon requires evidence of competence in basic skills, professional knowledge, and the specialty area(s) in which licensure is requested. Competence must be demonstrated as follows:

A. **BASIC SKILLS**—Submit passing scores on the Pre-Professional Skills Test (PPST), **OR** submit passing scores on the Praxis Computer-Based Test (CBT), **OR** submit verification of passing the California Basic Educational Skills Test (CBEST).

NOTES:

1. The basic skills test requirement is waived if you verify five years of full-time public school experience in a licensed position in another state.
2. A two-year postponement of the basic skills test requirement is granted upon request from the Oregon school district that offers employment.

B. **PROFESSIONAL KNOWLEDGE**—Submit a minimum score of 661 on the NTE Core Battery Tests of Professional Knowledge (30520).

NOTES:

1. The professional knowledge test requirement is waived if you verify five years of full-time public school teaching in another state.
2. A one-year postponement of the professional knowledge test is granted to foreign language, special education, and technology education teachers due to the shortage of applicants in those fields.

C. **SPECIALTY AREA**—Submit a minimum score on the MSAT for an elementary endorsement.

NOTES:

1. If you verify five years of public school teaching in another state in the endorsement area(s) requested on a license valid for the assignment; **TSPC will evaluate your transcript of academic preparation** in lieu of the required specialty area test score(s).

2. A one-year postponement of the specialty area test(s) is granted to foreign language, special education and technology education teachers due to the shortage of applicants in these fields.

STEP 4—PROVIDE EVIDENCE OF RECENT EDUCATIONAL EXPERIENCE

Recent experience may be verified by:

A. Submitting Form C-2 showing that you completed a teacher education program within the previous three years, **OR**

B. Submitting verification of one year of full-time public school teaching experience within the last three years on an out-of-state teaching license valid for the assignment, **OR**

C. Submitting transcripts verifying nine quarter hours of approved preparation completed within three years prior to application. The preparation must be appropriate to the license and endorsement being requested.

NOTES:

1. You can apply for evaluation without recent education experience; however, you must meet this requirement to be issued a license.
2. A one-year postponement of the recency requirement is granted to foreign language, special education, and technology education teachers due to the shortage of applicants in these fields.

STEP 5—ASSEMBLE ALL DOCUMENTS NEEDED FOR APPLICATION

All documents needed for evaluation of your application must be submitted in a single envelope. An incomplete application will be returned. You will need the following:

A. **Official transcripts of *all* college preparation including verification of degrees conferred.**

NOTES:

1. Your bachelor's degree must be from an approved institution. If you have five years of public school experience, a bachelor's degree from any college or university will be accepted.
2. Official transcripts bear the seal of the institution and signature of the registrar. Transcripts must be sent to you for submission to TSPC with your application.

B. **A photocopy of your license which is currently valid for teaching the subject area or special education in another state, *OR* Form C-2 completed by your teacher education institution.**

NOTES:

1. If your out-of-state license has expired, Form C-2 is required.
2. Your out-of-state certificate or license must be a regular license, not a temporary, emergency, or other special license limited due to outstanding requirements in the issuing state. If your certificate or license is substandard, Form C-2 is required.

C. **Original score reports from tests of basic skills, specialty area, and professional knowledge.** Refer to pages 366 for instructions and the tests required in Oregon.

NOTES:

1. Do not have test score reports mailed directly from Praxis or CBEST to TSPC. Score reports must be sent to you for submission to TSPC with your application. Your original score reports will be returned to you after recording.
2. Five years of full-time public school experience may satisfy test requirements needed for the Basic Teaching License under Step 3.
3. Test requirements are postponed for two years when a Reciprocal Teaching license is issued.

D. **Verification by a public school district(s) of contracted teaching experience on the Professional Educational Experience Report (PEER) form.**

NOTES:

1. Five years of full-time public school experience may satisfy test requirements needed for the Basic Teaching License under Step 3.
2. One year of full-time public school experience in the past three years qualifies as recent experience under Step 4.
3. Experience gained while student teaching and substitute teaching is not accepted.

E. **Completed affidavit attesting to knowledge of laws prohibiting discrimination.**

F. **Submit 2 Fingerprint Cards & Fingerprint Fee**

Oregon law requires that applicants who apply for an Oregon license as an educator must submit two fingerprint cards for checking Oregon and Federal Bureau Investigation criminal history records. **SEE: INSTRUCTIONS FOR FULFILLING OREGON'S FINGERPRINTING REQUIREMENTS.**

G. **Complete Application Form C-1 as follows:**

Provide all information requested on Form C-1. Check that you are applying for a Basic Teaching License. (Reciprocal Applicants check Basic.)

Complete the character questions attesting to your fitness to serve as an educator and provide all supporting materials, if required.

Sign and date the application within 90 days prior to submitting your materials to TSPC.

H. **Submit the Application Materials and Fee**

The application fee is assessed for evaluating your qualifications for an Oregon teaching license and is nonrefundable. **This fee is in addition to the processing fee for fingerprinting**. If you meet the requirements, a license will be issued at no additional cost.

Enclose all materials in a single envelope and mail them to TSPC, Public Service Building, 255 Capitol Street NE, Suite 105, Salem, OR 97310-1332

STEP 6—ALLOW THIRTY DAYS FOR PROCESSING

INTERSTATE CERTIFICATION COMPACT (ICC) RECIPROCAL TEACHING LICENSE

Oregon has a reciprocal agreement with 32 states that covers all elementary, secondary, and special education **teachers**. *Test requirements are postponed for two years when a Reciprocal Teaching License is issued.* The chart below illustrates requirements needed for the Reciprocal Teaching License.

RECIPROCAL TEACHING LICENSE

Alabama, Arkansas, California, Colorado, Connecticut, Delaware, Florida, Georgia, Hawaii, Idaho, Illinois, Indiana, Maine, Maryland, Massachusetts, Michigan, Montana, New Hampshire, New York, Nevada, North Carolina, Pennsylvania, Rhode Island, South Carolina, Tennessee, Texas, Utah, Vermont, Virginia, Washington, Washington D.C., West Virginia.

CURRENT LICENSE IN THE RECIPROCAL STATE -AND- ONE OF THE FOLLOWING BLOCKS IN THE RECIPROCAL STATE

1 year experience within previous 3 years	27 months experience within previous 7 years	1 year experience more than 3 years ago -AND- *9 quarter hours within previous 3 years	27 months esxperince more than 7 years ago -AND- *9 quarter hours within previous 3 years

TEACHER EDUCATION PROGRAM IN THE RECIPROCAL STATE -AND- ONE OF THE FOLLOWING BLOCKS

Teacher education program completed within previous 3 years	Teacher education program completed more than 3 years ago -AND- *9 quarter hours completed within previous 3 years

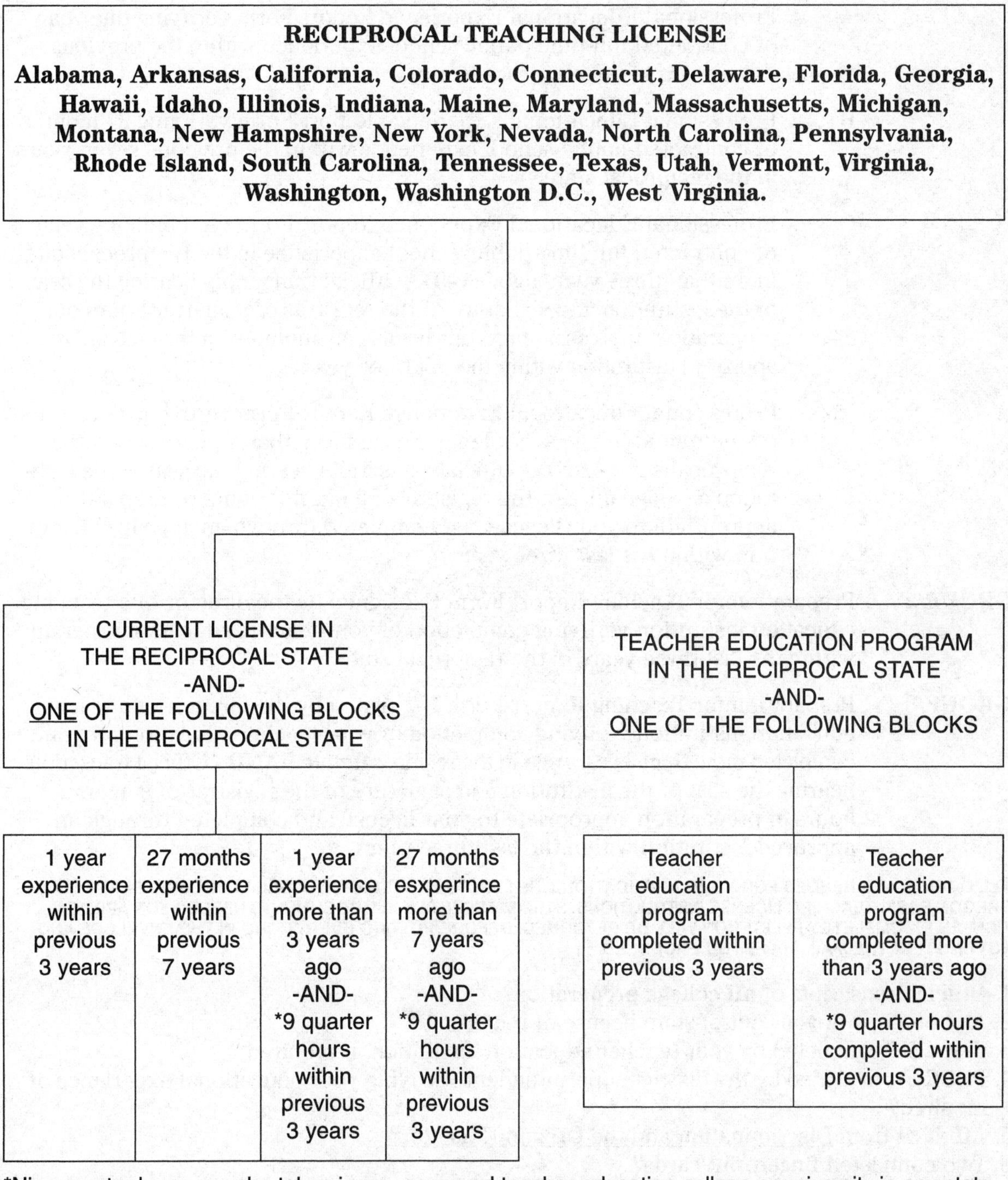

*Nine quarter hours may be taken in any approved teacher education college or university in any state.

RECIPROCAL TEACHING LICENSE

To make application for the Reciprocal Teaching License refer to the Oregon Basic Teaching License Instructions, Step 5 **assemble all documents needed for application**. In addition to the application materials submit **one** of the following groups for the Reciprocal Teaching License:

GROUP 1 A photocopy of your license, which is currently valid for teaching the subject(s) in another state, **AND *one*** of the following.

A. Professional Educational Experience Report Form verifying one year of contracted full-time public school experience within the previous three years in the reciprocal state.

B. Professional Educational Experience Report Form verifying 27 months of contracted public school experience within the previous seven years in the reciprocal state.

C. Professional Educational Experience Report Form verifying one year of contracted full-time public school experience in the reciprocal state more than three years ago - **AND** - Official transcripts bearing the seal of the institution and signature of the registrar of 9 quarter hours of preparation appropriate to your license and completed through an approved institution within the last three years.

D. Professional Educational Experience Report Form verifying 27 months of contracted public school experience more than 7 years ago in the reciprocal state - **AND** - Official transcripts bearing the seal of the institution and signature of the registrar of 9 quarter hours of preparation appropriate to your license and completed through an approved institution within the last three years.

GROUP 2 Preparation for Teaching Report Form C-2 signed by the director of a teaching education institution verifying completion of your teacher education program within the last three years in the reciprocal state.

GROUP 3 Preparation for Teaching Report Form C-2 signed by the director of a teacher education institution verifying completion of your teacher education program completed more than 3 years ago in the reciprocal state - **AND** - Official transcripts bearing the seal of the institution and signature of the registrar of 9 quarter hours of preparation appropriate to your license and completed through an approved institution within the last three years.

ALL DOCUMENTS NEEDED FOR YOUR APPLICATION MUST BE SUBMITTED IN A SINGLE ENVELOPE. REFER TO THE OREGON BASIC TEACHING LICENSE INSTRUCTIONS, STEP 5, ASSEMBLE ALL DOCUMENTS NEEDED FOR APPLICATION. AN INCOMPLETE APPLICATION WILL BE RETURNED. BEFORE PUTTING EVERYTHING IN THE ENVELOPE AND PUTTING IT IN THE MAIL, HAVE YOU ENCLOSED. . .

1. Official transcripts of **all** college preparation?
2. A photocopy of your out-of-state license, if required?
3. Form C-2 completed by your teacher education institution, if required?
4. PEER Form signed by the district superintendent verifying your educational experience, if required?
5. Affidavit from Discrimination and the Oregon Educator?
6. Two completed fingerprint cards?
7. A check or money order for the fingerprint fee?
8. Completed Application Form C-1?
9. A check or money order for the evaluation fee?

COLLEGES AND UNIVERSITIES IN OREGON WITH APPROVED TEACHER CERTIFICATION PROGRAMS

Institution	Address	Telephone
Oregon State System of Higher Education		
Eastern Oregon University	1410 L Avenue La Grande, OR 97850	(503) 346-3405
Oregon State University	Corvallis, OR 97331	(503) 737-5959
Portland State University	PO Box 751 Portland, OR 97202	(503) 725-4697
Southern Oregon University	1250 Siskiyou Blvd Ashland, OR 97520	(503) 522-6918
University of Oregon	Eugene, OR 97403	(503) 346-3405
Western Oregon University	Monmouth, OR 97361	(503) 838-8825
Oregon Independent Colleges Association (503) 639-4541		
Concordia University	2811 NE Holman St. Portland, OR 97219	(503) 280-8539
George Fox University	414 N Meriden Newberg, OR 97132	(503) 538-8383
Lewis and Clark College	SW Palentine Hill Rd Portland, OR 97211	(503) 768-7768
Linfield College	900 SE Baker Street McMinnville, OR 97128	(503) 434-2201
Northwest Christian College	828 11th Avenue East Eugene, OR 97401	(541) 684-7252
Pacific University	2043 College Way Forest Grove, OR 97116	(503) 359-2783
University of Portland	5000 N Willamette Blvd. Portland, OR 97203	(503) 283-7208
Warner Pacific College	2219 SE 68th Ave Portland, OR 97251	(503) 788-7443
Western Baptist College	5000 Deer Park Drive Salem, OR 97301	(503) 375-7019
Willamette University	900 State Street Salem, OR 97301	(503) 370-6343

13 GETTING A TEACHING JOB

There are specific steps you can follow to increase your chances of getting the teaching job you want. There are no guarantees, but you can definitely improve the odds. Let's begin with a discussion of job opportunities.

WHERE ARE THE TEACHING JOBS?

There are teaching jobs everywhere! This writer served on the board of education in a small suburban town with about 80 teachers in a K-8 school district. It was the kind of place most people would like to teach. There were between two and five teaching openings each year, for six years. But you could hardly find an advertisement or announcement anywhere.

About the only people who knew about the jobs were administrators and teachers in the district and surrounding districts, the few people who read a three-line ad that ran once in a weekly paper, and those who called to inquire about teaching jobs. Keep this information in mind. It is your first clue about how to find a teaching job.

The *Occupational Outlook Handbook*, released by the federal government, predicts that teaching opportunities for elementary and secondary school teachers will increase faster than all occupations as a whole during the next 10 years. The book predicts a much faster increase in jobs for special education teachers.

Other sources predict an increased need for mathematics, science, and bilingual teachers during this same period. Experience indicates that the opportunities for teachers certified in more than one area will grow much faster than average as well.

Some publications predict that the population of elementary age school children will increase about 10 percent by 2005. If the number of teachers were to increase at this rate over all, the number of teachers in the United States will grow from about 3,250,000 to about 3,560,000. In the 1990s, the teachers are apportioned approximately as follows: elementary school, 1,600,000; secondary school 1,300,000; and special education, 360,000.

More than half of American teachers are over 40. While predictions vary, the number of retirements during the next decade will probably be larger than we have seen in the last 20 years. I have spoken with principals who predicted that all the teachers in their school would retire by the year 2000.

The growth in the school age population and the increased retirement rate will probably produce a large numer of teaching jobs during the next decade. You need only one.

HOW CAN I FIND A JOB?

Before discussing this question, let's talk about rejection. Remember, you need only one teaching job. If you are interested in 100 jobs, you should be extremely happy with a success rate of 1 percent. A success rate of 2 percent is more than you need, and a very high success rate of 5 percent will just make it too hard to decide which job to take.

Rejection and failure are part of the job search process. Be ready; everyone goes through it.

OKAY, I'M READY FOR REJECTION. HOW DO I FIND A JOB?

Begin by deciding on the kind of teaching jobs you want and the geographic areas you are willing to teach in. There is no sense pursuing jobs you don't want in places you don't want to go.

Write your choices here.

These are the kind of teaching positions I'm interested in.

____________________ ____________________

____________________ ____________________

These are the places or locales I'm willing to teach in.

____________________ ____________________

____________________ ____________________

You can change your mind as often as you like. But limit your job search to these choices.

Follow the guidelines presented below. You must actually do the things outlined here. Reading, talking, and thinking about them will not help.

Make and use personal contacts

Find out about every appropriate teaching position

Apply for every appropriate teaching position—go to every interview

Develop a good resume

Use the placement office

MAKE AND USE PERSONAL CONTACTS

You will not be surprised to learn that many, if not most, jobs are found through personal contacts. You must make personal contacts to maximize your chances of finding the job you want. Take things easy, one step at a time, and try to meet at least one new person each week.

Find a way to get introduced to teachers, school administrators, board of education members, and others who will know about teaching jobs and may influence hiring decisions. The more people you meet and talk to, the better chance you will have of getting the job you want.

Get a mentor. Get to know a superintendent or principal near where you want to teach, and ask that person to be your mentor. Tell them immediately that you are not asking for a job in their district. (That will not stop them from offering you one if they want to.) Explain that you are just beginning your teaching career and that you need help learning about teaching jobs in surrounding communities and about teaching in general. Ask your mentor to keep their eyes and ears open for any openings for which you are qualified. You can have several mentors if you want to. Listen to their advice.

You already have a lot of contacts through your friends and relatives. Talk to them all. Tell them you are looking for a teaching job and ask them to be alert for any possibilities. Ask them to mention your name and your interest in a teaching position to everyone they know.

FIND OUT ABOUT EVERY APPROPRIATE TEACHING POSITION

The contacts you have and are making each week will help you keep abreast of some teaching opportunities. Follow these additional steps. Look in every paper every day distributed in the places you want to teach. Don't forget about weekly papers.

Call all the school districts where you want to teach. Ask the adminstrative assistant or secretary in the superintendent's or principal's office if there are current or anticipated job openings in the district. If you are in college or a recent graduate, visit or contact the placement office every week and ask your professors if they know about any teaching opportunities. Contact the offices of California County Superintendents (pages 378–381) and the Oregon Education Service Districts (pages 382–383) for more job leads.

APPLY FOR EVERY APPROPRIATE TEACHING POSITION—GO TO EVERY INTERVIEW

Apply for every teaching position that is of the type and in the location you listed. No exceptions! Direct application for a listed position is probably the second most effective way to get a job. The more appropriate jobs you apply for, the more likely you are to get one. It is not unusual for someone to apply for more than 100 teaching positions.

Go to every interview you are invited to. Going to interviews increases your chances of getting a job. If you don't get the job, it was worth going just for the practice.

Your application should include a brief cover letter and a one-page resume. The cover letter should follow this format: The first brief paragraph should identify the job you are applying for. The second brief paragraph should be used to mention a skill or ability you have that matches a district need. The third brief paragraph should indicate an interest in a personal interview. Every cover letter should be addressed to the person responsible for hiring in the school district.

DEVELOP A GOOD RESUME

A good resume is a one-page advertisement. A good resume highlights the things you have done that prospective employers will be interested in. A good resume is not an exhaustive listing of everything you have done. A good resume is not cluttered.

For example, say you worked as a teacher assistant and spent most of your time on lunch duty and about 10 percent of your time conducting whole language lessons. What goes on the resume? The whole language experience.

Your resume should include significant school-related experience. It should also include other employment that lasted longer than a year. Omit noneducation-related short-term employment. Your resume should list special skills, abilities, and interests that make you unique.

An example of a resume using a format that has proven successful appears in this chapter. This resume combines the experience of more than one person and is for demonstration purposes only.

An outline of a resume you can copy, to begin to develop your own resume, is also included in this chapter. If you are interested in two different types of teaching positions, you may have two resumes. Go over your final resume and cover letters with a placement officer or advisor.

Derek Namost
33 Ann Street
Kearning, CA 99999
(555) 555-5555

Objective: Elementary School Teacher
Special Education Teacher
Secondary History Teacher

Education: BS History—Collegiate College (minor in education) 1991
MS in Education at Long Key College in progress

Certification: Teacher of Special Education
Teacher of Elementary Education

Experience: **Lincoln School District,** 1995–present
Elementary School Teacher Fifth Grade

- Teach in a student-centered elementary school
- Prepare and teach individualized lessons geared to student needs
- Use computer software and CD-ROM's to teach mathematics and motivate students
- Prepare and implement whole language instruction
- Integrate instruction in science, language arts, and social studies

Southern Pines School District, 1991–1995
Secondary School Special Education Teacher

- Planned and taught modified classes for classified students
- Modified the curriculum to meet the individual needs of students
- Taught modified science and social studies courses to classified students
- Assisted students with class assignments, self-management, and study skills
- Collaborated with class and subject matter teachers

Watson School, Spring 1991
Student Teacher, Preschool Class

- Collaborated in teaching a class of preschool students

Honors: Kappa Delta Pi, Phi Delta Kappa

Coaching/ Advising: Coach, varsity soccer team 1992–95
Advisor, mathematics team 1992–95
Interested in coaching and advising after-school activities

Special Skills: Extensive experience using computers, including Macintosh and IBM computers, multimedia, and CD-ROM's

References: References are available on request

RESUME WORKSHEET

____

____

____

(______) ______ - ______________

Objective:

Education:

Certification:

Experience:

Honors:

Coaching/ Advising:

Special Skills:

References:

USE THE PLACEMENT OFFICE

If you are a college student or graduate, use the school's placement office. Set up a placement file that includes recommendation letters from professors, teachers, and supervisors. It's handy to have these references on file. If a potential employer wants this information, you can have them sent out from the placement office instead of running around.

College placement offices often give seminars on job hunting and interviews. Take advantage of these.

WHAT TIME LINE SHOULD I FOLLOW?

Let's say you are looking for a job in September and you will be certified three months earlier in June. You should begin working on your personal contacts by September of the previous year. You should start looking for advertisements and tracking down job possibilities during January. Have your placement file set up and a preliminary resume done by February. You can amend them later if you need to. Start applying for jobs in February.

ANY LAST ADVICE?

Stick with it. Follow the steps outlined here. Start early and take things one step at a time. Remember the importance of personal contacts. Remember that you need only one teaching job. Let people help you.

CALIFORNIA COUNTY SUPERINTENDENTS

County	Address	Telephone
Alameda	313 W Winton Avenue Hayward, CA 94544-1198	(510) 887-0152
Alpine	43 Hawkside Drive Markleeville, CA 96120	(916) 694-2230
Amador	217 Rex Avenue, #5 Jackson, CA 95642	(209) 223-1750
Butte	1859 Bird Street Oroville, CA 95965	(916) 538-7237
Calaveras	PO Box 760, 373 S Main Street Angels Camp, CA 95221	(209) 736-4662
Colusa	146 Seventh Street Colusa, CA 95932	(916) 458-0351
Contra Costa	77 Santa Barbara Road Pleasant Hill, CA 94523	(510) 942-3388
Del Norte	301 W Washington Blvd Crescent City, CA 95531	(707) 464-6141
El Dorado	6767 Green Valley Road Placerville, CA 95667-9357	(916) 622-7130
Fresno	Credential Department 1111 Van Ness Fresno, CA 93721	(209) 265-3005
Glenn	525 W Sycamore Willows, CA 95988	(916) 934-6575
Humboldt	901 Myrtle Avenue Eureka, CA 95501	(707) 445-5411
Imperial	1398 Sperber Road El Centro, CA 92243	(619) 339-6464
Inyo	135 S Jackson Street PO Drawer G Independence, CA 93526	(619) 878-2426
Kern	1300 17th Street Bakersfield, CA 93301-4533	(805) 636-4000
Kings	1144 W Lacey Blvd Hanford, CA 93230 (Government Ctr)	(209) 584-1441
Lake	1152 S Main Street Lakeport, CA 95453	(707) 263-3080
Lassen	472-013 Johnstonville Road North Susanville, CA 96130	(916) 257-2196

Los Angeles	9300 E Imperial Highway Downey, CA 90242-2890	(310) 922-6111
Madera	28123 Avenue 14 Madera, CA 93638	(209) 673-6051
Marin	1111 Las Gallinas Ave PO Box 4925 San Rafael, CA 94913	(415) 472-4110
Mariposa	County Office Bldg Highway 140 PO Box 8 Mariposa, CA 95338	(209) 966-3691
Mendocino	2240 Eastside Road Ukiah, CA 95482	(707) 463-4807
Merced	632 W 13th Street Merced, CA 95340	(209) 385-8300
Modoc	139 W Henderson Street Alturas, CA 96101	(916) 233-7100
Mono	Emigrant Street PO Box 477 Bridgeport, CA 93517	(619) 932-7311
Monterey	PO Box 80851 901 Blanco Circle Salinas, CA 93912	(408) 755-0301
Napa	1015 Kaiser Road Napa, CA 94558	(707) 253-6800
Nevada	112 Nevada City Hwy Nevada City, CA 95959	(916) 478-6400
Orange	PO Box 9050 200 Kalmus Drive Costa Mesa, CA 92626	(714) 966-4000
Placer	360 Nevada Street Auburn, CA 95603	(916) 889-8020
Plumas	50 Church Street PO Box 10330 Quincy, CA 95971-6009	(916) 283-6500
Riverside	3939 13th Street PO Box 868 Riverside, CA 92502	(909) 788-6530
Sacramento	9738 Lincoln Village Drive Sacramento, CA 95827	(916) 228-2500
San Benito	460 Fifth Street Hollister, CA 95023	(408) 637-5393

San Bernardino	601 North E Street San Bernardino, CA 92410-3093	(909) 387-4386
San Diego	6401 Linda Vista Road San Diego, CA 92111-7399	(619) 292-3868
San Francisco	135 Van Ness Avenue, Room 209 San Francisco, CA 94102	(415) 241-6151
San Joaquin	Ed. Center, PO Box 213030 Stockton, CA 95213-9030	(209) 468-4800
San Luis Obispo	PO Box 8105 San Luis Obispo, CA 93403-8105	(805) 543-7732
San Mateo	101 Twin Dolphin Drive Redwood City, CA 94065-1064	(415) 802-5300
Santa Barbara	PO Box 6307 4400 Cathedral Oaks Road Santa Barbara, CA 93160	(805) 964-4711
Santa Clara	1290 Ridder Park Drive San Jose, CA 95131-2398	(408) 453-6500
Santa Cruz	809 Bay Avenue, Suite H Capitola, CA 95010	(408) 476-7140
Shasta	1644 Magnolia Avenue Redding, CA 96001	(916) 225-0200
Sierra	#1 Bell Tower Square PO Drawer E Downieville, CA 95936	(916) 289-3526
Siskiyou	609 South Gold Street Yreka, CA 96097	(916) 842-5751
Solano	655 Washington Fairfield, CA 94533	(707) 421-6531
Sonoma	5340 Skylane Blvd Santa Rosa, CA 95403	(707) 524-2600
Stanislaus	801 County Center Three Court Modesto, CA 95355	(209) 525-5089
Sutter	County Office Bldg 463 Second Street Yuba City, CA 95991	(916) 741-5110
Tehama	PO Box 689 1135 Lincoln Street Red Bluff, CA 96080	(916) 527-5811
Trinity	PO Box 1256 Weaverville, CA 96093	(916) 623-2861

Tulare	2637 W Burrel PO Box 5091 Visalia, CA 93278-5091	(209) 733-6300
Tuolumne	175 South Fairview Lane Sonora, CA 95370	(209) 533-8710
Ventura	5189 Verdugo Way Camarillo, CA 93012	(805) 383-1901
Yolo	1240 Harter Avenue Woodland, CA 95776	(916) 668-6700
Yuba	938 14th Street Marysville, CA 95901	(916) 741-6231

OREGON EDUCATION SERVICE DISTRICTS

ESD	Address	Telephone
Clackamas	PO Box 216 Maryhurst, OR 97036	(503) 635-0541
Crook-Deschutes	1340 NW Wall Bend, OR 97701	(541) 382-3171
Douglas	1871 NE Stephens Street Roseburg, OR 97470	(541) 440-4751
Grant	835-A South Canyon Blvd John Day, OR 97845	(541) 575-1349
Harney	450 North Buena Vista Avenue Burns, OR 97720	(541) 573-2122
Jackson	101 North Grape Street Medford, OR 97501	(541) 776-8563
Jefferson	445 SE Buff Street Madras, OR 97741	(541) 475-6192
Lake	357 North “L” Street Lakeview, OR 97630	(541) 947-3371
Lane	PO Box 2680 1200 Hwy 99N Eugene, OR 97402	(541) 461-8200
Linn-Benton-Lincoln	905 4th Avenue SE Albany, OR 97321	(541) 967-8822
Malheur	363 “A” Street West Vale, OR 97918	(541) 473-3138
Multnomah	PO Box 301039 11611 NE Ainsworth Circle Portland, OR 97230	(503) 257-1531
North Central Region	PO Box 637 221 South Oregon Street Condon, OR 97470	(541) 384-2732
Clatsop	3194 Marine Drive Astoria, OR 97103	(503) 325-2867
Columbia	800 Port Avenue St. Helens, OR 97051	(503) 397-0028
Tillamook Regional	PO Box 416 2410 5th Street Tillamook, OR 97141	(503) 842-8423
Washington	5825 NE Ray Circle Hillsboro, OR 97124	(503) 690-5428

Region 9	422 East 3rd Street The Dalles, OR 97058	(541) 298-5155
Region 18	301 W North Street, No. 1 Enterprise, OR 97828	(541) 426-4997
Coos	1350 Teakwood Avenue Coos Bay, OR 97420	(541) 269-1611
Curry	PO Box 786 350 Mary Street Gold Beach, OR 97444	(541) 247-6681
Umatilla-Morrow	2001 SW Nye Avenue Pendleton, OR 97801	(541) 276-6616
Baker	2100 Main Street Baker City, OR 97814	(541) 523-5801
Union	10100 North McAlister Road Island City, OR 97850	(541) 963-4106
Willamette	3400 Portland Road NE Salem, OR 97303	(503) 588-5330
Yamhill	2045 SW Hwy 18 McMinnville, OR 97128	(503) 472-1431

NOTES

NOTES

NOTES

NOTES

NOTES

BEGINNING SPANISH FOR TEACHERS OF HISPANIC STUDENTS

Pamela J. Sharpe, Ph.D.

Here at last is a valuable self-instruction program for primary and secondary school ›achers who speak English only, but need some practical knowledge of Spanish so that ıey can work with Hispanic students. The boxed set consists of—

A 280-page illustrated combination textbook and workbook
376 dialogue flashcards bound into a separate book of perforated card stock paper
Four 90-minute cassettes
A 92-page audioscript book

The program presents 24 lessons ıat start with greeting children in panish and introducing yourself, iving children basic instructions ıcluding taking out and putting way school supplies, participating ı learning activities, praising hildren's good work, correcting heir mistakes and behavior, uestioning and comforting a child ʼho is injured, participating in oliday celebrations and special vents, communicating with Iispanic parents, and much ıore.

The main book's text and lustration are coordinated to match the ramatized conversations on cassette. It features ıany quizzes and exercises that will help you learn and etain the Spanish you need to know. The accompanying dialogue ards contain simple line drawings that depict a teacher and students engaged in a variety f classroom activities. Each card coincides with key words and phrases in the lessons and ogether will help you increase your memory retention.

ʼamela J. Sharpe, Ph.D., is Associate Professor of English as a Second Language and Bilingual ducation at Northern Arizona University in Yuma.

A quick, practical way to learn Spanish for use in a classroom setting.

ISBN 0-8120-8118-8 **$35.00 Canada $45.95**

Barron's Educational Series, Inc.
250 Wireless Blvd., Hauppauge, NY 11788
Order toll-free: 1-800-645-3476 • Order by fax: 1-516-434-3217
Canadian orders: 1-800-645-3476 • Fax in Canada: 1-800-887-1594

Visit us at www.barronseduc.com

Books and packages may be purchased at your local bookstore or by mail directly from Barron's. Enclose check or money order for total amount, plus sales tax where applicable and 15% for postage and handling (minimum $4.95). Prices subject to change without notice.

#74 1/98